PACIFIC THUNDER

OSPREY
PUBLISHING

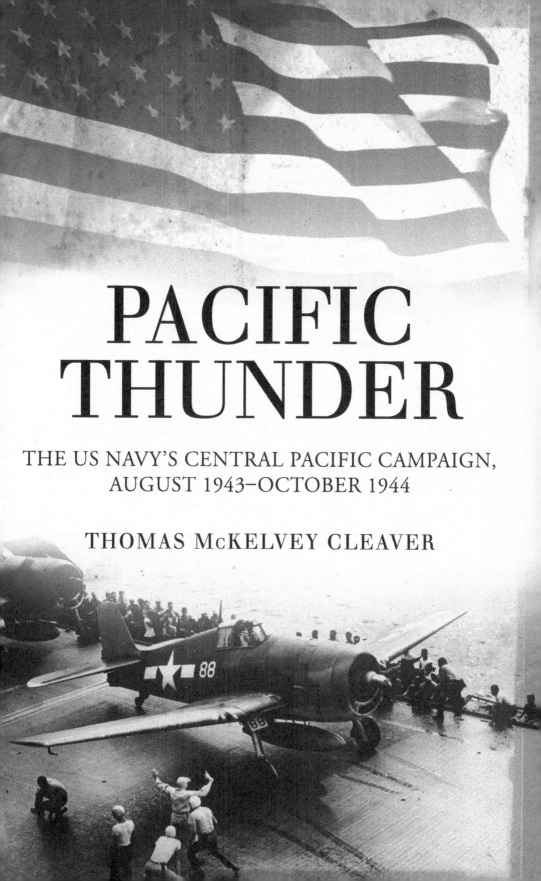

PACIFIC THUNDER

THE US NAVY'S CENTRAL PACIFIC CAMPAIGN, AUGUST 1943–OCTOBER 1944

THOMAS McKELVEY CLEAVER

OSPREY PUBLISHING
Bloomsbury Publishing Plc
PO Box 883, Oxford, OX1 9PL, UK
1385 Broadway, 5th Floor, New York, NY 10018, USA
E-mail: info@ospreypublishing.com
www.ospreypublishing.com

OSPREY is a trademark of Osprey Publishing Ltd

First published in Great Britain in 2017

ISBN: HB 9781472821843; PB 9781472821881; eBook 9781472821850;
ePDF 9781472821867; XML 9781472821874

18 19 20 21 22   10 9 8 7 6 5 4 3 2 1

Maps by bounford.com
Index by Zoe Ross
Originated by PDQ Digital Media Solutions, Bungay, UK
Printed and bound in Great Britain by CPI (Group) UK Ltd, Croydon CR0 4YY

Front cover: Top: US flag (Library of Congress); Bottom: Plane wave-off (NARA)
Back cover: Left: Alex Vraciu (NARA); Right: Curtiss Helldivers SB2C-1C circa 1944 (National History and Heritage Command)

Osprey Publishing supports the Woodland Trust, the UK's leading woodland conservation charity. Between 2014 and 2018 our donations are being spent on its Centenary Woods project in the UK.

To find out more about our authors and books visit www.ospreypublishing.com. Here you will find extracts, author interviews, details of forthcoming events and the option to sign up for our newsletter.

CONTENTS

LIST OF MAPS

The Pacific Theater, 1942–44

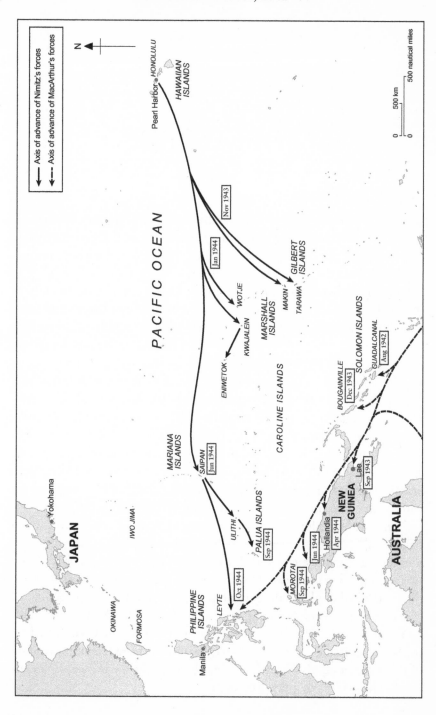

FOREWORD

Between September 1942 and September 1945, US Navy aircraft carriers were in action almost daily against the Japanese Empire. Those three years largely defined the sweep and scope of the Pacific War, the largest theater of operations in the world's largest conflict.

At 64,000,000 square miles, the Pacific Ocean covers about one-third of the planet's surface – more than the combined total of Earth's land area. Such is the enormity of the arena in which Thomas McKelvey Cleaver sets his dramatic survey of the Pacific carrier campaigns following the arrival of the "new navy" in the summer of 1943.

The story begins on a downbeat for American forces, with loss of the *Wasp* (CV-7) to an extraordinarily competent Japanese submarine captain off Guadalcanal, nine months after the stunning attack on Pearl Harbor, Hawaii, on December 7, 1941. Following that 20th-century version of "shock and awe," the Imperial Navy rode rough-shod over Allied forces across the eastern half of the Pacific, including the Chinese coast, Philippines, and Dutch East Indies. In fact, the war probably could not have been started without the six carriers that launched nearly 400 aircraft against Pearl.

With her battleships destroyed or damaged, America's only resort was a handful of "PacFleet" carriers – from three at the beginning to a maximum of four during the subsequent year. The naval millennium arrived in May 1942 when, for the first time, two fleets fought one another beyond visual range. The carrier had displaced the battleship atop the world's naval pyramid.

Following Japan's stunning reversal of fortune at Midway in June 1942, America launched its first offensive of the war at Guadalcanal in the Solomon Islands in August. Two carrier battles were fought for control of the waters around "Guadal," setting the stage for the inevitable voyage northward, leading to Tokyo Bay itself.

Yet *Pacific Thunder* goes beyond the battles, ships, and leaders who fought the titanic campaigns for oceanic control through 1945. Cleaver properly backtracks to describe the technical and institutional battles and innovations that produced the aircraft carrier. Both the US and Japanese navies, following in Britain's wake, spent two decades perfecting equipment and techniques in carrier aviation. Such was the carrier's primacy that it enabled the Pacific island-hopping campaigns of 1943–44, when the Pacific Fleet brought its own airpower with amphibious forces to seize crucial bases *en route* to Japan itself. Operating beyond range of land-based aircraft, the fast carriers and their smaller, slower escort-carrier team mates pioneered a wholly new martial art.

Throughout *Pacific Thunder* you will meet a democratic cast of characters in the global drama: "snipes" in the engineering spaces; aircrewmen as well as aviators; aces as well as admirals. Some of the stories have often been told, such as the First Battle of the Philippine Sea, better known as the Marianas Turkey Shoot. Others are rendered both in macro and micro scale, leading to the final missions over Japan itself. The facts of Cleaver's story float on this sea of memories.

Few of the players remain today, as time wins its inevitable victory over human beings. But thanks to Cleaver and his generation of historians, the sweeping, gripping story is being preserved. We who delve into the subject know that history has a shelf life, and we have passed the point of no return for the World War II veterans. But let readers remember this: *Pacific Thunder* sets an example for current and future recorders of human events. Almost certainly there are men and women living within your reach who have stories to tell, that deserve preserving. I urge you to follow Tom Cleaver's example in three simple words:

Do
It
Now.

Barrett Tillman
Author, *On Wave and Wing:
The 100-year Quest to Perfect the Aircraft Carrier.*

PREFACE

Looking back, I can date my fascination with naval aviation in the Pacific War to around age ten, when I discovered my father's copy of the *Life* magazine special issue "The Fighting Lady," with the magnificent photographs taken aboard *Lexington* (CV-16) by famed photographer Edward Steichen, director of the Naval Aviation Photographic Unit. Since then, I have been fortunate to be involved directly in naval aviation myself, where I got to know the first of many naval aviators I would meet over the decades since, who had served in the Pacific War and whose stories I would hear first-hand. The subject has been a passion of mine ever since.

The navy I served in was far closer to that of World War II than today's. The majority of the ships in the fleet were veterans of that war, as well as all the senior petty officers I worked for and most of the officers over the rank of Commander. On a late night watch, it wasn't hard for a young sailor to come up with a sincerely asked question that elicited a story it was impossible to forget, which is where I began my lifelong collection of those first-person accounts. When I walked the southern end of the island of Okinawa a mere 18 years after the battle, it was impossible to take a step anywhere without finding a bullet casing or other evidence of the desperate fight. There were still urban areas of Japan that had yet to be rebuilt from the fire raids; terrible sights that are impossible to forget. When I read World War II accounts of sailors in ships lacking air conditioning dragging their thin mattresses up to one of the main decks to get some sleep in cooler tropic air, only to be awakened by a soaking as the ship sailed through a rain squall, I know personally what that was like.

As one who grew up in the years following World War II, I am always surprised how little most of my fellow Americans under the age of 60 know about that epic conflict, particularly the war in the Pacific. When Americans think of the "Good War," they think of D-Day and the liberation of Europe, the war of the "Band of Brothers." Most Americans know nothing of the greatest naval battle in history, the Battles of Leyte Gulf, which involved over 300 ships and 200,000 sailors and airmen on both sides, nor even how to pronounce it (Lay-TEE). And they know even less about the battles across the Central Pacific over the previous year that led up to that epic confrontation.

Growing up when I did, one did not need to have a formal class in the history of the war. One's father, one's uncles, the fathers of one's friends were all veterans of the war, and some were even willing to talk about their experiences. There was *Victory At Sea* on the television; any Sunday when we stayed "too long" visiting my grandmother and there was a possibility of not getting home by 6pm to see that show (in the days before video recorders) would find me increasingly agitated until we got in the family car and were on the way home in time. The footage, Richard Rogers' music, Leonard Graves' narration, were impossible to forget. When my father bought the record of the music, I played it so much he had to purchase a second copy.

Many Americans today who do learn about the Pacific War turn away from it in revulsion. The mutual racially based contempt between Japanese and Americans is fearful to view nowadays. Dehumanizing the enemy to make him easier to kill is as old as humanity, but rarely was it practiced with a more depraved creativity than by both sides in the Pacific War.

For the United States Navy, the Pacific War was personal. Until 1944, every man who passed through Pearl Harbor could see first-hand the aftermath of December 7, 1941, the "date that will live in infamy." I have yet to meet a veteran of the Pacific War who saw those sights who did not swear to himself a personal oath of vengeance against those responsible. Such was not the case for Americans with regard to Hitler and the Nazis. No quarter was offered or taken between enemies in the Pacific. Men cheered the death of an attacking enemy when he fell. The crew of the battleship *Missouri* nearly mutinied when their captain decreed that the remains of the *kamikaze* pilot who had crashed into their ship should be treated with respect and buried at sea rather than thrown over the side with the garbage. My writing mentor, the late Wendell Mayes, who served as a fighter direction officer (FDO) aboard the carrier *Essex* told me how the crew would cheer when an attacking Japanese aircraft was blown out of the sky over the ship. For many contemporary Americans, such bloodthirstiness is difficult to comprehend.

There was a deep cultural difference between the two opponents, which can clearly be seen in the foundational anthems they sang. That of the United States Navy reads:

Almighty Father, strong to save,
Whose arm hath bound the restless wave,
Who bidd'st the mighty ocean deep
Its own appointed limits keep:
O hear us when we cry to thee
For those in peril on the sea.

The anthem of the Imperial Japanese Navy is far different:

Across the sea, corpses in the water;
Across the mountain, corpses in the field
I shall die only for the Emperor,
I shall never look back.

As Admiral Halsey put it, "The Americans fought to live; the Japanese fought to die."

Over the years since my time in the Navy, I have been fortunate to come to know many of the leading personalities of the Pacific War, most now long departed, through my writing for aviation history magazines over the past 40 years. It's a privilege to be able to put their stories together inside the larger context of the most successful naval campaign in history.

Thomas McKelvey Cleaver
Los Angeles, California
2017

CHAPTER ONE

TORPEDO JUNCTION

Tuesday, September 15, 1942: *Wasp* (CV-7) steams some 150 miles southeast of San Cristobal Island as part of Task Force 18, in company with the battleship *North Carolina* (BB-55), aircraft carrier *Hornet* (CV-8), light cruiser *Helena* (CL 50), heavy cruiser *Salt Lake City* (CL 25), and destroyers *Laffey* (DD 459), *Lansdowne* (DD 486), *O'Brien* (DD-415), *Mustin* (DD-413) *Farenholt* (DD-491) and *Anderson* (DD-411). The fleet's assignment is escort of transports carrying the 7th Marine Regiment to Guadalcanal. The bright blue waters of the Coral Sea are calm, with clouds on the horizon. Lookouts on all ships are extra alert; these waters are known to American sailors as "torpedo junction," following the torpedoing of *Saratoga* (CV-3) on August 28. Several Japanese submarines are known to be in the area. With *Enterprise* (CV-6) undergoing repairs at Pearl Harbor for damage suffered on August 24 in the Battle of the Eastern Solomons, the ships of Task Force 18 constitute the sum total of American offensive naval force in the South Pacific.

Prior to the US entry into the war in 1941, *Wasp* had participated in searches for the German heavy cruiser *Admiral Hipper* in late March and the battleship *Bismarck* in May, then transported Army Air Corps P-40s to Iceland in support of the American occupation in June. As a reduced-size version of the Yorktown-class aircraft carriers, *Wasp* was more vulnerable to combat damage than other American aircraft carriers. Thus, she had initially been deployed in the Atlantic along with *Ranger*, where Axis naval forces were less capable of inflicting decisive damage. In 1942 *Wasp* gained fame when she joined the British Home Fleet in April and twice ferried British Spitfire fighters to Malta, though her vulnerability to air attack meant she had been kept out of range of Axis aircraft operating from Sicily and Italy.

In May 1942, the US Navy lost *Lexington* (CV-2) at the Battle of the Coral Sea and a month later *Yorktown* (CV-5) was sunk at Midway. Whether or not she was properly designed to survive combat in the Pacific, *Wasp* transited the Panama Canal in June 1942 and joined *Saratoga* and *Enterprise* to support the invasion of Guadalcanal, the first offensive US action in the Pacific War.

To date, the only combat *Wasp* had seen was on August 7, 1942 while covering the Marine landings, when her aircraft destroyed seven Kawanishi H6K "Mavis" flying boats and seven Nakajima A6M2-N "Rufe" floatplane fighters at the seaplane base at Tanambogo, while also sending aloft support missions to defend the invasion fleet. *Wasp* had just missed the Battle of the Eastern Solomons when she was sent to refuel by Admiral Frank Jack Fletcher, a man who worried excessively about the fuel state of his ships; she returned just as the Japanese retired from the battle.

On this day, *Wasp* was responsible for operating defensive air patrols as the "duty carrier." Shortly after dawn, Signalman Third Class Tom Curtis looked down from the signal bridge and watched the morning search flight launch. The crew went to General Quarters an hour before sunrise, remaining at their stations until about 1000 hours, when the morning search returned. The ship's planes were refueled and rearmed for the midday antisubmarine patrol flight and eight F4F-3 Wildcats and three SBD-3 Dauntlesses were launched shortly after 1200 hours. At 1215, the pilot of an F4F-4 Wildcat in the Combat Air Patrol above the fleet spotted and shot down a "Mavis" flying boat that was searching for the US ships. At 1230 hours, *Wasp*'s crew went to watch condition 2, with the air department at flight quarters. Relieved from watch, Signalman Curtis went below to the Communications Division sleeping compartment. In the heavy tropical humidity, he stripped to his skivvy shorts before sliding into his rack and falling asleep.

The sailors of Task Force 18 weren't wrong to be worried about the submarine threat in "Torpedo Junction." The Type B1 fleet submarine I-19, commanded by LCDR Shogo Narahara, was in the immediate area and on the lookout for enemy ships. The veteran submarine had already been victorious in previous attacks on Allied naval forces and had participated in Operation *K-1*, planned as a second attack on Pearl Harbor using Emily flying boats from the Marshall Islands that would refuel from I-19 at French Frigate Shoals to bomb the American base on the night of March 4, 1942. The mission was only called off at the last minute when I-19 spotted an American ship anchored at the shoals. At 1345 hours local time, Captain Narahara was called to the control room by the report from the officer at the periscope that he had spotted smoke on the horizon. A quick look confirmed for Narahara that there was more than one source to the wisps of smoke he spotted on the northern horizon and he gave orders to close on the target.

At 1420 hours, Lieutenant David McCampbell, *Wasp*'s Landing Signal Officer, awoke from a short nap in his stateroom and headed back to the flight deck to bring aboard the eight Wildcats and three Dauntlesses of the midday search. *Wasp* maneuvered away from the fleet in order to turn into the wind so she could launch eight F4F-3 Wildcats and 18 SBD-3 Dauntlesses to relieve those on patrol. Lt (jg) Roland H. Kenton, USNR, of VF-71 flew the Wildcat that was the last aircraft to get off. McCampbell then rapidly completed recovery of the 11 returning planes.

Captain Narahara watched through the periscope as the enemy carrier heeled slightly and turned to starboard to rejoin the rest of the enemy fleet. At 1443 hours he fired off six Type 95 torpedoes from a distance of 1,000 yards.

As lookouts screamed the warning of inbound torpedoes, Captain Forrest P. Sherman ordered the rudder "hard a' starboard," but it was too late. Two of the six torpedoes passed ahead of *Wasp* and were spotted passing astern of the cruiser *Helena*. At 1445 hours, three hits were scored on *Wasp*, all in the vicinity of the aviation gasoline tanks and the ship's magazine. At 1451 hours, one of the first two hit *O'Brien* (DD-415) as she maneuvered to avoid the other. The sixth torpedo narrowly missed *Lansdowne* (DD-486) at 1448 hours; it was spotted two minutes later by *Mustin* (DD-413) as it penetrated *North Carolina*'s screen, before it struck the battleship at 1452 hours. Narahara's spread of six torpedoes was one of the most successful shots taken by a submarine on any side during the war.

LSO McCampbell recalled the instant the ship was hit: "I was crossing the flight deck as the first one hit, and I thought it was a bombing attack. I jumped down on the catwalk, then felt the next two and realized they weren't bomb hits."

At the same time, Signalman Curtis was thrown from his rack onto the deck, ending against a wall of lockers. "I immediately knew we had been torpedoed." Smoke quickly filled the compartment and Curtis, still clad only in his underwear and barefoot, made his way out.

Fiery blasts ripped through the forward part of *Wasp*, tossing aircraft about on the flight deck. In the hangar deck below, the spare planes stored in the overhead broke free from their restraints and dropped with such force that their landing gears were snapped off when they struck the deck. Fires broke out in the hangar deck and the flames were sucked below through open hatches. Tom Curtis arrived at the bottom of the ladder to the hangar deck just as the flames roared down toward him. "I managed to get to the portside ladder and got up to the hangar deck. Everything was on fire." Curtis climbed out of the hangar and made his way up an exterior ladder to the flight deck.

The heat of the gasoline fires detonated the ready ammunition stored at the forward antiaircraft guns on the starboard side. The Number 2 1.1-inch gun mount was blown overboard while the corpse of the gun captain was thrown onto the bridge, landing next to Captain Sherman and spattering him with blood.

Tom Curtis ran across the flight deck toward his station on the island as the ammunition exploded. "I stepped on a piece of hot shrapnel that burned and cut my foot." Running on pure adrenaline, the 22-year-old sailor climbed the ladder to the signal bridge. "The other guys were amazed to see me, practically naked, with my foot bleeding all over the deck."

Wasp's condition rapidly became more desperate. Crews fighting the fires in the forward section of the ship lost the fight when water was cut off due to the failure of the water mains. The fire reigned unchecked and set off ammunition and bombs as it reached the magazines, and aviation gasoline when the tanks were breached. The sea flooded in through the gaping holes in her side and *Wasp* took a 15 degree list to starboard. The sea around the ship was covered in fires as oil and gasoline spread from the ruptured tanks.

With no way to fight the fires on the ship, Captain Sherman slowed *Wasp* to 10 knots and ordered a turn to port in hope of getting the wind onto the starboard bow where it could blow the fires out to port. The fires continued to rage and the central damage control station was evacuated at 1452 hours when the sound-powered phone circuits were destroyed. At 1455 hours, the fire reached the main aviation gasoline tanks, which created another major flagration in the forward hangar deck. Thirteen minutes later, there were three major gasoline vapor explosions.

With all fire-fighting capability gone, Captain Sherman realized they must abandon ship. Task Group Rear Admiral Leigh Noyes agreed with the decision and at 1520 hours Sherman ordered "Abandon Ship."

On the flight deck, Dave McCampbell was leading fire-fighting parties when he saw other crewmen going over the side and ordered the men he led to join them. He crossed the deck to the LSO platform, where he and pilot Lieutenant Downs Wright attempted to lower a large 18-man raft that hung at the stern. Because the ropes were too short, the raft dropped the last ten feet into the sea and drifted off. McCampbell then lowered a line from the LSO platform and told the men they could go down the line or jump overboard. The LSO had been the intercollegiate diving champion as an Annapolis midshipman, and had always thought that if he ended up having to abandon ship that he would make a fancy dive off the ship. But when he saw all the debris in the water below, he realized the danger. "I grabbed my nose with one hand and the family jewels with the other and went in feet first."

When McCampbell got to the surface, he saw the ship drifting down on him and swam around to the upwind side and assisted other survivors to get aboard a raft. With too many aboard, the raft started to sink. A strong swimmer, he set off toward a destroyer that had stopped to rescue survivors, but it moved off before he could get to it. He found Captain Sherman hanging on to a waterproof mattress. At that moment, the destroyer *Farenholt* stopped nearby and dropped a whaleboat. He managed to get to the boat and was taken aboard, then they picked up Captain Sherman and brought them to the destroyer. McCampbell was covered in oil and was sent below to shower. When he returned topside, he saw more wounded men in rafts and went back in the water to rescue them with the help of the *Farenholt*'s chief engineer. Unfortunately, many died of their wounds during the night.

Tom Curtis donned a lifejacket when he received the order to abandon ship and went down a line from the flight deck, still wearing only his skivvies. "I spent two and a half hours in the water, thinking I was going to drown. All of a sudden, there was a destroyer heaving to not far away and I swam to her. When I tried to climb up the cargo net, my life jacket was so heavy from oil and watersoaked I couldn't do it. Two guys came down the net and cut if off me and pulled me aboard." Curtis was sent below to shower and clean off the oil that covered him. "They didn't do anything for my foot. I spent that night trying to hold a bandage to the leg of the kid next to me, but he died." In the morning, Curtis' injured foot was bandaged.

Wasp drifted as the fire spread throughout the carrier. The fleet could not remain while she sank, and *Lansdowne* was ordered to sink her. The destroyer fired two torpedoes that did not explode when they hit *Wasp*.

The torpedomen disabled the magnetic exploders of the remaining three torpedoes and set them to run at 10 feet. All three exploded on contact, but *Wasp* refused to sink until 2100 hours. Losses included 193 killed and 366 wounded. Twenty-five of 26 airborne aircraft landed on *Hornet*, while 45 were lost in the sinking.

On September 16, *Wasp*'s 1,946 survivors, who had been picked up by the *Farenholt*, *Laffey*, *Lansdowne*, *Salt Lake City* and *Helena*, were all put aboard *Helena*, which took the wounded to Espiritu Santo, then transported the rest to Noumea, New Caledonia, where they were put aboard a transport to return home. As Curtis later recalled, "It took that transport three weeks to get back to San Diego."

"In all that time, none of us had any clothes but what we had been given aboard the *Farenholt*," McCampbell remembered. "We arrived in San Diego and stayed at the Hotel Del Coronado til we got our pay records and our replacement uniforms. I had just the one shirt, a pair of pants, and socks til we got back to Norfolk."

Tom Curtis received a 30 day survivors' leave and departed San Diego with an official admonition not to tell anyone back home what had happened until he saw something in the newspapers. "My mother was really surprised when I arrived back home in Ohio with no notice. She asked what happened and I said nothing happened, I just got leave." Two days later, the loss of *Wasp* was reported in the newspapers. "When I told my mother that was why I was home, she was mad at first, and then happy I survived. I had to tell my mother's oldest and best friend that her son had died, which was probably the hardest thing I ever did, since we had grown up together." Once word got around that Curtis had been on the *Wasp*, he was interviewed by the local newspaper and a local radio station, and then asked to speak to local groups. "I didn't have hardly any time with my family, I was doing all that speaking. Most people back home weren't really aware of what the war was like, so the navy told me it was important for me to do that."

O'Brien survived her torpedoing but suffered severe structural damage. She managed to reach Espiritu Santo on September 16, where emergency repairs were carried out. On October 10 she departed for San Francisco. She put into Suva in the New Hebrides on October 13 and departed on October 16. By October 18, the rate of leakage from the damage continued to increase. The crew jettisoned as much topside weight as possible. At 0600 hours on October 19, her hull split open. The crew abandoned ship at 0630 hours and *O'Brien* sank at 0700 hours. All crewmen were successfully rescued.

North Carolina was struck just forward of her number one gun turret, which created a hole 32 by 18 feet, 20 feet below the waterline. Five men were killed but the ship avoided disaster. Skillful damage control quickly righted a 5.6-degree list and *North Carolina* was able to continue in formation at 26 knots. After making temporary repairs in New Caledonia, she arrived at Pearl Harbor, where she went into dry-dock for repair to the hull. She was able to return to the South Pacific in early January 1943.

In the weeks following *Wasp*'s sinking, Admiral Yamamoto gathered the Japanese carrier force at the main Japanese Central Pacific anchorage in Truk Atoll, confident that he could find the opportunity to reverse the Midway defeat here in the South Pacific. The veteran carriers *Shōkaku* and *Zuikaku* that had fought most recently at Eastern Solomons were joined by the fleet carriers *Hiyō* and *Junyō*, and the light carrier *Zuihō* in early October.

The situation for the Americans was critical after *Wasp*'s loss. On October 15 Admiral Nimitz wrote a bleak assessment of the situation in the Solomons: "It now appears that we are unable to control the sea in the Guadalcanal area. Thus our supply of the positions will only be done at great expense to us. The situation is not hopeless, but it is certainly critical."

The day before, Nimitz had decided that he must replace Vice Admiral Robert L. Ghormley, Commander South Pacific Force. He turned to Admiral Halsey, who had come out of hospital from the shingles attack that had sidelined him at Midway three weeks earlier. Halsey's fighting reputation sent American morale throughout the area skyrocketing on his arrival in Noumea on October 16. His first step was to assure General Alexander A. Vandegrift, who commanded the Marines on Guadalcanal, that the Navy would give all possible support. Two days later, Halsey's old flagship, *Enterprise*, arrived from Pearl Harbor after undergoing emergency repairs for the damage suffered at the Eastern Solomons.

Forty days after *Wasp* went to her watery grave, Americans and Japanese met in the last carrier battle of the opening phase of the Pacific War.

The Battle of Santa Cruz was part of an attempt by the Japanese to drive the Americans from Guadalcanal and end the stalemate that had existed since the Marine victory at the Battle of Edson's Ridge on September 14. The Imperial Army prepared a major ground offensive to take Henderson Field for October 20–25. Japanese carriers and other warships moved into position near the southern Solomon Islands to support this offensive with the hope of engaging Allied naval forces which responded to the ground offensive.

On October 20, the Japanese Army began their offensive, which became a battle for Henderson Field. The Japanese attack was defeated with heavy casualties by the night of October 24–25. Unaware of the earlier defeat on Guadalcanal, the Imperial Navy task force operating near the Solomons sent several ships to attack Henderson Field. Spotted by aircraft from the island, the ships were subjected to air attacks throughout the day, during which the light cruiser *Yura* was sunk and the destroyer *Akizuki* damaged.

Hornet, which had been the sole American aircraft carrier in the South Pacific following *Wasp*'s loss, had just been reinforced the day before by the arrival of *Enterprise* which had departed Pearl Harbor on October 16 and rendezvoused with *Hornet* and the rest of the Allied South Pacific naval forces on October 24, 273 miles northeast of Espiritu Santo. *Enterprise* brought with her the new fast battleship *South Dakota* (BB-57) as a replacement for the damaged *North Carolina*.

Task Force 17 was commanded by Rear Admiral George Murray with his flag aboard *Hornet*, while Rear Admiral Thomas Kinkaid commanded Task Force 16 with his flag aboard *Enterprise*. Together they formed Task Force 61. Kinkaid, who had participated in the Battle of the Eastern Solomons in August, was in command as the senior officer afloat (SOA).

In accordance with prewar carrier doctrine, the two task forces were separated from each other by about ten miles and would fight separate, uncoordinated actions as the battle developed. The carriers were escorted by *Portland* (CA-33), *Northampton* (CA-26), *Pensacola* (CA-24), *San Juan* (CLAA-54), *San Diego* (CLAA-53), and *Juneau* (CLAA-52) and 14 destroyers. *San Juan*, *Juneau* and *San Diego* were a new type of light cruiser, armed for a primary mission of air defense with 16 5-inch dual-purpose guns, rather than the 6-inch naval guns carried by standard light cruisers.

Admiral Willis Lee commanded Task Force 64 aboard the battleship *Washington* (BB-56), with *San Francisco* (CA-38), *Helena* (CL-50), and *Atlanta* (CLAA-51), plus six destroyers. This force was stationed south of Guadalcanal to intercept any IJN transports; with none sighted, Lee withdrew for fueling on October 24, and the task force played no part in the battle.

Regardless of the Army's failure on Guadalcanal and despite losing *Yura*, Vice Admiral Nobutake Kondō continued to maneuver the Mobile Fleet south of the southern Solomon Islands as part of the plan to force a fleet action with the Americans. After *Hiyō* suffered an accidental fire in her engine room on October 22 that forced her return to Truk, Admiral Nagumo still had four carriers to the Americans' two.

The Advanced Force, which was commanded by Admiral Kondō aboard the cruiser *Atago*, comprised the carrier *Junyō* and the battleships *Kongō* and *Haruna* and their escorts. Vice Admiral Chuichi Nagumo, who had commanded the Mobile Fleet at Pearl Harbor and Midway, commanded the carriers of the Main Force – the veteran sister ships *Shōkaku* and *Zuikaku* that had fought at Coral Sea and Eastern Solomons, and the light carrier *Zuihō*. Rear Admiral Hiroaki Abe led The Vanguard Force with the battleships *Hiei* and *Kirishima*, three heavy cruisers, one light cruiser, and seven destroyers.

A PBY Catalina flying boat located Nagumo's Main Body at 1103 hours on October 25. The three carriers were approximately 355 miles from Task Force 61, which was just beyond strike range. Realizing he had been spotted and not knowing where the enemy was, Nagumo turned north to stay out of range. On receipt of the sighting report, Kinkaid headed toward the Japanese at top speed, to close the range and attack that day. *Enterprise* launched a strike force of 23 aircraft at 1425 hours, but the strike force returned, unsuccessful, a few hours later.

The Battle of Santa Cruz took place on October 26, 1942, and proved everything that had been learned in the American fleet exercises before the war regarding the deadly speed of carrier warfare. At 0250 hours, the Japanese had reversed course; *Shōkaku* and *Zuikaku* were only 200 miles from their opponents at dawn. Both sides found each other at almost the same time. The Japanese Main Body was discovered by Scouting Ten commander LCDR James R. Lee and wingman Ensign William E. Johnson. Lee and Johnson reported the carriers, then maneuvered to attack, but eight defending Zekes intercepted the Dauntlesses before they could strike. Smart flying and shooting by Lee and Johnson resulted in three Zekes going down and the Americans escaped with only a roughing up. While Lee and Johnson evaded the Zekes, a *Shōkaku* Kate spotted *Hornet*.

Both sides launched immediate strikes. The Japanese strike included 21 D3A2 Val dive bombers, 21 B5N2 Kate torpedo bombers, and 21 A6M2 Zeke fighters from *Zuikaku* and *Shōkaku*, which were headed toward the Americans by 0740 hours.

At almost the same time, two SBD-3 Dauntless scouts flown by Scouting 10 pilots Lieutenant Stockton Strong and his wingman Ensign Charles Irvine spotted *Zuihō*. In accordance with American doctrine, after they made their reports they attacked *Zuihō* while the Japanese Combat Air

Patrol chased other scout aircraft. *Zuihō* took two 500-pound bombs that damaged the flight deck, putting her out of action for the rest of the battle and for quite some time thereafter. However, Strong and Irvine had arrived too late to prevent the carrier launching her strike.

Shōkaku launched a second strike of 19 Vals and eight Zekes at 0810 hours, while *Zuikaku* launched 16 Kates at 0840 hours. One hundred and ten Japanese aircraft headed toward the Americans.

The American commanders were well aware that the force that struck first would be the likely winner. At this point in the battle, they fell victim to the prewar doctrine that each carrier air group would launch individual attacks on the enemy, rather than operating as a combined force the way the Japanese did. Additionally, the extreme range meant that the US strike aircraft could not waste valuable gasoline assembling before heading toward the enemy. Combined with communication difficulties that resulted from the limited number of HF frequencies, the result was a disorganized American strike.

Hornet launched her first strike at 0800 hours, which consisted of 15 SBD-3 dive bombers, six TBF-1 Avenger torpedo bombers, and eight F4F-4 Wildcat fighters. *Enterprise* sent off three SBD-3s, seven TBF-1s, and eight F4F-4s at 0810 hours. *Hornet* launched a second group of nine SBD-3s, eight TBF-1s, and seven F4F-4s at 0820 hours.

The opposing formations passed within sight of each other at 0840 hours. Nine of *Zuihō*'s fighters attacked the *Enterprise* group while the Americans were still climbing for altitude. Four Zekes, three Wildcats, and two Avengers went down. Two Avengers and a Wildcat were so badly damaged they had to return to *Enterprise*.

Hornet's strike sighted the Vanguard Force at 0850 hours and carried on to discover the Main Force carriers shortly after. Three Zekes from *Zuihō*'s CAP hit the Wildcats and drew them away from the 15 Dauntlesses, which attacked without fighter escort. Four SBDs were shot down when 20 Zekes attacked the dive bombers. At 0927 hours, 10 SBDs attacked *Shōkaku*. The Dauntlesses scored six hits and wrecked her flight deck, as had happened at Coral Sea. The eleventh Dauntless near-missed the destroyer *Teruzuki* and caused minor damage. The six Avengers had been separated from the rest of the strike and so turned back. Returning to *Hornet* they found the heavy cruiser *Tone*; all the nearly-worthless Mark XIV torpedoes missed.

Shortly after, the surviving Avengers of the *Enterprise* strike missed the carriers but spotted the heavy cruiser *Suzuya*, which they attacked unsuccessfully. Within minutes, the second *Hornet* strike also missed the carriers and attacked the heavy cruiser *Chikuma*, causing heavy damage.

The air strikes launched by *Enterprise* and *Hornet* at Santa Cruz would go down in the record books as among the least-successful strike missions ever flown by US Navy aircrews, since only ten of 75 strike aircraft attacked and damaged a Japanese fleet carrier, while two scouts damaged a light carrier.

At 0830, the Americans received warning from the outbound strike that a Japanese strike was coming. *Hornet* was found by the Japanese strike leader at 0852 hours while *Enterprise* was hidden by a rain squall. Three minutes later American radar spotted the inbound attack 35 miles from the fleet. Thirty-seven Wildcats were ordered to engage the Japanese. Within minutes, the single high frequency radio net was swamped with calls and all but a few of the American fighters failed to engage the enemy before they began their attacks on *Hornet*. While the Wildcats managed to splash several Val dive bombers, the others were able to commence their attacks relatively unmolested by the defenders. This was particularly true of the deadly B5N2 Kate torpedo bombers, which could attack at 250mph and an altitude of 2,500 feet, unlike the American Avengers which were forced to attack at 100 feet and 100mph. Once a Kate was in its dive, it was difficult for a Wildcat that was positioned to stop an American-style attack to catch it before the torpedo was dropped.

When the 20 Kates and the 16 surviving Vals began their attacks, the American ships opened fire at 0909 hours. *Hornet* was hit dead center on the flight deck near the island at 0912 by a 551-pound semi-armor-piercing bomb dropped by a Val that penetrated through three decks then exploded and killed 60 men. Moments later, a high explosive bomb detonated on impact when it struck the flight deck. This created an 11-foot hole and killed 30 sailors. This was followed a minute later by a second armor-piercing bomb that hit near the first and also penetrated through three decks before it exploded; it caused severe structural damage but there was no loss of life.

At 0914 hours, *Hornet*'s defensive fire hit and damaged a Val. On fire, the dive-bomber's pilot intentionally continued his dive and hit *Hornet*'s stack; seven men were killed while burning aviation fuel from the crashed Val spread over the signal bridge.

The Kates maneuvered for a classic "hammer and anvil" attack from ahead that prevented the target turning away from one set of attackers without presenting itself to the other. Defensive fire knocked down several of the Kates, but *Hornet* was hit in the engineering compartments by two Type 95 torpedoes at 0913 and 0917 hours that knocked out all power and brought the carrier to a stop. A Kate that had been set afire deliberately crashed into her at the hangar deck level and started a fire near the main aviation fuel tanks. Five minutes later, the Japanese survivors departed, leaving *Hornet* dead in the water and in flames.

Just as the Japanese departed, *Enterprise* and her escorts emerged from the rain squall and she was spotted. The "Big E" immediately began landing the damaged and fuel-depleted CAP fighters as well as returning scout aircraft from both carriers while she prepared a second strike to launch as soon as possible.

At 1030 hours, *Enterprise* spotted the second Japanese strike formation on radar. She ceased landing operations at 1100 hours and ordered the remaining planes out of the area. *Hornet*'s fires were under control at this point with firefighting assistance from three destroyers, and the wounded had been evacuated to the destroyers. *Northampton* prepared to take the carrier under tow despite the impending attack.

As this was happening, *Porter* (DD-356) was maneuvering to pick up the crew of a ditched *Enterprise* TBF when she was hit by a torpedo from the downed aircraft. The explosion caused heavy damage and killed 15. The "Abandon Ship" order was passed and *Shaw* (DD-373) picked up the crew before sinking *Porter* with gunfire.

The Japanese strike arrived overhead at 1105 hours. *Hornet* appeared to be sinking, so the attackers concentrated on *Enterprise* with an attack that commenced at 1108 hours.

The Japanese were at a higher altitude than the defending Wildcats, which were unable to climb to the enemy's altitude before they reached *Enterprise* and only managed to shoot down two Vals before they initiated their attack. *Enterprise* was hit by two 551-pound bombs while a third was a near miss. The hits killed 44 and wounded 75. Two Dauntlesses were blown overboard, while the midships elevator was jammed in the "down" position, which prevented air operations.

The American defense was stronger than in the previous carrier battles, due to the fact that both *Enterprise* and *South Dakota* had recently had their 1.1-inch "Chicago Piano" anti-aircraft guns replaced by 40mm Bofors cannons.

Fifteen minutes later, 15 Kates commanded by Pearl Harbor and Coral Sea veteran LCDR Shigeharu Murata arrived over the American fleet. Lieutenant Stanley "Swede" Vejtasa had just shot down two of the escaping Vals from the previous attack when he and his wingman Lieutenant Harris spotted the Kates low over the ocean, racing towards their targets at 250 knots, ten miles from *Enterprise*. Diving on the Kates, the two shot down six before they ran out of ammunition, while other Wildcats accounted for another three. Vejtasa had set the Navy record of shooting down seven enemy planes on a single day. One of the Kates was set afire. Before it crashed, the pilot deliberately aimed the aircraft into the destroyer *Smith* (DD-378), which set the ship afire and killed 57. The ship was only saved when her captain steered her into the large wake of *South Dakota*, dousing the fires on her bow. She then resumed station.

The remaining Kates proceeded to attack *Enterprise, South Dakota*, and *Portland*. At 1144 hours, the surviving Kates lined up on *Enterprise* to attempt a "hammer and anvil" attack. Those Kates to starboard dropped their torpedoes first. Captain Osborne Hardison ordered full right rudder and the carrier combed the torpedoes – one by a mere 30 feet – then ordered full left to miss *Smith* and more torpedoes. Speeding at 28 knots, her stern shuddered with each radical turn. Finally, the carrier came in line with five other Kates, which forced the bombers into a long turn to get into launching position. Three of the five were shot down by *Enterprise* and *South Dakota* before they could launch. The fourth desperately tried to drop its torpedo while in a stall off the stern, but both torpedo and bomber fell into the sea harmlessly. Of the five, only one managed a good drop, but Captain Hardison paralleled the torpedo and it ran past fifty feet away.

At 1159 hours, *Enterprise* finally steadied her course, and prepared to begin landing the *Hornet* and *Enterprise* planes collecting overhead, despite the fact the midships elevator was still a huge hole in the deck. After a momentary delay when gunners on *South Dakota* mistakenly opened fire on six friendly Dauntlesses, LSO Lieutenant Robin Lindsey began bringing planes aboard. After only a few traps, the guns roared back to life. Eighteen Vals commanded by Lieutenant Maseo Yamaguchi with 12 Zekes from the carrier *Junyō* had finally found their target.

They scored a near miss on *Enterprise* that caused more damage. *South Dakota* was struck on a heavily-armored 16-inch gun turret that caused minor damage from shrapnel, but killed one and wounded 50, including the battleship's captain, Thomas Gatch. The cruiser *San Juan* was struck by a bomb that went completely through the ship before exploding under the hull, causing flooding and damage to the rudder. Eleven of the 17 attacking Vals were shot down.

Overall, *Enterprise*'s Fighting Ten claimed 17 shot down for the loss of seven Wildcats and four pilots. *Hornet*'s VF-72 claimed 28 for a loss of five pilots and ten Wildcats. The gunners aboard *South Dakota* shot down 26, while the *Enterprise* gunners took down 46, the record for any American carrier in the Pacific War. Japanese logs reveal the magnitude of losses: nine Zekes returned from the second strike in serviceable condition, while only two of the 27 that attacked *Hornet* returned, period.

LCDR Masatake Okumiya, *Junyō*'s air staff officer, described the return of the strike groups:

> We searched the sky with apprehension. There were only a few planes in the air in comparison with the numbers launched several hours before. The planes lurched and staggered onto the deck, every single fighter and bomber bullet holed. As the pilots climbed wearily from their cramped cockpits, they told of unbelievable opposition, of skies choked with antiaircraft shell bursts and tracers.

At 1235 hours, *Enterprise* turned into the wind to land aircraft. The sky overhead was crowded with *Enterprise* and *Hornet* Wildcats, Dauntlesses and Avengers, all critically short of fuel. In what is considered the finest performance ever by an LSO, Robin Lindsey brought in plane after plane at 30-second intervals. As they came out of the arresting wires, planes were carefully pushed past the open midships elevator to make room for others, though it was impossible to put them below since the forward elevator had been jammed "up." Despite orders to stop, Lindsey continued and bought aboard 95 airplanes from both carriers that packed the deck from the bow to where the last 12 had to catch the first or second wire to avoid crashing into the planes ahead, with the last coming aboard at 1322 hours with its engine dying of fuel starvation as it touched down.

With all planes aboard, and *Enterprise* unable to conduct air operations, and surmising correctly that the enemy still had one or more carriers capable of launching strikes, Admiral Kinkaid ordered a withdrawal. *Hornet*'s task force was ordered to retreat as soon as they were able.

Admiral Kondo ordered the Advanced and Vanguard Forces to head toward the Americans' last reported position at 1300 hours with the hope of a night engagement. The damaged *Zuihō* and *Shōkaku* headed to Truk.

Junyō launched a second strike of seven Kates and eight Zekes at 1306 hours, while *Zuikaku* launched a third strike of seven Kates, two Vals and five Zekes. These were followed by a final launch of four Kates and six Zekes at 1535 hours from *Junyō*.

At 1445 hours, after overcoming several technical problems, *Northampton* finally began towing *Hornet* out of the battle area at five knots with *Hornet* on the verge of restoring partial power. However, there was virtually no chance that the carrier could be towed successfully in the face of the enemy, so far from a friendly naval facility.

Junyō's second strike found the formation at 1520 hours. While six torpedoes missed, the seventh struck *Hornet* amidships at 1523 hours. The newly-repaired electrical system failed while the sea flooded into the gaping hole to create a 14-degree list. With this, *Hornet* was finally given up for lost. *Zuikaku's* third strike found *Hornet* as the order to "Abandon Ship" was given and hit the ship with a final bomb at 1720 hours.

Admiral Halsey learned from radio intelligence that the Japanese fleet was approaching and finally ordered that *Hornet* be scuttled. *Mustin* (DD-413) and *Anderson* (DD-411) fired multiple torpedoes and more than 400 5-inch shells unsuccessfully. With the leading Japanese ships only 20 minutes away, the burning hulk was abandoned at 2040 hours.

The Japanese surrounded *Hornet* by 2220 hours. When he realized this was the carrier that had launched the Doolittle Raid, Kondo considered taking her as a war trophy, but she was too badly damaged to take under tow. The destroyers *Makigumo* and *Akigumo* finished *Hornet* with four Type 93 torpedoes (later known as "Long Lance torpedoes" by the US Navy). *Hornet* finally sank at 0135 hours on October 27, 1942.

Kondo was unable to continue pursuit of the retreating Americans due to a fuel shortage. After meeting oilers off the northern Solomons, the fleet returned to Truk on October 30. The Imperial Navy claimed to have sunk three carriers, one battleship, one cruiser, one destroyer and one "unidentified large warship" while shooting down 79 American aircraft.

The United States Navy was now reduced to one damaged carrier afloat in the South Pacific. In ten and a half months of combat, only two of the seven carriers so carefully built over the previous fifteen years still survived. *Hornet* herself had lasted a year and six days from the day she was commissioned. She would be the last US fleet carrier sunk by enemy action.

After *Enterprise* received temporary repairs at New Caledonia, she returned to the Solomons two weeks later and provided air support during the Naval Battle of Guadalcanal, the the battle for control of Guadalcanal.

Shōkaku and *Zuihō* were damaged so severely they would not be able to return to operations for several months. *Zuihō* returned to Truk in late January 1943 while *Shōkaku* remained under repair until March 1943 and was not reunited with *Zuikaku* at Truk until July 1943. Though undamaged, *Zuikaku* and *Hiyō* were forced to return to Japan because they did not have sufficient trained aircrew to man their air groups. The most significant losses were the 148 pilots and aircrew members, including two dive bomber squadron leaders, three torpedo squadron leaders, and 18 other section or flight leaders. This was more aircrew lost than had happened in the three previous carrier battles. 409 of the 765 elite aviators who had participated in the attack on Pearl Harbor were now dead and their loss would never be made good.

Admiral Nagumo, the victor at Pearl Harbor and the vanquished at Midway, was reassigned to shore duty in Japan. His report to Admiral Yamamoto stated: "This battle was a tactical win, but a shattering strategic loss for Japan. Considering the great superiority of our enemy's industrial capacity, we must win every battle overwhelmingly in order to win this war. This last one, although a victory, unfortunately, was not an overwhelming victory."

The American loss of 26 aircrew would be made good and multiplied a thousand-fold by the time the Japanese met an entirely new American carrier fleet 20 months later.

CHAPTER TWO

FORGING THE SWORD

W hat would become the rules of carrier warfare were shaped by the United States Navy during the years between world wars I and II in the many Fleet Exercises held throughout the 1930s. Out of this process came the development of both the ships and aircraft that the navy would use in the Pacific War. The only thing that had not been decided before the war was the position of the carrier within the force structure. This was resolved through *force majeure* in the wake of Pearl Harbor, when carriers became the center of the striking force while the battleships lay blasted on Battleship Row. While the Americans trained in peacetime exercises, the Japanese carriers were increasingly involved in combat operations in China, which led to the Japanese naval air force using their carriers in an integrated multi-carrier task force, which was superior to the American practice of organizing a task force around a single carrier. When the superiority of the Japanese practice was demonstrated in the 1942 carrier battles, this tactic was adopted by the Americans as the final necessary addition. The Japanese, however, never adopted the carrier and its aircraft as the primary striking force in a battle fleet.

Carriers – originally converted from other vessels rather than built for purpose – had first been used by the Royal Navy in World War I, and only came to be seen as integral components of a navy in the years following the 1922 Washington Naval Treaty. From around this time, as the number and size of purpose-built carriers increased, Japanese and American military leaders started reassessing their role from scouting-and-observation auxiliary warships, considering that they might actually have a decisive impact on the outcome of a Japanese–American showdown that leaders of both navies expected would occur at some future point.

Lexington (CV-2) and *Saratoga* (CV-3) were developed from hulls initially intended for battlecruisers, but were converted to aircraft carriers due to the terms of the Washington Treaty. Each weighed about 33,000 tons and could operate more aircraft than any contemporary Royal Navy vessel; once launched, they were used extensively as experimental platforms that helped develop operating doctrine and tactics. Lessons had already been learned from the *Langley* as she only had one deck elevator and this meant that only six planes could be launched at a time, and it was essential to future operations that as many planes as possible could go up in quick succession. Therefore, *Lexington* and *Saratoga* were both built with two elevators, each operating twice as fast as *Langley's* single one, relatively quadrupling their operating capabilities. For the 1929 Fleet Problem, they each operated 73 aircraft as opposed to *Langley's* 36.

Nevertheless, *Langley's* operation was the product of careful thought and Captain Joseph M. Reeves, who took command of Aircraft Squadrons, Battle Fleet in 1925, decided that *Langley* must be able to operate more efficiently: he got aviators to take off and land more quickly; implemented the modern ideas of the deck park; the crash barrier; and specialized deck crew. *Langley* was consequently able to have 16 planes airborne by February 1926 and 22 in 1927.

Lexington (CV-2) entered service in January 1928, a month after *Saratoga* (CV-3). Both had a length of 888 feet and a beam of 107 feet; they were powered by 16 water-tube boilers which drove four turbo-electric turbines of 180,000 shaft horsepower and gave each a top speed of 33 knots. They would revolutionize naval aviation and establish the method of operating aircraft aboard a carrier that is still used today.

The US Navy has always operated two major fleets; that assigned to the Atlantic, and that assigned to the Pacific. Throughout the interwar years, the Pacific Fleet was always the stronger of the two, given the Navy's expectation that the most likely situation in which war would break out was a conflict with Japan. Thus, the annual Fleet Problems were held in the Pacific and all envisioned that the "Enemy Fleet," regardless of its color designation in the exercise, was really the Imperial Japanese Navy. These fleet exercises were where the details of War Plan Orange – the Navy's plan for war with Japan – were fleshed out and potential problems and possibilities were resolved. As new elements were demonstrated effective in a fleet exercise and adopted, these would then be published in the Fleet Tactical Publications studied by all officers. The result by the end of the interwar period was the creation of a doctrine which was based on the concept of controlling the pace of engagement through seizure of the tactical initiative. This doctrine emphasized coordination of all arms while stressing tactical flexibility.

The battleships that composed the heart of the Battle Fleet were considered the primary offensive force in the years before the Pearl Harbor attack. Since War Plan Orange foresaw a traditional fleet engagement between the American and Japanese battle lines, the initial studies leading to the development of the navy's war-fighting doctrine focused on the Battle of Jutland, the only major engagement between modern battleships. As the US Navy saw things in retrospect, the Royal Navy's failure to obtain a decisive outcome in the battle was the result of inadequate coordination and communication among the formations, poor approach dispositions of the battle line, and inability to seize the offensive and control the pace of engagement. This central analysis would dominate American naval warfare planning, and would survive the change in capital ship and method of attack that was seen in World War II.

For the US Navy, the central point of this analysis was that the key to success lay in aggressive offensive action that allowed control of the tempo of the engagement. As regards communications, it was seen that, with contemporary technology, it would be impossible to coordinate an entire fleet from a central location in the heat of battle. What was needed was officers who understood what to do in the midst of engagement without the necessity of direct orders in detail. Thus, the development of a common doctrine was seen as the way to guarantee that ship captains would be able to coordinate effort, since all would be working from the same playbook. As noted in the *War Instructions*, victory would be aided by "Indoctrination of the forces, so that there may be mutual understanding of the intentions and plans of the Commander in Chief and so that there may be coordination in the means and methods employed in carrying out the tasks assigned and of the necessary procedure when without orders."

Since the central battle strategy involved a fleet engagement, finding the enemy first was crucial to the ability to control the engagement. As the US Navy emphasized long-range fire once the fleet was engaged because such plunging fire gave the greatest possibility of a single hit being decisive, aerial spotting of the battle line's fire was crucial. This meant that the initial involvement of carrier aviation was centered on scouting and observation, with the carrier an auxiliary to the battle line. This coordination between aircraft and battleship was first successfully demonstrated on February 17, 1919, when the battleship *Texas* (BB-35) conducted a long-range firing exercise in coordination with an aircraft. Spotting data was radioed to the ship, and it was determined that aerial spotting was far more effective than spotting from the masts. Lieutenant Commander Kenneth Whiting testified before the General Board that the effectiveness of fire was 200 percent utilizing aerial observation of the fall of shot.

The development and dissemination of this doctrine came from two places. First was the Fleet Problems, which were conducted on an annual basis throughout the period 1931–40, and allowed for practical demonstrations of tactics and operational developments. Second was the Naval War College at Newport, Rhode Island. Here, tactical concepts could be tested and refined through tabletop exercises and simulations, which had the added benefit in a period of restricted finances of being both inexpensive and a quick way to test new concepts and train officers in their use.

The Naval War College was then and is today more laboratory than college. Admiral Harris Laning recalled that:

> Here we study only enough to learn the sound principles on which successful warfare is based, the greater part of the time being devoted to actual operations and experiments carried out in chart maneuvers or on the game board. It is through such war games, conducted in miniature, that we can see the whole picture, that the student learns how to apply to actual war situations the principles he has learned through this study.

Officers were selected to attend the Naval War College as a path to career development. Where that was not possible, the college issued correspondence courses for those in the fleet. Laning recalled, "if you couldn't be there as we couldn't, why you were enjoined to enroll in this correspondence course, Strategy and Tactics. Well, I did, and that's where I became aware of this philosophy."

As much as the naval aviators were successful in developing and demonstrating the ability of the aircraft carrier to operate independently and effectively as a strategic offensive weapon beyond that of a platform for the operation of scouting and observation aircraft, the mindset of the "Battleship Admirals" throughout this period precluded a major change in strategic and tactical planning. That would only come about by *force majeure* after December 7, 1941. There were no high-ranking career naval aviators to argue against this mindset, and only two admirals with any aviation background – King and Halsey. Both were considered "latecomers" by the career naval aviators, since they had only entered flight training at late stages of their careers, and had done so for career advancement. The career naval aviators, who had entered the field as junior officers, saw a difference in mindset and understanding of what was potentially possible with carrier aviation between themselves and the "latecomers." It was the difference of the dissenting "true believers" as opposed to the High Churchmen. These junior men would become the carrier commanders and task group commanders in the Pacific War.

The Navy was early in understanding the value of carriers operating together, though the concept of integrating air groups for operations was not adopted. Early in their careers, *Lexington*, which was then commanded by future World War II Chief of Naval Operations Captain Ernest J. King, operated with *Saratoga* during February 1931 in Fleet Problem XII, in which the carriers were assigned the defense of the Pacific Coast of Panama against a hypothetical invader. While both carriers inflicted damage to the invasion convoys, troops were successfully landed by the enemy force. In March 1932, *Langley*, *Saratoga* and *Lexington* conducted further maneuvers in the Caribbean. In these exercises, *Saratoga* successfully defended the Panama Canal against *Lexington*'s attack when Admiral Reeves set a trap with a destroyer and scored a "sunk" on March 22 when *Saratoga*'s air group caught *Lexington* without her aircraft, which were in search of *Saratoga*.

The exercises established the two main principles of carrier warfare: a carrier's primary role was to find and sink the opposing carrier, and that the carrier that made the first strike and prevented the enemy from further operation would be the winner. The operational result of this was the decision to develop the scout bomber, which would be able to find the enemy and then attack once the enemy carrier was discovered. The Japanese never discovered this concept and used floatplanes launched from battleships and cruisers in the traditional observation role to find the enemy fleet without the capability of following up with an immediate attack to damage the enemy carrier.

The ability of carriers to attack targets ashore was demonstrated on January 26, 1932, when *Saratoga* launched 86 aircraft to attack the Panama Canal, the key to the "two-ocean navy" strategy; the attack was judged to have seriously damaged the locks.

The future was demonstrated during Grand Joint Exercise No. 4 when *Lexington* and *Saratoga* struck Pearl Harbor with an undetected air strike on Sunday, February 7, 1932 which the judges determined destroyed ships in harbor. Fleet Problem XIII the next month had *Lexington* assigned to the "Black" Fleet in defense of the West Coast and Hawaii against "Blue" Fleet's *Saratoga*. The "combat" was decisive: *Lexington*'s planes caught *Saratoga* with her aircraft still aboard on March 15; *Saratoga* was ruled to have been badly damaged with her flight deck knocked out; she was ruled "sunk" that night by Black Fleet destroyers. Air Group 2 demonstrated the power of dive bombing when *Lexington*'s bombers were credited with severely damaging two Blue Fleet battleships. Again, the two primary rules of carrier warfare were driven home, while the dive bomber was shown to be the primary ship-killer.

Before commencement of Fleet Problem XIV, the Army and Navy conducted another simulated carrier attack on Pearl Harbor in which *Lexington* and *Saratoga* launched a strike at dawn on January 31, 1933, without being detected.

The need for underway replenishment capability was demonstrated in Fleet Problem XVI, conducted between April and June 1935 when, after five days of high-speed steaming, *Lexington* ran low on fuel. As a result, experiments with underway replenishment began later that year and demonstrated this capability was essential to future combat operations. The next year saw routine refueling of plane guard destroyers by *Lexington* and the new *Ranger* (CV-4) in Fleet Problem XVII.

Fleet Problem XVIII in 1937 had *Lexington* assigned to support the battle line rather than operating independently. She was judged crippled and nearly sunk by surface gunfire and torpedoes. This demonstrated the principle that the carrier must operate with its own independent task force.

Following a month in the South Pacific unsuccessfully searching for Amelia Earhart, *Lexington* and *Saratoga* attacked Pearl Harbor a third time at dawn on March 29, 1938, in Fleet Problem XIX. One has to wonder why measures were not taken to provide better defense of the important base, with the carriers having demonstrated in 1932, 1933, and 1938 how vulnerable the main American base in the Pacific was to seaborne aerial attack. Three and a half years later, the Imperial Japanese Navy would launch the devastating attack the American Navy had so successfully demonstrated.

A month after the third Pearl Harbor attack, San Francisco was successfully attacked by *Lexington* and *Saratoga* with neither carrier being spotted by the defending fleet. The attack was the first demonstration that aircraft carriers could perform a strategic role, which would see its full flower with the carrier attacks against the Japanese home islands in 1945.

Fleet Problem XX was held in the Caribbean during March and April 1939 and it gave a preview of how the fast carrier task force would operate in a Pacific war. The new carriers *Yorktown* (CV-5) and *Enterprise* (CV-6) joined *Lexington* and *Ranger* in a multicarrier task force which featured repeated underway refueling operations that extended the ships' range and duration of operation.

While war raged in Europe in 1940, Fleet Problem XXI gave a preview of just how vulnerable carriers were to attack when *Lexington*'s Air Group 2 caught *Yorktown* by surprise and crippled her, with *Yorktown*'s already-airborne Air Group 5 knocking out *Lexington*'s flight deck.

By the time war came in 1941, the American Navy was doctrinally prepared and her sailors and naval aviators understood the rules of carrier warfare: that the ship that could quickly operate the greatest number of aircraft had the best chance to find and overwhelm the enemy; that the side which first damaged the other's carriers would be the one most likely to win the battle; that the ability to defend the fleet was crucial to continued operations. The one fault was the failure to understand that carrier task forces should not operate individually; this would change after the four carrier battles in 1942.

Although the battle line, the heart of the fleet, was destroyed on December 7, 1941, the operating principles of doctrine that had been developed for that fleet were still readily applied to the remaining forces. The hallmarks of victory in the Pacific War for the American Navy were the emphasis on decisive offensive action, reliance on individual initiative of ship commanders, and development of decentralized command.

While the Americans learned the essential rules of carrier warfare during the 1930s, the Japanese Navy did not. Their failure began with the decision to equip *Akagi* and *Kaga* with multiple decks with the result that both ships spent the years 1932–35 in drydock being extensively rebuilt with the extra takeoff decks removed, rather than engaging in operational exercises. Shortly after their return to service, Japan went to war with China and the carriers were committed to combat operations off the Chinese coast, whence they struck Chinese targets inland in support of the Army, rather than participating in exercises where strategies and tactics could be reviewed and changed in light of experience, as their future American opponents did.

An important result of this lack of experience was the decision that scouting for the enemy fleet was a job for dedicated reconnaissance aircraft, primarily the floatplanes carried by the escorting cruisers. There was no possibility that such aircraft could be used similarly to the American scout bomber, which could attack the enemy carrier once found, potentially damaging the flight deck sufficiently to prevent further operations. Had the No. 4 scout plane launched by the cruiser *Tone* at Midway been a scout bomber, and had it damaged either *Yorktown* or *Enterprise* following discovery of the American carriers northeast of Midway, before either launched its strike force, the result of the Battle of Midway would have been entirely different.

After both navies commissioned their converted battle cruiser carriers, they began to design and construct aircraft carriers designed for the purpose from the outset. The American Navy's first carrier built as such from the outset was *Ranger* (CV-4). *Ranger*'s design dated to the late 1920s, when the real role of the carrier had yet to be revealed in the Fleet Problems and she was thus the product of the belief that the carrier's role was that of an auxiliary. The result was a ship less than half the size of *Lexington* or *Saratoga*, too small to carry proper armor protection and too slow to operate with the new carriers that were in the design stage at the time of her 1935 commissioning. As a result, *Ranger* was the only prewar carrier that never saw action against the Japanese.

The high point of American prewar carrier design was reached with the three fleet carriers of the Yorktown class. Class leader *Yorktown* (CV-5) was laid down on May 21, 1934 at the Newport News Shipbuilding and Drydock Company in Newport News, Virginia, which would construct all three. The design owed everything to lessons learned operating *Lexington* and *Saratoga*. She was equipped with three fast-acting elevators on the flight deck centerline to move aircraft between the flight and hangar decks. At 27,000 tons, she was not as large as *Lexington* or *Saratoga*, with length overall of 825 feet and beam a bit more than 109 feet. However, the Yorktowns could carry an air group larger than that of either predecessor, since the ships had a much larger hangar deck than did the former battle cruisers. The Navy had discovered that a large carrier was superior to a smaller carrier, since it could maintain a high speed and operate a larger air group. The Yorktowns were powered by nine Babcock & Wilcox boilers feeding four Parsons geared turbines providing 120,000 shaft horsepower and a top speed of 33 knots. In addition to high speed, a larger ship could carry sufficient armor protection against torpedoes and bombs to make it more likely to survive an attack than a smaller ship. Despite the fact that both *Yorktown* and *Hornet* were lost in combat, they proved to be tough ships that were so hard to kill that each was eventually given the *coup de grace* by their own defenders to prevent them falling into enemy hands. *Enterprise* (CV-6) managed to survive the worst the enemy could throw at her till the final battles against the *kamikazes* and even then she returned home under her own power.

Yorktown was launched in 1937, followed by her classmate, *Enterprise* in 1938. Under the terms of the Washington Naval Treaty and the subsequent London Naval Treaty of 1930, the Navy had 135,000 tons allocated to aircraft carriers, of which 15,000 tons were left unbuilt in 1937. *Wasp* (CV-7) was the result. She was a scaled-down *Yorktown* only 741 feet long with a beam of 80 feet and had none of the armor or torpedo protection carried by the Yorktowns. Her powerplant provided only 75,000 shaft horsepower that resulted in a top speed of only 29 knots. Construction began on April 1, 1936; the ship was launched on April 4, 1939 and commissioned on April 25, 1940.

Following repudiation by Japan and Italy of the proposed 1936 modifications to the 1930 Treaty of London, the limitations on tonnage were terminated. Ship designers were finally free to design ships to fit the mission, rather than the allowed tonnage. The Bureau of Ships decided to upgrade the capability of the Yorktown class. With passage of the Naval Expansion Act by Congress on May 17, 1938, an increase of 40,000 tons for aircraft carriers was authorized. This allowed construction of *Hornet* (CV-8) as the last of the Yorktown class and the design of *Essex* (CV-9) as the new fleet carrier. Laid down on September 25, 1939, *Hornet* was launched on December 14, 1940 and commissioned on October 20, 1941, the last American carrier commissioned before the war.

Laid down in 1940, *Essex* (CV-9) was the first of a very influential class of capital warship, 880 feet long and so wide as to only just fit through the Panama Canal – an operational necessity. In accordance with previous USN carrier design, this class had armor on the hangar deck which lowered the center of gravity and allowed the flight deck above to be big enough for the operation of air groups that were larger in aircraft number than prewar air groups.

The first three of the class – CV-9, CV-10, and CV-11 – were ordered from the Newport News Shipbuilding and Drydock Company on July 3, 1940. Ten more were planned in the wake of the Two-Ocean Navy Act that summer. Eight were ordered on September 9, 1940: CV-12–15 from Newport News; CV-16–19 from Bethlehem Steel Fore River Shipyard; while CV-20 and CV-21 were ordered on December 15, 1941, eight days after

Pearl Harbor, from the Brooklyn Navy Yard and Newport News, respectively. Following the US declaration of war, funds were quickly appropriated for 19 more. Ten were ordered in August 1942: CV-31 and CV-33–35 from Brooklyn Navy Yard; CV-32 from Newport News; CV-36 and CV-37 from Philadelphia Navy Yard; CV-38–40 from Norfolk Navy Yard. Three more were ordered in June 1943: CV-45 from Philadelphia Navy Yard; CV-46 from Newport News; and CV-47 from Fore River. Only two of these later ships were completed in time to see active service in World War II. Of the final six ordered in 1944, CV-50–55 were canceled before construction began. Following the carrier battles of 1942, four were renamed after they were laid down before they were launched. CV-10, originally named *Bon Homme Richard*, was renamed *Yorktown* for the carrier lost at Midway; CV-12, originally named *Intrepid*, became *Hornet* in memory of the carrier lost at Santa Cruz; CV-16, originally named *Cabot*, became *Lexington* in memory of the carrier lost at Coral Sea; CV-18, originally named *Oriskany*, became *Wasp*. In 1944, CV-37, originally named *Valley Forge*, became *Princeton* in memory of *Princeton* (CVL-23), lost at Leyte Gulf.

The midships deck-edge elevator was the most important operational improvement. It was introduced on *Wasp* (CV-7), and allowed replacement aircraft to be lifted from the hangar deck to the flight deck without having to use one of the two centerline elevators, which disrupted operations. Thus, a damaged airplane could be struck below while the deck stayed open for more landings, without aircraft parked forward having to respot. Alternatively, an airplane could be replaced before launch without disrupting the flight deck.

The new carriers' main defensive gun armament was composed of 12 5-inch/38-caliber guns: four in single-weapon open mounts, two forward two aft on the port side of the flight deck, while the other eight were in four twin mounts located fore and aft of the island on the starboard side. These guns were reinforced by as many as 17 quadruple-mount 40mm Bofors cannon (depending on the modernization of the individual ship), with 65 single-mount 20mm Oerlikon cannon along both sides of the flight deck for close-in defense.

The range of the 5-inch guns was 10 miles and the rate of fire was 15 rounds per minute, firing the proximity-fuse shell first introduced in January 1943, which detonated within 70 feet of an attacking aircraft. The 40mm guns had a higher rate of fire and greater hitting power than the 1.1-inch/75-caliber "Chicago pianos" which had originally been mounted on the earlier Lexington and Yorktown ships.

Effective radar made the decisive defensive difference from the prewar carriers that had only been equipped with early radars at the outset of the war. SK air-search and SC and SG surface-search radars were the original equipment, while SM fighter-direction radar was added later. The 5-inch batteries were originally controlled by two Mark 37 fire control directors with FD Mark 4 tracking radar. This gear proved inadequate in distinguishing low-level intruders from surface clutter and the systems were replaced with the Mark 12/Mark 22 combination. Mark 51 gyro-stabilized optical directors with integrated lead-angle calculators were used to control the 40mm batteries. A plan position indicator (PPI) radar display in the Combat Information Center (CIC) allowed a multicarrier task force to maintain a high-speed formation in heavy weather or at night. A dead reckoning tracer (DRT) was used for navigation and tracking surface ships, while identification-friend-or-foe (IFF) radar transponders in both aircraft and ships allowed fast identification of hostile ships and aircraft. Radio communication was vastly improved by use of the four-channel very high frequency (VHF) radio, which used channel variation to prevent enemy interception of transmissions while allowing simultaneous radio contact with other ships and planes in the task force.

VHF was a vast improvement over the earlier single-channel high-frequency radio, which had been easily swamped with radio transmissions in the 1942 battles because the system lacked the necessary capabilities. With this electronic support, young FDOs, such as Lieutenant (jg) Wendell Mayes who reported aboard *Essex* at Ulithi in October 1944, were able to transform carrier air defense from its pitiful state during the 1942 carrier battles.

Minor modifications were made throughout the war. The hangar deck catapult that blasted an aircraft out an opening on the port side of the ship was removed, but not before doing so became what Fighting 15 pilot Jim Duffy recalled as "my single most frightening experience of my entire Navy career," when every squadron member was required to make a catapult launch from *Hornet*.

While the ventilation system was substantially revised for operation in the tropics, Bombing 15 Aviation Radioman 3/c Ted Graham wrote in his diary that air conditioning was not considered important for enlisted men in their part of the ship. During infrequent refits in the United States, new and more powerful radars were installed, as well as more antiaircraft weapons. The hundreds of such changes made meant that, to the knowledgeable observer, no two Essex carriers were really ever the same.

Originally, the air group for an Essex carrier was composed of 36 F6F-3 Hellcat fighters, 24 SBD-5 Dauntless dive bombers which were replaced in 1944 by 24 SB2C-1C Helldivers, and 24 TBF/TBM-1C Avenger torpedo bombers. This balance of types was changed throughout the war as the number of fighters was increased, with a concomitant reduction in the number of dive and torpedo bombers. Operations in 1944 demonstrated that the Hellcat was capable of taking on the role of fighter-bomber with a load equal to that of a Helldiver. Combined with the Hellcat's increased range and the ability to self-defend, the number of Helldivers in a squadron was reduced to 18 in late 1944.

With war looming in 1941, President Franklin D. Roosevelt, who paid personal attention to the development of the new navy due to the interest he had acquired following his tour as Assistant Secretary in the Navy during World War I, questioned the fact that no new fleet carriers were expected to join the fleet before 1944. He suggested that some of the many light cruisers then under construction be converted to aircraft carriers. The Navy's General Board answered the presidential suggestion on October 13, 1941, in a report that stated such a conversion involved too many operational compromises and cited prewar studies which had concluded a carrier that small was too seriously limited with regard to armor protection and air group size to be effective. The president was undeterred, and ordered a second study. The Navy got the message. The October 25, 1941 Bureau of Ships report recommended the conversion, even though a cruiser-conversion aircraft carrier would necessarily have less capability than the coming Essex-class fleet carrier, since such a ship would be available as early as 1943. With America's sudden entry into the war following the Pearl Harbor attack, the need for more carriers was now urgent. Construction of the Essex carriers was accelerated and a Cleveland-class light cruiser under construction was ordered to be converted to a light aircraft carrier (CVL), which became *Belleau Wood* (CVL-24).

Two more light cruisers were ordered converted to carriers in February 1942, with another three in March and the final three in June. Now called the Independence class, the ships had a short, narrow flight deck with a small hangar below and an island which was the same as that used for the escort carriers (CVE). There was a substantial increase in topside weight which was compensated for by adding blisters to the original cruiser hull that increased the original beam by 5 feet. While a fleet carrier air group numbered 90 aircraft, CVL air groups had only some 30 aircraft. The original complement was 12 F6F-3 Hellcat fighters, nine SBD-5 Dauntless dive bombers, and nine TBF-1C Avenger torpedo bombers. Use of the Dauntless, with its non-folding wings, created operating difficulty on the flight deck and in hangar storage, with the result that the CVL air group was reorganized with 25 Hellcats and nine Avengers.

The primary value of the CVL was its availability. The ships experienced sea-keeping difficulties in Pacific typhoons and at least two CVLs came close to being sunk in storms. There was a relatively high aircraft accident rate due to operating from the short and narrow flight decks. These shortcomings were balanced by the fact they were fast ships since their cruiser hull and propulsion provided the speed necessary to stay up with the fleet carriers.

The Navy learned the hard way in 1942 that carriers should not operate separately from one other; in a major change of doctrine, it was determined that the best protection was the formation of a task group composed of three or four carriers, ideally two Essex-class heavy carriers and two Independence-class light carriers that could all combine their antiaircraft fire with their supporting battleships, cruisers and destroyers for an effective defensive umbrella. The combined aerial fighter strength allowed strike groups to be well escorted while also having a strong CAP capability. Two or more task groups operating together made a fast carrier task force. In 1944, four such task groups comprised the fast carrier task force known as Task Force 38 when the fleet was led by Third Fleet commander Admiral Halsey and Task Force 58 when part of Admiral Spruance's Fifth Fleet.

A third class of aircraft carrier became important during the Central Pacific campaign. The escort carrier was originally conceived as an auxiliary carrier, based on a merchant ship hull: the initial Sangamon-class CVEs were based on tanker hulls, while the Bogue class were based on the hull of the Type C3 cargo ship. The later and more numerous Casablanca class were based on S4-S3-BB33 merchant ship hulls, while the Commencement Bay class were larger, based on the Maritime Commission T3 type tanker hull with a displacement of 23,000 tons and a greater length of 557 feet with a general layout similar to the Sangamon class. Initially, these carriers were developed to provide antisubmarine aerial defense for Atlantic convoys. They were originally classified as auxiliary aircraft escort vessels (AVG) in February 1942, with the designation changed to auxiliary aircraft carrier (ACV) on August 5, 1942 before becoming escort aircraft carriers (CVE) on July 15, 1943. In the Pacific Theater, these smaller carriers were good for providing air support to the island invasions. Eventually, CVEs in the Pacific were organized into the Carrier Support Group, operating in task units of four to six CVEs with Escorting Destroyers (DD) and Destroyer Escorts (DE) in a task group of three or four task units. CVEs also provided yeoman service as aircraft transports to island bases, and transporting replacement aircraft to make up losses aboard the fleet carriers. A typical CVE "composite squadron" was composed of 16–18 FM-2 Wildcat fighters and 12–14 TBM-1C Avenger torpedo bombers.

Known as "jeep carriers," "Woolworth flattops," "Kaiser coffins," and "one-torpedo ships," the joke went around among their crews that CVE stood for the three most salient characteristics of a CVE: combustible, vulnerable, and expendable. In 1944, a journalist traveling aboard the *White Plains* (CVE-66) wrote, "A jeep carrier bears the same relation to a normal naval vessel that is borne to a district of fine homes by a respectable, but struggling, working-class suburb. There is a desperate effort to keep up appearances with somewhat inadequate materials and not wholly successful results." The Casablancas were the first CVEs designed and built as such from the keel up. Using a new submerged arc welding technique, a Liberty ship could be built in an average of 42 days, and Henry J. Kaiser promised that a CVE could be produced in 90.

Kaiser created the most important shipbuilding facilities in the United States during the war. His reputation for effective management of resources, and for projects completed on time and under budget preceded him as the primary contractor for the construction of the Hoover Dam, which had been completed in half the time originally expected. He had gone on from that to build cargo ships for the Maritime Commission in partnership with Todd Pacific Shipyards and the Bath Iron Works. Kaiser Shipbuilding was created in 1939 to meet the construction goals set by the United States Maritime Commission for merchant shipping in what was seen as a coming war. In 1940, he contracted with the British government to construct 31 cargo ships for the British merchant marine. Chosen to develop CVEs due to the company's experience in mass production of the Liberty ships and later Victory ships, Kaiser opened a new shipyard in Vancouver, Washington, for the construction of tankers and aircraft carriers.

However brilliant the means of construction, Kaiser took shortcuts on materials and components. CVEs had fewer watertight compartments than any other warship. Power was provided not by turbines but by inexpensive and idiosyncratic Skinner Uniflow steam engines that did not conform to Navy specifications and were unknown to the young engineering sailors being graduated from the Navy's schools. The thin steel the ships were built from had a high content of sulfur and phosphorus and was quite brittle. This meant that, when hit, it would burn quickly and break up fast. This was demonstrated in the loss of *Liscome Bay* (CVE-56), which was torpedoed by a Japanese submarine on November 24, 1943 and sank less than ten minutes after exploding.

Additionally, the ships lacked blower systems to ventilate the lower compartments and crews suffered whether they were in the freezing North Atlantic or the sweltering South Pacific. Of the 151 aircraft carriers built by the US Navy during World War II, 122 were CVEs, 38 of which were provided to the Royal Navy through Lend-Lease. Though none survive today, the Casablanca class holds the distinction of being the most numerous single class of aircraft carrier ever built, with 50 launched between November 3, 1942 and July 8, 1944. The Bogue class came in a close second, with 45 launched.

Of the 11 American aircraft carriers lost during the war, six were CVEs. Two were sunk by submarines (one Japanese, one German), one by surface gunfire and three by *kamikazes*.

At the outset of the war, the Imperial Japanese Navy had six fleet carriers. While *Akagi* and *Kaga* were similar in size and operational capability to *Lexington* and *Saratoga*, the next two – *Sōryū* and *Hiryū* – were comparable to *Wasp* in size and capability, and *Shōkaku* and *Zuikaku* were superior to *Yorktown*. The Shōkaku class was the best carrier in the world until the first Essex class ships entered service. Japan had no way to match the industrial capacity of the United States to replace wartime losses. After the outbreak of war, only two other large fleet carriers were built. *Taihō*, an improved *Shōkaku* with an armored flight deck, joined the Mobile Fleet in April 1944 only to be sunk two months later at the Battle of the Philippine Sea. Following the loss of *Akagi*, *Kaga*, *Sōryū*, and *Hiryū* at Midway, the third Musashi-class super-battleship, *Shinano*, was converted into the world's largest aircraft carrier. *Shinano* was launched in the fall of 1944 and sank while *en route* from Yokosuka to Kure for final fitting-out following commissioning. Additionally, three Unryu-class fleet carriers roughly equivalent to *Hiryū* were completed during the war, though they did not take part in any major fleet actions and only *Unryu* herself saw any operations.

Additionally, the Imperial Japanese Navy operated two carriers, *Junyō* and *Hiyō*, which were converted from ocean liner hulls; rated as CVs, they were approximately similar to the original *Wasp* in size. Eight carriers rated as CVL ranged in size from somewhat smaller to somewhat larger than the American *Ranger*. Five CVE-class carriers rounded out the fleet.

No matter how good the ship, a carrier's "punch" was the airplanes she carried into battle. The US Navy was fortunate that after 1943 the naval air force comprised airplanes that were superior to their land-based and carrier-based enemy counterparts. This resulted from decisions made in the years immediately before the war by naval aviators and aeronautical engineers who paid close attention to the revolutionary developments in air combat following the outbreak of war in September 1939.

The F6F Hellcat has a place in popular mythology as "the answer" to the Zeke, specifically designed to take it on in aerial combat. The truth is that the prototype had already made its flight before the first A6M2 Zero was captured and examined by American intelligence, so the production timescales do not support this.

In 1943, Grumman created the "Wilder Wildcat," originally the XF4F-8, but known as the FM-2 when produced by Eastern Aircraft. The 1,350-horsepower Wright R-1820-56 Cyclone replaced the Pratt & Whitney 1,200-horsepower R-1830 Twin Wasp and the aircraft was recognized by a taller vertical fin to cope with the increased torque. With a lightened airframe, the FM-2 became a real performer in air-to-air combat and possessed the best victory-to-loss ratio – 30:1 – of any US fighter. The FM-2 was the standard fighter in CVE composite squadrons from the spring of 1944 and served to the end of the war.

The F6F was originally intended as an upgraded F4F, ordered from Grumman by the Navy as an interim measure until the F4U-1 Corsair could come into service. Vought had lost its early prototype of the Corsair and was testing the XF4U-1, but this needed considerable development before it could come into service, so the Navy needed a fighter that could stand against all comers and approached Grumman. Grumman's Bob Hall convinced Leroy Grumman that the new fighter would need to be an entirely new design rather than an upgrade, and began development of a bristling fleet-defense fighter with enough fuel capacity to be able to fly for hours, with a wing of 334 square feet when the average fighter wing was less than 250 square feet; this would allow it to outmaneuver anything it ran into. The Bureau of Aeronautics quickly approved the project and Grumman started initial design of what would become the F6F Hellcat on June 30, 1941.

Though the F6F was not developed as an "answer" to the Zeke, the design benefited from the input of Navy pilots who had met the Japanese fighter in combat during early 1942. On April 22, 1942, Lieutenant Edward "Butch" O'Hare, the Navy's first ace, visited Grumman, where he spoke with the engineers and analyzed the expected performance of the Hellcat against the Zeke.

The XF6F-1 was powered by the Wright R-2600 14-cylinder Twin Cyclone radial engine. After meeting O'Hare, Grumman suggested a power increase which resulted in a decision on April 26, 1942 to put the superb new Pratt & Whitney R-2800 18-cylinder Double Wasp, perhaps the best piston engine ever built, in the second prototype. Power increased to the magic 2,000 horses.

Input from the Bureau of Aeronautics' Lieutenant Commander A.M. Jackson resulted in the designers mounting the cockpit higher in the fuselage for better visibility. The Hellcat thus had the best forward visibility of any piston-powered fighter in the war.

The XF6F-1 first flew on June 26, 1942, and quickly proved the need for additional power. The Double Wasp-powered XF6F-3 flew on July 30, 1942, proving itself a winner from the first flight. Tests of the Akutan Zero demonstrated that the F6F-1 would have been slower than the Japanese fighter; with the R-2800 the big fighter had a 30mph speed advantage at the altitudes where most Pacific fighting occurred.

The initial airframe design was so good that there were fewer changes between prototype and production version, and fewer changes between sub-types, than any other fighter on either side. The wide-track gear, which retracted hydraulically into the wing, was strong enough to let the fighter fall undamaged from 20 feet onto the flight deck; such events happened regularly during heavy weather in the Pacific where the deck pitched and heaved beneath a stalled-out Hellcat at the moment of landing. The low-set wing and raised cockpit provided the best visibility for combat and shipboard landing and was miles ahead of the F4U Corsair which gained the names "Old Hose Nose" and "Ensign Eliminator" for its difficult landing characteristics.

VF-15 ace Lieutenant John Strane recalled his first flight in a Hellcat: "My initial impression of the Hellcat was that I was in a completely different ballpark than the SNJ trainer or the F4F. The tremendous power, the comfort of the cockpit, the ease of handling of the plane throughout its entire flight envelope was unbelievable."

Regardless of the XF6F-3's crash on a test flight in August, the first production F6F-3 flew on October 3, 1942. Production output gathered steam quickly: ten Hellcats were delivered by the end of December 1942, 128 during the first three months of 1943, and 130 in the month of April; production increased quickly in the following months. Eventually, Hellcats were rolling out of the factory in Bethpage, Long Island, at 500 per month in 1944–45.

From the first introduction to combat in August 1943 through August 15, 1945, Hellcats shot down 5,000 enemy aircraft, 62 percent of all enemy aircraft shot down by Navy and Marine fliers, and 43 percent of all those shot down by Army and Navy fighters in the Pacific. It excelled when flown as a day fighter, a night fighter, or a fighter-bomber able to defend itself. A total of 305 Hellcat pilots became aces in the airplane in two years of combat, with a 19:1 victory-to-loss ratio. Truly, the Hellcat was an "ace maker."

The F4U Corsair finally arrived in early 1943. The F4U-1 was difficult to operate aboard a carrier because of stiff landing gear that created a damaging bounce in all but a perfect landing, and low-speed handling was dangerous; the stall came without warning when the right wing dropped quickly. VF-12, the first squadron to receive the fighter, changed to the F6F-3 because of these difficulties. VF-17 persisted and managed to de-bug the airplane. A triangular stall-warning strip on the right wing leading edge just outboard of the wing-fold gave solid warning of a coming stall; reducing the hydraulic fluid in the main gear oleo struts reduced the bounce. Still, the Corsair was more difficult for an average pilot to operate from a carrier than was the Hellcat. Fleet squadrons were quickly standardized on the Hellcat, while the Marines were happy to take the "cast-off" Corsair; it became the most important American fighter in the Solomons campaign, where it made a major contribution to wiping out the cream of the Imperial Japanese Naval Air Force. At the end of 1944, in the face of the *kamikaze* threat, the Marines brought their Corsairs aboard the fast carriers as reinforcements and Navy squadrons took the Corsair into combat in 1945. This was the F4U-1D, "tamed" for carrier operation with all the features originally pioneered by VF-17. The F4U was 60mph faster than the Hellcat and climbed faster, and it rapidly assumed the position originally expected of it in defending the fleet against the *kamikazes*, the worst threat of the war. In the summer of 1945, Marine squadrons took Corsairs aboard CVEs. While the American Navy rejected the F4U, the Royal Navy's Fleet Air Arm successfully operated the early unmodified F4U off CVEs 18 months before the US Navy brought the airplane aboard the fleet carriers; the airplane was universally liked in the Fleet Air Arm.

Second in importance in the fast carrier air groups was the Grumman TBF Avenger torpedo bomber. The Avenger had handling characteristics that made it easy to fly, reliable and rugged. It performed well both on forward air bases and all types of carrier, being excellent at close air support, torpedo strikes, antisubmarine and bombing operations.

Grumman began developing the plane as a replacement for the Douglas TBD Devastor, which had become outdated after just two years, such was the pace of aviation development at this time. The TBU-1 had a simply-designed rear turret and the internal bomb bay could carry a Mk XIV torpedo, four 500-pound general purpose bombs or a 1,600-pound armor-piercing bomb. Crucially, the 54-foot wingspan could be dramatically reduced to 18 feet by the power-operated folding wings, which were perfect for crowded carrier decks.

It quickly went into production as the TBF "Avenger" and the first production models were delivered to *Hornet* in March 1942. The four-plane detachment then saw action in the Battle of Midway in May, and while only one returned (too damaged to fly again), the TBF would accomplish much in the battles to come.

By June 1942, Grumman was turning out 60 TBF-1s a month and by the end of the year there were 646 Avengers serving in the fleet, while the company was able to maintain production of 150 a month through the middle of 1943. However, the commitment to full-scale production of the Hellcat in late 1942 meant another source had to be found to produce Avengers. General Motors had a four-factory complex in New Jersey that was turned over to aircraft production despite doubts on the part of Grumman that an automotive company could meet the far more demanding tolerance requirements of aircraft production as opposed to automobile production. Despite their doubts, Grumman's engineers set to work with the engineers of the newly created Eastern Aircraft subsidiary of GM. The auto engineers simplified assembly of the aircraft and production commenced in November 1942 with assembly of Grumman-built Avengers. By May 1943 Eastern was producing 100 of their own aircraft a month, designated TBM. By the end of the war, Eastern had produced 7,546 of the total 9,837 Avengers, including all of the final TBM-3. Crews could only tell Grumman from Eastern Avengers by the color of the cockpits.

Two dive bombers served in the air groups. The Douglas SBD-5 Dauntless was the newest version of the most successful dive bomber used by any air force in the war. At Midway, Dauntlesses from *Yorktown* and *Enterprise* had smashed the heart of Japanese naval aviation, sinking the *Akagi*, *Kaga*, *Sōryū*, and *Hiryū*. Flying from Henderson Field on Guadalcanal, they prevented the Japanese landing enough troops to dislodge the Marines.

By the time the SBD-5 entered production at Douglas's El Segundo factory in February 1943, its greatest days were behind it. The new version had a more powerful R-1820-60 engine and an increased fuel capacity of 370 gallons, but the wings were still non-folding and the airplane lived up to its nickname "Slow but Deadly." When the last of 2,965 SBD-5s rolled off the production line in April 1944, it was the most numerous Dauntless sub-type.

While the SBD-5 was the primary dive bomber aboard the fast carriers during the Gilberts campaign in November and December 1943, by the time the Marshalls campaign commenced in February 1944, it had been replaced by the Curtiss SB2C-1C Helldiver in several air groups. By June 1944, the Dauntless equipped only VB-16 aboard the new *Lexington* and VB-10 aboard *Enterprise* at the Battle of the Philippine Sea. The SBD remained in service with Marine squadrons assigned the task of bombing bypassed Japanese island bases in the Marshalls and Gilberts through most of 1944 and its final American combat service came in the Philippines, where those Marine squadrons provided the closest of close support to the 1st Cavalry Division in the advance on Manila.

The Dauntless replacement had originally been touted as a vast improvement. Unfortunately, early versions of the SB2C Helldiver were arguably the worst airplanes to operate off carriers during the war.

The result of a 1938 design competition to produce a definitive divebomber that would remedy the design flaws of all previous designs, capable of carrying a 2,000-pound bombload in an internal bomb bay, the winning Curtiss-Wright SB2C-1 proposal was fatally flawed by the Bureau of Aeronautics' requirement that two of the aircraft could be fitted onto a flight deck elevator 40 feet by 48 feet, the dimensions of the elevators on the planned Essex-class carrier. The challenge this created made the design requirements technically formidable and ultimately impossible to meet. At the time the company was informed they had won, Curtiss saw the victory as the fulfilment of all the preceding "Helldiver" aircraft produced since the F8C-1 of 1931.

The sad part of all of this was that the elevator requirement, which would be the rock on which the Helldiver ultimately foundered, was to be unnecessary, since there was never a time in the aircraft's service where two Helldivers would ride a flight deck elevator on any carrier. The result of this requirement was a strange-looking airframe with a fuselage too short to provide adequate directional control, which resulted in extended re-design of the tail surfaces that ultimately saw a huge vertical fin and rudder combined with oversized horizontal stabilizers and elevators to provide adequate control.

The problems inherent in the design were further compounded when the Helldiver became one of the first designs to be put into production "off the drawing board," without a prototype. The result would be that the first production aircraft were diverted to further development, and that all of the early SB2C-1 and SB2C-1C aircraft would be subject to an eventual 800 modifications after they rolled out of the factory in order to meet operational requirements. Changes in armament, armor, self-sealing fuel tanks and other operational necessities resulted in ever-reduced performance. Additionally, the engine chosen would eventually prove not to provide sufficient power with all this additional weight, making operation of the aircraft off a carrier "adventurous," in the words of one pilot.

The first order for 370 SB2C-1s was made on May 15, 1939, despite the fact that Curtiss's P-40 production commitment at its Buffalo, New York factory, meant the government had to build a new plant to produce the airplane at Columbus, Ohio, with consequent delay from the outset.

Wind-tunnel tests of the initial design soon demonstrated its unfitness for carrier operation, since the stalling speed of the wing was far too high for carrier operation. The wing was redesigned (with consequent delay) to increase total wing area by 10 percent, while Handley-Page slats were added for low-speed controllability. The Helldiver was nearly a year late when the XSB2C-1 was rolled out to the tarmac on December 13, 1940. During his first flight on December 18, test pilot Lloyd Childs quickly discovered that the stability problems had not been solved.

Three days later, before entering official trials, the prototype was destroyed as the result of wing failure in flight. The rebuild was completed in May 1941; further tests revealed the newly enlarged vertical fin and rudder was still insufficient for good directional control; over the next month a third tail 20 percent larger was built and installed, but it was still barely adequate.

June 30, 1942 saw the first production SB2C-1 rolled out, but production flight tests revealed the many "gremlins" still present, which meant the early production aircraft would have to be retained for additional trials by the manufacturer. The installation of more equipment and armor brought about a weight increase that saw top speed drop from 368mph to 322mph. With the additional weight, the R-2600-8 Twin Cyclone, 1,700 horsepower resulted in marginal take-off performance even from large Essex-class decks. The faulty design of the dive flaps, without the perforations that allowed the SBD to remain steady in a dive, meant the SB2C did not have the controllability to insure an accurate drop, but the airplane was forbidden to dive without use of the flaps.

The improved SB2C-1C that appeared in the fall of 1943 and arrived on carrier decks early in 1944 suffered a weight increase of 3,000 pounds when armor and self-sealing fuel tanks were added, with two 20mm cannon in place of four .50-caliber machine guns in the wings, with the result that top speed dropped from 322mph to 280mph. The SB2C-3 that appeared in the fleet in the summer of 1944 was distinguishable from its predecessor by a 4-bladed Curtiss-Electric prop in front of an R-2600-20 engine with 1,900 horsepower, which meant that takeoffs were no longer marginal (The French would later operate the "definitive" SB2C-5 off the short deck of *Bois de Belleau*, the former CVL *Belleau Wood* without difficulty during the first Indochina War). Unfortunately, the landing speed increased to 91mph, which was the highest of any carrier aircraft flown during the war; landing was also affected negatively by "problematic" aileron control at such a "low" speed. The late-production SB2C-3 and the substantially similar SB2C-4 that appeared in the fall of 1944 finally received perforated dive flaps that solved the directional diving instability. The SB2C-4 of 1944 was close to what the Navy had wanted in 1940; sadly, the day of the dive-bomber was coming to an end and within six months, there would be only a few carriers still operating the type.

When production began to hit its stride and Helldivers were rolling out of the factory faster than the necessary fixes the simultaneous testing program was showing were necessary could be adopted on the production line, the "Mod I" post-production program was established in fall 1942 to deal with internal fixes and control surface modifications. The "Mod II" program introduced in the spring of 1943 saw more than 800 technical changes for each airplane before it could be passed on to a squadron. Bombing 9 was the first squadron to convert to the Helldiver, on December 15, 1942 to replace the SBD-3s the squadron was operating. The problems encountered during the conversion were such that by March 1943, the reliable SBD-5 Dauntless returned to the squadron before Air Group 9 deployed for combat aboard *Essex*.

An example of what the front-line squadrons went through can be seen in the experience of Bombing 15, which received their Helldivers in November 1943 and had a month to be ready to go aboard ship. Lieutenant John Bridgers, newly appointed squadron engineering officer and thus responsible for insuring all the changes had been made, recalled, "The SB2C had three fewer engines and two more hydraulic connections than a B-17."

The Helldiver was not really an advance on the plane it replaced and it never met its original specifications, lacking the range, speed and firepower to do its job – the Navy considered abandoning it three times. Because of its poor flying capabilities it quickly became known as the "Beast" and for its operational capability as "Sumbitch Second Class". In the "Mission Beyond Darkness" during the Battle of the Philippine Sea, 45 Helldivers were lost when they ran out of fuel returning to their carriers. The scathing report the Truman Committee issued in 1944 after investigating Helldiver was the beginning of the end for Curtiss-Wright as an aircraft design and production company, which ceased forever in 1948 after the failure of the XF15C-1.

Helldivers poured from the factory even as dive-bomber squadrons in the fleet were reduced to 12–14 aircraft in late 1944, then removed from most carriers altogether by the summer of 1945 when they were replaced by Hellcat and Corsair fighter-bombers; the majority of SB2C-4s and SB2C-5s were flown from the factory to aircraft parks they wouldn't leave before being scrapped when production ceased on V-J Day with 7,130 produced.

At the beginning of the Pacific War, the Japanese had the most advanced carrier aircraft of any navy. The Mitsubishi A6M2 Type Zero Model 21 fighter was the best carrier fighter in the world, capable of taking on any other fighter then in existence with exceptional range and close-in combat maneuverability. The Nakajima B5N2 Type 97 carrier attack bomber was the best torpedo bomber, armed with the deadly Type 91 aerial torpedo; unlike the lumbering TBD-1 Devastator which attacked at an altitude of 100 feet and 100mph to protect its unreliable Mark XIII torpedo, the B5N2 could attack at speeds over 200mph and drop its torpedo from a maximum altitude of 2,000 feet. The Aichi D3A1 Type 99 dive bomber was among the best in existence, though its bomb load was half that of the Dauntless. All these aircraft gained their exceptional performance due to lightweight construction and lacked such equipment as armor plate and self-sealing fuel tanks considered essential in Western aircraft.

Once the "secret" of the Zero was revealed with the discovery of Petty Officer Koga's A6M2, crash-landed on Akutan Island in the Aleutians in July 1942, and its testing against American aircraft, it was revealed that the Zero was highly maneuverable below 250mph, but that the large ailerons became progressively heavier above that speed and were nearly immovable at speeds over 300mph. American pilots were taught to keep their speed above 250mph and remain in the vertical plane rather than attempt to "dogfight" the Zero.

The B5N2 and D3A1, known to the Allies respectively as the "Kate" and "Val," turned out to be easy victims of heavy American .50-caliber machine guns.

Newer types were produced as replacements but did not close the gap with the new American types that appeared in 1943. The Zero was modified as the A6M5 with a shorter wingspan and an engine with an additional 300 horsepower, but it had fallen behind both the Hellcat and Corsair in performance; no other Japanese fighter was produced in sufficient numbers to make a difference. The D4Y3 *Suisei* (Comet) Type Zero dive bomber, known to the Allies as "Judy," was meant to replace the Val. It was faster and carried a heavier bomb load, but arrived too late to affect carrier battles; it became the Imperial Japanese Naval Air Force's primary *kamikaze* attack plane. The Nakajima B6N *Tenzan* carrier attack bomber Model 11, known to the Allies as "Jill," entered production in 1943 to replace the B5N, which still remained in service. Due to protracted development, a shortage of experienced pilots, and the American achievement of air superiority by the time it entered service, the B6N never had the opportunity to fully demonstrate its combat potential.

With the high quality of Japanese naval aviators in the beginning, the technical weaknesses of their aircraft were not immediately apparent. However, with the loss of the cream of Japanese naval air power at Midway, and the continuing attrition of pilots and aircrews in the Solomons campaign that ended with the neutralization of Rabaul in February 1944, Japanese naval air power had been seriously compromised when the Central Pacific campaign moved into high gear in 1944.

The average Japanese naval aviator at the Battle of the Philippine Sea in June 1944 had less than 200 hours of flight experience; only a very few combat veterans survived to pass on their experience. The higher-powered aircraft like the Judy and Jill bombers were very difficult for these poorly trained pilots to operate. The Imperial Japanese Naval Air Force never recovered from the losses at the Marianas and only remained a threat after the Battle of Leyte Gulf in October 1944 due to the introduction of the *kamikaze* suicide attack tactic; while conventional attacks did occur, the loss rate was such that even those initially opposed to the organized use of suicide attack eventually conceded it was the tactic with the greatest likelihood of success.

Japan was never able to create a training program like that of the US Navy since it had not planned on a long war, as the Americans had. There were never sufficient naval aviators to allow any experienced pilots to return and work in the training program. The trained naval aviators who could operate from carriers were sacrificed when their units were sent to the Solomons and Rabaul. While the carriers remained idle at Truk or the Home

Islands during 1943, the air groups were repeatedly sent south to reinforce the depleted land-based air groups. In August and September 1943, the aircraft from Carrier Division 2 went to Rabaul, then on to Buin near Bougainville, where Zero pilots trained to operate from carriers suffered disastrous losses in daily pitched air battles. Staff officer CDR Masatake Okumiya wrote after the war that conditions at Buin were so much more primitive than Rabaul that pilots who lasted more than a week in combat died of exhaustion and disease. In October, what was left was withdrawn to defend Rabaul when the Allied air campaign to isolate that base swung into action. In early November, Carrier Division 1's planes and crews were sent to Rabaul, including the most experienced squadron leaders. By the conclusion of the American carrier raids on November 11, over half of these men had been shot down, with very few rescued. Okumiya, writing after the war, described the final days at Rabaul: "The days passed in a blur. Every day we sent the Zeros up on frantic interception flights. The young and inexperienced student pilots had become battle-hardened veterans … Not for a moment did the Americans ease their relentless pressure … Our losses mounted steadily, and the list of dead and missing pilots grew."

When the survivors returned to Truk in February 1944, they brought with them the disease of "defeatism." The young pilots sent as replacements were not as good as these earlier replacements had been; the leaders they so desperately needed lay in twisted wrecks in jungles or at the bottom of the sea. Additionally, the ranks of the pilot force were made up primarily of enlisted men. The young officers who would have been the leaders of new units had been lost in combat over Guadalcanal, the Solomons, and Rabaul. Japanese tradition did not allow commissioning of experienced enlisted men. Thus, the officers leading new units were without combat experience to pass on, while the number of experienced pilots steadily dwindled. Top surviving Imperial Japanese Naval Air Force ace Saburo Sakai wrote after the war that the 70 men who were washed out of his training program in 1938 would each have been better than any of the men graduated from the Japanese training program by 1943.

American naval aviators were perhaps exceeded only by their Japanese opponents at the outset due to the combat experience the Japanese had gained in China and the extreme rigor of the Imperial Japanese Navy's training program. Prior to 1940, American naval aviator training lasted 18 months, during which the student pilot flew all types of aircraft operated by the Navy; he could expect during his career to fly all these types operationally in different assignments. Other than the elite enlisted Naval Aviation Pilots

(NAP) who manned VF-2, the "Flying Chiefs," and were assigned to the unit for years, the average officer aviator changed assignments every two to three years. Until 1936, all officer trainees were Annapolis graduates who served two years of sea duty before they were accepted to flight training.

In 1936, the Aviation Cadet (AvCad) program began, which accepted pilot candidates for service in the Naval Reserve. These men reported directly for flight training. In the beginning, they too received the standard general training in all aircraft types. When the Naval Aviation Cadet (NavCad) program was introduced in 1940, trainees were "streamed" into fighters, dive bombers, torpedo bombers, or patrol bombers after they completed the mid-level of training when they had approximately 100 flying hours. Initially, these men were expected to serve four years of active duty before reverting to reserve status and were not allowed to rise to command responsibility in their squadrons. All squadrons were commanded by Annapolis graduates until 1943, when expansion required that outstanding prewar AvCads be promoted to command positions, though they were still a minority of the naval air leadership throughout the war.

In 1940, the US military had the foresight to plan a major expansion, and even then there was a shortfall at the start of the war. Both Germany and Japan had gone to war without plans for the conflict lasting for any extended period, and were unable to sufficiently expand quality pilot training. Whereas the Germans trained 10,000 pilots in the war, and Japan even fewer, America trained over 150,000; and in 1944 alone America produced 96,318 aircraft as opposed to Japan's *total* wartime production of 76,320. Maintaining superiority of numbers was considered crucial to the war in the Pacific.

Another important technical skill held by naval aviators was due to the fact that the US Navy was the only air force on either side that made a point of teaching fighter pilots proper gunnery from the outset. Although ex-Marine aviator Charles Older, who became the second ace of the American Volunteer Group, recalled that his squadron leadership in the Marines seemed far more interested in his ability to maintain perfect position in a parade ground formation, gunnery was considered important in the naval aviation community throughout the interwar years. A man's record in the annual fleet gunnery competition had a strong bearing on his future assignments. The "Flying Chiefs" of VF-2 made it a point of honor that every pilot qualified for the gunnery "E" for excellence each year.

Rather than merely emphasize the classic "stern chase" used since the earliest days of World War I, naval aviators were taught the difficult art of deflection shooting and were able to put it to good use throughout the war. The Luftwaffe never taught this skill, nor did the Royal Air Force, though in both air forces individual pilots did develop the ability to use this tactic on their own initiative. The Army Air Forces, on the other hand, made no attempt to formally teach gunnery before 1943. Richard I. Bong, Jr., the eventual American "Ace of Aces," returned from New Guinea in 1944 with a score of 27 as the first Army pilot to equal Eddie Rickenbacker's World War I score, and requested to be sent through the new gunnery school. After he finished the course, Bong declared that had he known what he now knew when he first went to the South Pacific, "my score would be double what it is." When he returned to combat, his gunnery skills were shown in each of his following 13 victories before he was taken out of combat and sent home for good. David McCampbell, the Navy "Ace of Aces" was a fleet gunnery champion in 1940 and trained so hard when he returned to flying fighters in 1943 that he later said that when he engaged in his first air combat in June 1944, "I knew I could shoot him down and I did." In his second combat, he shot down seven enemy aircraft in five minutes. Many other naval aviators posted similar performances.

The result of this training was that fighter pilots in the Navy were far more effective than their counterparts elsewhere. This was important, given that carrier warfare did not involve a "daily grind" of operations such as one might find in New Guinea with the Fifth Air Force or in England with the Eighth Air Force, but was rather a series of separate encounters generally over only a few days (or weeks in the case of the Marianas and Philippines invasions). The Navy's fighter pilots needed to maximize their opportunities since they had a limited time to achieve the goal of battlefield air supremacy.

The US Navy had been at war for 18 months when the new carriers arrived in summer 1943, which meant many junior and middle-ranking aviators had amassed valuable experience, which could be apportioned among the new squadrons. In the new air groups of 1943, a good mix was to have one third of pilots with operational experience; one third with training command experience as instructors; and one third new graduates. Most often, a unit might make one combat tour before the lieutenants and lieutenant commanders were sent into the training program, and the ensigns and lieutenants (junior grade) got middle-rank promotions and were sent to new squadrons as a cadre of experienced pilots.

An excellent example of how this system worked is seen in the career of Lieutenant Commander John S. "Jimmy" Thach. As a result of his experience in early combat, Thach developed a combat tactic later known as the "Thach Weave"; this allowed a two-man fighting element to give each other protection when engaged by the more maneuverable Zeke (Zero) fighter, while maintaining the opportunity to shoot down the enemy. Thach demonstrated the value of the tactic at Midway, where he shot down three Zekes and his wingman shot down a fourth while they were outnumbered by the enemy. After Midway, Thach was taken off operations and sent into the training command, where he instructed gunnery instructors in the maneuver and they in turn instructed their trainees. When the Central Pacific campaign went into operation in the summer of 1943, every Navy fighter pilot knew how to use the Thach Weave and Thach himself became the Senior Air Officer on the staff of Vice Admiral John S. McCain, Sr., when he became commander of Task Force 38.

John Bridgers was an excellent example of a man who joined through the NavCad program in the period just before the outbreak of war. A 1940 graduate of East Carolina Teachers' College, Bridgers really wanted to go on to medical school, but he had to find work, since his family was still dealing with the effects of the Great Depression. He later recalled in his memoirs, *Naval Years*:

> A beginning teacher in North Carolina received a monthly salary of $96.50. From this, one was expected to house, clothe, and feed oneself as well as suffer pension withholdings and pay taxes. While contemplating that, I learned I could make $105.00 per month in the navy as an aviation cadet with board, lodging, and clothing furnished. In a year, if successful in flight training, I would be commissioned as an ensign in the Naval Reserve with a $250.00 per month salary, again with lodging provided and an allowance for food, and with a half-month's bonus for flight pay. Further, for foregoing four formative years one typically spent on temporary employment, the reserve aviator would receive a $1,000.00 per year bonus at discharge: $4,000. To a son of the Depression, these seemed princely arrangements, and the flight bonus would provide a nest egg if I needed more college before medical school.

Bridgers graduated from flight training at Pensacola and was commissioned an ensign in the Naval Reserve on December 3, 1941 with specialization as a dive bomber pilot. He and his father were listening to the broadcast of the New York Giants football game that December Sunday afternoon on the NBC Blue Network when the broadcast was interrupted with the news no one who heard it ever forgot: Pearl Harbor had been attacked. "I knew my plans for medical school had been put on hold." During the next two years he participated in the Doolittle Raid, the Battle of Midway, the Guadalcanal and Solomons campaigns, and the Battles of the Philippine Sea and Leyte Gulf; just short of his 24th birthday he was promoted to the rank of Lieutenant Commander and the position of executive officer (XO) of Bombing 15, the dive bomber squadron in Air Group 15, the top-scoring naval air group of the war.

A war in the Pacific had been considered inevitable by the leaders of both the American and Japanese navies from the moment news spread of the Japanese having defeated the Russian fleet at the Battle of Tsushima Strait in 1905, the first time that an Asian power had defeated a Western power. In the years between the two world wars, the US Navy learned the rules and tactics of the revolutionary new form of warfare that would dominate the Pacific War. Even with that knowledge, understanding and technological development, the Navy would only hang on during the first year of the "inevitable war" by its fingernails, until its prewar planning caught up with the reality of war.

CHAPTER THREE

LEADERSHIP

The author of the Central Pacific campaign was Admiral Chester W. Nimitz, Commander in Chief, US Pacific Fleet (CINCPAC). Born in Fredericksburg, Texas, five months after the death of his father and raised in the German-speaking community there, his family struggled financially. He began working at age eight after school and on weekends as a delivery boy for a meat market and later as a desk clerk and handyman at the hotel his mother came to own and run in Kerrville. Graduating from high school with few prospects for further education, Nimitz was unsuccessful in applying for an appointment to West Point, but learned his congressman, James L. Slayden, had one Annapolis appointment available. Believing such an appointment was the only chance he had to receive a higher education, Nimitz was the number one applicant after taking the congressman's test and was appointed from Texas's 12th Congressional District in 1901. Graduating on January 30, 1905, a year behind William F. Halsey, Jr., Nimitz was seventh in a class of 114.

At this time, an academy graduate was not commissioned on graduation, and Nimitz was sent to the Philippines in 1906 to join the Asiatic Squadron, where he served aboard the battleship *Ohio* (BB-12). He was commissioned an ensign after two years' duty on *Ohio* and once commissioned, he volunteered for submarine duty and became captain of the early "Holland" submarine *Plunger* (later A-1) in May 1909. He was the original captain of *Snapper* (later C-5) when she was commissioned on February 2, 1910. Promoted to Lieutenant, he became captain of

Narwhal (later D-1) on November 18, 1910. He was made commander of the Atlantic Fleet Submarine Squadron in May 1912 and served in that position until March 1913.

As XO of the new fleet oiler *Maumee*, Nimitz conducted the first underway refueling when *Maumee* accompanied the first US destroyer squadron to Europe in 1917. Promoted to Lieutenant Commander that August, he was named Chief of Staff to Captain Samuel Robison, Commander Submarine Force Atlantic. Promoted after the war to XO of the battleship *South Carolina* (BB-26), Nimitz took command of *Chicago* (CA-14) as a Commander in 1920. After the war, Nimitz received extensive staff training. As a student at the Naval War College in 1922–23, the plan he developed for a hypothetical Pacific war in a class assignment later formed the basis of the one he would put to use in World War II.

Nimitz was promoted to Rear Admiral in 1938 and conducted experiments in the underway refueling of large ships, which became a key element of the Navy's success in the war to come during his time in command of Cruiser Division 2 in 1938 and Battleship Division 1 in 1939.

On December 17, 1941, Rear Admiral Nimitz was personally chosen by President Roosevelt, with whom he had worked on naval issues during the previous three years, to take command of the Pacific Fleet following the attack on Pearl Harbor. Promoted from Rear Admiral directly to full four-star admiral over senior admirals such as Vice Admiral Halsey, Nimitz arrived in Hawaii and raised his four-star flag aboard the *Grayling* (SS-209) on December 31, 1941. On March 30, 1942, the US Joint Chiefs of Staff (JCS) divided the Pacific Theater into three areas: the Pacific Ocean Areas, the Southwest Pacific Areas, and the Southeast Pacific Areas (later South Pacific Area). The Joint Chiefs designated Nimitz as "Commander in Chief, Pacific Ocean Areas," with operational control over all air, land, and sea Allied units in that area. General Douglas MacArthur was designated Commander in Chief, Southwest Pacific Areas. Throughout the rest of the war, there would be tension between the two men, with MacArthur constantly advocating that the main line of advance to Japan be through the Philippines, while Nimitz worked to implement the Navy's strategies that had been worked out in the prewar Orange and Rainbow plans for an offensive across the Central Pacific.

As commander of the Pacific Theater, Nimitz's responsibilities meant he would command from shore. His command philosophy was that an effective senior commander needed to choose competent subordinates, define their objectives, and provide them with the means necessary to meet those goals. He did not interfere with the conduct of any individual operation, holding that the commander on the scene would know best what tactical measures to take. Calm and affable, Nimitz was not one to promote himself with reporters. He got on well with both admirals and younger staff officers, while his concern for enlisted personnel was widely noticed. Many who dealt with Nimitz believed he knew them personally; while he did have a good memory for faces and names, he had learned early in his career to create a filing system of information on those with whom he served, and it was the responsibility of his flag lieutenant to go over this information with him before any meeting with subordinate commanders. Nimitz loved a good story and used his collection of stories, which were frequently described as "salty," for serious purposes. When the planning sessions over which he presided sometimes grew argumentative, he would bring out an appropriate anecdote that eased tensions, much in the way President Lincoln had done. As the presiding authority at staff meetings, he was not a man to flaunt his rank, listening more than speaking, seeking to elicit the reasoned opinions of commanders and planners both, while shepherding all toward consensus before signing operational orders.

Among Nimitz's greatest responsibilities was managing interservice rivalry in a multiservice command, which frequently revealed itself in interpersonal conflicts growing out of personal rivalries. He was scrupulously even-handed in hearing every point of view, and no matter how violent the argument, men left his office still on speaking terms. Interservice rivalry came to a head between the Marines and the Army over operational philosophy: while the Marines acted quickly as shock troops, the Army units in an invasion would move slowly, carefully setting the stage for the next move. Marine General Holland M. "Howlin' Mad" Smith, the "father of amphibious warfare," was placed in command of V Amphibious Corps with the Army units subordinate to his command. He constantly complained through the Gilberts and Marshalls campaigns about Army slowness in taking objectives. This difference came to a head on Saipan in June 1944 when he relieved Army General Ralph Smith of command of the 7th Infantry Division, a fight that was only finally sorted out at the highest level of the Joint Chiefs.

Nimitz's two senior commanders who led the fast carrier battle fleet across the Central Pacific could not have been more different. William F. Halsey, Jr., and Raymond A. Spruance were night and day to each other. Halsey never met a reporter he wouldn't spend 30 minutes talking to in language as bloody-minded and salty as possible, while Spruance gave one

30-minute interview during the entire war, saying he did so "not through ungraciousness, but rather to keep my thinking impersonal and realistic." He was never known to utter a curse word in his life.

Spruance was likely thinking specifically of Halsey and how his public image influenced his decision-making during the war when he later wrote:

> Personal publicity in a war can be a drawback because it may affect a man's thinking. A commander may not have sought it; it may have been forced on him by zealous subordinates or imaginative war correspondents. Once started, however, it is hard to keep in check. In the early days of a war, when little about the various commanders is known to the public, and some general or admiral does a good and perhaps spectacular job, he gets a head start in publicity. Anything he does thereafter tends toward greater headline value than the same thing done by others, following the journalistic rule that "Names make news." Thus his reputation snowballs, and soon, probably against his will, he has become a colorful figure, credited with fabulous characteristics over and above the competence in war command for which he has been conditioning himself all his life.
>
> His fame may not have gone to his head, but there is nevertheless danger of this. Should he get to identifying himself with the figure as publicized, he may subconsciously start thinking in terms of what his reputation calls for, rather than how best to meet the actual problem confronting him. A man's judgement is best when he can forget himself and any reputation he may have acquired, and can concentrate wholly on making the right decision.

Later historians have compared Halsey and Spruance as types with the two great British naval commanders of World War I, Beatty and Jellicoe. The two were a contrast in styles, with Halsey an aggressive risk taker while Spruance was calculating and cautious. Where Halsey did not differentiate between the greater glory of Admiral Halsey and the glory of the Navy, Spruance always kept the bigger picture in mind, believing a job well done was its own reward. Halsey was proud of the fact that an early 18th-century ancestor, Captain Jack Halsey, was named in *The History of the Lives and Bloody Exploits of the Most Noted Pirates* and began to play to that reputation. The carrier raids he carried out soon after Pearl Harbor were vastly overrated by a press hungry to report any American success in the midst of the disasters reported elsewhere. In the public imagination, he became not only a national hero but something of a superman, which was reinforced by his personal tendency toward bellicose statements couched in salty language, with the result that he became "Bull Halsey," Japan's nemesis.

Both men knew each other well over their naval careers and each considered the other a friend. Spruance, four years Halsey's junior, graduated from the United States Naval Academy in 1906, two years after Halsey; both came out of Annapolis into the expansion and modernization of the Navy that came in the wake of naval victories in the Spanish-American War. Halsey graduated in the lower third of his class where he was known as "everybody's friend" according to the 1904 *Lucky Bag*, a lack of standing that did not indicate his later success, while Spruance graduated solidly in the upper quarter of his class. Both men participated as junior officers in the 'Round the World Cruise of the Great White Fleet in 1907–08, with Halsey aboard *Kansas* (BB-21) and Spruance aboard *Minnesota* (BB-22). Both men then served aboard destroyers, where each first experienced command – Halsey as captain of *Du Pont* (TB-7) in 1909 and then commander of the 1st Group of the Atlantic Fleet Torpedo Flotilla in 1912–13, while Spruance commanded *Bainbridge* (DD-1) from March 1913 to May 1914. Promoted to Lieutenant Commander in 1917, Halsey commanded *Benham* (DD-49) and *Shaw* (DD-68) during World War I, where he won the Navy Cross for leadership when *Shaw* was struck by RMS *Aquitania* on October 9, 1918. Spruance spent the war years as Assistant Engineering Officer of the Brooklyn Navy Yard.

Both commanded other ships during the 1920s, but their careers as surface navy officers parted ways in 1934, when Captain Halsey was offered command of *Saratoga* (CV-3) by the Chief of the Bureau of Aeronautics, Rear Admiral Ernest J. King. Since, by law, all commanders of aircraft carriers and seaplane tenders were required to be either naval aviators or naval observers, Halsey went to Pensacola where he was expected to enroll in the easier naval observer course but instead entered the 12-week naval aviator course as a pilot trainee. Graduating from the course on May 15, 1935, he was at age 52 the oldest man to ever qualify as a naval aviator. He was remembered as a dangerously bad flier who could not read the instruments since he refused to wear his glasses under his goggles. Fortunately, his rank and position soon restricted him to flying with another aviator. During training, he crashed his plane and was awarded the decoration of "Flying Jackass," an aluminum breastplate in the shape of a donkey that he was to wear until another pilot received the award. When the time came, Captain Halsey refused to give up the award and took it with him to the *Saratoga*, where he posted it in his stateroom as a reminder of humility.

Promoted to Rear Admiral in 1938, Halsey commanded carrier divisions before being promoted to Vice Admiral in June 1940 and Commander Aircraft Battle Force. He was Commander Carrier Division 2 with his flag aboard *Enterprise* (CV-6) at the outbreak of war on December 7, 1941.

After serving as an instructor at the Naval War College from 1935 to 1938, Captain Spruance assumed command of *Mississippi* (BB-41), until he was promoted to Rear Admiral in December 1939. At the outbreak of war, Spruance commanded the four heavy cruisers of Cruiser Division 5 with his flag aboard *Northampton* (CA-26) as part of Task Force 16 based around the *Enterprise* and commanded by Vice Admiral Halsey.

During the opening months of the Pacific War, Task Force 16 carried out hit-and-run raids against the Japanese in the western Pacific, striking the Gilbert and Marshall Islands in February 1942, Wake Island in March, and protecting the Doolittle Raid against the Japanese homeland in April. These actions were critical to naval morale as they set a new tone of aggressiveness by American commanders while they provided invaluable battle experience for commanders and seamen both.

Returning to Pearl Harbor at the end of May, 1942, Halsey was exhausted from his time at sea, and suffered from a debilitating case of what has been described as both dermatitis and shingles, and was officially labeled "generalized allergic dermatitis" though it was likely psychosomatic in origin as a reaction to stress. It left him unable to remain in command of Task Force 16 in what would become the most important naval battle of the Pacific War, Midway. When he was ordered into hospital two days before the fleet was to depart for battle, Halsey recommended to Admiral Nimitz that Spruance be given command of the task force, despite his lack of experience in air warfare. Backed by Halsey's irascible Chief of Staff, Captain Miles Browning – one of the leading naval aviation strategists and tacticians – Spruance commanded *Enterprise* and *Hornet* alongside Task Force 17 commander Rear Admiral Frank Jack Fletcher aboard *Yorktown* in the battle that saw the heart of Japanese naval air power destroyed when the carriers *Akagi*, *Kaga*, *Sōryū*, and *Hiryū* were sunk by American dive bombers on June 4, 1942. Regardless of what he had done in promoting the career of Raymond Spruance, Halsey would never forget that he had lost the opportunity to cap his career with victory over the Japanese fleet. Speaking later at Annapolis shortly before he returned to active service after the bout of "generalized dermatitis," Halsey said that "Missing the Battle of Midway was the greatest disappointment of my life – but I'll sink those damned Jap carriers yet!" This obsession would lead to an unfortunate result when he did command the fleet in the last great naval battle of the war.

Spruance's most important decision of his career was made on the evening of June 4, 1942, when he turned his task force to the east rather than continuing west in search of the remainder of the Japanese fleet, stating that "We've done what we came to do." Had he continued west, he would very likely have run into the ambush Admiral Yamamoto had planned with his battleships. A night surface action against a superior force would have completely negated the day's success. Given his record at the time and later, Halsey very likely would have continued on, and there is reason to believe that Yamamoto set the ambush in the belief that Halsey was his opponent.

For his actions at Midway, Spruance was awarded the Navy Distinguished Service Medal and cited as follows: "For exceptionally meritorious service … as Task Force Commander, United States Pacific Fleet. During the Midway engagement which resulted in the defeat of and heavy losses to the enemy fleet, his seamanship, endurance, and tenacity in handling his task force were of the highest quality." Summing up Spruance's performance, naval historian Samuel Eliot Morison later wrote: "Fletcher did well, but Spruance's performance was superb. Calm, collected, decisive, yet receptive to advice; keeping in his mind the picture of widely disparate forces, yet boldly seizing every opening. Raymond A. Spruance emerged from the battle one of the greatest admirals in American Naval history."

Shortly after Midway, Spruance became Chief of Staff to Admiral Nimitz, and in September 1942 was promoted to Vice Admiral and appointed as Deputy Commander in Chief of the Pacific Fleet. Over the next year, Nimitz and Spruance would form a close personal bond, sharing the same quarters at Pearl Harbor and sharing a personal passion for physical activity that had them hiking the hills of Oahu nearly every evening after a day spent in planning conferences. Faced with naming a fleet commander for the coming Central Pacific campaign in May 1943, Nimitz informed Spruance at the end of one of their hikes that while he knew his staff chief longed to return to an active command, he didn't feel able to lose his presence on the staff. Obviously disappointed, Spruance took the news in his stride so well that Nimitz was personally impressed at the demonstration of his subordinate's commitment to the greater needs of the war over personal desires. The following day, Nimitz informed Spruance that he had changed his mind and would name him commander of the new Central Pacific Force.

Halsey returned to active service in September 1942, and the following October was appointed ComSoPac by Nimitz. With his public reputation, his appointment to the command caused an immediate spike in morale throughout the American forces engaged against the Japanese. Moreover, his decisive leadership in the desperate fighting of the Guadalcanal campaign during the most critical and tenuous period of the campaign, including the Battle of Santa Cruz in October, along with his willingness to risk the only two American battleships in the Pacific in the Naval Battle of Guadalcanal in November – which was the decisive naval engagement of the Guadalcanal campaign and doomed the Japanese garrison – was crucial to the eventual victory in February 1943. Halsey continued to lead the Solomons campaign to its successful conclusion with the invasion of Bougainville in November 1943 and the neutralization of Rabaul in February 1944.

In defense of Halsey, while his sense of personal proportion was indeed affected by the early fame he gained, he always maintained that attitude of being "everybody's friend," so positively noted in the 1904 *Lucky Bag*. He was revered by those he commanded for his approachability and his solicitous attitude toward his subordinates. Always daring, his attitude was not "Go!" but rather "Let's go!" He never passed the buck or shirked responsibility and never left a command without words of thanks and commendation for those with whom he had served. On leaving his position as commander of Third Fleet following the Philippines campaign, he began his farewell speech to the fleet by saying "I am so proud of you that no words can express my feelings."

Two months before Halsey became ComSoPac, Spruance was given command of the new Central Pacific Force, which would be centered on the new Essex- and Independence-class carriers and their air groups, for the coming Central Pacific campaign. The Central Pacific Force became the Fifth Fleet on April 29, 1944, at which time Admiral Nimitz instituted a command arrangement never seen before. Command of the "Big Blue Fleet" was to alternate between Spruance as Commander Fifth Fleet and Halsey, named Commander Third Fleet in May 1944. For the rest of the war, the fleet was identified as the Third Fleet with the fast carrier task force as Task Force 38 under Halsey, or Fifth Fleet and Task Force 58 under Spruance. While each was ashore in Hawaii as the other commanded the fleet, they and their staff were hard at work on plans for future operations.

Spruance's time in command coincided with the Battle of the Philippine Sea in June 1944, the first fleet action since Santa Cruz in October 1942. Spruance was criticized by aviators both during and after the action for his refusal to take the fleet away from the Marianas, where Fifth Fleet and Task

Force 58 were responsible for protecting the invasion forces, rather than moving west to confront the oncoming Japanese fleet. Had he done so, he would have placed the fleet in the exact position in which the Japanese hoped to find it, so they could use their planned tactic of "shuttle bombing," launching strikes from the carriers that would recover on Guam, to repeat the performance while returning to their carriers. Speaking with Samuel Eliot Morison after the war, Spruance said: "As a matter of tactics I think that going out after the Japanese and knocking their carriers out would have been much better and more satisfactory than waiting for them to attack us, but we were at the start of a very important and large amphibious operation and we could not afford to gamble and place it in jeopardy." Chief of Naval Operations Admiral Ernest J. King told Spruance immediately after the battle: "You did a damn fine job there. No matter what other people tell you, your decision was correct." The result of the Battle of the Philippine Sea – though unknown to the US Navy at the time – was the final destruction of Japanese carrier air power. Spruance had been victorious in command at the two most crucial carrier battles of the Pacific War.

By the time he took command of Third Fleet on August 29, 1944, members of his staff felt that William F. Halsey, Jr., was smarting from the successes of his former subordinate. While his time in command was initially successful with his rampage through the Philippines and the destruction of enemy air power on Okinawa and Formosa which isolated the looming battleground of the Philippines, his conduct during the Battles of Leyte Gulf inevitably colors his final reputation. Many fellow officers believed he was so eager to be the admiral who finally sank the Japanese carrier fleet that he took the Japanese bait and led his fleet away from its position as defender of the invasion of the Philippines at the moment the enemy came closest to a tactical victory in the final sea battle of the war, an event that became known throughout the navy's officer corps in an uncomplimentary way as the "Battle of Bull's Run." Nimitz was forced to step in and stop the controversy in order to avoid further divisiveness. Halsey's reputation took another hit in December 1944 when the Third Fleet was battered by what came to be known as "Halsey's Typhoon," with three destroyers lost and much damage to other ships in the fleet. There was, sadly, little love lost between the two men when Spruance returned to command Fifth Fleet on January 29, 1945, leading Fifth Fleet in taking Iwo Jima and Okinawa and striking the Japanese Home Islands directly. On May 29, 1945, Halsey returned to command Third Fleet, a position he held till the end of the war three months later, despite putting the fleet through another typhoon that saw two fleet carriers damaged so badly they were put out of action for the rest of the war, and suffering the indignity of having the Court of Inquiry recommend his removal as fleet commander. Again, Nimitz stepped in and kept Halsey in command, though he planned to have Spruance in command during the coming invasion of the Home Islands.

Halsey commanded the wholehearted loyalty of sailors and officers throughout the fleet due to his fighting reputation, much as Patton did with the Third Army in Europe. However, most senior officers preferred Spruance. Captain George Dyer served under both as captain of *Astoria* (CL-90). His memory of his commanders was representative of many other captains:

> My feeling was one of confidence when Spruance was there. When you moved into Admiral Halsey's command from Admiral Spruance's ... you moved [into] an area in which you never knew what you were going to do in the next five minutes or how you were going to do it, because the printed instructions were never up to date ... He never did things the same way twice. When you moved into Admiral Spruance's command, the printed instructions were up to date, and you did things in accordance with them.

The absolute confidence in his ability among those he commanded led Nimitz to describe his fleet commander as "an Admiral's Admiral."

Personally very active and a believer in exercise to clear the mind, Spruance regularly walked 8 or 10 miles a day in Hawaii. This activity frequently found staff officers of lesser physical condition accompanying him struggling to keep up. A man of simple personal tastes, he was a devotee of classical music, which he listened to at night in order to take his mind off the difficulties of the day. He was a lifetime non-smoker whose beverage of choice was hot chocolate that he made personally every morning. He was known to drink only a weak cocktail in the evening when he lived in the same quarters with Nimitz when he was Pacific Fleet Chief of Staff. He loved the companionship of his schnauzer, Peter, and had a reputation as a devoted family man. Working in the garden and greenhouse that was his personal pride and joy during his retirement, he dressed in old khakis and work shoes even when showing off the garden to visitors. During his retirement, he wrote of himself:

> When I look at myself objectively, I think that what success I may have achieved through life is largely due to the fact that I am a good judge of

men. I am lazy, and I never have done things myself that I could get someone to do for me. I can thank heredity for a sound constitution, and myself for taking care of that constitution. Some people believe that when I am quiet that I am thinking some deep and important thoughts, when the fact is that I am thinking of nothing at all. My mind is blank.

While William F. Halsey, Jr., became one of 12 senior commanders of World War II promoted to five-star rank in 1945 as Fleet Admiral, Raymond A. Spruance, whose achievements were at least equal to if not more important than those of his more famous compatriot, did not. His promotion to Fleet Admiral was opposed by the House Armed Services Committee Chairman, Congressman Carl A. Vinson of Georgia, who gave his strong support to his good friend Admiral Halsey. Spruance was vindicated upon his retirement in 1949 when Congress passed a law over Vinson's opposition granting the Admiral full pay and benefits for life in his retirement.

The final man whose leadership was crucial to victory in the Central Pacific campaign was Vice Admiral Marc A. Mitscher, who commanded the fast carrier task force.

Mitscher was one of many Annapolis graduates who proved the obverse of early academic achievement at the academy as an indicator of later success. Remembered as "an indifferent student with a lackluster sense of military deportment," Mitscher endured severe hazing during his plebe year due to his being from Oklahoma, during which he picked up the nickname "Pete" which would follow him the rest of his life. He was forced to resign from the academy at the end of his sophomore year for amassing 159 demerits and failing his class work. He reapplied at the insistence of his father and was accepted on the condition he re-enter as a first year plebe. He graduated 113 of 131 in the class of 1910.

Interested early on in aviation, it took Mitscher over five years after his graduation to manage an assignment to flight training, where he became Naval Aviator No. 33 on June 2, 1916. He participated in early experiments involving operation of seaplanes from ships. Within a year, Lieutenant Mitscher was in charge of seaplane flight training at NAS Dinner Key, Florida, at the time the second-largest naval air station. Promoted to Lieutenant Commander in July 1918, he joined the staff of the Aviation Section in the office of the Chief of Naval Operations.

In 1919, Lieutenant Commander Mitscher was the pilot of NC-1, one of three US Navy flying boats attempting the first crossing of the Atlantic.

The aircraft departed NAS Rockaway, New York, on May 8, 1919 and flew to Newfoundland, whence they departed on May 16 headed for the Azores. Encountering heavy fog that caused him to lose sight of the horizon, Mitscher landed the NC-1 in a heavy oceanic chop that had appeared calm from altitude and snapped a control cable when the flying boat touched down. The six-man crew retreated onto the upper wing because of the rough seas until they were rescued by the Greek cargo ship SS *Ionia*. Taken under tow, NC-1 foundered three days later. NC-3, flown by Lieutenant Commander John C. Towers, was also forced down by the weather and her crew taxied their aircraft across 200 miles of open sea to reach the Azores. Of the three flying boats that made the attempt, only the NC-4 successfully completed the crossing to arrive at Lisbon, Portugal on May 28, 1919, and flew on to arrive at Plymouth, England, on May 31. For his part in the effort Mitscher was awarded the Navy Cross.

In 1922, after commanding NAS Anacostia outside Washington DC, Mitscher was assigned to the Bureau of Aeronautics where he assisted Rear Admiral William A. Moffett in defending the Navy's air interests against General Billy Mitchell's call for a separate air service to control all aviation assets. His knowledge of aircraft was of crucial importance in the Navy's being able to answer Mitchell's challenge and retain their own air force. Mitscher later testified for the prosecution in Mitchell's famous court-martial. Following this, he served aboard *Langley* (CV-1) where he participated in the development of carrier operations. In 1928, he took command of the air group assigned to the newly launched *Saratoga* (CV-3), and made the first landing aboard the new carrier. Promoted to captain in 1938, Mitscher was named to command the *Hornet* (CV-8) in 1941 after serving as Assistant Chief of the Bureau of Aeronautics.

Mitscher took *Hornet* to the Pacific in March 1942, where she transported and launched the 16 B-25 bombers of the Doolittle Raid on April 18, 1942 as part of Task Force 16 commanded by Admiral Halsey. Six weeks later at the Battle of Midway, the *Hornet* air group, the least-experienced of the three air groups committed to the battle, turned in the worst performance, completely missing the opportunity to strike the Japanese on June 4, when Air Group 8 Commander Stanhope Ring failed to find the Japanese at the incorrect coordinates he had been given. Running low on fuel, the strike force broke up, with some attempting to return to *Hornet* while others headed toward Midway Island. The ten F4F-4 Wildcat escorts all ran out of fuel and had to ditch at sea, while several of the SBD-3s heading to Midway also ran out of fuel and ditched on their approach to the island. Many of the SBDs that tried to return to their carrier were unable to locate her and disappeared into the vast Pacific. While all these aircraft were lost, a number of pilots and gunners were later rescued. Of the strike force, only Torpedo 8 reached the enemy fleet, where the squadron flew into immortality when all were shot down, with only one survivor. The *Hornet* air group had lost half its force without achieving any combat result.

This was a "black mark" in Mitscher's record of command, but he had already been named a Rear Admiral and was promoted to that rank in the aftermath of the battle. Following six months in command of Patrol Wing 2, he was sent to New Caledonia to become Commander Fleet Air Noumea in December 1942.

Halsey and Mitscher had a long history together, even before Task Force 16. In April 1943, Halsey named Mitscher Commander Air, Solomon Islands, in command of US Army, Navy, Marine, and New Zealand aircraft in the air war over the Solomon Islands. Halsey said of the assignment, "I knew we'd probably catch hell from the Japs in the air. That's why I sent Pete Mitscher up there. Pete was a fighting fool and I knew it." Mitscher later said that this assignment was his toughest duty of the war.

Mitscher took command of Carrier Division 3 of the Central Pacific Force at the end of 1943 just after the invasion of Tarawa, and took part in the invasion of Kwajalein and Eniwetok and the strike on the major Japanese Central Pacific base at Truk. In April 1944, when the Central Pacific Force became the Fifth Fleet, he was promoted to command Task Force 58, in charge of all the fast carriers to replace Vice Admiral Charles Pownall, commander of Task Force 50 – the original designation of the fast carrier force as part of the Central Pacific Force – who had come to be seen as an insufficiently aggressive commander during the Gilberts and Marshalls campaigns.

Though reserved and quiet in his personal demeanor and known as a man of few words, Mitscher possessed a natural charisma and authority. A raised eyebrow was all it took to indicate he was displeased with a subordinate's effort and he could stop a man in his tracks with a single question. Not one to engage in small talk, he would never discuss mission details at the mess table. Signalman Tom Curtis, who survived the sinking of *Wasp* (CV-7) and ran the signal bridge on Mitscher's flagship, *Lexington* (CV-16) in 1944, was privileged to be one of the few with whom Mitscher engaged in personal conversation when he was invited to have coffee with the Admiral; he recalled that the one thing Mitscher could become animated about was fishing, a hobby he had taken up in the 1930s, and that the Admiral exhibited a dry sense of humor. For personal relaxation, Mitscher read murder mysteries and was a fan of the work of Dashiell Hammett.

As a commander, Mitscher was intolerant of incompetence and would relieve officers he believed were not making the grade, but was lenient over what he considered honest mistakes. He placed tremendous value on the pilots of his air groups, whom he held in great respect for the risks they accepted in attacking the enemy. Not forgetting the abuse he had suffered as a midshipman, he believed that harsh discipline ruined more men than it made and felt particularly that pilots could not be successfully handled through enforcement of rigid rules, since what made a good pilot was an independence of spirit that inflexible discipline destroyed. Regarding aerial operations, however, he was insistent on rigid "air discipline" and would break any violator.

Mitscher's wartime Chief of Staff and later Chief of Naval Operations, Arleigh A. Burke, said of his commander:

> He spoke in a low voice and used few words. Yet, so great was his concern for his people – for their training and welfare in peacetime and their rescue in combat – that he was able to obtain their final ounce of effort and loyalty, without which he could not have become the preeminent carrier force commander in the world. A bulldog of a fighter, a strategist blessed with an uncanny ability to foresee his enemy's next move, and a lifelong searcher after truth and trout streams, he was above all else – perhaps above all other – a Naval Aviator.

At the end of the Okinawa campaign, Admiral Nimitz said of Mitscher, "He is the most experienced and most able officer in the handling of fast carrier task forces who has yet been developed. It is doubtful if any officer has made more important contributions than he toward the extinction of the enemy fleet."

Mitscher's subordinate task group commanders were – with the exception of Admiral Harrill, who was replaced within two months of his arrival in Task Force 58 – outstanding officers, several of whom themselves later went on to leave an indelible mark in very senior positions on the Navy in which they served.

Mitscher's counterpart as Task Force 38 commander was Vice Admiral John S. McCain, Sr. Like Mitscher, McCain was another whose performance as a midshipman at Annapolis was not an indicator of his later career; he graduated 79 of 116 in the class of 1906 and was labeled the "skeleton in the closet of the Class of '06" in the yearbook. A surface officer for most of his career, he entered flight training in 1936 and was 52 when he pinned on his Golden Wings before taking command of *Ranger* (CV-4) in 1937. He was known as the shakiest pilot in the Navy. Promoted to Rear Admiral in 1941, he commanded the Aircraft Scouting Force of the Atlantic Fleet.

Named Commander Aircraft South Pacific in May 1942, McCain was responsible for the conduct of air operations in the Guadalcanal campaign. In October 1942, he was named Chief of the Bureau of Aeronautics and became Deputy Chief of Naval Operations for Air as a Vice Admiral in August 1943. He joined the fleet in August 1944, when Admiral Halsey raised his flag as Commander Third Fleet and became Commander Task Force 38 on October 29, following the Battles of Leyte Gulf when Mitscher returned to the United States for health reasons. He would hold the command until Mitscher returned as commander of Task Force 58 on January 26, 1945, and would again command the carriers under Halsey during the final three months of the war.

Short in physical stature with a thin frame, McCain was known for his gruffness and expansive use of profanity. He liked to drink and gamble, but also demonstrated courage and was regarded as a natural, inspirational leader of men. In the words of one biographer, McCain "preferred contentious conflict to cozy compromise."

One of the best and certainly the most aggressive of Mitscher's fighting admirals was Rear Admiral Joseph James "Jocko" Clark. He claimed one-eighth Cherokee ancestry and was a registered member of the Cherokee nation. When appointed from Oklahoma, he was the first person of Native American ancestry to graduate from Annapolis in 1917 as a member of the accelerated class of 1918. Achieving command of a destroyer in 1922, he transferred to naval aviation and won his Wings of Gold in 1925. He commanded Fighting 3 aboard *Saratoga* during the time that future Chief of Naval Operations Ernest J. King commanded the carrier, a personal connection that later allowed for quick promotion once King was named the Navy's Commander in Chief. Named captain of the aircraft carrier *Suwannee* (ACV-27), one of the first of the fleet of CVEs, at the invasion of North Africa and later taking her to the Pacific where she participated in the Solomons campaign, Clark was ordered to take command of the new *Yorktown* (CV-10) and served as captain from her commissioning in April 1943 through the early stages of the Central Pacific campaign. Clark was promoted to Rear Admiral in January 1944 and given command of Task

Group 58.1 that March with his flag aboard the new *Hornet* (CV-12). His aggressive leadership was demonstrated when he was the first commander to order "turn on the lights" to help guide his strike force back to the fleet during the "Mission Beyond Darkness." He led the air campaign against Iwo Jima in June and July that denied the Japanese full use of the island air base during the Marianas campaign. Clark maintained his task group command until the end of the Okinawa campaign, returning to the United States in June 1945.

Rear Admiral Ralph E. Davison graduated in the Annapolis class of 1916. He entered flight training at Pensacola in September 1919 and pinned on his Wings of Gold on March 17, 1920. At Pensacola, he trained with a fellow member of the class of 1916, Frank W. "Spig" Wead, who would become well known in the 1930s as the screenwriter of such classic aviation movies as "Helldivers of the Navy" and "Test Pilot." Davison was promoted to Rear Admiral in November 1943; he commanded a task group of the CVE Carrier Support Force during the Gilberts and Marshalls campaigns, and joined the fast carriers as a task group commander in August 1944. He was considered a quiet, brilliant, aggressive officer and was the first of the promising young CVE task group commanders to move up to command of a fleet carrier task group. His Chief of Staff, Captain James Russell, said of him, "[He was] a very considerate man, a wonderful man, a very learned man, cool in battle. He had one fault. He liked his whiskey. In Ulithi, he'd go ashore and would be mellow most of the time we were in port. But we'd get out to sea and he went back to work, terrific under attack, a wonderful commander."

Davison commanded Task Group 58.2 at the Battles of Leyte Gulf. Despite a brilliant command record, when he missed an important flight in 1945 due to his penchant for drinking while off-duty, he was promptly removed from command and assigned to training posts for the remainder of the war.

The exception among Mitscher's task group commanders was Rear Admiral William K. Harrill, who commanded Task Group 58.4 during the Marianas campaign from his flagship *Essex* (CV-9). His nickname in the service was "Whiskey" Harrill and he was renowned for his inability to make a decision. While there was such doubt about his fighting spirit that his task group didn't even participate in the "Mission Beyond Darkness", the actual reason for the lack of participation is even worse: Harrill mismanaged the fuel state of his task force such that they could not participate in the action. An excuse was found to get him out of the way, as

Dave McCampbell recalled:

> During the week following the Marianas Turkey Shoot, Admiral Harrill
> came down with a stomach ache. Asked by [*Essex* commander] Captain
> Oftsie if there was anything really wrong with the Admiral, the chief
> surgeon replied that he *might* have appendicitis. Oftsie ordered the surgeon
> to remove Harrill's appendix, saying "He's better off out of the way." After
> a few days, he was unsure if he should go back to duty or remain in bed.
> Oftsie ordered the surgeon to put Harrill in the senior officer's room of the
> ship's sick bay, which had a head [restroom] at either end, neither of which
> was in use at the time. Oftsie ordered that the doors to both be opened.
> "Then Whiskey will get so confused about which one he ought to use that
> he'll put in for a transfer." At Eniwetok, he departed for a shore desk back
> in the States. No one mourned his leaving.

Admiral Harrill was replaced by Rear Admiral Frederick C. "Ted" Sherman,
who had commanded the old *Lexington* (CV-2) at the Battle of the Coral
Sea in 1942, and commanded Task Force 38 with *Saratoga* and *Princeton*
when they made the epic first strike on Rabaul in November 1943.
Sherman was remembered as a "by the book" commander who was not
so hidebound that he could not deviate from the book when events so
required. Sherman's main complaint about his new command concerned
VF-27, the fighter squadron that came aboard *Princeton* shortly before he
took command. The squadron, commanded by Lieutenant Commander
Frederic A. Bardshar, was unique among all squadrons in the fast carrier
task force. Something of an eccentric among Academy grads, Bardshar
was not a "by the book" leader. When he discovered that one of his Naval
Reservist pilots, Lieutenant (jg) Robert Burnell, was an accomplished
artist, he asked Burnell to come up with a distinctive squadron marking,
which was a definite no-no in the squadrons that operated aboard the fleet
carriers, as a way of promoting unit morale. Burnell came up with a play on
the F6F's name and created a Hell Cat, with bloodshot eyes and dripping
fangs in a blood red mouth, utilizing the natural geometry of the F6F
engine cowling with its well-known "grin." Participating in the Marianas
Turkey Shoot, "Halsey's Rampage" across the Philippines, Okinawa and
Formosa, and the Battles of Leyte Gulf, VF-27's score of 220 victories
was the best of any CVL fighter squadron of the war. The record didn't
matter when *Princeton* was sunk on October 24, 1944 at Leyte Gulf; the
nine VF-27 Hellcats that had been airborne when their ship was attacked

were recovered aboard *Essex*. That night, following Admiral Sherman's directive, they were shanghaied into Fighting 15 and their distinctive faces were quickly covered with navy blue paint. Sherman also kept up a running argument throughout Air Group 15's tour aboard *Essex* with David McCampbell over the role of the Commander Air Group (CAG). Sherman felt it was unseemly that the CAG seemed able to combine his responsibilities as strike group coordinator with his growing fame in air combat, which eventually led to McCampbell becoming the US Navy "Ace of Aces" with 34 victories. Sherman gave McCampbell a direct order that he was not to engage in aerial combat unless it was necessary to defend the strike group formation – which only slowed him down slightly.

The other two task group commanders during the Central Pacific campaign were Rear Admiral Alfred E. Montgomery and Rear Admiral John W. Reeves. The former was a graduate of the Naval Academy class of 1912, who entered the submarine service in July 1915, rising to command USS F-1 during World War I. Transferring to naval aviation, he pinned on his Wings of Gold in June 1922.

He commanded observation and torpedo squadrons through the 1920s and 1930s before becoming XO of the aircraft carrier *Ranger* (CV-4) in November 1936, serving until June 1938; he moved up to command *Ranger* from June 1940 to June 1941. He was assigned as Chief of Staff to Commander Aircraft, Atlantic Fleet in June 1941, being promoted to Rear Admiral in May 1942. In August 1943 he was promoted to command of Carrier Division 12, flying his flag on *Essex* (CV-9) in August 1943, and commanding Task Group 50.3 in the Gilbert Islands campaign. On November 11, 1943, his three carriers – *Essex*, *Bunker Hill* (CV-17), and *Independence* (CVL-22) – made the second carrier air strike on Rabaul. He was named commander of Carrier Division 3 in March 1944, which became Task Group 58.2 with his flag aboard *Bunker Hill*.

Rear Admiral John W. Reeves, Jr., commanded Task Group 58.3. He graduated from Annapolis in the class of 1910 and became a naval aviator in 1923, then commanded squadrons aboard *Saratoga* and *Lexington* in the 1930s. He was the first commanding officer of *Wasp* (CV-7). Promoted to Rear Admiral following his departure from *Wasp*, he was commander of the Alaskan Sea Frontier and responsible for direction of the Aleutians campaign following the Japanese invasion of Attu and Kiska in June 1942, until the islands were successfully retaken in 1943. In March 1944 he joined Task Force 58 and became commander of Task Group 58.3 with his flag aboard *Enterprise*.

During the Central Pacific campaign, first Spruance and then Halsey would be opposed by Vice Admiral Jisaburō Ozawa, commander of the carriers in the Imperial Japanese Navy's Mobile Fleet. At 6 feet 7 inches in height, Ozawa was much taller than the average Japanese and was considered one of the three ugliest officers in the Navy; his nickname within the Imperial Japanese Navy was "Onigawara" ("Gargoyle"), after a stylized type of roof tile imprinted with the face of a devil to ward off evil spirits. He took the task of warding off the "evil spirits" of his American opponents very seriously, and historians have credited him as being the most capable of the Japanese fleet commanders. Unlike many Japanese commanders, he was known for being compassionate toward his sailors, as well as for his courage.

Graduating 45th in a class of 179 cadets in the 37th class of the Imperial Japanese Naval Academy at Eta Jima on November 19, 1909, Ozawa served as a midshipman on the cruisers *Soya* and *Kasuga* and battleship *Mikasa*, Admiral Togo's flagship at the Battle of Tsushima Strait in 1905. He was commissioned an ensign on December 15, 1910, then promoted to sub-lieutenant on December 1, 1912, and to lieutenant on December 13, 1915. He specialized in torpedo warfare in his studies. After graduation from the Naval War College in 1919 and promotion to Lieutenant Commander on December 1, 1921, he took command of the destroyer *Take* and subsequently commanded *Shimakaze* and *Asakaze* before becoming chief torpedo officer on the battleship *Kongō* in 1925. He became a full Commander on December 1, 1926 and served in staff positions until 1933, during which time he visited the United States in 1930. Promoted to Captain on December 1, 1930, he took command of the heavy cruiser *Maya* on November 15, 1934, and the battleship *Haruna* in 1935.

Promoted to Rear Admiral on December 1, 1936, he was named Chief of Staff of the Combined Fleet in 1937 and Commandant of Eta Jima in 1939. He was promoted to Vice Admiral on November 15, 1940. During his assignment as Chief of Staff of the Combined Fleet, he was the first high-ranking officer to recommend that the separate Japanese aircraft carrier divisions be organized into a single operational entity so that they could train and fight together.

At the outbreak of the Pacific War, Ozawa commanded the First Southern Expeditionary Fleet which covered the invasion of Malaya and the Dutch East Indies. In January–March 1942 his fleet was involved in the invasions of Java and Sumatra. During March and April he led his fleet on a successful commerce-raiding expedition in the Indian Ocean.

On November 11, 1942, following the Battle of Santa Cruz, Admiral Ozawa was appointed Commander in Chief of the Third Fleet and relieved Admiral Chuichi Nagumo as commander of the carrier forces. In this position, he would fight Admiral Spruance at the Battle of the Philippine Sea in June 1944 where his carrier force was effectively neutered by the loss of three aircraft carriers and the majority of the fleet's aircraft. In October 1944, he would take the carriers to sea for the last time to lure Admiral Halsey away from defending the Philippine invasion fleet, a task he accomplished successfully while losing the last of Japan's aircraft carriers, other than a few new ships which arrived too late to participate in combat operations.

On May 29, 1945, Vice Admiral Ozawa refused promotion to four-star admiral when he was named the last Commander in Chief of the Combined Fleet, a position he held until the surrender in September 1945.

One final Japanese Admiral needs mention. Admiral Takeo Kurita, perhaps Japan's most competent surface force commander, is prominent in US naval history as the admiral who reversed course when he could have steamed to victory at Leyte Gulf. While it is true his force could very likely have inflicted tremendous damage among the ships of the invasion fleet and the forces ashore had he continued on to sink the rest of the CVEs of Taffy-1 and 2, it is likely the Center Force ships would have finally met Admiral Willis Lee's TF 34 battle line before they could have returned to San Bernardino Strait following such a fleet action, where they would have been the losers of what would have been the last and greatest battle line fight in history.

A graduate of Eta Jima in 1910, Kurita by 1940 commanded the leading squadron of Japanese heavy cruisers and was victorious with them in the Battles of the Java Sea in 1942 that ended any Allied hope of holding on to the Netherlands East Indies. He later commanded the battleship force that bombarded Henderson Field on Guadalcanal in October 1942, the most successful Japanese blow against American forces on that crucial island. More importantly, by the time he took command of the heavy surface forces of the Second Fleet in 1943, he was prescient enough to recognize there was little hope of Japan successfully ending the war on any favorable conditions. He considered the Japanese Navy's effort at Leyte Gulf a waste of ships and lives, particularly since his fleet could not get to Leyte Gulf until five days after the landings, which left no more than empty transports for his battleships to sink. He openly resented Admiral Toyoda and the others who, from safety in Tokyo, sent him and his sailors to fight to the death for no good purpose.

Following his return to Japan, Kurita was removed from command that December to protect him from possible assassination and he became the last commander of the Japanese Naval Academy, Eta Jima. In this position, he likely gave his best service to his country, telling his young midshipmen that it was not their duty to die for their country for no purpose, but to live and rebuild it after the war. Many of those young men who listened to him rose to positions of leadership throughout Japanese society in the years after the war and contributed to the creation of today's Japan.

CHAPTER FOUR

FIRST CONTACT

A year after the Battle of Santa Cruz, the "new" US Navy, the ships constructed following the passage of the "Two-Ocean Navy" Act in 1940, entered combat in the Pacific. On September 30, 1943, Task Force 14 stood out of Pearl Harbor, heading west. The fleet centered on six new aircraft carriers: *Essex* (CV-9) was joined by her sister ships *Yorktown* (CV-10), named for the carrier lost at Midway, and *Lexington* (CV-16), namesake of the first American carrier lost in combat. Accompanying these three large fleet carriers were the light carriers *Independence* (CVL-22), *Belleau Wood* (CVL-24), and *Cowpens* (CVL-25). What would become known as the "fast carrier task force" headed into the Pacific trade winds, aiming for Wake Island, the first US possession lost to Japan nearly two years earlier, in December 1941.

Aboard *Essex* was Fighting 9, the first squadron to equip with the new F6F-3 Hellcat fighter. Among the young pilots of the squadron was Lieutenant (jg) Hamilton McWhorter III, who had fallen in love with airplanes and flying when his uncle had let him take a ride in a Ford Trimotor at age eight in 1929. Entering the University of Georgia in 1939, he had immediately enrolled in the recently started Civilian Pilot Training (CPT) Program and gotten his private pilot's license. At the end of his sophomore year in June 1941, when he had the necessary two years of college to apply, McWhorter enlisted in the Navy's NavCad program, and was ordered to begin flight training at Pensacola that August. Armed with his CPT pilot's license, McWhorter bypassed primary flight training and started in the basic flight training course that October.

A farm boy whose father had given him his first shotgun at age nine, McWhorter had long before developed a shooting eye. "We hunted dove and quail, and it got to be where pulling lead on a moving target was just instinctive to me." His "eye" was demonstrated during gunnery training at Pensacola, where he consistently scored well with the .30-caliber machine gun carried by his SNJ trainer. "I am sure that had a lot to do with my being selected for fighter training at NAS Miami. I reported in there on Christmas Eve 1941 and the accelerated schedule of seven-day work weeks and ten-hour flying days made the training go fast." McWhorter pinned on his Wings of Gold as a naval aviator on January 28, 1942 and was commissioned an ensign on February 9, 1942, "the day after the Annapolis class of 1942 received their commissions, so we would never outrank them."

Fighting 9 was newly equipped with the Grumman F4F-4 Wildcat when McWhorter joined that March, the first version of Grumman's first monoplane fighter to feature folding wings. After carrier qualification aboard *Long Island* (CVE-1) that summer, the squadron went aboard *Ranger* (CV-4) in late September and entered combat during Operation *Torch*, the invasion of North Africa, on November 8, 1942. After four days of successful combat against the Vichy French, *Ranger* returned to the naval base at Norfolk, Virginia, in late November.

Shortly thereafter, the pilots of VF-9 first met the Grumman F6F Hellcat. McWhorter recalled, "When we came back from North Africa, we were scheduled to be the first squadron equipped with the F4U Corsair, but Vought wasn't producing them fast enough, so we became instead the first squadron to be given the Hellcat." Comparing the Hellcat with its Wildcat predecessor, McWhorter said it was "like stepping out of a Model-T into a Cadillac. The plane made carrier operations so much easier."

Fighting 9 had learned the hard way in North Africa the value of aerial discipline and good gunnery. Throughout the spring of 1943 pilots trained hard as they got to know the Hellcat. "We did at least one gunnery mission every day, and sometimes two." VF-9 became carrier-qualified aboard the brand-new *Essex* in February. By the time the ship deployed to Hawaii in May 1943, the pilots had more than 50 hours each in the F6F. Lieutenant Commander Phil Torrey took command of VF-9 at NAS Barbers Point on Oahu in June and they trained harder over the summer, with most pilots gaining an additional 40–50 concentrated hours in their new mount over about 60 days. They passed their "final exam" with flying colors on August 31, 1943 when *Essex*, in company with the new *Yorktown* and the light carrier *Independence* launched the first new carrier strike against Marcus Island, only 700 miles from Tokyo.

Thirty minutes before dawn on October 5, 1943, Task Force 14 was a bit over 100 miles east of Wake Island. *Essex, Yorktown, Lexington,* and *Independence* turned into the wind and each launched three fighter divisions. The 47 Hellcats joined up in the pink light of dawn high over the fleet that steamed on the dark sea below and turned west toward their target. *Essex* and *Yorktown* proceeded to launch some 70 SBD-5 Dauntlesses and TBM-1C Avengers for the strike that would follow the fighter sweep.

Japanese radar detected the inbound sweep 50 miles out. As Wake Island hove into sight on the western horizon, the Hellcats were intercepted by 27 Mitsubishi A6M5a Zeke fighters.

In the initial attack, Phil Torrey got one, then evaded two more that jumped him. McWhorter dove into the gaggle of Zekes. "One of them just appeared in front of me. I came up behind him and let him have a one-second burst." The exploding Zeke was his first victory, and the second of 5,223 enemy aircraft that would fall to the Hellcat's guns over the next 23 months of combat. When the fight was over 15 minutes later, the Hellcats had shot down 22 of 34 Zekes, demonstrating beyond doubt that the new fighter could more than hold its own against the enemy's best.

After Wake Island, the Pacific carrier offensive began to build up steam. In late October, American forces in the Solomons were preparing to invade Bougainville, the last major Japanese base in the northern Solomons, on November 1 in the aptly named "Operation *Shoestring*." American forces would be stretched to the maximum limit, with naval forces in the South Pacific Theater now diverted to the Central Pacific for coming operations.

When word that the Americans had landed at Cape Torokina in Empress Augusta Bay on Bougainville reached Japanese naval headquarters at Rabaul on the morning of November 1, Vice Admiral Tomoshige Samejima, commanding the Eighth Fleet, immediately embarked 1,000 Special Naval Landing Force troops on five destroyers at Rabaul and ordered them to proceed to Cape Torokina to make a counter-landing. Samejima sent an escort force under the command of Vice Admiral Sentaro Omori, composed of the heavy cruisers *Myōkō* and *Haguro* and the light cruiser *Agano* of the 10th Cruiser Squadron, with the destroyers *Naganami, Hatsukaze,* and *Wakatsuki,* and the light cruiser *Sendai* with the destroyers *Shigure, Samidare,* and *Shiratsuyu* of the 3rd Destroyer Squadron. Most of the ships in the Japanese fleet, which had been hastily assembled from the ships on hand, had never trained or fought together before. During the night voyage to Torokina, the Japanese force was spotted by an American submarine and by a search plane. Worried that he had lost the element of surprise, Omori radioed to ask permission from Samejima to return the slow-moving transports to Rabaul while he continued on with his combat force to attack the transports he assumed were still in Empress Augusta Bay. Samejima agreed and Omori pressed ahead.

At Bougainville, American Rear Admiral A. Stanton "Tip" Merrill commanded Task Force 39, which consisted of Cruiser Division 12 and two destroyer divisions. Cruiser Division 12 comprised light cruisers *Montpelier* (CL-57), *Cleveland* (CL-55), *Columbia* (CL-56), and *Denver* (CL-58). Destroyer Division 45 consisted of *Charles Ausburne* (DD-570), *Dyson* (DD-572), *Stanley* (DD-478), and *Claxton* (DD-571); they were commanded by the legendary Captain Arleigh A. "31-Knot" Burke and known as "The Little Beavers." They were accompanied by Destroyer Division 46: *Spence* (DD-512), *Thatcher* (DD-514), *Converse* (DD-509), and *Foote* (DD-511).

With receipt of the submarine report, the Americans had evacuated most of the landing craft and troop transports to the south. Task Force 39 assembled southwest of Empress Augusta Bay and steamed slowly north. Radar contact was made by the Americans at 0230 hours on November 2. Destroyer Division 45 was ordered to attack; at 0245 hours they fired a salvo at the enemy. Simultaneously, the *Sendai*-led Japanese 3rd Destroyer Division fired 18 torpedoes. Both American groups successfully dodged them (except for a hit on the destroyer *Foote*), using radical maneuvers to neutralize the torpedo threat. The 3rd Destroyer Squadron then turned into the path of the onrushing 10th Cruiser Division, which broke up the Japanese formation. The Japanese ships became separated in the confusion into three groups: north, center, and south. At 0245 hours, the American light cruisers opened fire on the Japanese under radar control. The action became confused; the Japanese used optical means to identify ships, while the American radar was not as helpful as expected. Several Japanese ships collided with one another, while American ships narrowly missed collisions with ships of their own force.

After an hour, Japanese cruiser fire was heavy and increasingly accurate, forcing the American cruisers to maneuver behind a smoke screen that successfully interfered with the Japanese optically-controlled gunnery, while the American ships took hits that were not critical. Throughout, the American ships missed opportunities to attack Japanese ships out of fear they were attacking their own. At 0320 hours, Omori, worried about being caught on the open sea in daylight by American aircraft, ordered a retreat. At daylight the Americans broke off pursuit of the Japanese stragglers and all ships, many low on fuel and ammunition, were ordered to rendezvous.

The rest of November 2 was spent defending the landing beaches from strong Japanese air attacks. The Americans had held off the Japanese fleet, but only narrowly. On November 3, Admiral Halsey learned from a reconnaissance flight that more cruisers and destroyers had arrived at Rabaul from Truk to reinforce the Eighth Fleet and renew the attack on the Allied forces. Lacking the forces to successfully oppose this fleet if it attacked, Halsey requested emergency help from Admiral Nimitz at Pearl Harbor, later stating that the threat the Japanese cruiser force at Rabaul posed to the Bougainville invasion was "the most desperate emergency that confronted me in my entire time as ComSoPac."

Nimitz's Central Pacific Fleet was already committed to the coming invasion of the Gilbert Islands later in November, but he managed to release Task Group 50.3, composed of *Essex*, *Bunker Hill* (CV-17), and *Independence*, under the command of Rear Admiral Alfred E. Montgomery. The carriers departed Pearl Harbor on November 3. The only carrier force immediately at hand in the South Pacific was Task Force 38, which had been providing air cover for the invasion. Task Force 38 was centered on *Saratoga* and *Princeton* (CVL-23), under the command of Rear Admiral Frederick C. Sherman, who had commanded the first *Lexington* at Coral Sea. *Saratoga* and *Princeton* were refueling near Rennell Island when Sherman received the order to raid Rabaul the evening of November 4. Other than the surprise raid at Pearl Harbor, no successful attack against such a well-defended land target had ever been made by carrier aircraft. The mission was considered highly dangerous for the aircrews and placed the carriers themselves at risk, but the fate of the invasion hung in the balance.

Racing north at 27 knots, Sherman's carriers launched their strike from 57 miles northwest of Cape Torokina at 0900 hours on November 5. Favorable weather provided sufficient wind for an easy launch while also providing cloud cover that confused Japanese snoopers into a belief that only cruisers were present. All 97 aircraft aboard the two carriers – 52 F6F-3 Hellcats from *Saratoga*'s VF-12 and *Princeton*'s VF-23, 23 TBF-1C Avengers from both carriers, and 22 *Saratoga* SBD-5 Dauntlesses – were launched while two land-based squadrons from Barakoma and Vella Lavella arrived overhead to provide cover.

Almost complete surprise was achieved, which was lucky since it turned out that more than 150 enemy aircraft were present. Seventy Zekes met the formations, but missed their main chance because they expected the

Americans to split up before attacking. By the time they saw the Americans hold formation through the heavy flak, it was too late for a successful interception. Below in the harbor, the ships were unprepared for such an attack. Despite heavy antiaircraft fire and a large formation of defending fighters, American losses were only five Hellcats and five Dauntlesses.

The attack was followed an hour later by a Fifth Air Force raid from New Guinea composed of 27 B-24 Liberators escorted by 58 P-38s. As a result of the two attacks, six of the seven Japanese cruisers in Simpson Harbor were damaged, four heavily by the Navy. *Atago* was near-missed by three 1,600-pound bombs that caused severe damage and killed 22, including her captain. *Maya* was hit by one bomb above an engine room that caused heavy damage and killed 70. *Mogami* was hit by one 500-pound bomb and set afire with heavy damage and 19 dead. *Takao* was hit by two 500-pound bombs that caused severe damage and killed 23. *Chikuma* was slightly damaged by several near misses. In the aftermath of the attack, Admiral Mineichi Koga was forced to order the damaged cruisers back to Truk for repair. The attacks ended the Japanese warship threat to the Allied landing forces at Bougainville.

The leader of Air Group 12, Commander Turner F. Caldwell, returned to *Saratoga* in a shot-up TBF Avenger that was put over the side after he successfully landed aboard. VF-12 commander Lieutenant Commander Joseph L. "Jumpin' Joe" Clifton reported himself very pleased with the success of his Hellcats in defending the bombers. That night, Halsey sent a message to Sherman: "My utmost admiration for your brilliant performance during recent operations. Your strike was another shot heard round the world. When the *Saratoga* is given a chance, she is deadly."

After three days at sea on a high-speed run, Task Group 50.3 dropped anchor at Espiritu Santo in the New Hebrides Islands south of Guadalcanal in the early evening of November 5, where they learned of the strike against Rabaul that day by *Saratoga* and *Princeton*. The next day, the aircrews learned they would make a second strike against Rabaul. McWhorter remembered, "We were very concerned when we heard we were going there. They lost ten or eleven airplanes in that strike. We were told we could expect to find 80–90 Zekes there. What no one knew was the Japanese had flown in all the Zekes from their carriers at Truk to Rabaul the day after that raid. When we got there, we were up against approximately 160 Zekes."

At dawn on November 11, 1943, Sherman's Task Force 38 was operating under cover of a weather front near Green Island when they launched a dawn strike of 55 Hellcats, 25 Avengers and 21 Dauntlesses that had to contend with clouds most of the way, to discover that Simpson Harbor was almost completely cloud-covered. The bombers concentrated on three cruisers visible in the rain and hit one. Seventy Zekes were up and chased the raiders in and out of the weather, but only caught seven; five of these returned to the carriers with battle damage while VF-12 scored one victory. After they recovered the strike, Task Force 38 retired to the south without being detected by the Japanese.

Essex, Bunker Hill, and *Independence* were in the Solomon Sea 165 miles southeast of Rabaul when they launched their strikes at 0945 hours: 185 aircraft operating as separate groups from each carrier. The strike force included SBD-5 Dauntlesses from Bombing 9 and 16 new SB2C-1 Helldivers of Bombing 17 on their combat debut, alongside TBF-1C Avengers from the three torpedo squadrons, escorted by Hellcats from the three carriers. McWhorter remembered, "We ran into trouble right from the start. En route to the target, we were at 12,000 feet when a dozen Zekes found us and tried to lure the fighters away, but we stuck with the mission."

When the *Essex* strike arrived over Rabaul there were no Zekes in their vicinity, but the antiaircraft fire was very heavy. Below, McWhorter saw a long line of Japanese warships leaving the harbor at high speed:

> I went after a heavy cruiser, and came in off her starboard beam. It seemed like every weapon on the cruiser and all the other warships were firing at me and I could actually see the eight-inch shells coming at me. I opened fire from about 2,500 feet out, and fired about a four-second burst at the open AA [antiaircraft] gun batteries, then zoomed over her. I thought that incredible flak barrage was going to get me for sure.

The heavy cruiser McWhorter attacked was *Atago*, which had remained at Rabaul after the November 5 strike and was torpedoed and heavily damaged in this attack.

The fight wasn't over by a long shot. Sixty-eight Zekes had been launched to intercept the Americans. As he headed for the rendezvous point, McWhorter saw a huge World War I-style dogfight west of the harbor, involving about two dozen Hellcats and about 50 Zekes:

> I saw a Zeke ahead that was scoring heavily on another Hellcat. I came in behind him and fired a short burst. I saw the Zeke explode, but couldn't tell if the Hellcat escaped. Then, all of a sudden, I heard a sound like when someone throws a handful of large rocks on a galvanized tin roof. It was the

sound of bullets hitting my plane! I snapped into a split-S to get away from whoever was on my tail, and as I dove out straight down there was another Zeke passing right in front of me and he blew up when I fired a short burst. It seemed like I'd been in that fight for an hour, but all of a sudden I was alone and when I looked at my watch, the whole thing hadn't lasted a minute.

In total, Fighting 9 claimed 14 Zekes shot down.

Bunker Hill's Air Group 17 followed *Essex's* strike. VF-18, commanded by Lieutenant Commander Sam L. Silber, stayed close to the bombers, but managed to score two Zekes. *Independence's* VF-22, supplemented by a 12-plane detachment from Fighting 6, scored four Zekes for three Hellcats. The six Zekes actually lost contrasted with American claims from the three squadrons for 30.

Overall, the strike was a success. The Japanese suffered one destroyer sunk, with another destroyer and light cruiser badly damaged, and three other ships slightly damaged, including the heavy cruiser *Atago*. The attacking squadrons lost only 11 aircraft.

While the strike forces were away from the fleet, air cover was provided by the F4U-1A Corsairs of VF-17, which had been the original fighter squadron aboard *Bunker Hill* until the Corsairs were pulled off the carrier in Hawaii shortly after their arrival in the Pacific, due to there not being sufficient F4U spares in the supply chain to support the airplanes in the fleet. The "Jolly Rogers" had arrived in the Solomons in October and taken part in the air battles over the Bougainville invasion. The pilots were happy when they were relieved of their patrols and allowed to bring their Corsairs back aboard *Bunker Hill* and *Essex*, where they were treated to hot showers for the first time since leaving the ship six weeks earlier, as well as lunch in the wardroom that beat the C-rations they had been getting used to ashore. VF-33's Hellcats also provided CAP, with the Hellcats landing aboard *Independence* for refueling.

Shortly after lunch, *Essex's* radar spotted an incoming raid 119 miles distant, which was following the returning planes from the morning strike. Pilots of VF-33 overhead reported "millions of them!" The Japanese had launched a strike of 67 Zekes, 27 Val dive bombers, 14 Kate torpedo bombers, and a few G4M1 Betty twin-engine bombers. The strike was intercepted by the 12 Hellcats and 24 Corsairs defending the fleet. The Vals evaded the defending fighters but found the American antiaircraft accurate and deadly. No ships were hit, but Admiral Montgomery was compelled to cancel a second strike against Rabaul shortly after the launch began. Ensign C.T. Watts of VF-18 had only begun to retract his wheels from his launch when a Val appeared in front of him and he shot it down. Lieutenant (jg) Rube Denoff of VF-9 had a similar experience when he was launched from *Essex*. "I didn't have time to even retract my wheels before I had a Val in front of me." He shot it down, then connected with his wingman and proceeded to shoot down a Kate before he was hit by "friendly fire" from his carrier and forced to make an emergency landing aboard *Essex*. Radio control over the fleet broke down and the defending fighters found themselves flying toward flak bursts to engage the enemy.

American claims for 90 shot down in the attack were as excessive as the claims over Rabaul, but the Japanese lost eight Zekes and 31 Vals and Kates, despite some mistakes made by the American FDOs that resulted in 12 Hellcats being vectored to investigate a bogey which turned out to be 12 Hellcats from the second strike that had not been recalled.

For the pilots of Fighting 9, things were different that night on *Essex*. "Up until then, the torpedo bomber and dive bomber pilots usually had little use for us 'hot shot' fighter pilots," McWhorter recalled. "But that night they came to our ready room with cigarettes, gum, and candy. We had escorted them into Rabaul and back and only one dive bomber had been lost to AA fire."

When asked to compare the Rabaul strike with later events in his career as the first Hellcat Ace and a top-scoring Navy fighter pilot, McWhorter replied, "On a terror scale of 1–10, Rabaul was an 8. It was definitely my most memorable mission."

CHAPTER FIVE

BUTCH IS DOWN!

Considered by many contemporaries to be the outstanding example of a naval aviator in World War II, as well as a leader who influenced others who came after through both personal contact and professional example, Edward H. "Butch" O'Hare was seen as a flier of standout ability from the day he graduated from Pensacola in May 1940 with his Wings of Gold and was assigned to Fighting 3 aboard *Saratoga*.

Lieutenant John S. "Jimmy" Thach, then XO of Fighting 3, took young Ensign O'Hare as his wingman. At the time, every Navy fighter squadron XO emphasized gunnery training, unlike their Air Corps compatriots. O'Hare was the best gunnery student Thach had ever encountered during his ten-year career in naval aviation, during which he had established his reputation as the Navy's leading expert on the topic of aerial gunnery. In the fleet gunnery competition held in November 1940, eight of 16 Fighting 3 pilots qualified for the coveted "Gunnery E." Ensign O'Hare won the fleet trophy for best gunnery and was soon promoted to lieutenant (jg).

When war came to the Pacific on December 7, 1941, Thach had been promoted to Lieutenant Commander and was the commanding officer of VF-3, while newly promoted Lieutenant O'Hare was his senior division leader. In early 1941, *Saratoga* had gone into the Bremerton Navy Yard for modernization and the squadron had operated from *Enterprise* out of San Diego. In June they got rid of their Brewster F2A-2s and re-equipped with the Grumman F4F-3 Wildcat, which O'Hare flew for the first time on June 21, when he took delivery at the Grumman plant in Bethpage, Long

Island. He flew the airplane across the country, stopping at Washington DC, Dayton, Ohio, and St Louis, Missouri, where he met his future wife. In September, *Saratoga* came out of the yards but much time was spent fitting out and the squadron spent most of its time at NAS North Island. The day no naval aviator would forget, December 7, *Saratoga* had only arrived in San Diego the previous Friday. The next day, December 8, she stood out of the harbor past Point Loma and Air Group 3 brought Fighting 3's 18 Wildcats, Scouting and Bombing 3's 36 SBD-3 Dauntless dive bombers and Torpedo 3's 18 TBD-1 Devastator torpedo bombers aboard, then headed for Hawaii at flank speed.

Flying the flag of Rear Admiral Aubrey Fitch as flagship of Carrier Division 1, *Saratoga*'s sailors and airmen stared grimly at the devastation of the Japanese attack: the capsized *Oklahoma* where rescue crews still worked to open holes in the ship's hull in a desperate attempt to rescue survivors trapped within, the beached *Nevada*, the devastated *West Virginia* and *Tennessee*, the sunken *California* and the ravaged wreck of the *Arizona*, the twisted wrecks of aircraft at Ford Island Naval Air Station and the burned-out hangars; they swore to themselves the personal oath of vengeance against Japan taken by every sailor who went through Pearl Harbor during the war and saw that sight.

Saratoga joined *Lexington* in Task Force 14 under Rear Admiral Frank J. Fletcher and the two carriers departed Pearl Harbor the next day to reinforce Wake Island. *Saratoga* carried the Brewster F2A-3s of VMF-221 which were to join the F4F-3s of VMF-211 on the besieged island. Rendezvous with the slow *Neches* (AO-3) and heavy seas slowed *Saratoga*'s task group; further delay was caused by the necessity of refueling her DEs on December 21 after they failed to connect with *Neches* due to the weather. Admiral Fletcher received word on December 23 of Japanese carrier air strikes on Wake; unwilling to risk two of the Pacific Fleet's three aircraft carriers in a battle against an enemy carrier fleet of unknown size, acting Pacific Fleet commander Vice Admiral William S. Pye instructed the carriers to return to Pearl Harbor. The Japanese second attempt to land on Wake on December 24 was successful and this time they took the island bastion. On Christmas Day, the F2A-3s of VMF-221 departed *Saratoga* for Midway. Among the young Marines who left the ship on that first Christmas of the war was newly promoted First Lieutenant Marion E. Carl, who would later become a leading Marine ace at Guadalcanal.

Upon her return to Pearl Harbor on December 29, *Saratoga* became the flagship of Task Force 14 upon Rear Admiral Herbert F. Leary's assumption of command while Admiral Fitch joined the Pacific Fleet staff. The task force put to sea on New Year's Eve and patrolled in the vicinity of Midway.

Saratoga was 420 miles southwest of Hawaii on January 11, 1942, *en route* to meet up with *Enterprise* when she was spotted by the Japanese fleet submarine I-6 and torpedoed. Three boiler rooms were flooded by the explosion that killed six crewmen and reduced her speed to 16 knots. *Saratoga* reached Pearl on January 13. Temporary repairs were made over the next three weeks while her four twin 8-inch gun turrets were removed and installed as coastal defense shore batteries on Oahu. She sailed to the Bremerton Navy Yard on February 9, 1942 for permanent repairs.

Fighting 3 remained at Ford Island. *Lexington*'s Fighting 2 was still operating the Brewster F2A-3, which had proven itself too fragile for extended operations at sea. The "Flying Chiefs" returned to the United States aboard *Saratoga*, where the experienced senior enlisted pilots who were the squadron's heart were commissioned and sent into Training Command to spread their experience among new aviators.

Lexington was now flagship for Task Force 11 commander Vice Admiral Wilson Brown; the force left Pearl Harbor on January 31 to rendezvous with Admiral Halsey aboard *Enterprise* as Task Force 16 returned from the successful raid against Kwajalein, and to cover a convoy headed to Canton Island. Jimmy Thach led Fighting 3 aboard *Lexington* off Diamond Head, with one Wildcat damaged when landing.

Newly arrived Pacific Fleet commander Admiral Chester W. Nimitz ordered Task Force 11 to join ANZAC forces in the Coral Sea. The force was joined by the heavy cruiser *San Francisco* (CA-38) on February 10, when Admiral Brown was ordered to attack the newly captured Japanese base at Rabaul on the island of New Britain. *Pensacola* (CA-24) joined the fleet on February 17; the plan of attack included a bombardment of the port by the two cruisers while *Lexington*'s air group made their attack.

Lexington and the rest of the task force were 453 nautical miles northeast of Rabaul on the morning of February 20, when a snooper was picked up at a range of 35 miles by the CXAM radar. Four Wildcats led by Thach were launched to intercept, while four more were launched to orbit over the task force under the leadership of VF-3's XO, Lieutenant Commander Don Lovelace. Thach led his Wildcats in and out of the clouds and squalls until the Kawanishi H6K "Mavis" was spotted in a rain squall. Thach executed an overhead pass from starboard with his wingman executing a similar pass from portside. The big flying boat's fuel tanks caught fire and it span down to crash into the ocean.

Lovelace and his wingman caught a second Mavis 50 minutes later and shot it down. Clearly, the fleet had been discovered; the Rabaul strike was canceled. *Lexington* and her escorts continued on course toward New Britain to lure a Japanese attack. The US Navy was about to discover whether or not a carrier task force could survive a determined land-based attack.

At 1630 hours, radar spotted 17 twin-engine Mitsubishi G4M1 Type 1 Land Attack Bombers that would soon be known as the "Betty" from the 4th Air Group at Rabaul approaching in one nine-plane formation from starboard and one eight-plane formation from port, 25 miles out and coming on. The timing for the Americans could not have been worse. Lovelace's division was just entering the landing pattern after four Wildcats led by Lieutenant Noel Gaylor had relieved them.

The Bettys lost precious minutes as they overflew the Americans, then turned to attack from astern. Lovelace's Wildcats were burning the last of their fuel when they hit the Japanese and disrupted the bomb run; the nearest bomb exploded when it hit the sea 3,000 yards from *Lexington*. Gaylor's four Wildcats made the unwelcome discovery of the Betty's 20mm "tail stinger," losing two defenders.

Six Wildcats that included O'Hare were launched with Thach in the lead. O'Hare was ordered to orbit the task force with Lieutenant (jg) Marion F. Dufilho, while Thach led the others into an attack on the eight-plane formation where he shot down two. O'Hare and Dufilho watched in frustration as the others chased the survivors. At this point, 16 of Fighting 3's 18 Wildcats were airborne.

At 1700 hours, radar picked up the nine-plane formation 12 miles out on the task force's disengaged side. O'Hare and Dufilho were vectored to intercept and ordered to "Buster" (fly at maximum speed). The F4F-3 had a sluggish climb, but they managed to get to an altitude 1,500 feet above the attackers when they caught them 9 miles out. The two fliers made a starboard high-side pass as the bombers angled down in a shallow dive toward *Lexington*.

Dufilho discovered his guns were jammed and dove away as O'Hare lined up his first target. The winner of the 1940 Fleet Gunnery Competition was entering the match of his life. O'Hare closed to 100 yards as defensive tracers streaked past and opened fire, hitting the starboard engine of the last Betty in the Vee-of-Vee's. The engine was hit by such concentrated fire that it literally jumped out of its mountings. While that Betty span down, O'Hare opened fire on the one ahead, which caught fire and dropped out of formation. Pulling out of his dive, he put his sights on the rearmost bomber on the far side of the Vee; a third burst blew up the port engine and the Betty fell toward the sea below. He rolled, turned for a second pass and torched number four. Thach reported that the action was so fast he saw three bombers falling in flames when he joined the fight.

O'Hare turned for a third high-side pass as anti-aircraft fire from the task force surrounded him and the surviving bombers opened fire at him. As his guns rattled empty, O'Hare blew up the formation leader. The four survivors dropped their bombs 100 yards astern of *Lexington* and turned to escape, but not before Thach's four claimed two more.

Lieutenant Edward H. "Butch" O'Hare had just become the first US Navy ace in the first major naval air battle of the Pacific War. Awarded the Medal of Honor for saving *Lexington*, he was the only one of eight Wildcat pilots so honored during the war who was carrier-based.

When O'Hare climbed out of his cockpit he asked for a glass of water and downed four before he was called to the Admiral's bridge for congratulations. Fighting 3 lost two F4Fs and one pilot as they shot down 15 of 17 attacking Bettys, including two that ditched before they got back to Rabaul. O'Hare directly shot down four; his fifth was one of the two that ditched, which validated his claim. When he checked the Wildcat, Thach determined O'Hare had used only 60 rounds for each plane shot down. The prewar emphasis on gunnery training was fully validated.

Following the attack, Task Force 11 altered course after dark to rendezvous with the tanker *Platte* (AO-24) early on February 22. An Aichi E13A "Jake" floatplane managed to track the task force for a short time after dark but the six Mavis flying boats could not locate the American ships in the darkness and the task force met with *Platte* and her escorts, HMAS *Australia*, HMAS *Canberra*, and USS *Chicago* (CA-29) as planned. Admiral Brown's request for reinforcement by another carrier if another raid on Rabaul was attempted was met by Admiral Nimitz's prompt order to Task Force 17, commanded by Rear Admiral Frank Jack Fletcher aboard *Yorktown*, to rendezvous north of New Caledonia on March 6, 1942 and join *Lexington* in a second attempt on Rabaul.

The Americans received word on March 8 that Rabaul Harbor was empty; the Japanese invasion fleet was now off the villages of Lae and Salamaua in Papua, New Guinea. Wilson prepared to attack the invaders from a position in the Gulf of Papua south of New Guinea. The mission involved crossing the Owen Stanley Mountains, the "spine" of New Guinea and not known for good flying conditions. The morning of March 10, *Lexington* sent off eight Wildcats, 31 Dauntlesses, and 13 Devastators at 0745 hours; these were followed 21 minutes later by *Yorktown's* eight Wildcats, 32 Dauntlesses, and 12 Devastators. The *Lexington* strike force arrived first, sinking three transports and damaging several other ships before the *Yorktown* strike arrived 15 minutes later. Antiaircraft fire got one Dauntless while a Nakajima E8N1 "Dave" observation floatplane was shot down by a Wildcat. A Mavis spotted *Lexington* later that afternoon, but bad weather prevented an attack.

Following the New Guinea mission, Task Force 11 was ordered to return to Pearl Harbor; *Lexington* exchanged six Wildcats, five Dauntlesses, and one Devastator for two *Yorktown* Wildcats in need of overhaul before she left and arrived back at Pearl Harbor on March 26.

During a short refit, *Lexington's* four 8-inch twin gun turrets were removed and replaced with additional antiaircraft weapons. The reconstituted Fighting 2 rejoined the ship in mid-April. No longer the "Fighting Chiefs," the squadron was known as "Ramsey's Lambsies" for their commander, Lieutenant Commander Paul Ramsey. To bring the newcomers "up to speed" in terms of combat experience, 11 experienced VF-3 pilots were transferred on April 12 when the squadron's strength was increased from 18 to 27 Wildcats. *Lexington* sortied from Pearl Harbor on April 15 for her rendezvous with destiny in the Coral Sea.

With Fighting 3 now ashore at NAS Barber's Point, Thach began training new replacements up to combat standard. Butch O'Hare was soon called to Washington to receive the Medal of Honor from President Roosevelt. He then began what would become the standard mandatory nationwide publicity tour for all official heroes after him throughout the war, during which he spoke to civic groups and appeared at local rallies to raise money selling Victory Bonds. During the tour, he visited the Grumman factory at Bethpage, Long Island and was photographed in an F4F-3 painted to look like the Wildcat he had flown on his Medal of Honor mission (in the years since the war, these publicity photos have frequently been mistaken by "experts" for photos of the real airplane). He also spent time with Grumman's design team which was working on the new F6F Hellcat and gave them the benefit of his combat experience. His essential contribution was raising the cockpit to provide good sight over the nose for gunnery and carrier landings.

O'Hare was promoted to Lieutenant Commander in June 1943 after a year "on tour," and given command of his old VF-3, now back in Pearl Harbor after participating in the Battle of Midway and seeing combat in the Guadalcanal campaign the year before. The next month, Fighting 3 became the first front-line squadron in the Pacific to transition to the new F6F-3 Hellcat. They worked up on the new fighter at Naval Auxiliary Air Station (NAAS) Pu'unene on Maui, where a few weeks later Lieutenant (jg) Alexander Vraciu, a first-generation Romanian immigrant's son from Chicago, reported for duty. As Jimmy Thach had chosen O'Hare three years earlier, he chose Vraciu as his wingman after interviewing the newcomer and checking his flight proficiency. Over the next five months they flew together, O'Hare passed on to Vraciu all he had learned in the hard crucible of combat.

While O'Hare was taking command of Fighting 3 in Hawaii, across the continent, a new Fighting 2 was re-established on June 1, 1943 at NAS Atlantic City, New Jersey. Known as the "Rippers," this Fighting 2 was the last fighting squadron activated during World War II that bore the same designation as a previous unit. The pilots were a perfect example of the way in which the Navy expanded its air force during the war. With a policy of only appointing Annapolis graduates to command a unit and to senior posts within, it was frequently the case that the squadron commander and XO were Annapolis men. While some might have combat experience, it was more likely at this point in the war that they would come from Training Command. The division leaders were generally newly promoted lieutenants with combat experience, while the Lieutenant (jg) section leaders were a mix of combat veterans or instructors. Newly-graduated, Ensigns were assigned as wingmen. Ensign Don Brandt remembered, "We fresh-caught ensigns mostly lived in awe of our superiors and hoped to emulate them."

Lieutenant Commander William "Bill" Dean, Annapolis class of 1934, became a naval aviator in 1936. Prior to assuming command of Fighting 2, he had been at NAS Miami where he worked closely with future Fighting 17 "Jolly Rogers" leader Lieutenant Commander Tom Blackburn, developing the training syllabus for future fighter pilots. Dean took command after Blackburn left to command VC-29 aboard the *Santee* (CVE-29) during the North African invasion. Thus, his background was excellent for a man whose job was to lead the graduates of his training program into the "final exam" of actual combat. Dean was alone among American fighter squadron commanders in the Army, Navy, or Marines during the war, in creating opportunity for all the pilots in the unit to score victories as the best way to create high morale. Unlike other squadron commanders, he had no "favorites" and was remembered for being as willing to fly a CAP assignment as to lead a fighter sweep. Don Brandt remembered, "Commander Dean led by example, and never asked anyone to take an assignment he wouldn't take himself. We loved him."

Several veterans of Fighting 10 formed Fighting 2's core of combat experience. That squadron had been commanded during the Solomons campaign by Coral Sea veteran Lieutenant Commander James "Jimmy" Flatley, who was as well known in the flying navy as was the other "Jimmy", John Thach, and an equally good teacher of fighter pilots. Fighting 10 was aboard *Enterprise* at the Battle of Santa Cruz and was later sent to Guadalcanal at the height of the struggle for that island. The Fighting 10 alumni included Lieutenant John E. Eckhardt, Annapolis '38, who became Fighting 2's XO; Lieutenant L.E. "Tex" Harris, Annapolis '39 and almost an ace with a score of four over Guadalcanal and Lieutenant (jg) Bill Blair were assigned as senior division leaders.

Flight operations officer Lieutenant (jg) Roy M. "Butch" Voris, another Fighting 10 veteran who would became a leading ace in the new unit had been born in Los Angeles in 1919. His childhood hobby was building and flying model airplanes made of balsa and tissue paper. He discovered Eddie Rickenbacker's World War I account, *Fighting the Flying Circus*, and spent many hours watching airplanes fly at Mines Field – today's Los Angeles International Airport before he finally became a NavCad in 1941. He recalled in a 2004 interview, "When the war clouds were rolling in, I was living in San Francisco. I walked past a big recruitment sign that said 'Fly Navy' with a pilot looking off into the wild blue yonder standing on the wing of the plane." Graduating from Pensacola with his Wings of Gold in February 1942, he joined VF-10 that July. He landed on Guadalcanal after Santa Cruz when the squadron was sent to reinforce the "Cactus Air Force." "I shot down my first Zero at Guadalcanal. But I didn't see one coming up behind me and I got shot up and knocked out of the sky. I didn't bail out – they'll shoot you out of your parachute and if you go into the water the sharks will eat you. I was full of shrapnel wounds and had a dead stick – I'd lost the engine – but I got back to Guadalcanal. I was a lucky boy." The assignment to Fighting 2 marked his return following recovery from those wounds. Seventy years later, Don Brandt remembered Voris as "the best leader, and the best teacher, I ever ran across in the Navy." After the War, Voris founded the Blue Angels Flight Demonstration Team.

Lieutenant (jg) Arthur "Van" Van Haren, Jr., joined after Pearl Harbor, In a service that at the time actively discriminated by ethnic background in choosing officer candidates, he was one of very few of Latino heritage. An apt pupil, "Van" remained after graduation at Pensacola as a flight instructor with the opportunity to hone his flying and gunnery skills. He was a "high-time Hellcat pilot" when he arrived in VF-2 that summer of 1943, since he had ten hours in the new fighter at Pensacola. Commander Dean was more than happy to put Van Haren's instruction skills to use, assigning him to oversee the transition from Wildcat to Hellcat.

While the new aviators were learning about the new airplanes, the new navy arrived in the Pacific. *Essex* dropped anchor at Pearl Harbor in May 1943 with Air Group 9 aboard. *Yorktown* transited the Panama Canal on July 11 and arrived at Pearl on July 24 with a new Air Group 10. *Lexington* arrived on August 9 with Air Group 16. The light carrier *Independence* arrived on July 22, followed by *Princeton* on August 9.

The Navy was now ready to implement what had begun life in 1919 as War Plan Orange, one of many plans created to deal with possible future developments, which was adopted as the Navy's official plan of battle in the Pacific in 1924. War Plan Orange envisioned an amphibious campaign across the Central Pacific, creating bases in the Gilbert and Marshall Islands chains, before taking bases in the Marianas and fighting a major fleet action against the Imperial Japanese Navy, leading to a blockade of Japan itself. The plan had originally foreseen a fleet action in the classic manner between opposing battle lines, but this now changed in light of the events at Pearl Harbor that saw aircraft carriers take the primary offensive role in the fleet.

While War Plan Orange was officially dropped as a formal plan in 1939, the strategies and actions developed in the plan were adapted into the five "Rainbow" war plans developed between 1939 and 1942, with War Plan Orange being the major basis of the Rainbow-Four plan. War Plan Rainbow-Five, which was the foundation of United States strategy in World War II, foresaw a war with the United States allied to Britain and France, with offensive operations in Europe and defensive "holding" operations in the Pacific. In the event, this strategy was not followed as closely as originally expected, with the Navy pushing hard for increased operational authority as conditions in the Pacific changed.

Chief of Naval Operations Admiral Ernest J. King wanted to start the Central Pacific campaign in 1942. This was delayed by the need to land on Guadalcanal to secure the sea route to Australia, but King never lost sight of his main goal. He was correctly seen by General Sir Alan Brooke, Chief of the Imperial General Staff, as the American most opposed to the "Germany First" strategy adopted by Churchill and Roosevelt.

King's desire for all-out war in the Pacific as opposed to the agreed "holding action" saw initial victory at the Casablanca Conference in

January 1943, where George Marshall supported King against the British when he presented the "70–30 plan" that allocated Allied troops, shipping, and equipment "70 percent in the Atlantic theater and 30 percent in the Pacific theater." At the Trident Conference held in Washington in May, Admiral William Leahy became the de facto "chairman" of the US Joint Chiefs. On May 13, Leahy informed the British that any limitation on US freedom of action in the Pacific "would not be acceptable to the United States Chiefs of Staff." With only token forces actively engaged against the Japanese, the British lacked standing to influence strategy in the Pacific.

In a presentation at the close of the conference on May 21, King outlined a plan that would see the Marianas under US control by the summer of 1944, with the new B-29 bombers commencing action against Japan proper by the fall. On June 14, 1943, the Joint Chiefs instructed Admiral Nimitz to prepare to invade the Marshall Islands with a tentative sailing date of November 15, 1943.

MacArthur was outraged that this would reduce forces for his planned offensive in New Guinea, while Halsey was concerned that he would lose naval forces in the South Pacific. In the end, the Central Pacific Force rescued Halsey with the Rabaul strikes, and supported MacArthur's final New Guinea landing at Hollandia in April and his landing on Mindoro in September 1944.

By July 1943, Nimitz's staff reported that an invasion of the Marshalls could not happen before early 1944 and argued for delay on the grounds that the Fifth Fleet would be sufficiently strong by January 1944 to face the Japanese fleet should they offer battle over the invasion. King was adamant that action be taken before the end of 1943. Admiral John Towers, who commanded naval air forces in the Pacific, and his Chief of Staff, former *Wasp* commander Captain Forrest P. Sherman, presented a plan to retake Wake Island. Admiral Spruance presented a plan to invade the Gilberts. The result was a decision to invade the Gilberts in November in place of the Marshalls, announced on July 20, 1943 as Operation *Galvanic*. Time was short, with only four months to plan what was the largest and most complex amphibious operation ever attempted to that time.

By early August, Fighting 3 was ready for combat in the Hellcat. Redesignated Fighting 6 at the end of July, the squadron was divided in half; three divisions under O'Hare went aboard *Independence*, while the other three went aboard *Princeton*, thus providing both carriers with Hellcats to replace the Wildcats of their fighter squadrons.

The first strike by the new fast carrier task force, now known as Task Force 50, was carried out against Marcus Island on August 31, 1943, with strikes flown by *Essex*, *Yorktown*, and *Independence*. O'Hare's Hellcats were held back as CAP over the task force. The other half of VF-6 aboard *Princeton* participated in the occupation of Baker Island from September 1–4.

Still divided and still aboard *Independence*, O'Hare's detachment finally saw combat as part of Task Force 14 during the Wake Island strike conducted by *Essex*, *Yorktown*, *Independence*, and the newly arrived *Cowpens* (CVL-25) on October 10, 1943 which marked the combat debut of the F6F against the Zeke. O'Hare shot down one of the 50 Zekes that rose to oppose the strike, then later chased and shot down his sixth Betty bomber when it attempted to attack the fleet. O'Hare's wingman, Alex Vraciu, also scored in this fight. When O'Hare chased the Zeke he shot down below the clouds, Vraciu lost sight of his leader and followed a second Zeke to Wake Island. After it landed, he strafed the enemy fighter on the ground and then destroyed a Betty parked on the runway.

While these initial operations occurred, Fighting 2 completed their advanced gunnery training at NAS Quonset Point, Rhode Island in July, then did carrier qualification in August at NAS Norfolk, Virginia, with each pilot completing three landings aboard *Charger* (CVE-30) in Chesapeake Bay. On September 6 they left Quonset Point for San Diego and arrived at NAS North Island the night of September 8. The next day they flew to NAS Alameda in San Francisco Bay and went aboard a CVE for transport to Hawaii, sharing deck space with USAAF P-47 Thunderbolts.

The squadron arrived at Pearl Harbor on September 18 and were first stationed at NAS Barber's Point before they moved to NAAS Pu'unene on Maui where they rejoined Bombing 2 and Torpedo 2 for advanced training as an air group. The air group went aboard the new *Lexington* at the end of October and put in an impressive performance during a Marine landing exercise on November 1.

Butch O'Hare was promoted to command Air Group 6 when he returned to Hawaii after the Wake Island operation. Ordered to go aboard the newly repaired *Enterprise* for the Gilbert Islands invasion, O'Hare requested that the promising newcomers of VF-2 be temporarily transferred to Air Group 6 so he would have a cohesive, trained fighter squadron instead of the broken, disorganized unit VF-6 had become. On November 10, Fighting 2 went aboard *Enterprise*.

Though he was now CAG, O'Hare still insisted on being called "Butch." At first, he flew a TBF-1 Avenger command aircraft with crewmen gunner

Aviation Ordnanceman 1/c Del Delchamps and radioman Aviation Radioman 2/c Hal Coleman. With its good radio equipment, docile handling, and long range, the Avenger made an ideal command aircraft for the CAG, who was traditionally seen as the strike coordinator, not an active combatant. However, before *Enterprise* headed into combat, Task Group 50.2 commander Rear Admiral Arthur W. Radford allowed O'Hare to use a Hellcat as his command aircraft instead of the Avenger. He drew Grumman F6F-3 Hellcat, BuNo 66168 and the side number "00" was painted on. VF-2's Ensign Warren Andrew "Andy" Skon became his wingman.

The invasion fleet grew when Task Group 50.3: *Essex, Bunker Hill,* and *Independence,* newly returned from New Guinea and their epic November 11 strikes at Rabaul, rendezvoused with the other carriers of Task Force 50 on November 13.

On November 18, a day before D-Day, the task force began air strikes against targets in the Gilberts. That afternoon, as 12 Hellcats of VF-9 returned to *Essex,* Lieutenant (jg) Hamilton "Mac" McWhorter looked up at the right moment. "I saw a biplane on floats flying the opposite direction about 4,000 feet above and to the left of us. I recognized it immediately as a F1M2 "Pete" floatplane so I decided to go after him." The highly maneuverable Pete was a difficult target; several American pilots in the Solomons had discovered the hard way that it was far from easy to bag a Pete:

> The Pete was in a shallow dive heading for the clouds below and I was closing in on his port quarter just waiting to get into firing range. He then made a hard right diving turn and increased his dive angle, which turned my firing run into a perfect overhead pass. Before I could fire, he disappeared into some clouds and I thought I'd lost him, but just then I saw a dark blur in the clouds and opened fire on that, not seeing whether I had hit him or not. I dove on through the clouds and looked back and there he was beneath the clouds, spinning down in flames.

The Central Pacific campaign began in earnest on November 19, 1943 with the invasion of Tarawa and Makin atolls. The *Enterprise* air group struck Makin. The first wave of SBD-5s from Bombing 6 and TBM-1Cs from Torpedo 6, with the fighters led by CAG O'Hare, saw VF-2's "Tex" Harris become an ace when his division caught a Dave floatplane which he set aflame for Fighting 2's first and his fifth victory. The installations on Makin were hit by strafing Hellcats and dive-bombing Dauntlesses, while the Avengers dropped four 500-pound bombs each in glide bombing attacks.

Andy Skon took a hit in his Hellcat's wing that exploded some ammunition without further harm to him or the airplane. The three strikes saw antiaircraft fire silenced and all targets destroyed. Antiaircraft fire hit Ensign Wayne Harrold's Hellcat on the second strike; he disappeared during the return flight to become Fighting 2's first combat loss. Makin was under American control by November 21; island natives welcomed the soldiers as liberators, though Marine General Holland W. "Howlin' Mad" Smith, who held overall command of the ground forces, was enraged by Army General Ralph Smith's leisurely campaign against negligible opposition.

November 19, 1943 would be one of the most memorable in Mac McWhorter's career. While his division was on a combat patrol north of Tarawa, they received a call to intercept a low bogie. Dropping to 2,000 feet, the bogie turned out to be a Betty bomber flying about 10 feet above the water. "Once again, they didn't spot us until we were in an advantageous position. I made a flat side pass coming in on his starboard beam, aiming at the engines and nose, and gave it about a one second burst. The port engine flamed and the Betty hit the water and burned." The Betty was victory number five and Hamilton McWhorter became the first pilot to score five kills in the Hellcat. Back aboard *Essex*, the armorers discovered he had only fired 86 rounds to down the Betty. His squadron nickname became "One Slug."

The most important combat position, between the Gilberts and Marshalls, had been assigned to Task Group 50.1 – *Yorktown*, *Lexington*, and the newly arrived *Cowpens* (CVL-25) – to intercept any Japanese attacks while mounting strikes against airfields in the Marshalls. The three carriers launched strikes against Jaluit and Mille, sites of the two largest airfields in the eastern Marshalls on November 19. With no aerial opposition, the strafing Hellcats and glide bombing Avengers left the fields in smoking ruins.

At Truk, Combined Fleet commander Admiral Koga had considered opposing any American invasion in the Gilberts or Marshalls, but he did not have the strength to do so now, in light of the naval and air losses sustained at Rabaul. Japanese air power in the Gilberts and Marshalls was considerably reduced after transfers to Rabaul, but bomber units on airfields in the western Carolines and Marianas were ordered to move into the eastern Marshalls and seek out the enemy fleet.

Sixteen Betty bombers were belatedly spotted against the setting sun as they deployed against Task Group 50.3 when the carriers were landing the last strikes of the day. *Bunker Hill*'s VF-18 CAP was vectored to the bombers and shot down six while the antiaircraft gunners in the task group scored three, but not before they dropped their deadly Type 91 torpedoes. *Independence* was struck in her stern, with serious damage. The 12 VF-6 Hellcats still airborne, including O'Hare's former wingman Alex Vraciu, landed aboard *Essex*. After emergency repairs were made, *Independence* steamed to Funafuti on November 23 for further temporary repairs. She would be out of the war under repair at Mare Island Navy Yard in San Francisco until July 1944.

When Japanese bombers attempted attacks throughout the night of November 20–21, *Enterprise* launched Fighting 2's Commander Dean and wingman Lieutenant (jg) Danny Carmichael into the pre-dawn grayness at 0445 hours on November 21 to intercept the bogeys plotted on radar. Lieutenant Arthur Van Haren and his wingman took off shortly after. Sixteen miles out, Dean and Carmichael spotted a Betty at 10,000 feet; Dean made a high-side attack on the bomber and flamed it for his first victory of an eventual 11.

Later that day, Fighting 5's skipper, Commander Charles Crommelin, took off from *Yorktown* leading seven other Hellcats; they headed toward Mille to see how many bombers remained on the airfield, with orders to observe and report, not attack. The aggressive Crommelin made a low pass over the airfield on the pretense of going in for a closer look. Spotting a Betty taxiing toward the runway, he opened fire and set it aflame. Banking around for another strafing run, he took a 20mm direct hit in his cockpit that destroyed most of his instruments and shattered the canopy. With shrapnel wounds in his face, neck, chest, and right arm, Crommelin lost sight in his left eye and could barely see out the right. While the windscreen was intact, spider webs of cracks obscured his vision forward. Barely able to see, he pushed the shattered canopy back and leaned out. He leveled off at 300 feet and was joined by a wingman who escorted him the 120 miles back to *Yorktown*, where he made a perfect approach and snagged the three wire, an incredible performance. Captain Joseph James "Jocko" Clark later reported that "He was lifted from the cockpit in a semiconscious condition, suffering from severe shock and loss of blood." After a lengthy recuperation in the United States where his left eye was saved, Crommelin returned to flight operations in early 1945.

Because of these nocturnal attacks, Task Group 50.2 commander Admiral Arthur Radford, O'Hare, and *Enterprise* air officer Commander Tom Hamilton worked to develop an ad hoc counter-tactic that resulted in the first carrier-based night fighter operations by the US Navy. O'Hare's plan involved a three-plane formation of two Hellcats led by an Avenger using its sea-search radar to find the airborne enemy. The two Hellcats on the Avenger's wing would then be vectored onto any enemy found by the radar operator in the Avenger. The unit was called a "Bat Team."

The plan required the fighter director officer in the CIC to spot any incoming enemy formations at a sufficient distance to allow the "Bat Team" to be launched. The radar-equipped Avenger would then lead the Hellcats into position close enough for the F6F pilots to spot the enemy's exhaust flames, at which point they would close in and shoot down the bomber.

Three days after the invasion, VF-16 commander Lieutenant Commander Paul Buie led 12 Hellcats of the "Pistol-Packin' Airedales" off *Lexington* at 0930 hours on a CAP. Second division leader Lieutenant (jg) Ralph Hanks, who had been assigned this exalted position following his division leader's failure to safety his guns when he landed aboard the carrier the day before, resulting in his spraying the deck with machine gun fire, remembered, "It was a beautiful day over a calm Pacific, with a few scattered cumulus clouds. My division joined quickly as we climbed to our assigned CAP station, 12,000 feet over the ship." Two and a half hours later, *Lexington*'s FDO radioed he had a contact. Buie was vectored to what he later called "a fighter pilot's dream": 4,000 feet above a formation of 30 Zekes that were unaware of the American presence. Leading his fliers in a coordinated side and overhead attack, Buie personally splashed two; in the melee that followed, 15 more Zekes went down. VF-16's score of 17 was the biggest bag of enemy aircraft in one fight by Navy fighters to date and fully demonstrated the Hellcat's capability as a fleet-defense fighter.

Among the victorious Hellcat pilots was Ralph Hanks, whose actions in the fight demonstrated that Buie had been right to promote the young flier. Diving on a flight of three Zekes, he shot down the right wingman. Turning airspeed into altitude, he zoomed back up as a Zeke dove past him. "I rolled hard to keep him in sight, easily cut across his turn and took a big lead on him, and fired a burst. He instantly blew to pieces." Turning, he spotted a Zeke on the tail of another Hellcat. "Closing on his tail was easy, he apparently never saw me. A long burst from his six o'clock brought fire and smoke and I had to roll high to avoid debris and flame." Rolling inverted, Hanks took an instant to view an incredible sight, "There were burning airplanes and detached wings, brightly flashing, falling, tumbling, showing their red meatballs in the sun. There were fires on the water, white splashes in the water, deep red balls of fire and black smoke – all against beautiful puffy white clouds on the horizon. It was a colorful, beautiful sight." An instant later, Hanks spotted a Hellcat far behind a Zeke, firing uselessly at the enemy. "I dove nearly vertical on the Zeke, but he flicked away. Then I spotted one jinking like he thought he was being chased. I obliged him and came up behind and gave him a burst and he went down." Hanks split-essed away and came upon a "vic" of three Zekes. "I closed in fast and opened fire slightly out of range at the wingman. My tracers were passing down both sides of his fuselage, but then they converged and produced a ball of black smoke and fire." Spotting another Zeke, he turned and opened fire, "but all I got was a few shots and then I was out of ammo."

In his first aerial combat, a fight that lasted a total of five minutes, Ralph Hanks had scored five confirmed victories to become the first Navy "ace in a day," after O'Hare, by scoring five victories on the same date. When he landed back aboard *Lexington*, Buie took him up to meet *Lexington's* commander, Captain Felix Stump. "I was introduced as 'Five-shot Hanks' and that was my nickname on the ship for the rest of the cruise." Famed photographer Edward Steichen, who was aboard *Lexington* with his photo unit to film what became the well-known documentary *The Fighting Lady*, photographed Hanks with his captain and squadron commander, and then with his fellow pilots. The result of the second shot was one of the iconic photos of the Pacific War: victorious young pilots waving their fists in celebration of victory, standing beside the tail of one of their Hellcats.

Enterprise's first "Bat Team" interception was attempted on November 24 at 0300 hours. Dean and Butch Voris took off in company with a Torpedo 6 Avenger. After several fruitless hours of being vectored against targets found by the *Enterprise* FDO, the three landed at 0800 hours. That night the fleet tracked three different attacking formations overhead, but clouds prevented the launch of defending fighters while the Japanese couldn't spot the ships below.

While Japanese air power was largely unable to inflict damage to the American fleet, the Japanese submarine force demonstrated it was still as dangerous as it had been in "Torpedo Junction" the year before. Carrier Division 24, known as the Carrier Support Force, had been organized prior to Operation *Galvanic*, to bring a large group of CVEs together so their composite air groups could provide air support for an extended period to the Marines once they made it ashore. The fast carrier task force did not want to be tied down to one geographic location, lest the enemy get a better opportunity to inflict major damage on the fleet. The small carriers were indeed more expendable than the fleet carriers, thus they could take station off an invasion beach and provide the needed support. As predicted, their presence in one place did attract unwanted attention.

Throughout Operation *Galvanic*, late afternoon sorties required night landings, and aviators who were not trained for night operations looked for any friendly deck. With heavy thunderheads throughout the area of the invasion on the afternoon of November 23, Admiral Pownall ordered flight operations canceled. Five FM-1 Wildcats from *Liscome Bay* (CVE-56) lost their way in the deteriorating weather and also lost their ship's homing beacon signal. When they spotted *Yorktown*, they requested permission to land aboard so they could return to their carrier the next day. As the last light of day gave them the opportunity to come aboard, the first three Wildcats trapped successfully. The pilot of the fourth failed to lower his tail hook, and was given a wave-off that he didn't respond to. He came down on *Yorktown*'s deck hard and bounced, then gunned his throttle in an unsuccessful bid to get airborne, hit the deck again and somersaulted over the barrier into parked aircraft. It was one of those instants that demonstrated there was never a safe time on an aircraft carrier during flight operations. Several airplanes were hit and destroyed, and four airedales (the slang term for the flight deck crewmen who positioned the aircraft on deck) were killed outright. The Wildcat burst into flames that spread quickly through the damaged airplanes and soon spread across the flight deck amidships. Within 20 seconds, fire control parties had foam on the fire, but the aircraft were all fully fueled and armed for the morning strike. Ammunition started cooking off and bullets whistled across the deck. Magnesium flares went off, illuminating the ship.

Captain Clark kept *Yorktown* heading into the wind to prevent the fire spreading to more airplanes parked on the forward flight deck, later writing that "the intense heat was unbearable on the island superstructure. If the island caught fire, navigation and ship control would be nearly impossible." Firefighters in asbestos suits walked into the flame and foamite was spread on the deck three inches deep, while burning aircraft were dragged to the side of the flight deck and pushed overboard. The fire burned for 30 minutes before it was put out at 1905 hours. Amazingly, the ship had suffered no serious damage and she was ready to launch aircraft the next dawn.

That night, the submarine I-175 arrived off Makin, having departed Truk on November 18 when word of the pre-invasion strikes was received.

At the same time, a temporary task group centered on the three jeep carriers commanded by Rear Admiral Henry M. Mullinnix, composed of *Liscome Bay*, *Coral Sea* (CVE-57), and *Corregidor* (CVE-58), was steaming at 15 knots 20 miles southwest of Butaritari Island. Reveille sounded aboard the ships at 0430 hours on November 24. At 0445 hours, *Liscome Bay* traded positions in the patrol line with *Coral Sea* as she prepared to assume the role of "duty carrier" for launching patrols. Minutes later, as the gray pre-dawn light brightened into the first pink promise of another spectacular tropic sunrise, the crews went to their routine dawn General Quarters at 0505 hours while the deck crew aboard *Liscome Bay* prepared two Avengers for launch.

At approximately 0510 hours, a lookout aboard *Liscome Bay* shouted, "Here comes a torpedo!" Minutes later, I-175's torpedo struck just abaft the after engine room. Surviving crewmen crowded up ladders from below decks to the hangar deck when the aircraft bomb stowage detonated from the fire caused by the torpedo; a major explosion engulfed the ship and sent shrapnel flying across the rest of the task group as far as 5,000 yards. Aboard the destroyer *Hoel* (DD-533) crewmen at their battle stations gaped at the sight in amazement. *Liscome Bay* was brighter than the rising sun. Lieutenant John C.W. Dix, *Hoel*'s communications officer, later wrote, "It didn't look like a ship at all. We thought it was an ammunition dump. She just went whoom – an orange ball of flame."

Ten minutes after she was hit, *Liscome Bay* listed to starboard and then sank at 0533 hours. Fifty-three officers and 591 enlisted men, including Admiral Mullinnix, Captain Wiltsie, and famed Pearl Harbor hero Ship's Cook 3/c Doris Miller, who had shot down a Japanese plane on December 7, 1941, went down with their ship. Of her crew of 916, only 272 were rescued by *Morris* (DD-417), *Hughes* (DD-410), and *Hull* (DD-350).

Forever after, the crew of *Coral Sea* (later renamed *Anzio*) believed *Liscome Bay* had taken a torpedo meant for them. Throughout the CVE fleet, sailors now knew that the "joke" about being combustible, vulnerable, and expendable was no joke and took to staying out of the lower spaces of their ships except when required by duty. Sixteen-year-old Seaman 2/c M.G. "Charlie" Charles, who had lied about his age when he joined the Navy the previous July and was now the most popular man aboard *Coral Sea* since he had been assigned the duty of running the ship's store and operating the ice cream machine, recalled in later years that "It didn't matter what they were doing on the hangar deck with the planes at night, guys brought their mattresses up and slept anywhere they could find space. Nobody wanted to be down below if it happened again."

During the day of November 24, VF-16's luck continued. Again leading three divisions on CAP at nearly the same position as the day before, squadron leader Buie was vectored by the FDO onto a formation of 20 Zekes and two Betty bombers at 23,000 feet. This time, the enemy held the altitude advantage. Buie turned the formation to meet the oncoming Zekes. Although one F6F went down, the Japanese never got the chance to maintain their advantage. The fight turned into a vertical scrap that ranged from 28,000 feet down to 5,000 feet. When it was over, VF-16 had scored 13 confirmed and six probables, giving them a two-day score of 30 confirmed and setting the bar high for other squadrons. VF-16's two fights constituted the last air battles during the invasion.

The most important event of Fighting 2's tour aboard *Enterprise* happened the night of November 26–27. Just after sunset, a large group of enemy aircraft was picked up on radar. As the call to man planes echoed through the ship, O'Hare was eating dinner in the ward room. He ran to Fighting 2's ready room and assigned himself as one of the intercept pilots, along with Andy Skon. Torpedo 6's commander, Lieutenant Commander John C. Phillips, flew the Avenger, with radar specialist Lieutenant (jg) Hazen B. Rand and turret gunner Aviation Ordnanceman 1/c Alvin Kernan. The three aircraft left *Enterprise* between 1958 and 2001 hours.

Confusion reigned. The two Hellcats had trouble finding the Avenger and joining on it, while the FDO aboard ship had difficulty guiding them to the targets. O'Hare and Skon were finally able to position themselves behind the Avenger. There was danger of friendly fire in this situation and O'Hare radioed Phillips, "Hey, Phil, turn those running lights on. I want to be sure it's a yellow devil I'm drilling." During the next 30 minutes, Rand guided the Avenger onto two Bettys; unfortunately the Hellcats couldn't gain visual contact long enough to shoot. However, Phillips shot down both Bettys with the Avenger's two wing-mounted .50-caliber weapons. The other Bettys were alerted by the explosions of the two, and separated in the darkness.

At 2030 hours, Commander Dean led a second "Bat Team" into the darkness with Voris his number two and an Avenger flown by VT-6's XO. The FDO was unable to assemble this team while keeping track of O'Hare's formation.

Shortly after Phillips managed to shoot down the second Betty, Skon saw the shadowy shape of O'Hare's Hellcat to his right when the CAG moved into the TBF's five o'clock position. At the same time, gunner Kernan spotted a Betty above and almost directly behind O'Hare. He opened fire and a Japanese gunner fired back. O'Hare was caught in the crossfire.

Seconds later, the Hellcat slid out of formation to port and pushed down at about 160 knots, then vanished in the dark. Phillips received no reply to his repeated calls. Skon reported that he had seen O'Hare's lights go out as he veered off and down into darkness. Phillips later reported that as the Hellcat dropped out of view it appeared to release something that dropped almost vertically at a speed too slow for anything but a parachute, then something "whitish-gray" appeared below, perhaps the splash of the aircraft plunging into the sea.

Phillips reported the situation to *Enterprise* – "Butch is down!" At dawn three search planes were launched, but neither O'Hare nor his aircraft was ever found. A PBY Catalina also conducted a search on November 29 with no result. The Navy's first and most famous ace was officially reported missing in action, the most likely cause then considered to have been the result of "friendly fire" when Gunner Kernan mistakenly shot him down.

Alvin Kernan described this night in detail from the perspective of the man who fired the Avenger's gun seconds before O'Hare disappeared in his memoir, *Crossing the Line: A Bluejacket's World War II Odyssey.* In 1997, extensive interviews of Skon, radar officer Rand, and gunner Kernan were done by researchers Steve Ewing and John B. Lundstrom for their book *Fateful Rendezvous: The Life of Butch O'Hare.* They concluded that "Butch fell to his old familiar adversary, a Betty. Most likely he died from, or was immediately disabled by, a lucky shot from the forward observer crouched in the Betty's forward glassed-in nose … the nose gunner's 7.7mm slugs very likely penetrated Butch's cockpit from above on the port side and ahead of the F6F's armor plate."

The "Bat Team" concept became obsolete with the arrival of radar-equipped F4U-2 Corsairs of VF(N)-101 aboard *Enterprise* two months later.

Task Groups 50.1 and 50.2 were detached to deal with the night attackers by striking their base on Kwajalein. The two task groups rendezvoused on December 1 to form Task Force 50. Admiral Pownall planned a dawn attack on December 4. The six carriers penetrated the Marshalls without being spotted and began launching their strikes at 0630 hours. Lieutenant Commander Edgar Stebbins was first over the target 90 minutes later and counted 30 ships in the lagoon, including two cruisers.

The Japanese were taken completely by surprise; the few Zekes that got airborne were quickly dispatched. Fighting 2 pilots Lieutenant "Griff" Griffin and Lieutenants (jg) "Randy" Carlson and William "Shorty" LaForge each shot down a Zeke in the sudden melee. Commander Dean's four Hellcats destroyed four Kawanishi H8K "Emily" flying boats, while Tex Harris's division destroyed three A6M2-N "Rufe" floatplane fighters that they caught still moored in the lagoon. Ensign Gene Redmond was hit and lost fuel; he eventually ditched near a destroyer and was quickly rescued.

Avengers sank three ships while Hellcats strafed the seaplane base on Ebeye Island. At the conclusion of the strikes, Stebbins discovered an airfield on Roi with 60 Betty bombers that had not been touched. He radioed a recommendation for a second strike, but this was overruled by Admiral Pownall, who determined the fleet would depart as planned. The Japanese response arrived at noon with a formation of 15 Kate torpedo bombers; seven were shot down by the CAP and ship's antiaircraft fire. When a second formation of Kates arrived, they were hit by the CAP, but four of them attacked *Yorktown*. Three were shot down and the gunners were firing at the fourth when Admiral Pownall ordered them to cease fire because the cruiser *San Francisco* was in the line of fire. Jocko Clark was dumbfounded – did the Admiral not see the airplane attacking the ship he was on? He disregarded the order and the Kate was shot down moments later by a 40mm mount, crashing just astern of *Yorktown*. Photographer's Mate Al Cooperman caught the enemy bomber just at the moment the Kate was hit and caught fire with a photograph that became one of the most famous in the Pacific War; *Life* magazine later featured it as "the photo of the week." *Yorktown*'s gunfire did kill one and injure 22 aboard *San Francisco*.

At 1300 hours, the planned strike against Wotje was launched, and recovered at 1500 hours as the fleet headed north in increasingly heavy seas. The strikes scored three transports sunk, hits on a cruiser, and approximately 40 Japanese aircraft destroyed. The Japanese propaganda broadcaster known to the Americans as "Tokyo Rose" claimed (once again) to have sunk the "Big E," as the *Enterprise* was now known, along with two cruisers and 23 aircraft shot down in the raid.

By 1945 hours, the first of the Roi bombers was spotted on radar. For the next several hours, wave after wave of enemy aircraft tracked the ships, dropping flares and launching torpedoes. *Essex* reported in her log "what happened was the longest sustained night torpedo attack of the war to date. For seven-and-a-half hours, enemy planes were continually pressing attacks, and *Essex* personnel remained at battle stations until 0200 hours – almost 24 hours after starting the attack on Kwajalein."

Around 2140 hours, a three-quarter moon rose in the east and illuminated the wakes of the ships. The night sky over the fleet was torn by blasts of antiaircraft fire and several attackers were shot down. Multiple torpedoes were launched but all were evaded and the fleet suffered no damage. *Yorktown* evaded two torpedoes. Her escort, the antiaircraft cruiser *Oakland* (CLAA-95) requested permission to drop astern and light the ship to draw off attackers; over the next 30 minutes *Oakland* shot down 12 Bettys with her formidable armament.

Another Betty penetrated the screen. Captain Clark turned *Yorktown* directly at the attacker as it dropped its torpedo, which narrowly missed the carrier, while the gunners shot down the Betty. A second bomber came in, passed low over *Yorktown*, and dropped her torpedo, which struck *Lexington*.

Lexington's log captured the night in nearly poetic language:

At 1925 bogeys began closing and other ships in the task group began firing. Both groups were maneuvering at high speeds on evasive courses, and firing by the screen was continuous. To those with topside battle stations it seemed like a long-drawn-out, unreal dream, the ship silently steaming through the water, throwing out a brilliant phosphorescent wake, the moonlight reflected against the planes on the flight deck, and all the while the night broken by bright streamers of tracer bullets and the flash of five-inch bursts from the ships of the screen firing at unseen targets.

At 2150 hours a Betty dropped float lights in the water to guide the attackers into the target. At 2232 four parachute flares appeared on *Lexington*'s port beam, "... beautifully placed to silhouette the ship, and it was obvious we had been picked out as the target." At 2235 hours, *Lexington* opened fire. "Bogeys were closing in fast on the starboard bow." One torpedo bomber crashed into the sea and exploded 200 yards ahead of the carrier while a second was hit and exploded 500 yards astern. The third closed to 1,800 yards and dropped its torpedo before it was hit and crashed into *Lexington*'s starboard beam. That torpedo missed, but a moment later a fourth Betty was spotted on the starboard beam. Heavy fire was directed toward the attacker but a torpedo was seen to drop and the Betty got away at high speed directly over the ship.

At 2237 hours, the torpedo hit *Lexington* in her stern. The ship immediately settled 5 feet to starboard and lost steering control. With her rudder jammed hard left, she began to turn in a wide circle to port, streaming a dense cloud of smoke from ruptured gas tanks on the fantail. Temporarily protected by this accidental smoke screen, damage control parties fought to regain steering control. Twenty minutes after taking the hit, the rudder was brought amidships through the use of an emergency hand-operated hydraulic unit which had been designed by *Lexington* damage control officer Lieutenant P.N. MacDonald and installed by her crew during the last availability. The device was instrumental in saving the ship from further damage by permitting her rapid withdrawal from the area. Steering only with the main engines, *Lexington* headed east at 20 knots. "The entire retirement to Pearl Harbor was made in this manner." Over the next few months, every carrier in the fleet was equipped with MacDonald's invention.

After temporary repairs at Pearl Harbor, *Lexington* put Air Group 16 ashore and arrived at the Bremerton Navy Yard on December 22 for permanent repairs. Tokyo Rose announced for the first time that *Lexington* had been sunk, leading to her nickname the "Blue Ghost." Repairs were completed by February 12, 1944, at which time *Lexington* took Air Group 19 aboard and transported them to Hawaii, where Air Group 16 rejoined the ship. At the end of February, *Lexington* arrived in the new fleet anchorage at Majuro Atoll, where Admiral Mitscher came aboard and she became flagship of the newly named Task Force 58. Mitscher would remain aboard until October 31, 1944.

Task Force 50 returned to Pearl Harbor from Operation *Galvanic* on December 9, 1943. VF-2 launched from *Enterprise* before she entered Pearl Harbor and landed at NAS Barber's Point. Dean recommended Butch Voris for a Distinguished Flying Cross, and Harris, Griffin, LaForge, and Carlson for Air Medals. Fighting 2 and the entire fast carrier task force had met the test of combat.

On December 20, 1943, a solemn Pontifical Mass of Requiem was offered for Butch O'Hare at the St Louis Cathedral. The Navy promoted Commander Phillips to lead Air Group 6 on December 4, and later awarded O'Hare, Phillips, Skon, Rand, and Kernan each a Navy Cross for their role in protecting the carrier and carrying out the Navy's first combat night fighting mission, with O'Hare being cited for leading the daring mission. Cynics concluded that the Navy, forced to choose between courts-martial or medals for the Avenger crew, chose the latter, being unwilling to publicly admit that its biggest hero had been killed by friendly fire.

During the three days it took to return to Pearl Harbor, Jocko Clark and several other officers wrote a memorandum documenting Admiral Pownall's lack of aggressiveness and the danger in which the Admiral had placed the fleet as a result, citing several specific decisions and including aerial photos of the 60 Bettys at Roi that Pownall had refused to attack.

The memorandum, which was circulated unsigned among senior officers of the CINCPAC fleet following arrival at Pearl Harbor, did not directly discuss Pownall's nerve, but Clark made no bones about personally calling the Admiral "a yellow son of a bitch."

Lieutenant Herman Rosenblatt, Clark's air intelligence officer, was a prewar lawyer who had worked for the Roosevelt family and knew both the President and First Lady, and was close to two of the President's sons; his uncle, Sam Rosenman, was one of President Roosevelt's most trusted aides and speech writers. Rosenblatt traveled to Washington and made the case against Pownall to the highest levels. Such an act on Clark's part was very close to "crossing the line" but he was unrepentant. Questioned after the war, Admiral Clark stated, "I was very fortunate in having a pipeline to the president. He [Pownall] had a chance to score a victory and he passed it up. I think many commanders make mistakes, and I guess maybe I made some myself, but if you don't have the will to win, you have no business in the war."

Nimitz had already made up his mind. Jocko Clark was promoted to Rear Admiral on January 1, 1944. On January 3, 1944, Pownall was relieved of command and replaced by Marc Mitscher. As Admiral King had stated at the Trident Conference, 1944 would be the decisive year in the Pacific War.

CHAPTER SIX

THE SPRUANCE HAIRCUT

The new year of 1944 saw the United States Navy in a far better position than it had been a year before. Where American forces were just managing to defeat their opponents on Guadalcanal at the end of 1942, 1943 had seen the entire Solomons wrested from the Japanese, at a cost that would reverberate through the Imperial forces for the rest of the war. Though no one could know it on this New Year's Eve, in less than 60 days Rabaul would be neutralized. The amphibious campaign in the Central Pacific had demonstrated the ability to take and hold enemy territory, with the Gilberts once again Allied territory as planners set their sights on the Marshall Islands to the immediate west.

Roger Bond, who served as a quartermaster on the *Saratoga* for most of the war, recalled after the war that there was a dividing line in experience of the Pacific War. "I think that for anyone who participated in the war, there were actually two wars. If you went out to the Pacific, say, after January 1944, you had a completely different experience and viewpoint than those before, because it really was two different operations."

With the arrival in Pearl Harbor on January 10, 1944 of the brand-new *Intrepid* (CV-11), Task Force 58 now had five fleet carriers: *Enterprise*, *Yorktown*, *Essex*, *Intrepid*, and *Bunker Hill*, and four light carriers: *Belleau Wood*, *Cabot*, *Monterey*, and *Cowpens*, embarking more than 500 Hellcats, Dauntlesses, Helldivers, and Avengers. Supporting the fast carriers were seven battleships, numerous cruisers and destroyers, 217 ships in all, the greatest armada that had ever been seen in naval history. The new navy was far stronger than the navy that had fought Japan to a stop in 1942, and almost twice the size of the Central Pacific Force that had led the invasion of the Gilberts less than 60 days earlier.

The new year brought a change in name for the Central Pacific Force in early March. Now known as Fifth Fleet, the fast carrier task force was now Task Force 58. Task Force 58 was now so large it was divided into four striking forces, each larger than the carrier fleets that had fought each of the crucial battles of 1942. Task Group 58.1 was commanded by Rear Admiral J.W. "Black Jack" Reeves, Jr., aboard his flagship *Enterprise*, with *Yorktown* and *Belleau Wood*; Task Group 58.2, under Rear Admiral Alfred E. Montgomery aboard flagship *Essex*, with *Intrepid* and *Cabot* (CVL-28); Task Group 58.3, led by Rear Admiral Frederick C. Sherman aboard flagship *Bunker Hill*, with *Monterey* (CVL-26) and *Cowpens*; and Task Group 58.4 under Rear Admiral Samuel P. Ginder aboard *Saratoga*, with *Princeton*, and *Langley*. The fleet was so strong that the earlier carrier strategy used as recently as the Gilberts campaign of "hit and run" no longer made strategic sense. The fleet could maintain position off any enemy position and maintain air and naval superiority for so long as it was needed. The aspirations of naval aviators over the 20 years preceding the war were now reality.

After the capture of Makin and Tarawa in the Gilbert Islands, the next step in the United States Navy's campaign in the Central Pacific was the Marshall Island chain. The strategic importance of the Marshalls had been recognized by US Navy planners back in 1921 during the development of War Plan Orange, the first plan for what was seen even then as an inevitable conflict with Japan. The islands had been purchased by Imperial Germany from Spain in 1899, as part of the overall purchase of Micronesia. The Imperial Japanese Navy had occupied Kwajalein, the largest atoll in the world with some 93 islands within its coral barrier reef, during World War I and the Marshalls had been assigned to Japan by the League of Nations as the Eastern Mandates in 1919. Afterwards, the islands became a mystery to the outside world after Japan closed them to international commerce in the 1920s. Navy planners presumed the Japanese had built illegal fortifications throughout the islands, but the precise extent of such fortifications was unknown until aerial reconnaissance became possible at the end of 1943.

Strategically, Japan regarded the Marshalls as part of the "outer ring" of the Empire. After losing the Solomons over the course of 1943 and with the end of a Japanese presence in New Guinea only a matter of time, the Japanese high command determined that the Marshalls were expendable. Nonetheless, the island bases there were reinforced over the latter half of

1943 to make their capture by the Americans more costly. By January 1944, Admiral Masashi Kobayashi, the regional commander at Truk, had deployed 28,000 troops to defend the Marshalls, though there were few aircraft for support following the carrier raid on December 4, 1943.

Navy planning for the Marshalls campaign originally foresaw amphibious landings on the eastern islands of Maloelap, Wotje, Mille, and Jaluit, with Kwajalein in April. Kwajalein lagoon was so vast that the entire Pacific Fleet could be based there. Taking the atoll was to be the first step in developing major advanced naval bases across the Pacific to support the planned invasion of the Marianas in mid-summer.

While Admiral Nimitz was famous for rarely overruling his top advisors, and never against their unanimous opposition, he did exactly that at the CINCPAC meeting of December 7, 1943 at which he announced the Navy would bypass the eastern Marshalls and strike directly at Kwajalein at the end of January 1944. Spruance opposed the idea on the grounds that the bypassed islands would threaten the lines of communication from Hawaii and the Gilberts as the Japanese based aircraft on those islands to harass the transports supporting the new base at isolated Kwajalein. Additionally, the fast carriers were committed to supporting Halsey for the coming invasion of Kavieng in New Britain and MacArthur's final amphibious landings in New Guinea, which meant the force would be separated and what he would have left would not be strong enough if the Japanese at Truk decided to contest the invasion. Marine General Holland M. Smith believed from his experience at Tarawa and Makin that his Amphibious Corps should be concentrated on one island target at a time, while invading Kwajalein would require taking Kwajalein and Roi-Namur islands simultaneously. Amphibious force commander Vice Admiral Richmond Kelly Turner supported the arguments of both Spruance and Smith.

Nimitz, however, had intelligence his commanders didn't. Although the Japanese had poured troops into the eastern Marshalls, this had been done at the expense of the garrisons in the central Marshalls, particularly at Kwajalein, which meant the main target was easier to attack while the outer islands could be neutralized at leisure through air power. His final argument was, "We're going into Kwajalein because the Japanese aren't expecting us there." Indeed he was right. After the war, Commander Chikitaka Nakajima of the Combined Fleet staff told his American interrogators, "There was divided opinion as to whether you would attack Jaluit or Mille. There were some who thought you might go to Wotje. But no one thought you would go right to the heart of the Marshalls and attack Kwajalein."

Not only had Nimitz decided to take Kwajalein as a future fleet anchorage, he planned to take Majuro Atoll, 250 miles southwest of Kwajalein in the western Carolines, which would position the fleet to strike the Marianas. When General Smith protested he did not have the manpower to attack the atoll, Nimitz assured him that he did, and turned to Captain Edward Layton, the head of CINCPAC intelligence. When Layton told Smith that the total Japanese force on Majuro was "six," Smith thought he was referring to 6,000. "No," Layton insisted, "six." His radio intelligence had intercepted a ration request from the Majuro garrison that indicated they were consuming six rations per day. Only a single battalion would be necessary to take Majuro.

With the experience of Tarawa behind them, the three commanders in charge of what was now known as Operation *Flintlock* determined that the mistakes made at the first invasion would not be repeated now. The Marshalls as a region were to be subjected to what would come to be known as the "Mitscher shampoo," while the island targets themselves would be given what would be called by reporters who saw the results the "Spruance haircut."

Attrition of Japanese air power in the Marshalls had begun with the carrier strike on December 4, 1943. Following that, the United States Army Air Forces Seventh Air Force, operating from Canton and Ellice Islands and establishing forward bases at Tarawa and Makin, flew their first B-24 raid against targets in the Marshalls by the end of December. The missions were long, but they were virtual milk runs as the Japanese had no aircraft with which to oppose them. On January 21, 15 B-24s dropped 30 tons of bombs on Roi-Namur and Kwajalein; on January 22 ten B-24s dropped 20 tons on Roi; on January 29 five B-24s dropped 13 tons on Kwajalein, while seven B-24s added a final 21 tons to all three islands. PB4Y-1s, the Navy's version of the B-24, mined the sea routes throughout the Marshall chain and conducted aerial reconnaissance.

The carriers swept through the Marshalls in mid-month. While few Japanese aircraft were encountered over Kwajalein, *Cabot's* Fighting 31 discovered some action over the atoll as the invasion forces gathered. VF-31, formed the previous spring to become the second Navy squadron fully equipped with the Hellcat, came aboard *Cabot* on December 20, 1943 as the light carrier was preparing for her first deployment with the fast carrier task force. The squadron was led by one of the most colorful naval aviators, Lieutenant Commander Robert A. Winston. A reporter for the *New York Times* in the early 1930s, Winston had joined the US Navy in 1935 as a naval reservist "AvCad" at the relatively "advanced" age of 28. Eventually flying Grumman F3F-2s with Fighting 6 aboard *Enterprise* before his reserve obligation ended in 1939, Winston was the author of *Dive Bomber*, which is still considered the best account of prewar naval flight training and operations. When the book achieved best-seller status upon publication in 1940, the motion picture rights were purchased by Warner Brothers. The resulting movie, a Technicolor classic of prewar naval aviation starring Errol Flynn and Fred MacMurray that was released in 1941, shared little with the book it was "adapted" from other than the title.

After delivering Brewster F2A-1 fighters to Finland during the "Winter War," Winston escaped from Paris a few days before the Germans arrived in June 1940 and returned to active naval service shortly before Pearl Harbor. Assigned duty as Director of Naval Public Relations after Pearl Harbor due to his background and reputation, Winston managed to finagle himself back into active aviation at age 35 and took command of newly commissioned VF-31 in May 1943.

By January 29, 1944, Winston had been promoted to command Air Group 31. That morning, he led 12 Hellcats off *Cabot* two hours before dawn to provide cover for the invasion. Leading the lower four-plane division with his wingman, Ensign Cornelius "Conny" Nooy, Winston spotted a group of aircraft he identified as SBD Dauntlesses. Approaching to within 100 yards, Nooy noticed the red circles on their wings and called them out as Zekes. Winston opened fire on the trailing Zeke, missing his target but breaking up the enemy formation.

Winston later recalled what then happened:

A string of tracers worked toward me and went through my left wing. I banked sharply to the right, almost into another red stream of bullets from a Jap on my right. I yanked the release to drop my belly tank, without first switching over to an internal fuel supply. A moment later my engine sputtered and went cold. At first I thought that it had been hit, then I remembered the belly tank and switched to a full tank. Just then Nooy's plane flashed in front of me. There was a Zeke on his tail, firing. As the Jap crossed my sights I fired a string of tracers that he seemed to fly into until they went right into his cockpit. He rolled over and disappeared. More tracers streamed past me. I whipped over in a cartwheel turn toward Nooy, who was ready with a similar turn. As I passed in front of Nooy he clipped the Jap off of my tail.

When the fight was over, VF-31 claimed five victories among five pilots, as well as three probables. Winston's victory was the first of five he would score to become an ace, while Conny Nooy was on his way to becoming the top-scoring ace whose squadron was based on a light carrier.

On January 28, Admiral Fred Sherman's Task Group 58.3 finished off any chance of aerial opposition at Kwajalein. The dawn sweep by the task group's Hellcats found no enemy aircraft, while the Helldivers of *Bunker Hill*'s VB-17 and the Avengers of all three carriers blasted the airfield so thoroughly that no aircraft would be able to operate from it over the next three days leading up to the invasion. Next day, Sherman's fliers administered the same treatment to Eniwetok, remaining until February 2 while they battered and then pulverized the atoll's airfields and ground installations. By February 2, there was nothing left but heaps of rubble and palm trees denuded of their foliage. One Helldiver pilot reported "the island looked like desert waste."

At dawn on January 31, support force commander Rear Admiral Richard C. Connolly's flagship, the battleship *Maryland* (BB-46), took position 2,000 yards off the northern beaches of Roi Island; as General Smith put it, "So close that his guns almost poked their muzzles into the Japanese positions." Captain Truman Hedding later explained, "We learned a lot about softening up these islands before we sent the Marines in. We really worked that place over. They developed a tactic they called 'the Spruance haircut.' We just knocked everything down; there wasn't even a palm tree left." Over the 72 hours of bombardment prior to H-Hour, 15,000 tons of bombs and naval shells – more than a ton for each man of the Japanese garrison – were dropped on the islands. As one wag put it, "Never in the field of human conflict was so much thrown by so many at so few." When the Marines and Army troops landed, the islands had been so thoroughly battered that the geographic points on their maps could no longer be identified.

Kwajalein Atoll was invaded on January 31, 1944, with landings on the main island of Kwajalein at the south end of the atoll, and the twin islands of Roi-Namur at the northern entrance to Kwajalein lagoon. Roi was declared secure by nightfall and Namur by the afternoon of the next day. The Army's 7th Division took three days to secure Kwajalein by February 3, a slow performance that had Marine General Smith at his "Howlin' Mad" best. Lightly defended Majuro was taken on January 31 with no US losses.

The invasion had proceeded with such ease and light casualties that further operations in the Marshalls were advanced. Eniwetok Atoll was taken on February 19–21 rather than waiting for the original schedule of May.

Taking Kwajalein, Eniwetok, and Majuro atolls completely changed operations for the Pacific Fleet. Prior to this, the fleet's ability to strike the enemy involved how far the target was from Pearl Harbor, and the fact that a damaged ship had to return all the way to Pearl for repairs. Jocko Clark remarked that before the Marshalls, the carriers could only strike the enemy approximately once a month, considering travel time from and to Hawaii. By the end of February 1944, all three lagoons were available as anchorages, with Service Squadron 10's ships available for re-supply efforts. Additionally, ships at sea could range farther west, since the fleet oilers were now based in the Marshalls. By late 1944, possession of these advanced bases would see ships of the Pacific Fleet routinely making sustained operational cruises of 60 and even 90 days.

For the crews, these bases meant there was even less opportunity for a man to "get away from it all" than when a ship was in Pearl Harbor. There were no "weekend passes to London" in the Pacific Theater. In Honolulu, a sailor on liberty could at least get cold beer in a local bar, and the only limit on the number he might consume would be the money in his pocket. At Majuro, Eniwetok, and Kwajalein, a sailor on "liberty" on one of the small islands was allowed a ration of two bottles of beer, both warm. Off-ship dining was limited to spam sandwiches. The drink of choice became Coca-Cola. Seventy years after the war, SCUBA divers who visit these harbors can still find thousands of Coke bottles on the seabed, thrown off the piers by bored sailors.

Enlisted diarists like radioman Ted Graham from Bombing 15 recorded that recreational activities on the islands were mostly limited to baseball games, horseshoe pits, and the like. On many of the islands, it was recalled that the sand fleas were particularly aggressive. Many men ended up staying on their ships for the duration of their deployment to the western Pacific; in some cases where ships never returned to the United States for overhaul or repair, this could mean for the duration of the war.

The only men on the ships who could look forward to return to the United States were the aircrews in the air groups, who normally spent approximately five to six months aboard their carrier before being relieved from their tour. *Essex*, for example, only returned to the United States once after her initial deployment to the Pacific in June 1943, a six-week period of overhaul and repair at the Bremerton Navy Yard in March and April 1944. By the end of the war, most of her crew had last seen home 16 months previously.

The success of Operation *Flintlock* erased the near-disaster of Tarawa from the planners' minds, and led to a fundamental re-thinking of the future of the war. At the Quebec Conference in November 1943, Admiral

King had obtained Allied approval for an invasion of the Marianas in the summer of 1944. Although the islands had not figured prominently in any of the Orange war plans or the later Rainbow plans, King was convinced the Marianas were the strategic keystone of the Pacific War since they would block Japanese access to remaining bases in the South Pacific, while providing an advance base for the Pacific Fleet submarine force that would nearly double the number of operational days for the submarines in their hunting grounds of the western Pacific by reducing travel time to and from their base. Additionally, the three main islands were suitable for the construction of large airfields that could be used as bases for the B-29 Superfortress that would place all of Japan within striking range.

Interestingly, King was not supported by any of the Pacific commanders in this position in the period after Tarawa and before Kwajalein. Douglas MacArthur was determined that after the Marshalls, the US Navy would support his drive north from New Guinea into the Philippines, once he was appointed Supreme Commander in the Pacific. MacArthur's deputy General Richard Sutherland argued that the Marianas were too far from the new bases in the Marshalls and that mounting such an invasion fleet would drain valuable shipping resources for the invasion of Mindanao. Additionally, the fleet would be operating beyond the cover of land-based aircraft and would be vulnerable should the Japanese come out to fight. MacArthur went so far as to go over George C. Marshall's head and argue directly with Secretary of War Stimson and Roosevelt himself that such an invasion would make the costs of Tarawa look light in comparison, and that his strategy of bypassing strong enemy positions would reduce American casualties. In January 1944, MacArthur presented a statement of his views to Secretary Stimson:

> These frontal attacks by the Navy, as at Tarawa, are tragic and unnecessary massacres of American lives ... The Navy fails to understand the strategy of the Pacific, fails to recognize that the first phase is an Army phase to establish land-based air protection so the Navy can move in ... Mr. Roosevelt is Navy-minded. Mr. Stimson must speak to him, must persuade him. Don't let the Navy's pride of position and ignorance continue this great tragedy to our country. Give me central direction of the war in the Pacific and I will be in the Philippines in ten months.

Fearing that the Gilberts campaign was a preview of further bloodshed, even Nimitz was not in support of the Marianas campaign. On January 27,

1944, three days before the invasion of Kwajalein, a conference of senior Pacific commanders was held in Pearl Harbor. MacArthur was represented by his staff chief General Sutherland, his naval commander Admiral Kinkaid, and his air commander General George Kenney. It was apparent at the outset that few in attendance looked positively on the proposed Marianas campaign. Admiral John Towers, Commander Naval Air Forces Pacific (ComNavAirPac), supported MacArthur's argument that B-29 missions from the Marianas would be a "stunt" because the bombers would have to fly at high altitude since they would not have fighter escort, which would mean a lack of sufficient accuracy of any bombing. Admiral Kinkaid pointed to a lack of good harbors in the Marianas to support such a campaign. At the close of the conference on January 28, Nimitz signed onto a memorandum recommending against the Marianas campaign. MacArthur's representatives left Hawaii satisfied they had won.

In Washington, Admiral King responded to the memorandum with a letter to Nimitz: "I read your conference notes with much interest, and I must add with indignant dismay." George Marshall and Army Air Forces commander General H.H. "Hap" Arnold were similarly opposed. The Marianas invasion was still on.

The invasion of Kwajalein three days later proved that the Navy could make an amphibious assault with acceptable losses, even at the enemy's doorstep and beyond the range of land-based air support.

Two weeks later, the Navy demonstrated that the fast carriers could go wherever they wanted, stay as long as necessary, and decimate any enemy forces they encountered.

CHAPTER SEVEN

GIBRALTAR OF THE PACIFIC

Beyond the Marshalls lay the unknown, mysterious main Japanese naval and air base in the Pacific: Truk Atoll, which in the 20 years Japan had been in control had taken on the name "Gibraltar of the Pacific," an indication of its importance to Japanese ambitions. Though the name was correctly pronounced "Trook," it would be universally known by Americans as "Truck."

Truk Atoll lies 7 degrees north of the equator in the southwestern Pacific, 1,000 miles northeast of New Guinea and 3,300 miles southwest of Hawaii. The atoll itself is made up of dozens of islands, surrounded by a great barrier reef, though only seven islands, each marked by a volcanic peak, the tallest of which is nearly 1,500 feet above sea level, are of any size or support any significant population. The barrier reef is roughly triangular in shape and 140 miles around; it forms a vast deep-water lagoon of more than 800 square miles. Visibility through the water in the lagoon is more than 50 feet. With abundant rainfall and sunshine, and an average year-round temperature of 81 degrees, the islands are green and lush. All of this makes Truk a Pacific paradise.

Truk was discovered by Europeans in January 1565, when the Spanish explorer Alonso de Arellano sailed into the lagoon aboard his galleon, the *San Lucas*. News of the discovery was lost until Francisco de Lezcano arrived at Yap in 1686 and named the islands "Las Carolinas," in honor of the Spanish King Charles. While Spain claimed Truk and the rest of the Carolines, they were not brought under formal Spanish control until 1885. Over the intervening 300 years, explorers from Portugal, England, France, the United States, Russia, and Germany visited Truk. By the mid-19th century, European and American traders, whalers, and missionaries were living and working at the atoll. Japanese traders arrived during the 1890s.

The United States assumed control of Micronesia, including the Caroline Islands and Truk, as a result of the Spanish-American War. However, with American ambitions focused on the Philippines, Micronesia – excepting Guam, site of the one good harbor in the Marianas – was sold by Spain to Germany in the 1899 German-Spanish Treaty for $4.2 million. German rule was little-remarked and short-lived. On July 6, 1914, the Imperial German Navy's armored cruiser SMS *Gneisenau* dropped anchor in Truk lagoon, where she met her sister ship SMS *Scharnhorst* and the light cruisers of the German Navy's East Asia Squadron. Squadron commander Vice Admiral Count Maximilian von Spee, an avid naturalist, made the most of his opportunity to study the life in the lagoon and on the surrounding islands. On August 1, the ships received the warning "threatened state of war." The crews went to work in a frenzy to prepare. All peacetime furnishings came off: wood paneling and tapestries were torn from wardroom walls while sofas, stuffed armchairs, carpets, and sideboards were taken ashore. On August 3, Admiral von Spee was informed that a state of war existed between Germany and Great Britain. At dawn on August 6, Von Spee's ships departed, to meet the rest of the East Asia Squadron at Pagan Island in the Marianas, from whence they sailed on to meet their fate in the Battle of the Falklands that December.

In accordance with a secret treaty with Great Britain which was made in July 1914 that allowed Japan to take control of German territories in China and the Pacific in return for Japan declaring war on Germany and joining the Allies, the Imperial Japanese Navy arrived in Truk in September 1914, following the Japanese declaration of war with Germany on August 23, 1914. While this move was made without the official approval of the Japanese government at the time (though there was an unofficial desire to take advantage of the opportunity presented by the treaty), the fact that the Navy was nearly autonomous regarding higher governmental control under the Meiji Constitution allowed the service to proceed to turn the atoll into a military base and fleet anchorage. Japan then proceeded to take all of Micronesia, including the Marshall Islands which had been granted to Germany by Spain in the 1880s, and the Marianas other than American-controlled Guam. The seizure was illegal under international law and only supported by the secret Anglo-Japanese treaty. The Imperial Japanese Navy directly controlled the islands until 1921, though the seizure had been recognized internationally by the newly created League of Nations in 1919, when Japan was granted control of the South Pacific Mandate.

Though the mandate prohibited fortification or colonization of the islands, Japan began settling thousands of Japanese throughout Micronesia beginning in 1921. Japanese colonists took control of the best agricultural land on the seven islands of Truk Atoll while the Imperial Japanese Navy established its Pacific headquarters on Dublon Island. By the outbreak of the Pacific War in December 1941, there were approximately 100,000 Japanese civilians in Micronesia and only some 50,000 native Micronesians.

In further violation of the mandate, the Carolines were closed to international commerce in the 1920s and the Imperial Japanese Navy began building airstrips and fortifying key islands throughout the archipelagos of Micronesia. By the time they were finished in the late 1930s, Truk Atoll was the site of Japan's greatest fleet anchorage outside of the home islands. It was not, however, the great fortified bastion implied in the reference to it being the "Gibraltar of the Pacific." This fact was unknown outside the Imperial Japanese Navy.

Conspiracy theorists have claimed that Truk was the real objective of Amelia Earhart in her 'round-the-world flight in 1937. According to these tales, Earhart and her navigator, Fred Noonan, were on a secret mission for President Franklin Roosevelt and the Department of War to photograph Truk but were shot down by the Japanese and captured. There has never been any evidence presented that would support these theories.

In July 1942, Truk became headquarters for the Combined Fleet, with Admiral Yamamoto flying his flag as commander from the battleship *Yamato* anchored in the lagoon. When Yamamoto was killed on April 18, 1943, his replacement, Admiral Mineichi Koga, flew his flag from *Yamato*'s sistership *Musashi*, also anchored in the lagoon.

To the US Navy in 1942 and 1943, seeing Truk as the Gibraltar of the Pacific was no exaggeration. It appeared impregnable and sailors spoke the name in awe-struck tones. Dangerous long-range reconnaissance flights flown by B-24s from bases in the Gilberts in December 1943 managed to bring back photos that allowed intelligence officers to map out the air bases and the various anchorages in the lagoon. Analysts began to realize there was not as much there as expected.

Navy planners were not aware of the Japanese decision to sacrifice the Marshalls, and expected a possible naval response from Imperial Japanese Navy units at Truk. Thus, it was imperative that the "Gibraltar of the Pacific" be neutralized. The attack was set for February 17, 1944, which was also D-Day for the invasion of Eniwetok Atoll. In terms of audacity on the part of the attackers, this strike demonstrated how far the fast carrier task force had come since the Rabaul attack only 97 days earlier.

When the fliers of Task Force 58 got word of the proposed attack on Truk, aptly codenamed Operation *Hailstone*, they were eager but apprehensive. Planners estimated a total of 185 Japanese aircraft at Truk, but the real number was 365; however, there were not pilots for all of these aircraft and many were under repair. Task Force 58 carried 250 Hellcats. As VB-10's XO, Lieutenant James D. Ramage, recalled, "For the previous two years of the war, the very thought of approaching Truk seemed fatal." VF-9's Mac McWhorter remembered that when he was informed of the operation, "My first instinct was to jump overboard." *The Buccaneer*, the *Essex* shipboard newspaper, published a cartoon of the captain announcing the attack on Truk, followed by a panel in which the entire crew abandoned ship. *Yorktown's* Air Group 5 commander, Lieutenant Commander Edward Owen, wrote later that "by D-day I think everyone was a tiger."

The strike force consisted of Task Group 58.1, commanded by Rear Admiral J.W. "Black Jack" Reeves, Jr., with *Enterprise, Yorktown*, and *Belleau Wood*; Task Group 58.2, commanded by Rear Admiral A.E. Montgomery, with *Essex, Intrepid*, and *Cabot*; and Task Group 58.3, led by Rear Admiral Frederick C. Sherman, with *Bunker Hill, Monterey*, and *Cowpens*. Two hundred seventy-six F6F-3 Hellcat fighters, 140 SBD-5 Dauntless and 27 SB2C-1 Helldiver dive bombers, and 126 TBM-1C Avenger torpedo bombers equipped the air groups, totaling 569 aircraft. Task Group 58.4 under Rear Admiral Samuel P. Ginder with *Saratoga, Princeton*, and *Langley* were assigned to cover the landings on Eniwetok and would not participate in the Truk strike.

The fliers in Task Force 58 had no way of knowing the Japanese were even more apprehensive than they were. When word was received that Kwajalein had fallen, the leaders of the Imperial Japanese Navy feared their American opponents were now in a position to launch a strike at Truk. The majority of the Combined Fleet was ordered to leave the atoll on February 10. While a dozen cruisers and destroyers remained behind, the carriers and battleships sailed for Palau. Even with these departures, the lagoon was still packed with cargo and troop ships, while the airfields and all other ground installations on the islands in the lagoon were on high alert. The Japanese had 68 Zekes on Moen Island, 27 on Dublon Island, 20 on Eten Island, and 46 on Param Island for a total of 161 defending fighters up and ready, plus another 180 aircraft of various types waiting for pilots or repairs. There were also approximately 100 operational Betty, Kate, and Jill bombers.

Task Force 58 reached the launch point, 90 miles east of Truk, two hours before dawn on February 16, 1944. Fighting 6, which had been reunited as a squadron after the Gilberts campaign, had gone aboard *Intrepid* (CV-11) when the new carrier arrived in Pearl Harbor on January 10, 1944. Alex Vraciu, an ace after the Gilberts campaign, recalled the morning "was clear, cool and beautiful as we launched."

The first of 72 F6F Hellcats launched at 0645 hours. Leading Fighting 10's 12 Hellcats alongside 12 from VF-6 was the commander of Air Group 10, Commander William "Killer" Kane. A member of the Annapolis class of 1933 that would provide so many of the Navy's mid-level leaders during the war, Kane's nickname was the result of his record as a football player and wrestler at the Naval Academy. He had been at Pearl Harbor when the Japanese attacked and had entered combat at Guadalcanal 18 months previously.

As the golden light of dawn brightened the sky over Truk Atoll, the biggest air battle in the history of the Pacific War up to that time broke out. At 0800 hours, Kane's Hellcat strike force arrived over Moen Island and spotted Japanese fighters already aloft. The Hellcats fell on 40–50 Japanese fighters, shooting the Zekes out of the sky by twos and threes. Kane and his wingman, Lieutenant (jg) Vern Ude, shot down five Zekes in five minutes before turning their attention to strafing planes on the ground.

As the rest of Fighting 6 dove after Kane's Hellcats, section leader Alex Vraciu spotted Zekes 2,500 feet overhead. When no one responded to his warning call, he and wingman Ensign Lou Little broke into the enemy formation which scattered in the attack. In a series of quick fights, Vraciu gunned down two Zekes and a Rufe, while Little also nailed a Zeke. Vraciu then spotted another Zeke that ducked into a nearby cloud. After several inconclusive moments in which he spotted the enemy fighter darting in and out of the clouds, Vraciu climbed up-sun and waited for the Zeke to reappear. When it did, he dropped on it from six o'clock and lit it afire with two bursts. Vraciu had nearly doubled his score, to nine. "At that moment, I was the leading Navy ace of the war. The fighting over Truk was the wildest action I participated in, Turkey Shoot included."

Yorktown's CAG Owen remembered that:

As we started to strafe airfields, quite a melee developed as the Japs began getting into the air. Actually, there were so many Jap airplanes moving that it was almost confusing to select a target and stay with it until it was shot down, without being lured to another target just taking off, or apparently attempting to join up in some kind of formation. After a few minutes it was difficult to find uncluttered airspace. Jap aircraft were burning and falling from every quarter and many were crashing on takeoff as a result of strafing them on the ground. Ground installations exploded and burned, and all this in the early golden glow of dawn. At times it all looked like it might have been staged for the movies.

A total of 47 Hellcats from five squadrons were quickly engaged as more Japanese fighters clawed their way into the sky. Some American pilots claimed they saw Japanese pilots parachuting in colorful pajamas, which was claimed as evidence of how complete the surprise was. The fighting was so intense that Vraciu reported seeing one Hellcat shoot down another Hellcat.

Fighting 9's Lieutenant (jg) William J. Bonneau, who had scored three victories during the Rabaul strike in November, was a section leader in the first strike. While he was covering a division of Hellcats making a strafing run, a gaggle of Zekes fell on Bonneau's division. In the ensuing action he shot down four enemy fighters in flames. His plane was damaged, with flap control and hydraulic pressure shot away, though he managed to get back to the fleet and bring the Hellcat aboard *Essex*.

Bonneau's wingman, Lieutenant (jg) Eugene Valencia, got separated in the fight and was chased out to sea by six Zekes that fired at him continuously without result. Valencia finally decided that "They couldn't hit an elephant if it was tied down for them." He racked his Hellcat around and made a head-on pass, knocking down one. Hauling around tighter, he shot down two more and the surviving three dove away. Back aboard *Essex*, Valencia was questioned by the Grumman tech rep about his feelings regarding the Hellcat. Grumman's publicity department insured that Valencia's answer was widely quoted: "I love this airplane so much that if it could cook, I'd marry it."

Fighting 10's Lieutenant (jg) Robert Harman also scored four, two each in two missions over Truk. On the morning strike he shot down a Zeke and a Rufe. That afternoon, while escorting a strike against the airfield on Moen Island, four Zekes attacked Harman's division. He engaged in a rare 15-minute one-on-one fight in which the two opponents were so evenly matched that neither could gain the advantage. In the last turn, Harman managed to reef his fighter in tight and get off a burst that hit the enemy fighter, which crashed into the mountainside.

Fighting 5's Lieutenant Robert Duncan, who had scored the Hellcat's first victories in the October fight over Wake Island when he shot down nine-victory ace Warrant Officer Toshiyuki Sueda and his wingman, was the fourth pilot to score a quadruple victory over Truk to become a six-victory ace while escorting *Yorktown*'s Dauntlesses and Avengers in the early afternoon. "We soon saw about 15–20 Zekes above and they came down to engage us," Duncan later recalled. "Their front man came head on at me which was unusual because Japs usually didn't like to make head on shots." Duncan proceeded to shoot both the lead pilot and his wingman out of the air. "The third man that I got took off to run away and I went after him. I got so close on his tail that when I fired on him he just blew up right in my face. I thought I was going right through that explosion, and I jerked back on the stick and blacked out in the process." Climbing back through 8,000 feet, a fourth Zeke rolled inverted and bored in. Duncan pulled up sharply and fired head-on, though only the three guns in his right wing still worked. He banked around for another shot in time to see the Zeke strike the hills of Dublon Island.

Vraciu's status as leading US Navy ace didn't last an hour. Fighting 9's Mac McWhorter and his wingman, Lieutenant (jg) Bud Gehoe, were inbound to Truk escorting an Avenger on a photo mission when McWhorter spotted a flight of three bogeys in the distance coming toward them. Turning into the strangely marked orange-and-black aircraft to get a closer look, the bogeys turned out to be Zekes. "I truly couldn't believe it when they came at us head-on and never fired a shot. I don't see how they could have failed to spot us." With economical bursts, McWhorter downed two in about five seconds while Gehoe got the third. Later he saw another Zeke, came in behind it, fired, and it went down in flames. With that victory, McWhorter was the first Hellcat double ace.

At dawn, there had been 365 aircraft at Truk. By 1400 hours, the Hellcats had claimed 204 destroyed in the air and on the ground, with 130 shot down in aerial combat. Fighting 9 claimed top honors with a total bag of 36. The Hellcat pilots owned the air over the "Gibraltar of the Pacific" from mid-afternoon on through the final strikes the next day.

While the squadrons of the first wave tangled with Japanese fighters from sea level on up to 12,000 feet, Task Force 58 began launching the second wave of dive bombers and torpedo planes.

Among the strike aircraft were SBD-5 Dauntlesses of *Enterprise*'s Bombing 10, led by "Jig-Dog" Ramage with his gunner, Aviation Radioman 1/c Dave Cawley. The squadron leader, Lieutenant Commander

Dick Poor, led the first strike, launched at 0800 hours. Ramage's strike was launched from *Enterprise* at 0858 hours. Ramage later recalled, "There is always an apprehension of the unknown, and we knew so little about Truk. There were no current maps of the atoll. My strike consisted of 12 fighters, 12 dive bombers and eight torpedo planes. Our targets were ships in the Dublon Anchorage."

Enterprise was only 80 miles from the outer islets of the atoll. "The course to Dublon anchorage was 250 degrees magnetic. Prior to launch, we received the unwelcome news that most of the Japanese fleet had left but that there were plenty of ship targets that remained. Also, our F6Fs were having a field day with the Zekes. It was up to us to do our job."

As the Dauntlesses passed over one of the outer islets, a green-brown Zeke zoomed by on a parallel course to starboard. "I could see heavy AA coming up from the anchorage area and surrounding islands when 'Wwhoosh!' I saw a horrendous mushroom cloud rising from the roadstead. Someone had blown up an ammo ship. The fireball that resulted went up 300 feet. As I looked over the targets, I picked out the biggest ship of a group of about a dozen. She was a tanker at anchor."

Gunner Cawley remembered:

The tropic sunrise as we launched from *Enterprise* was beautiful. We approached from the east, and action started as we were at about 12,000 feet, nearly over the center of the lagoon. Our targets were in the anchorage adjacent to Dublon Island. Unlike most of the islands we had seen and attacked, which were low, flat atolls, the Truk Islands were volcanic with quite high peaks. Just before we reached the roll-in, we were in quite heavy AA, diving very close to a steep hill or peak on Dublon.

Ramage signaled his wingmen, Lieutenants (jg) Bill Schaefer and Oliver Hubbard, to fall back:

We did not roll in from an echelon because we liked to keep our defensive Vee as long as possible. I split my dive flaps and settled my pipper on a position just forward of the bridge. I manually released my 1,000-pound general purpose bomb at 2,000 feet and turned left on pullout to see the results. The tanker was covered with smoke and water splashes. I could not count the hits; one had detached the stern from the ship and she was definitely going down by the stern. The tanker was empty and hence hard to sink.

The ship attacked by Ramage's division was in fact the aft-engined cargo ship *Seiko Maru*. VB-10's second division was led by Lieutenant Lou Bangs. The three SBDs dove on what they identified as a CVL but was in fact *Akitsushima*, a seaplane tender.

Low over the waters of the lagoon during the getaway, Ramage's division was attacked. Cawley remembered:

> We dropped low over the water and were taken under fire by a rusty hulk of an old cargo ship or tanker. It was covered with antiaircraft and machine guns, and they were all firing at us. We were very close. I strafed it as best I could as we turned north to the open area of the lagoon. Only then did I have a chance to look back at our target and the planes following us. I spotted one of our SBDs about a half mile behind us, still in his vertical dive. At the pullout point, his dive varied about ten degrees and he dove almost vertically into the water. I saw more of our planes diving and bombs exploding, and more AA.

As the planes joined up to return to *Enterprise*, Cawley was able to determine that the SBD that he had seen shot down was the one flown by Lieutenant (jg) Donald Dean and Aviation Radioman 2/c J.J. McGorry.

After their pullout, Bangs' division was attacked by four Zekes and a Rufe. Aviation Radioman 2/c Honea, gunner for Ensign Bob Wilson, shot down one Zeke and damaged a second.

When they recovered aboard *Enterprise*, Bombing 10 learned they would be going out on an afternoon strike. Again, Ramage led the second formation of Dauntlesses. He recalled:

> We had a second strike that afternoon. By that time, the shipping was pretty well beaten up. We found the 13,000-ton *Hoyo Maru*, hit her on the centerline just forward of the stern and set her afire. Bangs' division scored two hits on the aviation stores ship *Kiyozumi Maru*, likewise leaving her on fire and sinking.
>
> In pulling out, we continued to search out smaller craft to strafe with both the twin .50s firing forward and the gunners' twin .30s aft. We chanced on two patrol craft about 100 feet long and chewed them up, leaving them on fire. Since we had fired all our ammo in our forward guns, I put the squadron in a circle and our gunners took care of what was left with their twin .30s.

Cawley witnessed a strike on the Japanese light cruiser *Katori* by Avengers:

> I saw a cruiser up to the north of Truk lagoon. I watched it on the clear calm sea as an Avenger attacked with four 500-pound bombs. They were dropped in a row with two missing, one hit and one exploding close aboard. There was considerable smoke from AA, fires and bombs. When I sighted the cruiser, she was low in the water and barely moving. Since we were without bombs and ammo, I opened up on guard channel, saying "Any strike leader from 51-Bobcat, there is a damaged Japanese cruiser just to the north of the lagoon. Come sink it." Immediately on guard channel came back, "Bobcat leader, this is Bald Eagle (Mitscher). Cancel your last. Do not, repeat do not, sink that ship. Acknowledge." I was stunned! I later found out that Admiral Spruance wanted to move his surface ships up for target practice on the cripple. I guess the battleships had to participate in some way!

Katori was sunk the morning of February 17 along with the destroyer *Maikaze* and the auxiliary cruiser *Akagi Maru* by the battleship *New Jersey* (BB-62) and the heavy cruisers *Minneapolis* (CA-36) and *New Orleans* (CA-32), 40 miles northwest of Truk anchorage when they were caught escorting a convoy of damaged merchantmen attempting to escape to Yokosuka, Japan. *Maikaze* was sunk with all hands, while the survivors of the other sunken Japanese ships reportedly refused rescue efforts by the American ships. Spruance's trip around the atoll was one of his rare acts to be seen as a misstep, since the ships were put at risk for small reward, while providing air coverage for them while they circumnavigated the atoll detracted from the overall strike force. This event would lead to Nimitz's decision that a task force or task group commander who was a surface fleet officer would henceforth be required to have an aviator as chief of staff, while a commander who was an aviator would have to have a surface fleet officer as chief of staff so that all viewpoints were taken into consideration when a commander made such a decision in the future.

Enterprise had something else in store for the Japanese. In the summer of 1943, Lieutenant Commander Bill Martin had shifted from commanding officer of Scouting 10 to command Torpedo 10 when the scouting and bombing squadrons were combined into one bombing squadron. As a junior officer, Martin had written the first instrument training manual for carrier aviators, and was recognized as the authority on the subject. He believed carriers should do more with night attack, and that the Avenger offered an aircraft with which to prove his ideas. That fall, he trained his crews in night carrier operations. As Lieutenant (jg) Charles E. Henderson III remembered:

> Bill drove us hard. Nothing but instruments and night operations. At Maui we did long night searches and attacks against friendly ships. As our skills developed, we improved our equipment. Bill's imagination fired us with innovation. We regrouped the instruments, developed indirect red lighting, an alarm buzzer on our radio altimeters, and a night gunsight. What we couldn't requisition we stole.

Now, Martin took his case to Admiral Reeves, who recommended to Mitscher that Torpedo 10 be scheduled for a night strike against the Japanese ships remaining in Truk lagoon the night of February 16–17.

At 0410 hours on February 17, 12 TBM-1Cs were catapulted from *Enterprise* for a night masthead-level attack. The strike was led by the XO, Lieutenant Van Eason, since Martin was unable to fly due to having broken his elbow in a ball game. The plan was that individual runs would be accomplished by radar with the bomb release point determined by the pilot, assisted by radar. Once over Truk, radar reception was hindered by the many coral islets. Additionally, many ships were anchored close to the larger islands which caused merged radar echoes. Most of the pilots searched for 30 minutes or more before they identified their targets. The Avengers carried four 500-pound bombs with 4-second delay fusing and the pilots released their bombs at 250 feet.

Shore batteries put up heavy but inaccurate fire as the Avengers flew over the lagoon. The anchored ships did not open fire until the attackers were within 400 yards. One Avenger, flown by Lieutenant (jg) J. Nicholas, did not return and the cause of loss was unknown. Back aboard ship, damage assessment indicated that the attackers had sunk two oilers and six cargo ships, with six additional cargo ships damaged. As Martin put it, "The great thing was that half of our bombs were hits that night. It was more than you normally get during a daytime attack, with attendant higher losses." Postwar interrogations revealed that the squadron's estimate of success was accurate.

This first night strike effort was considered a major success that fully proved the tactic. As a result, Air Group 41 would become the first dedicated night air group, operating off *Independence* (CVL-22) from July 1944 to February 1945. The success of Air Group 41 led to the formation and deployment of Air Group 90, a dedicated night attack carrier air group that would operate from *Enterprise* in 1945.

Enterprise also carried a detachment of four F4U-2 Corsair night fighters from VF(N)-101, the Navy's first dedicated carrier night fighter squadron, led by Lieutenant Commander Richard E. Harmer, VF(N)-101's skipper. These were modified F4U-1 "birdcage" Corsairs, the Corsair model the Navy had specifically rejected for carrier duty, and they had not gone through the "de-bouncing" program that Fighting 17 had discovered was the cure for the Corsair's aversion to a carrier deck or been equipped with the stall-warning strip on the left wing that allowed for safe carrier landings when the squadron was assigned to *Bunker Hill* in 1943. Following the problems with night attacks experienced in the Gilberts invasion, the Corsairs had joined *Enterprise's* Air Group 10 on January 4, 1944. They were equipped with a handmade microwave XAIA radar unit that was mounted in a bulbous fairing on the front edge of the starboard wing, with a rudimentary 3-inch radar scope in the center of the main instrument panel. Despite the air department's reluctance to engage in night operations that disrupted daytime operations, Admiral Reeves insisted on two "bats" being launched at night. The Corsairs did not achieve any victories during their deployment in the Marshalls campaign, but they pointed the way to future development of night fighting capability and would score a total of five night victories before leaving the ship just prior to the Marianas campaign. The squadron independently discovered the "cure" for the bounce that VF-17 had found and, by the second month aboard *Enterprise*, the Corsair was as safe for landing as the Hellcat. This knowledge would have a major effect on carrier operations after the Battles of Leyte Gulf, when Marine Corsairs were conscripted to provide additional fighter cover for the fleet in the face of the *kamikaze* threat.

While *Enterprise* was experiencing success, *Intrepid* had the fight of her life to survive that night. A Betty torpedo bomber managed to discover the new carrier in the darkness and put a Type 91 torpedo into her starboard quarter, 15 feet below the waterline. This flooded several compartments and jammed her rudder hard to port. By running her port engines at full power and stopping her starboard engines or running them at half ahead, Captain Thomas L. Sprague managed to keep her roughly on course. The crew moved all the aircraft on deck forward in order to increase her headsail and further aid in control. The damaged carrier set course for Pearl Harbor. On February 19, strong winds overpowered the improvised steering and swung

Intrepid back and forth, forcing her to weathercock and leaving her with her bow pointed toward Tokyo. Captain Sprague later confessed: "Right then I wasn't interested in going in that direction." At this point, the crew fashioned a jury-rig sail of wood, cargo nets, and canvas to further increase her headsail, allowing *Intrepid* to swing about and hold her course. With her crazy-quilt sail, the carrier stood into Pearl Harbor on February 24, 1944. Following temporary repairs, she left Pearl Harbor on March 16 for repair at Mare Island in San Francisco. She would rejoin the fleet in time to participate in the Battles of Leyte Gulf.

The schedule for February 17 called for a pre-dawn fighter sweep repeating the first day's action. Again 72 Hellcats swept in, but since the Japanese had lost almost all their aircraft the previous day, the squadrons strafed the airfields, going after the remaining aircraft or hulks and facilities and shooting up anything that moved in the lagoon or ashore, with Fighting 10 strafing Moen, Eten, and Param airfields. This time, the first strike by each of the fleet carriers was made up of 12 F6Fs and 12 dive bombers. Avengers went in on the second strikes, bombing airfields and shore installations.

Ramage recalled the mission:

I led the strike which circled outside the lagoon until it was light enough to attack the remaining shipping. The first division went down on an oiler, the 10,000-ton *Fujisan Maru*, which surprisingly was underway. After one to three hits, the ship went dead in the water. The second division dived on the auxiliary *Matsutan Maru*, also underway, and hit her amidships. These two ships were the only sizable ships remaining afloat in the harbor. On the way out, we set a 44-foot patrol boat afire and it blew up as a result of strafing.

Later strikes found nothing of note so far as targets were concerned, and when they departed nearly every structure on every island in the atoll had been knocked down.

In total the two-day attack on the "Gibraltar of the Pacific" sank three light cruisers: *Agano*, *Katori*, and *Naka*; four destroyers: *Oite*, *Fumizuki*, *Maikaze*, and *Tachikaze*; three auxiliary cruisers: *Akagi Maru*, *Aikoku Maru*, and *Kiyosumi Maru*; two submarine tenders: *Heian Maru* and *Rio de Janeiro Maru*; submarine chasers CH-24 and *Shonan Maru 15*; aircraft transport *Fujikawa Maru*; and 32 merchant ships. Some ships were destroyed in the anchorage and some in the sea surrounding Truk Atoll. Many merchant ships were loaded with reinforcements and supplies for garrisons in the Central Pacific area. Very few troops aboard the sunken ships survived and little of their cargoes was recovered.

The cruiser *Agano*, which had survived the November 11, 1943 Rabaul raid, was spotted soon after departing Truk enroute to Japan when the attack began and *Skate* (SS-305) sank her. Five hundred and fifty-three survivors were rescued by the destroyer *Oite*. As the destroyer returned to Truk with the survivors, aircraft spotted her and she was attacked and sunk. Only 20 of *Oite*'s crew survived while all the *Agano* survivors were lost.

Throughout the two days of strikes against Japan's most important base in the Pacific, the US Navy suffered the loss of only 40 men and 25 aircraft. Eleven of the men killed were crewmen aboard *Intrepid*.

Mac McWhorter recalled that, "We were sure Truk was going to be tough, but looking back on it, I have to say that the quality of the Japanese pilots we faced that day was nowhere near the quality we'd faced three months earlier at Rabaul." What had happened to change things was the air campaign against Rabaul from mid-November 1943 to late January 1944. All the Japanese air groups aboard the carriers at Truk had fed aircraft, pilots, and crews into the meatgrinder at Rabaul, and taken losses so bad that on February 24, after the Truk strike, the Japanese were forced to evacuate their air forces from the island base. While the Japanese pilots weren't as good as those met on November 11, 1943, Fighting 9 had gotten better.

There would be hard fighting to come, but with the losses sustained at Rabaul, combined with the losses at Truk, the Imperial Japanese Naval Air Force was a shadow of the force that had swept the Pacific in 1942. By February 1944, all US Navy fighter squadrons in the Pacific were led by men with combat experience, while their most junior pilots had over 600 hours of flight time in their logbooks by the time they reported to their squadron. There were almost no experienced leaders in the Imperial Japanese Naval Air Force, and the average pilot came to his squadron by February 1944 with no more than 200 hours of training. Most were barely able to take off from and land on an aircraft carrier. The Truk strikes put the Japanese carrier force out of commission until the Marianas invasion, while they tried to train replacement pilots to make up for the losses sustained at Rabaul and Truk.

At this moment in March and April, an amazing opportunity presented itself that might have changed the war, but such was not to be. Following the Truk strike, Combined Fleet commander Admiral Meinichi Koga decided to move the fleet from Palau, which was too exposed to possible American strikes, and base the ships at the Tawi-Tawi anchorage in the southern Philippines. Koga decided to transfer his headquarters from *Musashi* to Davao on the island on Mindanao. On the night of March 31, 1944, Koga and most of his senior staff and cryptographers boarded three H8K Emily flying boats to travel from Palau to Mindanao. The three aircraft flew into a tropical storm off Cebu and two were lost. The two Mavises carried Admiral Koga in one and Koga's Chief of Staff, Vice Admiral Shigeru Fukudome in the other. Fukudome's Mavis crashed off the island of Cebu and the admiral made it ashore, where he was captured by Filipino guerillas. Crucially, among the items carried by Fukudome on the flight that were lost in the crash was an updated Navy code book, a signal book, and a copy of "Plan Z," the master operational plan for the Japanese defense of the central Pacific, which Koga had determined would be centered on the use of land-based Japanese air units, since the carrier force was woefully unprepared for combat.

On April 10, with Japanese forces on Cebu hot on the heels of the guerillas, the American commander, Lieutenant Colonel Courtney Whitney, arranged to return Fukudome and the other prisoners to the Japanese in return for a cessation of the massacre of Filipino civilians. Three days later, the Filipinos who had found the box containing Plan Z and the code book when it washed ashore, turned them over to Whitney. The codebook was recognized for what it was when the guerillas discovered the Japanese were offering a 50,000 peso reward for its return. On April 27, Whitney arranged for the items to be picked up by the submarine *Crevalle* (SS-291) and taken to Australia. The pickup was made on May 11, and *Crevalle* arrived at Darwin on May 19; the documents were in headquarters in Brisbane later that day. Allied codebreakers looked forward with anticipation to the arrival of the codebook, since they had been stymied by changes to the Imperial Japanese Navy code since the summer of 1942 and had not "read the enemy's mail" in any detail since the week before the Battle of Midway, but unfortunately the code book had been separated from the Z Plan when found by Filipinos. Whitney radioed that they had the document in Cebu and a second submarine pickup was arranged, but the code book did not arrive in Australia until the end of May.

Unfortunately for the Americans, with Fukudome back in Japan and the plan and code book still missing, the Japanese Navy moved quickly to change both, so that by the time the code book arrived in Australia, the Japanese had changed their code again, effective on May 1. Thus, the Americans would never regain the ability to read enemy messages and would be forced to continue to depend on "traffic analysis" to give an indication of enemy intentions throughout the rest of the war. The continued inability to read Japanese naval code would have an important effect on the outcome of the two fleet actions to come, since the US Navy would have no way of knowing the enemy's true strength or intentions, or the actual battle losses and their impact on future operations.

Admiral Toyoda assumed direct command of the fleet on May 1 and changed the Z Plan. Fortunately his changes were not so radical that Admiral Spruance was prevented from successfully basing his plans for fleet movement on the translation of the Z Plan that had been airdropped on the deck of his flagship while the fleet was halfway between Majuro and Saipan.

Throughout the years prior to the outbreak of the Pacific War, Japanese Admiral Yamamoto, one of very few senior Japanese leaders with direct experience of living in the United States, had argued passionately against a war, on the grounds that Japan could never keep up with American production. Finally, with war inevitable, he said "I will run wild for six months. After that I can promise nothing." The Japanese would now experience the reality of their most famous Admiral's warning as it became clear to all but the die-hards in the coming months that Japan had no chance of winning the war.

CHAPTER EIGHT

THE CAPTAIN FROM HELL

Wile the battle over Wake Island, the Rabaul raid, the invasion of the Gilberts and Marshalls, and the strikes against Truk and the western Carolines were happening in late 1943 and early 1944, a smaller drama was unfolding, unlike any other that happened in the Navy during World War II and one that would have major consequences in how the war was experienced by the two top-scoring naval air groups.

Miles Rutherford Browning, a pioneer in the development of naval aviation as one of the original fliers to operate from *Langley*, who was intimately involved during the 20 years before the Pacific War in the development of aircraft types and the strategy and tactics on which the Navy's victory would be based, is an historian's nirvana of the consequences of personal shortcomings on professional success and failure. His citation for the Distinguished Service Medal cites: "His judicious planning and brilliant execution was largely responsible for the rout of the enemy Japanese fleet in the Battle of Midway." And yet nearly every naval aviator who ever dealt with him would remember him as "The worst individual I ever met in my entire naval career," in the words of Lieutenant (jg) Ken Glass, a junior pilot in Torpedo 2 when he met Browning, who went on to a 30-year career as a naval aviator. That the "facts" in the citation are in fact not true, and that the citation was the result of a campaign by his friend and commander William Halsey to resuscitate a personally botched public reputation, only adds to the story.

Browning was the son of a successful New York City stockbroker, who attended Annapolis as a member of the class of 1918, which was graduated a year early following the entry of the United States into World War I in 1917. During the war, Browning served on the *Oklahoma* (BB-37), then became a plank owner (a slang term for membership in the original commissioning crew) on *New Mexico* (BB-40). In June 1918, he was assigned as the senior American Naval Officer aboard the French cruiser *Lutetia* while she operated with Cruiser Force, Atlantic Fleet until the Armistice that November.

After four years of increasingly responsible sea duty, Lieutenant Browning married San Francisco socialite Cathalene Isabella Parker, stepdaughter of Vice Admiral Clark H. Woodward, on May 20, 1922. The professional connection was as important as the social connection, though the marriage would not last. In spite of the strong social pressures against divorce at the time, particularly in the naval officer corps, the first (of four) Mrs. Brownings would depart within five years.

In January 1924, Browning entered flight training at Pensacola, where he demonstrated exceptional skill as a pilot but also exhibited a "wild streak" that struck his fellow aviators as "potentially dangerous." Awarded his Wings of Gold on September 29, 1924, he reported aboard the *Langley*, where he became involved in the scouting function; over the next five years he served in scouting squadrons attached to cruisers and battleships after his time aboard *Langley*.

In July 1931, Browning was assigned to the Bureau of Aeronautics to serve in the Material Division (Design), where he spent the next three years participating in the design and testing of new combat aircraft, during which he survived a test flight crash in 1932. He was one of the group of "progressives" who advocated the development of a high-performance fighter, with maneuverability secondary to speed that would be fast enough to quickly overtake and shoot down enemy planes. Unfortunately for Browning and the other progressives, the Bureau of Aeronautics continued the emphasis on maneuverability, climb, and flight ceiling at the expense of speed. Had the Bureau of Aeronautics been more receptive to the ideas of the progressives, the Navy might have entered World War II with a more advanced high-performance fighter than the Wildcat.

In June 1934, Browning became commanding officer of VF-3B (the "B" indicating assignment to the Battle Fleet) aboard *Langley* and later on *Ranger*, the first carrier built from the keel up as an aircraft carrier, the design of which he had participated in. In June 1936 he reported to the Naval War College in Newport, Rhode Island for postgraduate studies, despite his removal as Fighting 3's commanding officer in circumstances that questioned his fitness for command. There was never any explanation of why Browning received such protection; one can only surmise that the "progressives" were taking care of their own whenever possible in the continuing battle to modernize naval aviation.

Browning's removal from command of Fighting 3 was the kind of scandal that ended most careers. Obsessed with having the squadron excel at the 1936 National Air Races, he had required that his pilots fly in close formation at night and follow him through a maneuver so dangerous they were forbidden to mention it. Word got out and days before the races he was transferred despite his pleas. In 1937, at the end of his first year at Newport, he was assigned as one of the first naval instructors at the Air Corps Tactical School at Maxwell Field where he was responsible for training a new generation of Army aviators who were destined for higher command in what was possible with naval aviation. He did this while he continued his own advanced studies in combat theory, national security policy, airborne command and control, and joint military operations at the War College.

Browning laid out his tactical logic regarding a carrier battle with the Imperial Japanese Navy in a 13-page, single-spaced, typewritten thesis on carrier warfare prepared in 1936, in which he anticipated the flaw in the execution of Japanese carrier flight operations that would later be exploited at Midway. Upon graduation from the Naval War College, he was ordered to Rear Admiral William F. Halsey, Jr.'s staff in the new assignment of air tactical officer. In June 1938, he became commander of Air Group 5 aboard the new *Yorktown*, serving in that position until 1940. When Halsey became Commander Aircraft, Battle Forces, Browning joined his staff as operations and war plans officer and became Chief of Staff in June 1941. From the outbreak of war until June 1942, Browning provided tactical counsel to Halsey in that position.

Under the aggressive leadership of Halsey and Browning, *Enterprise* took the offensive following Pearl Harbor. In February and March 1942, Browning planned and directed daring air raids on Japanese bases at Kwajalein, Wotje, and Maloelap in the Marshall Islands, as well as enemy installations in the Gilbert Islands, Marcus Island, and Wake Island; the resulting publicity over these events turned the then-unknown Halsey into a national hero. Halsey freely gave credit for much of his military success to his Chief of Staff and recommended Commander Browning for spot promotion to the rank of captain. *Life* magazine dubbed him "America's mastermind in aerial warfare." Browning's promotion to captain was approved following the Doolittle Raid, in which Browning played a major role in both planning and execution.

When Halsey was unable to sail in command of Task Force 16 at the Battle of Midway, Browning remained aboard *Enterprise* and worked with Halsey's replacement, Admiral Spruance. Following the victory at Midway, Halsey made certain Browning received official commendation for planning and executing the battle, even though much of his advice was not followed and might have changed the outcome for the worse if it had been. Spruance, however, was another naval officer who had difficulty dealing with Browning, though he was able to recognize the value of what historian Samuel Eliot Morison termed Browning's "slide-rule brain."

The one part of the battle where Browning's advice did matter came when the Japanese struck Midway that morning. He correctly deduced the Japanese would commit to a second strike on Midway Island, which would provide the opportunity to catch them off guard due to the delays he knew they would experience in fueling and rearming their aircraft since the aircraft would be taken below for refueling rather than remain on the flight deck; it was the operational failure on which he had based his prewar paper. Browning's argument convinced Spruance to launch *Enterprise*'s aircraft so they would arrive over the fleet while the enemy was so engaged. Thus, the *Enterprise* dive bombers had the good luck to catch the Mobile Fleet's carriers at their single most vulnerable moment. The fact that their CAPs were at low altitude after defending against the attacks of the Devastator torpedo bombers of Torpedo 3, Torpedo 6, and Torpedo 8 was an unforeseen added bonus. With the fortuitous arrival of the *Yorktown* SBD strike a few minutes later, three of the four carriers were sunk, just as Browning had predicted could happen in his 1936 tactical thesis.

Browning's fatal flaw was that he was a man of tremendous contradictions. Through all the years of what appeared to be a brilliant career, he became known as "the most intemperate man in the Navy" and actually seemed keen to cultivate his reputation for being hated, hateful and insulting. He was frequently drunk, which seemed to exacerbate all these problems. In a navy where a single divorce was considered career suicide, he was involved in three marriages and three divorces in the 20 years between 1922 and 1942. Had it not been for the war, it is likely he would never have been promoted past Commander.

Following the Battle of Midway, Browning engaged in an outrageous public affair in the constricted social milieu of Hawaii with the wife of a fellow officer, Commander Francis Massie Hughe, who caught Browning and his wife Jane *in flagrante delicto*. Hughe was a skilled boxer, and he administered a severe beating to Browning. Following her divorce in

1943, Jane became Browning's fourth and last wife. Finally, his career seemed to be "beached" as a result when he was removed from Spruance's staff aboard *Enterprise*.

When Halsey returned to active service in September, he called for his irascible comrade and Browning was saved. He followed Halsey to become Chief of Staff for the ComSoPac. By the end of 1942, Browning's tactics and his aggressive advice to his aggressive commander contributed to the Japanese defeat in the Guadalcanal campaign. However, Nimitz was convinced that Browning bore responsibility for the running of the Battle of Santa Cruz, which had resulted in the loss of *Hornet* and the damaging of *Enterprise*. Again, Halsey gave Browning credit for his success. In a letter written to Admiral Nimitz on January 1, 1943, concerning Browning's precarious career situation, Halsey wrote, "Miles has an uncanny knack of sizing up a situation and coming out with an answer." While admitting that his Chief of Staff was "decidedly temperamental," Halsey begged Nimitz not to break up "this partnership," concluding that, "I am almost superstitious about it."

In January 1943, Browning managed to incur the personal enmity of Secretary of the Navy Frank Knox, who was shocked by the Chief of Staff's disrespectful behavior during a visit to Halsey at his headquarters in Noumea. Knox saw Browning as a "psychological basket case" in the Secretary's own words, and a threat to national security if he remained in his position. Knox went so far as to counsel the Admiral to rid himself of his obnoxious Chief of Staff, as had many others before. However, Halsey continued to value Browning's professional expertise and was willing to put up with what he termed "eccentricities." He resisted Knox and advocated instead that Browning be advanced to the wartime rank of Commodore. This set up a situation where Browning had incurred the personal opposition of the Secretary of the Navy, a man who possessed a long reputation of being no one to cross, extending back to his days as publisher of the *Chicago Tribune*.

When Knox returned to Washington, he was determined to see Halsey given a "sane and competent Chief of Staff." He told Chief of Naval Operations and Commander in Chief of the Navy Admiral Ernest J. King – an officer well known for his own "eccentricities" and expressions of anger – that he wanted Browning gone.

King found a way to separate Halsey and Browning by making Browning an offer he couldn't refuse: command of the new *Hornet* (CV-12). Browning left Halsey's staff in July 1943 to assume the command. Halsey was given the services of Rear Admiral Robert B. Carney, who would rise eventually to Chief of Naval Operations, as his new Chief of Staff.

As word of Browning's new assignment became known, other senior aviators complained about his being given *Hornet*. In response, King insisted that "the idea was to get rid of him at once, whatever the price." Knowing of such an attitude on the part of one's superiors might give a new captain pause to reflect on his past and consider what he might do to take better advantage of his opportunity, but Miles Browning was not that man. Given his past, it was predictable that Browning would manage to destroy his relations with the ship's officers, the men whose support was crucial for his success. His presence on the bridge was unpleasant, every order being a snarl; he had no qualm about publicly berating division heads; and even launched a personal attack at a senior crew member over the public address system. Those who served under him reacted first with fear, and ultimately with hatred.

The newly formed Air Group 15 was assigned to Browning's carrier in December 1943. They were the first to experience the "hornet's nest" aboard the ship. The fliers in the group did not form a good impression of the commander of their new home in the wake of the quick loss of two SB2C-1C dive bombers in landing accidents. The losses resulted from the fact that the average pilot in Bombing 15 had had less than 20 hours in the type, in addition to the known difficulties of operating the "Beast." Browning called CAG William Drane to the bridge and informed him that he did not want to see any aircraft using more than 400 feet of deck for takeoff. When Drane protested that this was virtually impossible for the underpowered Helldivers in anything but a very strong headwind, Browning informed him that the "book" stated that was what the airplane was capable of and brooked no further contrary opinion.

Everyone was alienated by Browning's micro-management of the air group. Bombing 15's commander, Lieutenant Commander Dew, fell ill within a matter of weeks from the stress of dealing with Browning and was transferred.

The group faced the problem of finding Dew's replacement. Three other squadron commanders turned down the opportunity, having heard of Browning's *modus operandi*. It took every argument fighter leader Dave McCampbell and torpedo squadron leader VeeGee Lambert could assemble to get Lieutenant Commander James Mini, a former Annapolis tight end who would rise to Rear Admiral and Commandant of Midshipmen at Annapolis 15 years later. Mini had recently returned from a fleet assignment and was looking forward to shore duty, but finally allowed McCampbell to cajole him into taking the job.

Squadron pilot John Bridgers remembered, "Commander Mini was the worst pilot and the best officer I ever served with. He was always a minute from disaster, yet he would always take the difficult missions." Mini came aboard a day before *Hornet*'s departure for the Pacific and was thus forced to learn everything about his difficult mount aboard ship. His first landing resulted in his Helldiver bouncing over the arresting wires and ending upside down in the barrier. Mini immediately climbed into another and made three successful takeoffs and landings, which made quite an impression on the squadron pilots who witnessed the event. Under his inspirational leadership the squadron became a record-setter, but that was in the future.

Hornet and her air group departed Norfolk, Virginia, on January 13, 1944, headed south for the Panama Canal and on to the Pacific. Once underway, things went from bad to worse. The next two weeks saw two of the Helldivers crash on takeoff with no survivors. Bombing 15's morale sank and the situation became worse when Ensign Frank Eisenhart made a hard landing and his Helldiver lost its tailhook, bouncing over the crash barrier and striking Ensign David Hall's just-landed Helldiver, chopping off Hall's rudder with the prop and damaging the elevators.

The limited space Browning allowed for the Helldivers to take off meant that they would often disappear from sight as they left the bow before having to stay low to build up speed and gradually climb to altitude. Four more takeoff crashes had occurred by the time *Hornet* arrived in Panama on February 10, 1944, resulting in the deaths of two pilots and a rear-seat gunner. Though the Hellcats and Avengers didn't suffer similar events, all fliers remained on edge from Browning's ceaseless abuse.

During passage from Panama to San Diego, there were four more accidents involving Helldivers over the space of three days. Ensign Calvin Platt lost power on takeoff and went into the water; while he managed to escape the sinking Helldiver, his crewman, Aviation Radioman 3/c Tony Czerwiec, wasn't as lucky. Two other accidents involved landing gear collapse when the dive bombers hit the deck too hard in rough sea conditions. *Hornet* was three days out from San Diego when the Helldiver flown by Ensign John Peabody and Radioman George Cobbe went into a spin during dive-bombing practice; both were lost when the plane sank immediately on impact with the ocean. *Hornet* docked at NAS North Island on February 27, 1944, where she took aboard replacement Helldivers and flight crews before departing for Pearl Harbor two days later.

While *Hornet* was docking in San Diego, Fighting 2's skipper Dean had a narrow escape from death in a mid-air collision with Ensign John M. Edwards during air combat training on February 27. Edwards' cry "My prop is gone!" was the first any other pilots knew that something was wrong. Squadron engineering officer Lieutenant Charlie Harbert saw a Hellcat without a wing flutter down moments later. A figure emerged from the cockpit at almost the last minute and a parachute blossomed; Dean swung twice before he hit the water. None saw what happened to Edwards; he never returned. Once again, the fliers were reminded that everything they did was intrinsically dangerous. Within a week, Dean had returned to the squadron despite suffering a broken rib.

When *Hornet* docked at Ford Island on March 4, 1944, the future of Air Group 15 was dark. Captain Browning's official recommendation that they be taken off the ship and given more "training opportunity" was a professional slap in the face to the group leadership. The price they paid to remain together and in the combat zone was Commander Drane's removal as CAG. Fortuitously, his replacement was the commanding officer of Fighting 15, Lieutenant Commander David McCampbell, who later recalled Browning as the "Captain from Hell." The review of the group's performance by the staff of Commander Air Forces Pacific centered on the record of Bombing 15. Browning's recommendation was approved and Air Group 15 were on their way to Maui.

A replacement had to be found quickly. Air Group 2 had been scheduled to go aboard *Essex* when she returned from her deployment with Air Group 9, but this had changed when *Essex* was ordered to Bremerton, Washington, for overhaul. Since the group had their bags packed, they received the assignment to go aboard *Hornet*.

Fighting 2's Ensign Don Brandt was puzzled by what they found when they went aboard the *Hornet*. "The guys from Air Group 15 seemed awfully happy to be getting kicked off that ship, which seemed rather strange to us." Once the ship had departed Pearl Harbor and joined the fast carrier task force, Browning continued to require that aircraft use no more deck space than the "book" called for when launched; Bombing 2 suffered as had Bombing 15 throughout their time under his command.

When *Hornet* departed for the western Pacific on March 12, 1944, she was now the flagship for Rear Admiral J.J. "Jocko" Clark, who was another of the many officers who detested Browning for the marital affair in Hawaii. Ken Glass of Torpedo 2 recalled that "Our shared misery under Browning somehow brought the group together in a way we had not been together before, and made us better and more capable than we had been."

The kind of shipboard trouble that was not easily resolved began within days. Tragedy struck shortly after the launch of the morning CAP when *Hornet*'s task group crossed the International Dateline on March 18. Ensigns H.L. "Lefty" Carlson and Glendale D. "Cookie" Williams collided when they attempted to join up on Lieutenant L.E. "Blood" Doner, the division leader. Lieutenant (jg) Connie Hargreaves in number four was shocked when he saw the two Hellcats disappear into the ocean off *Hornet*'s port bow.

Hornet and her air group dropped anchor in the new fleet anchorage at Majuro Atoll on March 20, 1944 and soon received news they would depart on March 22 for strikes on the Palaus in the western Carolines, which would be followed by strikes on Yap and Woleai in the eastern Carolines. Task Group 58.1 under command of Rear Admiral Clark, with his flag aboard *Hornet*, crossed the equator at 1433 hours on March 25, when four Hellcats led by Commander Dean attempted unsuccessfully to intercept a Japanese snooper.

On March 29, ship and air group prepared for their baptism of fire. Two Mavis snoopers were shot down that afternoon by the CAP. At 1700 hours, two divisions, one led by "Tex" Duff, the other by "Tex" Harris, were launched to intercept a group of bogeys spotted on radar. Lieutenant (jg) F.T. "Gabe" Gabriel of Duff's division spotted a Betty and set it afire, leaving a fiery trail across the sky into the ocean below. Hellcats from other carriers shot down four other Bettys, while Harris's division were unable to close with what they identified as four Nakajima Ki-44 "Tojo" fighters (most likely they were Oscars, since the Tojo was at the time confined to air defense duty in the Home Islands). That evening, Ensign Thomas L. Morrisey, Fighting 2's intelligence officer, recorded the final pre-strike briefing in the squadron ready room: "Targets for strikes on 'K Day' have been assigned, plotting boards are being put in order, and flight leaders can be seen cornering their respective flights to give them final instructions." Don Brandt recalled that sleep came uneasily for many that night.

Air Group 2's first combat strike was launched at Palau on March 30, 1944, led by Fighting 2. Lieutenant (jg) Andy Skon's division strafed an ammunition ship that exploded, while the only Zeke spotted was shot down by Lieutenant (jg) J.T. "Mike" Wolf. It was obvious the previous day's snoopers had been able to get off their reports, since the warships the fliers expected to attack were gone; in fact, they had departed for the new Combined Fleet anchorage at Tawi-Tawi the week before. Torpedo 2 lost two Avengers on takeoff, with one lost to antiaircraft over the harbor.

Ken Glass remembered, "it was a rough initiation for the torpedo squadron into the big leagues."

The day also saw Lieutenant Edward L. "Whitey" Feightner of Fighting 8 attain ace status. Flying with Fighting 10 at Guadalcanal in 1943, Feightner had scored four. Following Air Group 10's return to the United States in the summer of 1943, Feightner returned to the Pacific in March 1944 as engineering officer with Fighting 8 aboard *Bunker Hill*. Palau was the baptism of fire for the squadron, whose pilots were equipped with an amazing device, the first "G-suits," known for their looks as "zoot suits" or "Z-suits." Lieutenant Scott McCuskey, a veteran of Coral Sea with VF-42, had been among the first to test the new "Z-suit" in the spring of 1943 while he was an instructor at Cecil Field, Florida. The suits weighed about 5 pounds and had bladders over the pilot's calves, thighs, and abdomen, that filled with air as G-force increased, thus restricting loss of blood from the head. McCuskey had immediately recognized the suit's value, which allowed him to pull about 1.5 G more than he could without it.

When he reported to VF-8 that summer, he inquired about getting the Z-suits and was told they were unavailable and that furthermore the West Coast evaluation team had recommended against them. McCuskey convinced squadron commander Lieutenant Commander William M. Collins of their value. "I called the Berger Brothers in Harford, Connecticut, who I had met at Cecil Field, and they personally provided the suits. Permission was granted by the Navy for us to equip the F6Fs on an experimental basis."

When Feightner spotted two Zekes over the island of Peleliu, he dived on them and used the superior maneuverability the Z-suit provided to outmaneuver both and destroy one that caught fire while he claimed the second as a probable. The rest of the squadron decisively demonstrated the suits' value when they shot down 11 with three probables; two of the victories were scored by McCuskey. It would still be another year before the fully developed suits would find fleet-wide use.

The Palau strikes finished successfully on March 31. Fighting 2's only victory was scored by Lieutenant (jg) "Griff" Griffin, who shot down what was listed as a Ki-44 "Tojo" but was in all likelihood another Oscar while the rest of the squadron strafed ground targets. The CAP was successful when Ensign "Stinky" Davis shot down another Mavis.

That morning, Ken Glass discovered the "hard" way of getting away from Captain Browning:

I was assigned for the dawn antisubmarine patrol. Just as I lifted off, the engine died. I was able to turn away to port, so that when we hit the water, the ship went past us about 50 yards away and we weren't run over or swamped by the wake. All three of us managed to get out, and after about ten minutes in the water we were picked up by the plane guard destroyer. We then had a period of ten days where the sea was too rough and dangerous to transfer personnel from ship to ship by breeches buoy, so we had an enforced vacation. Being away from the captain was wonderful.

Jill torpedo bombers launched from Yap attempted to attack Task Force 58 that evening. Four VF-31 Hellcats from *Cabot* led by Lieutenant Commander Winston were vectored 75 miles west onto a formation of nine Jills. Winston shot down three while his wingman Conny Nooy equaled that score and the other three were shot down by the other two pilots.

Ninety-three aerial victories were scored over Palau during the two days of strikes, including 29 scored by Fighting 5 from *Yorktown* and 25 by VF-30 in their final combat while based aboard *Monterey*.

On April 1, Task Force 58 hit Woleai, Yap, and Ulithi in the western Carolines, while returning to Majuro. With three days of combat operations under their belt, Fighting 2 had suffered no losses, while the fleet's Hellcats had scored 111 aerial victories and 46 destroyed on the ground at the three atolls. The fast carriers anchored in Majuro lagoon on April 6.

Admiral Clark wrote a report to Nimitz on his return to Majuro that he had saved Browning on three occasions: once when he prevented the captain running the ship aground, the next issuing orders that avoided a ramming, and finally the interception of an insubordinate message Browning had written to Mitscher that would have resulted in Browning's removal had it been delivered. Clark and Mitscher awaited Browning's next misstep.

On April 13, Task Force 58 headed south-southwest to support the invasion of Hollandia on the northwestern New Guinea coast. This operation would see the end of General Douglas MacArthur's New Guinea campaign with the destruction of the last Japanese base on the world's largest island.

Preparatory strikes were launched on D-minus-1, April 20, 1944. Earlier that morning, *Hornet* refueled her accompanying destroyers. Newly promoted Lieutenant (jg) Morrisey recorded that "the ship's band serenaded the tin cans from the hangar deck with 'Two O'Clock Jump.' " Just after dawn, *Hornet*'s first strike hit Wakde, near Hollandia. They sank two Japanese transports offshore, and knocked out many Japanese aircraft by strafing the nearby airfield. During the next two days, strikes were flown in support of the invasion forces and the group suffered no losses. Task Force 58 claimed 103 Japanese aircraft destroyed on the surrounding airfields.

Despite the success in February, Task Force 58 was not finished with Truk. Following the Hollandia–New Guinea operation, Admiral Nimitz decided the time was ripe to give the atoll another heavy working-over. While everything that floated was now at the bottom of the lagoon, Truk had the only major ship repair facility in the South Pacific, with service facilities and other military installations needing neutralization. Although it had been decided Truk would be bypassed, it remained a potential major operating base.

On April 23, Nimitz gave orders for a second strike at Truk, scheduled for April 29. Lieutenant (jg) Connie Hargreaves, who had been assigned to VF-18 aboard *Bunker Hill* for the February strikes, briefed his squadron mates in VF-2 about his experience, noting that they would likely encounter heavy flak.

The first Americans over Truk were eight Hellcats from *Langley's* VF-32, led by CO Lieutenant Commander Eddie Outlaw making a sweep ahead of 24 bomb-carrying Hellcats from *Lexington* and *Enterprise*. Some 100 Japanese fighters had been recovered from Rabaul following the February strikes and returned to Truk, of which 62 were airborne when VF-32 arrived overhead at 10,000 feet. Second division leader Lieutenant Hollis "Holly" Hills spotted a formation of 25–30 Zekes in three-plane vees a formation approaching 4,000 feet below. He kept his division high for cover when Outlaw's division dived on the Zekes. The enemy pilots showed no air discipline and all four Americans scored on their first pass. The remaining Zekes then maneuvered into two Lufbery circles. Outlaw made vertical dives from the rear to shoot down three, while section leader Lieutenant (jg) Donald Reeves also dropped three.

Hills shot down one Zeke, spotted his squadron commander with two Zekes on his tail, and shot them both down. Free of the Zekes, Outlaw then shot down two more to make "ace in a day," while Lieutenant Dick May scored two to finally become an ace after scoring three over Guadalcanal. VF-32 claimed 20 destroyed and two probables for one F6F damaged.

Holly Hills was a very different naval aviator from the norm. A native of Pasadena, California, he had enlisted in the Royal Canadian Air Force in Toronto on September 5, 1940 after being turned down by the Navy as an AvCad. Promoted to sergeant pilot in June 1941, he went to the UK that July, where he joined 414 Squadron, Royal Canadian Air Force, which was at the time equipped with the Curtiss Tomahawk II, an early version of the P-40. That fall, 414 became one of the first squadrons to equip with the new North American Mustang I, the first version of the famous P-51 series to see combat. Hills and the squadron flew low-level tactical "recce" missions over northern France and the Low Countries during the next 11 months before they were assigned to participate in the Dieppe raid in August 1942. On August 19, Hills and three other Mustang pilots encountered four of the dreaded Focke-Wulf Fw-190s, the Luftwaffe's newest and best fighter. In a turning fight at tree-top altitude, Hills shot down one of the attacking Fw-190s. It was the first aerial victory scored by a pilot in a Mustang, of which there would be many more to come.

In 1943, Hills returned to the United States. With a tour of combat operations in the European Theater of Operations behind him and an aerial victory, the Navy changed its mind and Hills became a naval aviator that fall, joining VF-32 after receiving his Wings of Gold. He would score again at the Marianas Turkey Shoot to become an ace, one of a very select fraternity of naval aviators to serve in more than one Allied air force and score against more than one enemy air force during World War II.

"Jig-dog" Ramage, still XO of Bombing 10 aboard *Enterprise*, recalled the difference between the first and second Truk strikes:

> This time we had lots of information on targets. We were scheduled against installations mainly on the islands of Moen, Dublon and Fefan. There was no air opposition to speak of, although I did see a pinkish-brown Zero take off from Eten on the first day.
>
> We wrecked the place! We started out the "treatment," as Mitscher called it, with the usual fighter sweep on April 29. The *Enterprise* fighters were led by VF-10 skipper Lieutenant "Bud" Schumann. The Japanese had flown in a substantial number of fighters since the first Truk attacks, but they didn't last long. My first strike, 1B, was scheduled against warehouses east of the Moen strip. My second strike, taking off at 1630 hours, was directed at revetments, aircraft and facilities on Moen air strip. By this time, it was clear that not much of value remained to be hit.

Ramage's gunner, Dave Cawley, had reason to remember April 30, 1944:

> Mr. Ramage, my pilot, was scheduled to lead the third strike on April 30. As normal before an attack, we all prepared to test our machine guns by firing two or three rounds from each gun. I aimed the guns into a clear area, released the safety and fired. Each gun fired a couple of rounds when there

was an extra-loud "whack," and I stopped firing. I felt as if someone had hit me across the front of my thighs as hard as you could swing a baseball bat. I cut my flight suit and there was a hole in my leg about two inches deep. It hadn't started to bleed, so I got my first aid kit and filled the wound with sulfa powder and put a bandage over it. I decided to say nothing of my problem, which was caused by the breech of one machine gun exploding.

There was little or no shipping around, but lots of major installations and fuel tank farms. The AA was very heavy and the weather was poor and deteriorating. When we landed, I went to sick bay. Later, a young doctor on reading an x-ray showed me where the ejector claw from my left machine gun lay against the thigh bone of my left leg. The doctor probed and dug for half an hour, which started some heavy bleeding, but he couldn't get the object out of my leg. The next morning they said I had two choices: leave the metal in my leg, or schedule a full-blown operation to surgically remove it. The latter would take me off the flight schedule indefinitely. I chose the former. I still carry the chunk and it has not bothered me.

Ramage tried to get Cawley a Purple Heart for his wound but was not successful when the wound was ruled non-combat related. "He was back on the flight schedule within three days."

Air Group 2 ran into the heaviest antiaircraft fire they had come across yet in the Pacific on the first day of strikes during their attack on Param Island. Fortunately, all Fighting 2 Hellcats returned safely, some with flak damage. The only emergency occurred when Bill LaForge lost engine power on pullout from a strafing run. He did everything he could think of to restart the engine as he contemplated ditching in the middle of the lagoon to a kind reception by the Japanese. Fortunately, it caught and he pulled up when he was at 500 feet over the water and rejoined the squadron for the return to the ship. Sadly, heavy flak caught two Torpedo 2's Avengers; no one got out of the burning airplanes.

Rain squalls on April 30 prevented any strikes being launched until 1000 hours. The day's action over Truk saw no American planes lost; it was obvious the base was a mere shadow of its former reputation. The lack of fighter opposition indicated that the Japanese must be husbanding their naval air forces for future action.

Ramage recalled the second day:

By the second day, a large tropical front had set in and the ceiling over the Dublon Navy Yard was about a thousand feet. I led my SBDs in straight and level and, at our maximum speed of about 180 knots, dropped on the installations. Since the shipping had all been sunk on the previous raids, the AA was concentrated around the remaining obvious targets. It was intense. Dublon has a 1,100-foot peak and they were firing straight at us during our run. We were all holed, but I think Lou Bangs' division got the worst of it from our own bomb fragments. The drop altitude was logged at 700 feet.

As we passed out of the atoll to the south, I could see numerous aircraft in the water, several within the atoll. There were several SOCs [Seagulls] and OS2Us [Kingfishers] from the cruisers and battleships on the water rescuing downed airmen. We were fortunate not to have losses in Bombing Ten. After landing back aboard the Big E, I went to the bridge and told the exec, Commander Tom Hamilton, and skipper Captain Matt Gardner about the strike, emphasizing the number of aircraft in the water. They took me up to the flag bridge where Admiral Reeves said, "I think we have run into the law of diminishing returns." He called Admiral Mitscher on TBS [Talk Between Ships] to recommend that further operations be canceled, as the benefits in continuing the raids were not worth the risk. Within 15 minutes, Mitscher canceled the remaining strike, though rescue operations, including fighter CAP, continued throughout the rest of the day. I mention this incident as an example of why we loved Marc Mitscher … More than half of the 46 airmen shot down were rescued, some inside the lagoon.

Ramage also remembered that task group commander Admiral "Black Jack" Reeves was very aggressive about further strikes:

If Admiral Reeves had his way, there would have been another Truk raid, despite the decision to bypass the now-useless base. On 18 May, our squadron Intelligence Officer, Lieutenant John Curtis, showed me a purloined dispatch, from Reeves to Mitscher, which I quote from memory: "Would I be stretching my glide too far to recommend you detach task group 58.3 to strike Truk?" This struck me as not being very wise, as there were no targets afloat or ashore worth the probable losses. Also, we knew that Truk was to be bypassed. I asked Curtis to find out Mitscher's response. It was not long in coming. Mitscher replied, "I will not be badgered into an unwise decision."

Alex Vraciu, who had requested a transfer to another squadron when Fighting 6 was forced to return to Hawaii aboard the *Intrepid* following her torpedoing in February, had managed to end up in VF-16 when *Lexington* returned from repair. When he first landed aboard the carrier, his Hellcat sported an "A" gasoline ration sticker on the windshield. The "A" sticker allowed a wartime motorist back home to buy four gallons of gas a week. Leading a division on the first day at Truk, Vraciu shot down two Zekes, which made him the leading Navy ace currently in combat with a score of 11.

The final claim for the second Truk raid was 65 aerial victories and 85 destroyed on the ground. Five aircraft were lost in air combat and 21 to the heavy flak. No important ships were found, and at the end of the strikes only a dozen Zekes were left flyable. The "Gibraltar of the Pacific" would serve as a target for new air groups "breaking in" as a first mission for the remainder of the war; B-24s and P-38s from the Seventh Air Force would attack the base from the Marianas after Saipan was secured. Bombing 10's Ramage explained, "That was the end of Truk. Its large garrison that survived the raids was left to starve as we took the war farther west to the Marianas."

Task Force 58 hit the island of Ponape on May 1 while returning to Majuro. Previous attacks had gutted the island's defenses and the flak was negligible. Air Group 2 suffered another deadly accident when a Helldiver returned with a 100-pound bomb under the left wing which had failed to drop. When the pilot touched down, the bomb fell loose and exploded; two of the flight deck crew were killed and 25 injured. In the middle of that, a second Helldiver went into the barrier when its tail hook pulled out. Butch Voris landed next; he hit his brakes hard enough when he failed to catch one of the first wires that his Hellcat nosed over and its spinning prop gouged the wooden flight deck. There was never a safe time when operating aircraft at sea.

Task Force 58 re-crossed the equator on May 3, 1944 during the return to base. Since there were no immediate operational assignments, *Hornet* put the war aside for a day while Davy Jones came aboard with King Neptune and his Court. The ship's company and air group "pollywogs" were duly initiated into the Ancient Secrets of the Deep and became "Honorable Shellbacks." The fleet dropped anchor in Eniwetok lagoon on May 4, completing the final sweep prior to the next major operation in the Central Pacific campaign.

With the final strike on Ponape, Task Force 58 had completed a four-month rampage across the Central Pacific, during which the fast carriers struck at will in a convincing show of power and competence which fully demonstrated that the visionaries aboard the *Langley* 20 years earlier had been right about what a carrier fleet could accomplish. There had been spectacular dogfights, with record numbers of Japanese aircraft destroyed, as a result of which Japanese naval aviation was virtually finished.

Captain Browning's end came while *Hornet* was anchored at Eniwetok following the Truk strikes. Some 1,500 crewmen were on the hangar deck the night of May 7, watching the movie *A Guy Named Joe*, starring Spencer Tracy. Someone opened a carbon dioxide canister as a joke at a quiet moment in the film. When others heard the hissing noise, which sounded like a lit fuse, one man yelled "There's a bomb loose!" Pandemonium ensued as the sailors fought and struggled to evacuate the hangar deck with the result that, in the confusion, several men jumped or were pushed overboard.

Captain Browning, who was in attendance, grabbed the microphone and berated the men verbally, adding to the confusion. Informed by the ship's First Lieutenant that there were men overboard, he refused to have a whaleboat lowered to rescue them, despite Admiral Clark making that recommendation directly. As a result, two crewmen drowned, while 15 suffered injuries including broken arms and legs. Clark returned to the flag bridge and radioed Mitscher, "Here is the overt act I have been waiting for."

Browning's action was finally too much, even for the Navy. He was found guilty of negligence by a hastily formed Board of Inquiry. Samuel Eliot Morison called the ensuing ruin of Browning's career, "one of the great wastes to the American prosecution of the war." Task Force 58 commander Admiral Marc Mitscher requested his immediate relief following the board's finding. It was a decision supported by the Browning-hating senior chain of command clear up to and including the Secretary of the Navy.

The men on *Hornet* learned on May 27 that Browning would be relieved. There were no open celebrations, but Ken Glass remembered that "there were smiles all over the ship on that news." Captain William D. Sample took command of *Hornet* on May 29. Air Group 2 veterans remembered him as the polar opposite of Browning, a captain who led by personal example and held the welfare of his crew foremost. Under Sample's command, *Hornet* became one of the Navy's outstanding ships during the rest of the war.

Miles Browning, known as both a brilliant strategist and a failure as a human being, was "beached" for the rest of the war at the Command and General Staff College at Fort Leavenworth, Kansas, with the assignment of instructor in carrier battle tactics. Amazingly, he was promoted to Rear Admiral on his retirement in 1947. He toured Japan in 1949, where he caused more dismay when he stated that "alleged" radiation damage from the atomic bombs was a "myth," pointing as proof to the fact there were no long-term effects to blooming gardens and that a number of tall chimneys were left standing in Hiroshima and Nagasaki.

In 1950, the man who didn't believe in negative effects from atom bombs was appointed Director of Civil Defense for the state of New Hampshire, where he devised a plan to house 500,000 displaced residents of Boston in New Hampshire in private homes in the event of an atomic disaster. He resigned the position shortly thereafter and in 1952 was diagnosed with systemic lupus erythematosus. In 1954, he died at age 57. As an interesting sidelight, his only daughter, Cathalene Parker Browning from his first marriage, was later the mother of American comic actor Chevy Chase.

Commander Jackson D. Arnold, Annapolis '34 and a naval aviator since 1937, fleeted up from commander of Torpedo 2 to become commander of Air Group 2 on May 31 after CAG Roy L. Johnson took the position of air officer aboard *Hornet*.

By the time Air Group 2 returned to the United States from their Western Pacific deployment in early October 1944, they were recognized as the then-leading air group in the Navy, with a score of planes shot down and ships destroyed that bettered that of Air Group 9.

Air Group 15 was assigned to the newly reconditioned *Essex*, and went aboard her on May 3, 1944, following six weeks of intensive training at NAAS Pu'unene on Maui. Over the next six and a half months, they would become the only big carrier air group to participate in both the Battle of the Philippine Sea and the Battles of Leyte Gulf, the two greatest naval battles of history. They would also participate in Admiral Halsey's destruction of Japanese air power in the Philippines, Okinawa, and Formosa during September and early October before the Philippines invasion.

Upon their relief by Air Group 4 in mid-November 1944, Air Group 15 was the all-time top-scoring naval air group of the war. Their CAG, David McCampbell, was recognized as the Navy "Ace of Aces." Looking back in retrospect, Jim Duffy said "It was the luck of the draw. That six-week delay meant we were there for all the big fights. It wasn't that we were so much better than any other group, we just had more opportunity to demonstrate how good we were."

In a perverse manner, the "captain from hell" was responsible for the operational creation of the two air groups that would most successfully demonstrate all his prewar predictions about the power and capability of naval aviation.

CHAPTER NINE

LIFEGUARDS

For aircrew anywhere, a major worry was what would happen if they were shot down. This was particularly true in the Pacific, since the Japanese did not treat prisoners in accordance with the Geneva Accords regarding prisoners of war. In accordance with the Code Bushido, which held that it was a great disgrace for a warrior to allow himself to be captured by the enemy, since it meant he had lost all personal honor, the Japanese did not recognize any responsibility for humane treatment of those aircrew they captured. There were numerous documented instances of captured aircrew being tortured or executed, frequently by beheading with a samurai sword; there were even confirmed instances of cannibalism. In addition to these fears, there was the possibility of being lost at sea in a crash.

There is a tradition in the Navy of not leaving men behind if it is possible to rescue them. In the face of this deadly Japanese response to captured prisoners of war, every effort was made to develop a means of rescue. In the days before helicopters, this meant the use of seaplanes and flying boats, in addition to ships. Since it was not advisable for a surface ship to operate in proximity to a Japanese target being struck by aircraft, this duty of "lifeguard" fell to submarines, either those on patrol in the vicinity of a strike that would be ordered to search for downed aircrew, or submarines sent to stand off a target with the specific assignment of rescuing downed airmen.

Lifeguard submarines would arrive on station in the target area ahead of the attack, often able to provide last-minute weather and enemy movement information to the attacking forces. Aircrews were given the submarine's radio frequencies, location, and bearing references, and code name. If a plane was hit and going down, the airmen or another pilot could transmit the location of the downed aircrew to the waiting submarine. Upon receiving information about downed aircrew, the responding submarine would have to surface, often before combat had ended, thus potentially exposing itself to fire from enemy aircraft, shore batteries, or ships. The crew had to go out on deck, throw lines to the airmen, haul them up on deck, and get them safely below. In some cases, members of the submarine crew had to use rubber rafts to retrieve downed airmen.

During the course of the war, there were several dramatic rescues performed by both submarines and aircraft. These stories gained wide reference in the fleet, with aircrew worries about their rescue being set at ease with the knowledge of what had been accomplished elsewhere to rescue those shot down in enemy territory.

The first submarine rescue happened on October 7, 1943 during the first fast carrier raid on Wake Island when USS *Skate* (SS-305) rescued Lieutenant (jg) Richard G. Johnson. The submarine went on to rescue an additional five airmen during the same operation, proving the value of the concept of submarines as "lifeguards" for airmen. Between October 1943 and the end of the war nearly two years later, 86 different US submarines rescued 520 US and Allied airmen. USS *Tigrone* (SS-419) set the rescue record with 31 on several lifeguard missions, including the last pilot rescued during the war, who was picked up off the Japanese mainland on August 14, 1945.

One of the most dramatic rescues involved the famous submarine USS *Harder* (SS-257) and her legendary captain, Lieutenant Commander Samuel D. "Sam" Dealey in the rescue of Ensign John D. Galvin of VF-8 at Woleai Atoll on April 1, 1944.

Harder's fourth war patrol was conducted as she sailed from Pearl Harbor to join the submarine forces at Fremantle, Australia. Since she was passing through the western Carolines, *Harder* was assigned as the lifeguard submarine covering the strikes by Task Force 58 against the island of Woleai. On April 1, 1944, *Harder* was notified that a naval aviator, Ensign John Galvin of Fighting 8 from *Bunker Hill* (CV-17), had been shot down and was in a raft just off Tangaulap, a small enemy-held island just west of Woleai Atoll. With Galvin's squadron mates providing air cover, Dealey brought *Harder* in close ashore on the surface. There was no aviator in a raft to be found, but lookouts spotted a reclining figure on the beach in dark clothing. As it turned out, this was Ensign Galvin, who was injured from the bailout and exhausted from being buffeted by the merciless sea, and had been tossed inside the reef and close to shore by the winds and waves where he ended up on the beach and passed out. Awakened by a low-flying American plane that dropped him a message, Galvin looked out and saw *Harder* approaching beyond the reef. As he later related, "They had no reason to think I was who they were looking for. My green G-suit looked nearly black from the water, and my face looked darker than it was due to all the dried blood on it from my having been washed over the sharp coral reef."

Galvin's flying mates overhead were running low on gas and would soon have to return to *Bunker Hill*, leaving *Harder* without air cover. Dealey radioed Spruance on his flagship: "Prolong air attack and provide air cover and we will effect the rescue."

By now it was obvious the "Zoomie" on the beach might not be able to get out to the reef, and that another way of rescue had to be found. Dealey slowly approached the booming surf as it struck the coral, maneuvering cautiously as the sonar operator reported the sea bottom was too close to measure. When the men in the forward torpedo room heard the sound of the bow scraping against rocks, Dealey put *Harder* aground against the reef and held her in position stern-on to the waves using the screws in a masterful display of seamanship. Ashore, a Japanese machine gun opened up. Dealey himself suffered a near-miss that parted his hair, fired by one sniper in the treeline.

Deciding that he would have to send a rubber boat into the lagoon to reach Galvin, Dealey called for volunteers to man the craft. Everyone volunteered, and Lieutenant Sam Logan, the torpedo officer, Seaman 1/c J.W. Thomason, and Machinist's Mate 2/c Francis X. Ryan were chosen. Once the boat was brought out on deck and inflated, it was discovered there were no oars. The men in the raft would have to paddle with their hands under Japanese fire. At noon, they went over *Harder*'s side and began swimming the boat toward the beach 1,200 yards away, laying a line behind them to the ship so they could be towed back. Once they reached shallow water, Logan stayed with the boat while Thomason and Ryan made their way to the beach.

In the meantime, another aircraft dropped a raft to Galvin, who inflated it and got back into the water, where he ended up drifting farther away on the tide. Finally, Logan and Ryan managed to grab Galvin's raft and start pushing it toward the submarine.

A Curtiss SOC-3 Seagull then managed to complicate the rescue when it landed in the lagoon to help and ended up taxiing over the line to *Harder*, cutting it and stranding rescued and rescuers inside the reef. Thomason was the only one with the strength left to swim back 800 yards to *Harder* to get another line, though he was exhausted when he arrived. Gunner's Mate 1/c Freeman Paquet, Jr., then volunteered to swim back to the men in the lagoon with the fresh line. After a two-hour ordeal, the crew aboard *Harder* were able to haul their shipmates and the rescued Galvin through the reef and back aboard ship. Galvin spent the next 33 days aboard *Harder*, where he spent the first week decoding messages, after which he stood watch as Junior Officer of the Deck. He would be one of very few men qualified to wear both the naval aviator's Wings of Gold and the silver Submarine Combat Pin.

A month after *Harder*'s incredible performance, one of the all-time legendary events of submarine and aviation history happened during the second series of strikes against Truk at the end of April.

Great things were expected of USS *Tang* (SS-306) from the day she was commissioned at the Mare Island Navy Yard on October 15, 1943. Her commanding officer was the already-legendary Lieutenant Commander Richard H. "Dick" O'Kane, who had made a name for himself as XO of USS *Wahoo* (SS-238) working in partnership with his commanding officer Lieutenant Commander Dudley W. "Mush" Morton, one of the truly great submarine commanders of the war on any side. *Wahoo* became the most successful Pacific Fleet submarine of the first two years of the war. Sadly, four days before *Tang* ran up her commissioning pennant, a Japanese antisubmarine patrol aircraft attacked a submarine in La Perouse Strait at the time *Wahoo* was to return from her second patrol into the dangerous Sea of Japan. (On October 31, 2006, the US Navy declared that the sunken Gato-class submarine found earlier that year 213 feet down in the strait was *Wahoo*; she had been sunk by a direct hit from an aerial bomb on the conning tower.) Kane saw himself as Morton's avenger over the eight months he and *Tang* fought the Japanese.

Joining the Pacific Fleet submarine force at Pearl Harbor in January 1944, *Tang*'s first patrol had set a record for success, sinking five ships and wiping out a Japanese convoy. She began her second patrol on March 16, assigned to cover the Palaus, Davao Gulf, and Truk Atoll. She had only spotted five ships she was unable to attack before she received orders to act as lifeguard submarine for the second Truk strike. She arrived off the atoll on April 29 and the first day of strikes on Truk came the next day. *Tang* was busy from the opening shots.

At 1025 hours on April 30, she received the first report of a downed plane and headed for the reported position 2 miles off Fourup Island at emergency speed. *Tang*'s logbook recorded, "Bombers working over Palau and Ollan Islands were most reassuring, and with numerous fighters to guide us, we were able to locate the life raft promptly about four miles west of its reported position." At 1156 hours, the deck crew pulled Avenger crew Lieutenant (jg) S. Scammell, Aviation Machinist's Mate 2/c J.D. Gendron, and Aviation Radioman 2/c H.B. Gemmell on board.

Answering another call at 1559 hours, *Tang* proceeded at emergency speed to round Kuop Island and reach a life raft outside the reef on the east side of Truk:

Fifteen minutes later, however, a second raft was reported to the north of us in the approximate position of our first recovery. As the latter could be reached during daylight, we returned at emergency speed to this position two miles east of Ollan and one mile off the reef. The hovering bomber and two fighters seemed perturbed that we wouldn't follow them over to the actual position, some five miles inside the reef.

After a 20-minute search with periscopes and from atop the shears did not locate the raft, *Tang* headed south again to return to the second rescue location.

The covering aircraft had now been recalled, leaving the men aboard *Tang* "a bit naked." Rather than submerge to pass Ollan Island, O'Kane ordered the 4-inch deck gun manned and *Tang* opened fire on the gun emplacements on the southwest end of the island:

The first shell burst nicely low in the trees intended to conceal the emplacements. Fired 20 rounds of H.E. and commented when retiring, quite agreeably amazed at the ability of the 4" to stay on the target. At 3,500 yards trained in and turned tail, a bit prematurely, however, for the Nips crawled out of their holes and let fly at us. Their first splash was about 1,000 yards short, the second we didn't spot.

Tang submerged for 40 minutes, then surfaced and proceeded toward the east side of Truk at emergency speed. At 2143 hours:

From position six miles ease of Feinif Island on the eastern reef, commenced zigzag search to the southwest at ten knots. Fired green Very stars every fifteen minutes at the turns and midway of each leg, hoping for any sort of answer from one of the rafts. The only reply, sighted on some occasions, was a series of red or white lights in the neighborhood of Uman Island, which changed bearing rapidly as if flashed along a runway.

The log noted on May 1 that "One of the pilots we recovered the following day had sighted our stars, but was afraid to answer them."

At 0330 hours on May 1, *Tang* headed east to position herself for the second day's strike, 10 miles closer to the atoll than on the previous day. At 0600 hours, lookouts sighted the conning tower of a Japanese submarine proceeding south around Kuop Island from Otta pass. *Tang* submerged and commenced her approach:

> Tracked him on straight course 180 at 12 knots. When the generated range was 3,000 yards and angle on the bow 30 starboard, suddenly lost sound contact. Took a quick look to observe our bombers and fighters overhead and to confirm our fears that the enemy had dived. Dropped to 150 feet and rigged for silent running, but was unable to regain contact. Headed southwest for an hour at standard speed.

Tang surfaced and proceeded toward the reported raft position from the evening before. Since aviators operated on a policy of "attack first and ask questions later" whenever a submarine was spotted, the crew spread a large American flag on the deck to identify *Tang* as friendly to any aviators who spotted her.

At dawn, Lieutenant (jg) John Burns was launched in his VO-6 OS2U-3 "Kingfisher" observation seaplane from the battleship *North Carolina*, along with another Kingfisher flown by Lieutenant John J. Dowdle, Jr. Their mission was to search for downed airmen from the previous day's strikes. At around 0800 hours, a pilot in a raft was spotted by Lieutenant Dowdle; it was Lieutenant (jg) Ralph Kauze. Dowdle and Burns circled the downed flier while they waited for the arrival of *Tang*.

When it appeared the submarine had been delayed, Dowdle landed to bring the pilot aboard. While they were on the water, a gust of wind capsized the Kingfisher, putting Dowdle and his radioman, Aviation Radioman 2/c Robert E. Hill, into the water when a float was knocked off. Burns and his radioman, Aviation Radioman 2/c Class Aubrey J. Gill, spotted Dowdle and Hill, and Burns set his Kingfisher down in 5-foot seas. He taxied over to the damaged Kingfisher, where Dowdle and his crewman had managed to retrieve their raft, and Hill threw a line to them, then another to Kauze, whom they had originally come to rescue. Burns advanced his throttle

Wasp (CV-7) was sunk on September 15, 1942, by the Japanese submarine I-19. Her LSO was David McCampbell, later the Navy's Ace of Aces. (Naval History and Heritage Command)

Enterprise (CV-6) under attack by Japanese aircraft at the Battle of Santa Cruz, October 25, 1942. (NARA)

The light carrier *Langley* (CVL-27) steams in formation with *Ticonderoga* (CV-14). (NARA)

Princeton (CVL-23) under way in 1944. (US Navy National Museum of Naval Aviation)

Intrepid (CV-11) was badly damaged twice by the Japanese but came back to combat both times. Today she is a floating museum in New York Harbor. (Naval History and Heritage Command)

Lexington (CV-16), named in honor of the carrier lost at the Battle of the Coral Sea, was known as "the blue ghost of the Japanese coast" for her dark blue camouflage, and the number of times the Japanese claimed to have sunk her. She was Admiral Marc Mitscher's flagship during the two greatest naval battles of history, the Battle of the Philippine Sea and the Battle of Leyte Gulf. (NARA)

Six great carriers together at Ulithi (from foreground to background): *Wasp, Yorktown, Hornet, Hancock, Ticonderoga,* and *Lexington*. (NARA)

An SBD-5 of VB-16 flies past the battleship *Washington. Lexington* (CV-16) is in the background. (US Navy National Museum of Naval Aviation)

A Curtiss SB2C-1C Helldiver of VB-2 damaged by anti-aircraft fire loses its engine after a hard landing aboard *Hornet* (CV-12). (NARA)

Airedales aboard *Hornet* (CV-12) sweat under the tropic sun while respotting F6F-5 Hellcats of VF-2 for launch. (NARA)

Helldivers from *Yorktown*, c. 1944. (Naval History and Heritage Command)

TBM Avengers from *Essex*'s VT-4, January 1945. (NARA)

Admiral Chester W. Nimitz, CINCPAC, awards the Navy Cross to Doris Miller, Steward's Mate 1/c, aboard a US Navy warship in Pearl Harbor, May 27, 1942. (Naval History and Heritage Command)

Shown from left to right are: Admiral Raymond A. Spruance, Vice Admiral Marc A. Mitscher, Fleet Admiral Chester W. Nimitz and Vice Admiral Willis A. Lee, Jr. (Naval History and Heritage Command)

Admiral William Halsey Confers with Task Force 38 commander Vice Admiral John S. McCain, at Halsey's desk on board the Third Fleet flagship *New Jersey* (BB-62), December 1944. (NARA)

Vice Admiral Marc Mitscher, commander of Task Force 58. (NARA)

Rear Admiral J.J. "Jocko" Clark was the most aggressive carrier commander in the Fast Carrier Task Force. (NARA)

Air Group 15 commander, David McCampbell, US Navy Ace of Aces. (NARA)

SBD Douglases of VB-6 and VF-5 aboard *Enterprise* are spotted for take-off towards Wake Island, February 24, 1942. (NARA)

Air Group 10 commander Jimmy Flatley ready for take-off from *Yorktown* (CV-10) during strikes against Marcus Island, August 1943. (NARA)

Lieutenant Edward H. "Butch" O'Hare and VF-3 squadron commander John S. Thach at Oahu air base, spring 1942. (NARA)

Lieutenant Commander Edward H. "Butch" O'Hare was the first US Navy ace of the Pacific War. He was lost in a "friendly fire" incident in the Gilberts in November 1944 attempting a night interception of Japanese Betty bombers. (NARA)

Harder (SS-257) stuck against the reef at Woleai. The Curtiss SOC-3 Seagull has just taxied over and snapped the lifeline to the men in the lagoon attempting to rescue Ensign John Galvin of VF-8. (US Navy National Museum of Naval Aviation)

Tang's Commanding Officer, Lieutenant Commander Richard H. O'Kane (center), poses with the 22 aircrewmen his vessel rescued off Truk during the raids on 1944. (Naval History and Heritage Command)

SBD-5 Dauntless of *Lexington*'s VB-16 over Wake Island on October 5, 1943. (NARA)

Japanese warships refueling at Simpson Harbor are attacked. This image was captured by P.T. Barnett, who died in an air battle shortly afterwards. (US Navy National Museum of Naval Aviation)

An F6F-3 Hellcat of VF-16 ready for launch from *Lexington* (CV-16) during the Gilberts Invasion, November 1943. *Yorktown* (CV-10) is in the background. (NARA)

After crash landing on *Enterprise* on November 10, 1943, Ensign Byron Johnson escaped without significant injury. (NARA)

A Japanese bomb explodes off *Essex*'s port quarter during the Japanese air attack following the Rabaul raid of November 11, 1943. (Getty Images)

A VF-12 Hellcat starts its take-off run aboard *Saratoga* (CV-3) during the Rabaul raid of November 5, 1943. Grumman TBF-1 Avengers await preparation for launch behind. (Library of Congress)

Above The pilot of a VB-12 Douglas SBD-5 Dauntless revs his engine to full power for take-off from *Saratoga* during the Rabaul strike of November 5, 1943. (Getty Images)

Right The flak-damaged elevator of a VB-9 SBD-5 Dauntless upon return from a Rabaul strike of November 11, 1943. (Getty Images)

Ensign Jim Duffy recalled that his launch by catapult from *Hornet*'s hangar deck, which was required of each pilot in VF-15 by Captain Miles Browning in December 1943, was "the single most terrifying event of my entire naval career." (US Navy National Museum of Naval Aviation)

Pilots pleased about their victory during the Marshall Islands attack aboard *Lexington* (CV-16), after shooting down 17 out of 20 Japanese planes heading for Tarawa, November 1943. Left to right, they are: Ens J. Seyfferle, Lt (jg) A.R. Fizalkowski, Lt (jg) A.L. Frendberg, LCDR Paul D. Buie (Commanding Officer), Ens John W. Bartol, Lt (jg) Dean D. Whitmore, Lt (jg) Francis M. Fleming, Lt (jg) C.B. Birkholm, Lt (jg) Sven Rolfsen, Jr. plus two others not named in the group to right of LCDR Buie. The planes are F6F-3 Hellcats. (NARA)

The Orote Peninsula on Guam. Naval aviators would find the Japanese antiaircraft fire here particularly dangerous during the Marianas invasion. (NARA)

Hornet (CV-12) arrives in Pearl Harbor with Air Group 15 aboard, March 1944. (NARA)

Left David McCampbell as the newly appointed AG-15 CAG, on the wing of his first F6F-3 Hellcat, "Monsoon Maiden," Maui, Hawaii, April 1944. (Singer Collection via Philip Downs)

Below The Mobile Fleet's Carrier Division 3 maneuvers under attack by US Navy aircraft on the afternoon of June 20, 1944. (NARA)

Japanese shipping in Manila Harbor during the first US air strike, September 20, 1944. (Naval History and Heritage Command)

Downed airmen aboard a Kingfisher floatplane await rescue by *Tang*, May 1, 1944. (NARA)

Crewmen dive off USS *Hornet* (CV-12) while anchored at Majuro Atoll fleet anchorage, May 1944. (NARA)

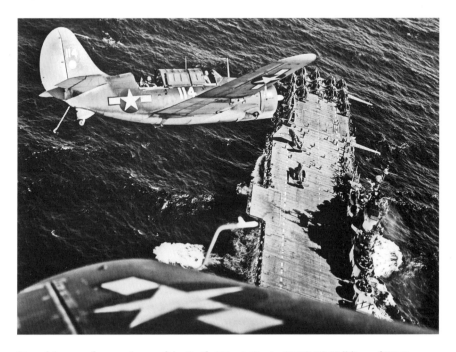

One of the most famous photos of the Pacific War: A Curtiss SB2C-1C Helldiver of VB-2 over *Hornet* (CV-12) during the Marianas invasion, June 1944. (NARA)

SB2C-1C Helldivers en route to their targets on Saipan, June 11, 1944. (Getty Images)

Left Lieutenant (jg) Alex Vraciu raises his hands to indicate the six Vals he shot down on June 19, 1944. (NARA)

Below *Lexington* (CV-16), as photographed by the gunner of an SBD-5 Dauntless just after take-off on the Mission Beyond Darkness, June 20, 1944. (NARA)

Bottom A Japanese B6N2 Tenzan (Jill) torpedo bomber attacks *Essex* on October 14, 1944, off Formosa. (Singer Collection via Philip Downs)

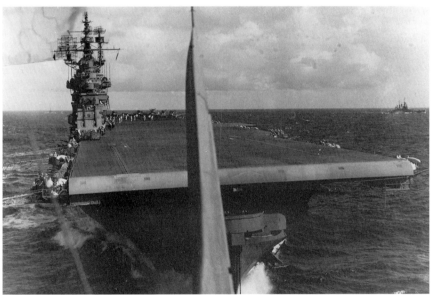

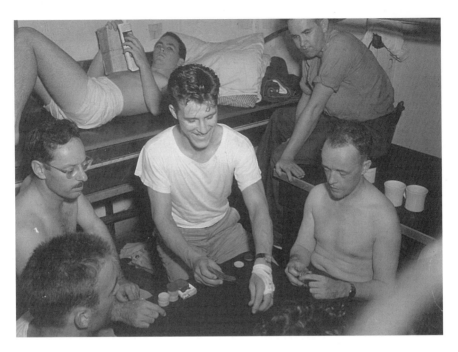

AP Photographer Joe Rosental (left, with glasses), later famous for taking "The Flag Raising On Iwo Jima" was aboard *Essex* for the AG-15 tour. Left to right are: photoplane pilot Art Singer (extreme left forward), Joe Rosenthal, VF-15 pilots "Sto-Baby" Stuart, Paul Robbins, Bill Hicks and "Tommy" Thompson, playing poker in the *Essex* photo lab on October 22, 1944. (Singer Collection via Philip Downs)

Princeton (CVL-23) seen on fire from *Essex*, October 24, 1944. (Singer Collection via Philip Downs)

Princeton explodes after being scuttled by torpedoes fired by *Reno*, October 24, 1944. (NARA)

Future 41st President of the United States Lieutenant (jg) George H.W. Bush of VT-51 prepares to be brought aboard *Finback* (SS-231) after being shot down over Chichi Jima on September 2, 1944. (Getty Images)

Lieutenant Art Singer (right) and two other VF-15 pilots prepare for the mission against the Japanese carriers, October 25, 1944. (Singer Collection via Philip Downs)

Gambier Bay (CVE-73) under fire from the Japanese cruiser *Chitose* during the Battle off Samar, October 25, 1944. (NARA)

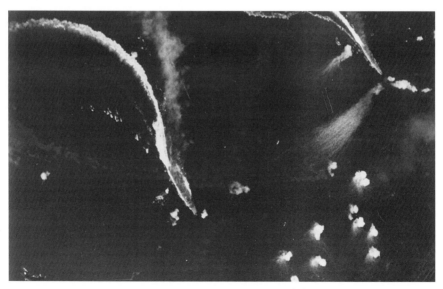

The Japanese carrier *Zuikaku*, last survivor of the Pearl Harbor attackers (left), maneuvers under attacks from Task Force 38 on October 25, 1944. Her sinking marked the final Navy revenge for Pearl Harbor. (NARA)

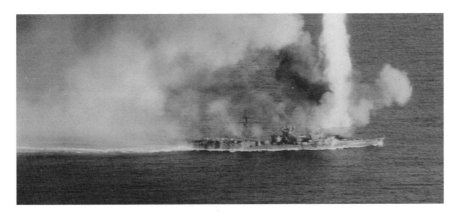

Zuikaku under attack from Air Group 15 on October 25, 1944. (Singer Collection via Philip Downs)

The Japanese aircraft carrier *Zuiho* after several hits by Task Force 38 planes during the battle off Cape Engano, October 25, 1944. (Singer Collection via Philip Downs)

The Japanese Battleship/Aircraft Carrier *Ise* under attack by SB2C Helldivers of Air Group 15, October 25, 1944. (Naval History and Heritage Command)

West Virginia (BB-48) fires a salvo from her 12 16-inch guns during the Battle of Surigao Strait, October 25, 1944, during the last battle line naval engagement in history. (NARA)

Ticonderoga (CV-14) at sea off the Philippines on November 5, 1944, just prior to her first strike against the Japanese. (Naval History & Heritage Command)

Above A Japanese destroyer burns while sinking off Leyte, after being attacked by American planes, November 11, 1944. The destroyers *Hamanami*, *Naganami*, *Shimakaze* and *Wakatsuki* were sunk on that day in Ormoc Bay. (US Navy National Museum of Naval Aviation)

Left VB-15 Commander Jim Mini briefs the final Air Group 15 mission to Manila Bay as VF-15 photoplane pilot Lieutenant Art Singer looks on. November 13, 1944. (Singer Collection via Philip Downs)

A Japanese *kamikaze* attack hits *Intrepid* (CV-11), November 25, 1944. (Naval History and Heritage Command)

On the next day, November 26, the crew of *Intrepid* had the somber task of burying at sea the officers and men who perished in the *kamikaze* attack. (NARA)

slowly and began towing the rafts farther away from shore, out of range of Japanese guns.

At 0828 hours, *Tang* arrived on the scene. The logbook recorded that the submarine:

> Proceeded at emergency speed for life raft reported two and a half miles southwest of our favorite Ollan Island. Before we reached the scene, a float plane from the *North Carolina* capsized in the cross chop in the attempt to rescue. The other *North Carolina* plane made a precarious landing and on our arrival was towing both rafts clear of the island. This action was most helpful, for we expected competition from Ollan, and nearby fighters were already strafing the gun emplacements for us.

Burns taxied over to the submarine and off-loaded the rescued airmen before taking off again. *Tang* took a few minutes to sink Dowdle's damaged Kingfisher with her 20mm antiaircraft guns. Once airborne, Burns spotted three more rafts in the lagoon and radioed their positions to *Tang*, which set off for the rescue.

En route to Burns's location, the submarine received further reports of downed airmen and maneuvered to rescue them, which delayed their arrival at the position Burns had reported:

> At this time, a smoking torpedo bomber was spotted hitting the water about seven miles to the east. Proceeded down the bearing at emergency speed, and opened fire on nearby Ollan as we passed. They had removed the trees intended to camouflage their position, evidently feeling it was no longer a secret. It gave us an unobstructed point of aim, however, and our 4" H.E. with a few common sandwiched in, supported by strafing fighters and topped off with two bombers, must have discouraged them for they did not return any fire.

On the way to where Burns had reported finding downed fliers, at 1004 hours *Tang* sighted a life raft and survivors ahead under circling fighters. At 1020 hours, Avenger crew Commander A.R. Matter, Aviation Radioman 2/c J.J. Lenahan, and Aviation Machinist's Mate 2/c H.A. Tompson were on board:

> Proceeded at emergency speed to round Kuop to reach three life rafts reported off the eastern reef. As our track took us close by our submarine

contact of the morning, we requested and promptly got air coverage. Blown high, with safety, negative and the fuel group dry, and even our Fairbanks-Morse smoking a bit, we rolled through this spot at 21 knots fairly confident that the Jap would get no more than a fleeting glimpse.

Worried by *Tang's* delayed arrival and not wanting to leave the men he had found adrift so close to the enemy-held shore, Burns decided to land. He picked up F6F Hellcat pilot Lieutenant (jg) Robert T. Barber. Further strikes had now arrived over the atoll, and Burns kept an eye out for further rescues. He didn't have long to wait as first one and then a second Avenger ditched nearby, with their crews scrambling into their life rafts. Burns taxied over to their position and Gill threw them a tow line, but as Burns applied power, the rafts were in danger of being swamped so he slowed to minimum power to keep them away from nearby islands. *Tang* arrived at Burns' location at 1328 hours. On the way they had gotten a call about other downed aviators. When Burns assured them he could remain where he was, *Tang* headed off:

> Followed our escorting planes to a raft off Mesegon Island in the bight between Kuop and Truk. As we thoroughly expected to be driven down, rigged a free running line and life ring to the SD [radar] mast for towing the raft clear while submerged, but our strafing escorts evidently discouraged any opposition.

At 1345 hours, Lieutenant H.E. Hill was recovered. Things were still very busy:

> Then headed for a fighter pilot reported in the water just off the eastern reef of Kuop. By the time of our arrival planes had dropped a rubber boat to him, but he was too weak to do more than climb aboard. After pulling perhaps our most grateful passenger aboard, Lieutenant (jg) J.G. Cole, backed upwind clear of the reef and headed for the waiting float plane at emergency speed.

Burns was now in trouble. As the wind came up, he had to use more power, which swamped the rafts. The fighter pilot and the two three-man Avenger crews climbed onto the little Kingfisher, positioning themselves on the wings and clinging to the fuselage. When Burns attempted to taxi away from the islands into the open sea, the Kingfisher began to spring leaks as the result of the pounding of the waves against the main pontoon and tail, and the airplane began to list to one side, threatening to capsize.

Burns gave up trying to taxi and held enough power to keep the airplane aimed into the waves. Just as it seemed the Kingfisher was about to capsize and sink, *Tang* arrived:

> No difficulty was experienced in bringing the following on board: Lieutenant R.S. Nelson; Lt (jg) R. Barber; Lt (jg) J.A. Burns; Ensign C.L. Farrell; J. Livingston, ARM1c; R.W. Gruebel, AMM2c; J. Hranek, ARM2c; O.F. Tabrun, AMM2c; and R. Hill, ARM2c. The action of Lt (jg) Burns, in making the rescue possible by deliberately placing himself in as precarious a position as any of the downed personnel will be made the subject of a special report.

After sending Burns and Gill below so they would not have to witness it, O'Kane ordered the Kingfisher sunk by gunfire at 1515 hours. *Tang*'s work was far from over:

> Proceeded at emergency speed to round Kuop to the last reported raft south of Ollan Island. As all planes were recalled as of 1630, and we could not reach the raft until sunset, requested two night fighters to assist in locating it. Our passage through the area of our morning contact was not quite as comfortable without air coverage, but again 21 knots took us through in a hurry. The night fighters joined us at sunset as we were approaching the last reported position three and a half miles south of Ollan, and immediately commenced their search. Fifteen minutes later one of the fighters circled then fired several red Very stars four miles northwest of us. Closed at emergency speed, spotting the raft from atop the shears, as it was now too dark for periscopes. At 1830 hours, with Lieutenant D. Kirkpatrick and R.L. Bentley, AOM2c, on board, dismissed the planes and commenced slow speed search west of the atoll.

By sunset on May 1, 1944, *Tang* had picked up 22 of the 35 aircrew shot down in the Truk strikes. It was the all-time record for lifeguard rescues. As one *Tang* crewman remembered, "We had a crew of 97, and with 22 more on board, talk about 'hot bunking'!"

When *Tang* docked at the Pearl Harbor Submarine Base with her 22 guests filling the after deck of the conning tower, Admiral Nimitz was there along with Admiral Charles Lockwood, commander of the Pacific submarine force, to welcome them. All 97 members of the *Tang* crew were awarded the Air Medal for their effort, while O'Kane was awarded the Navy Cross, as was Kingfisher pilot John Burns. Headlines on the front pages of newspapers across the country and a full article in *Life* magazine followed.

The next thrilling submarine rescue came seven weeks later, during the invasion of the Marianas. On June 13, 1944, Air Group 2 aboard *Hornet* was heavily engaged in strikes against Japanese installations on Guam. Normally two strikes a day were flown, but this day a third was requested. Air Group 2 Commander Arnold asked for volunteers. Among those who stepped forward was VF-2's Ensign Don Brandt, who had joined the squadron on Hawaii just as they deployed aboard *Hornet* back in March.

Arnold led the mission, with Brandt as his wingman. Brandt checked his watch as they approached Orote Point: 1013 hours. "It was 13 minutes after the hour, and I was at 13,000 feet in Hellcat number 13. As we pushed over in a bombing run, antiaircraft fire intensified." Arnold recalled, "Ensign Brandt's Hellcat was hit almost immediately. As he opened his canopy to bail out, I called to him not to do so, since I didn't think he could land in the water from his position, and parachuting onto shore would mean certain capture and almost certain death at the hands of the Japanese, who we had been briefed were taking no prisoners." As Brandt remembered, "I dove to get away from the flak, increasing speed to 360mph. I was afraid I couldn't get out at that speed, but when I unfastened my harness and slid open the canopy, wind pressure sucked me out immediately." Flung upside down when the parachute opened because one riser was jammed beneath the backstrap, Brandt struck the water head first and went under. "I had to pull my knife and slash at the harness to escape to the surface. The 'chute billowed and pulled away, taking my raft with it, then sank as it became waterlogged."

At 1014 hours, Arnold called the lifeguard, *Stingray* (SS-186), which was operating only a few miles offshore, to request they pick up his wingman. He then ordered the dive bombers to hit the shore positions, where there were several large guns that could endanger the submarine. A division of Hellcats strafed a Japanese boat that tried to set out from shore to capture Brandt.

In the water, Brandt managed to inflate his Mae West, and discovered that the wind was pushing him away from shore. "I was one unhappy Ensign when I saw the planes turn back to the carrier." The Japanese didn't fire at him during the next hour as he drifted in the bay, waiting for his rescuers to arrive.

At 1115 hours, another *Hornet* strike force appeared overhead, with SB2Cs going after Japanese warships in the harbor. Helldiver pilot Lieutenant (jg) LeMoyne spotted Brandt and abandoned his attack to drop a large raft to the pilot. *Stingray*'s captain, Lieutenant Commander Sam Loomis, learned from the radio reports that Brandt was still within range of the guns. The submarine continued her submerged run toward the bay.

Brandt, now alone in the middle of Agana Harbor, expected the Japanese would soon come out in a boat to get him. "I knew if the sub was coming it couldn't pick me up, being this close in to shore and in the middle of the harbor." He continued paddling toward the harbor entrance.

Fortunately, rescue was possible since the Marianas, being the result of a collision of two tectonic plates, have a steep drop-off to the Marianas Trench, the deepest place on earth. Because of this, *Stingray* could enter Agana Harbor directly while submerged.

The crew could hear the sound of exploding shells as Captain Loomis raised the periscope and moved slowly toward the life raft. Brandt paddled away, much to Loomis' frustration. "I suddenly noticed this periscope rise out of the water about two feet high heading right at me and I thought they were going to hit me, so I tried to get out of the way." Brandt paddled away again when *Stingray* made a second pass.

Loomis checked the time: 1430 hours. Darkness was a long time away and he could not surface this close to shore in daylight, nor could *Stingray* remain much longer in such shallow water with Japanese air or surface attack an imminent possibility. Loomis had to get the pilot now or leave him, and the only way to do so was to get him to grab the periscope. He ordered another pass.

In his patrol report, Loomis wrote: "1453: Pilot missed the boat again. On this try he showed the first signs of attempting to reach periscope. Maybe shellfire has made him think that a ride on a periscope might be all right after all. I am getting disgusted, plus a stiff neck and a blind eye. 1500: Heard another shell."

At 1516 hours, Loomis recorded, "Fourth try. Ran into pilot with periscope and he hung on!" Brandt recalled, "It slowed to a stop, and I paddled over. I took the life rope on the raft and looped it around the periscope, and we started moving toward the harbor entrance! I later learned the submarine ran in reverse all the way since there wasn't room in the harbor to turn around."

In the meantime, Arnold had quickly refueled and rearmed. He later recalled,

We returned about 1500 and spotted Don still in his raft in middle of the harbor. We commenced runs on the beach to keep their heads down. I was cussing out the skipper of the submarine for his lack of action, then I flew low and realized Don was moving through the water a lot faster than the wind could carry him. I made a second pass and spotted the silhouette of the submarine under him. They were towing him out of the harbor!

Arnold and the others circled to protect the submarine and Brandt. Loomis reported:

Towed him for one hour during which he frantically signaled for us to let up. His hand was cut badly and it must have been tough going hanging onto the bitter end of the line with one hand while bumping along the whitecaps. 1611: Lowered towing scope, watching pilot's amazed expression with other scope. 1613: Surfaced. 1618: Picked up Ensign Donald Carol Brandt, USNR [US Naval Reserve], suffering from deep wound in left hand. Glad to finally get him aboard. He said that during first and third approaches he was afraid periscopes were going to hit him and he tried to get out of the way and come in astern of me. He's taken quite a running, and taken it well. We're on speaking terms now, but after the third approach I was ready to make him captain of the head.

Brandt and his friend Lieutenant John Searcy, who had been shot down and rescued the day before, were reunited aboard *Stingray*. Over the next 30 days, they would have quite an odyssey in returning to the group. Dropped off at Eniwetok at the end of June, they were able to convince authorities not to return them all the way to Hawaii, and hitchhiked their way to Majuro, then on to Saipan in an adventure that lasted over three weeks. "We climbed out of the airplane we'd flown in from Majuro there at the airfield on Saipan, and saw an Avenger from *Hornet*, which had flown in to pick up mail. They were happy to fly us out to the ship."

Perhaps the most famous of the 520 airmen rescued by American submarines during the war was future 41st United States President Lieutenant (jg) George H.W. Bush, rescued by USS *Finback* (SS-230) on September 2, 1944. Bush was, at age 19, the youngest naval aviator on operations, serving in Torpedo 51 aboard USS *San Jacinto* (CVL-30), known throughout the fast carrier task force as the "flagship of the Texas Navy." The air strikes of early September were the last against the Bonin Islands until the 1945 invasion of Iwo Jima, flown in support of the coming invasion of Peleliu scheduled for September 15.

Inbound to the target in his TBM-1C Avenger, named "Barbara" for his fiancée, Bush kept control when the airplane was hit by antiaircraft fire, and continued his attack, dropping his four 500-pound bombs on a radio-communications installation. As he pulled out of the attack, antiaircraft fire riddled the plane and set it on fire. Bush was able to get a mile out to sea and successfully bail out, but his two crewmates, Lieutenant (jg) William White, an intelligence officer there to make first-hand observations of the strike, and Aviation Radioman 2/c John Delaney, did not get out of the burning bomber. Unfortunately, this was not an uncommon event with in-flight emergencies involving the Avenger, which stemmed from the design of the airplane. White, riding in the dorsal gun turret, had to climb down out of the turret into Delaney's radio compartment, from where both men would bail out through the crew door on the right side of the fuselage. With the plane on fire, the time it took to accomplish all that was too long to allow a successful escape. Other aircraft saw one man – most likely Delaney – exit out the rear hatch but his parachute failed to deploy. As pilot, Bush had only to push open his sliding canopy, climb out onto the wing and jump.

Bush landed offshore of the island but in sight of the defenders, who were notorious for their brutal treatment of prisoners. Fortunately, the veteran *Finback* was assigned as lifeguard for the strike. Having departed Majuro Submarine Base on August 16 for her tenth war patrol, *Finback* was commanded by Lieutenant Commander Russell Williams, Jr., and had already been successful as a lifeguard, when Avenger pilot Lieutenant Thomas R. Keene and his crewmen, Aviation Radioman 3/c J.R. Doherty and Aviation Ordnanceman 3/c J.T. Stovell, flying from USS *Franklin* (CV-13) were rescued on September 1.

It took *Finback* two hours to get to Bush after being informed of the loss. Fortunately, other aircraft from Air Group 51 had remained overhead and strafed the Japanese boat that put out from Chichi Jima to attempt his capture. Bush was pulled aboard from his rubber raft by Torpedoman 1/c Donnet Kohler. The following day *Finback* rescued Lieutenant (jg) James Beckman, a Hellcat pilot from *Enterprise*. After their rescue, the airmen became "shipmates" as *Finback* continued her patrol for the next 30 days. During their time onboard, the fliers stood standard watches as JOOD. During this time *Finback* sank the cargo ships *Hakuun Maru* and *Hassho Maru* on September 11.

In a letter to his mother, Bush wrote, "I am now standing Junior Officer of the Deck watches and I really love them. I am not in any way a qualified submariner as you can well imagine, but am armed with a pair of binoculars …" On October 2, *Finback* put in to Midway Island on her return to Pearl Harbor and dropped off her rescued fliers. Bush had an adventure similar to that experienced by Don Brandt in getting back to *San Jacinto*, which he caught up with two weeks later at Ulithi, in time to take part in the Battles of Leyte Gulf.

October 12, 1944 turned out to be the best and worst of days for Ensign Clarence L. "Spike" Borley, the youngest pilot in Fighting 15 aboard *Essex*. Target for the day was Formosa.

Twenty minutes after departure, Borley's division leader reported fuel pump failure and aborted with his wingman. Borley's section leader, Lieutenant (jg) Pigman, decided to continue. Over Formosa, the Hellcats got into a fight with a large formation of Japanese fighters. "I did not get into any dogfights, but rather I was able to see and hit four different airplanes without engaging in a fight." The result was the downing in quick succession of a Zeke, a Tojo, and two Oscars. Coupled with his victory scored two days before over Okinawa, he was the youngest American ace, having turned 20 the previous July 27.

Borley had a more difficult time ahead of him. He had to ditch his plane in the Formosa Strait after being hit by flak while strafing Japanese aircraft. Over the next four days he lost his food and water and became the only person ever to survive drifting through a typhoon in a one-man raft. By October 16, Borley was hallucinating and contemplating suicide out of fear he would be captured and reveal information he had of the coming Philippines invasion, but then in the late afternoon he was finally picked up by USS *Sawfish* (SS-276), 75 miles from where he had crashed. The submarine was 10 minutes from submerging and leaving when he was finally spotted. He worked his way on the submarine as a control room watch stander and then spent ten days hopscotching from Majuro to Pearl Harbor, arriving a day before Air Group 15 arrived home aboard *Bunker Hill*.

Rescues continued to the end of the war. *Tang's* impressive rescue record was challenged by *Tigrone* (SS-419). *Tigrone* was so new she was on her second war patrol at the end of May 1945 when she was assigned as a lifeguard off southern Honshu. On the afternoon of May 24, *Tigrone* received a call from a severely damaged PBY Catalina flying boat that had nosed into a wave trying to take off from a rescue operation. She took aboard 16 survivors: the crew of the Catalina and the now twice-rescued passengers. On May 25, she rescued a P-51D Mustang pilot based on Iwo Jima. On May 28 she rendezvoused with a Navy PB4Y-2 Liberator in distress that ditched 500 yards from the submarine; five crewmen were rescued. The next day she received orders to search for survivors of other downed aircraft. Night fell before they could be located but on May 30, despite 30-foot waves, the submarine at last located seven Army aviators who had been washed overboard from their raft several times during the night but had climbed back in each time. Heavy seas made the rescue difficult and time-consuming, but finally the exhausted fliers were brought aboard safely. On June 1, *Tigrone* arrived at Iwo Jima, where she dropped off 28 rescued "zoomies," a new lifeguard record.

Returning to patrol, *Tigrone* recovered a pilot on June 26 only six minutes from the time his parachute blossomed. Over the next two days, she took on rescued aviators from other submarines and headed for Guam, where she arrived on July 3, having rescued a total of 30 aviators.

One of the final rescues again involved Kingfishers from the *North Carolina*. On August 9, 1945, the day Nagasaki was bombed, the battleship was operating off the northern coast of the main Japanese home island of Honshu, shelling shore facilities in company with other battleships while the fast carriers flew air strikes. The weather was bad, with rain, fog, low ceilings, and poor visibility. By the end of the day, 11 pilots had been shot down in the area of Ominato, but it was impossible to launch rescue flights in the bad weather.

At dawn the next day, *North Carolina* launched her two Kingfishers to find the survivors, flown by Lieutenant (jg) Almon Oliver and Lieutenant Ralph Jacobs, escorted by four F6F-5 Hellcats and four F4U-1D Corsairs. The two flew alone in their planes so they could take rescued fliers aboard and return them to the fleet.

While headed in, they ironically took "friendly fire" from the submarine assigned as the lifeguard submarine, which could not undertake the rescue itself. As they flew on, they came under fire from Japanese batteries ashore. Oliver recalled, "Upon arrival in the area, one of the fighters spotted a pilot on the beach waving madly. By this time the destroyers at the naval base and antiaircraft fire from the airfield and the nearby Army bases opened up with a fury. There was a strong wind blowing into the beach and the surf was quite high." They had spotted Lieutenant (jg) Vernon Coumbe, who had spent a tense night ashore, 2 miles from a major Japanese naval base. Jacobs ordered Oliver to remain airborne and risked high winds and choppy surf to splash down. "There was a strong wind blowing into the beach and the surf was quite high." Automatic weapons fire whipped the air around the plane while shells hit the water nearby. Jacobs taxied near the beach as Oliver maneuvered evasively overhead. "From my vantage point it appeared that the pilot was having difficulty getting through the surf and the Japanese were firing what appeared to be 5-inch shells all around the plane on the water. After some time the plane started a take-off run, but soon it was porpoising badly and unable to get airborne. I then flew alongside and discovered there was no pilot aboard."

Coumbe had been unable to get through the surf to the plane. Jacobs had climbed out and then tried to throw a line to the pilot with one foot in the cockpit and one on the wing. In the midst of the attempt, he lost his balance due to the blast from a nearby shell and fell in the water, managing in that process to knock the throttle to full open. Oliver recalled:

> Now both pilots were waving wildly from the beach. I landed, taxied to the beach, blipped the engine and backed through the surf onto the beach. I told Jacobs to help the other pilot into the plane and I would send help for him. This idea didn't sit well and I soon had two very large and very wet people crammed into the back seat. How they managed to get into the cockpit, I'll never know, but the alternative was unacceptable at the moment.

The Kingfisher's center of gravity was so far aft with the two passengers in back that it "flew like a pregnant duck," burning fuel at a higher-than-normal rate. Oliver realized the difficulty he would have with navigation, weather, and fuel while flying in such an unbalanced condition, and decided to land at sea near the lifeguard sub. "After some deliberate thought, however, I decided to try to make it back to some ship in the fleet. Fortunately we picked up the ZB signal and made it back to the ship." Flying on for another two and a half hours, he managed to land alongside *North Carolina* with "one cup of gas" in the tank. It had been a very close call for all three as Oliver made the only rescue from Japan proper. Both Kingfisher pilots received the Distinguished Flying Cross for their efforts.

On July 31, 1945, *Tigrone* began her third and final war patrol. She arrived off Honshu on August 9 to learn that the Soviet Union had entered the Pacific War. On August 14, she made the final rescue of a naval aviator of the war, giving her the all-time record of 61 rescues as a lifeguard.

CHAPTER TEN

OPERATION FORAGER

A dmiral Koga's loss and the loss of the Gilberts and Marshalls, added to the destruction of Truk as a major Pacific base, led to profound changes in the leadership of the Imperial Japanese Navy and some modification of their plans to oppose further American offensives in the western Pacific. This would lead directly to the Battle of the Philippine Sea, the largest naval battle in history to that time. Koga's loss was officially noted when Admiral Soemu Toyoda was appointed Commander in Chief of the Imperial Japanese Navy.

In 1943, following the Battle of Santa Cruz, the Combined Fleet had been reorganized, with the Second Fleet composed of the surface warships – battleships and cruisers – under the command of Vice Admiral Nobutake Kondo, who was relieved in August 1943 by Vice Admiral Takeo Kurita. The Second Fleet was subordinate to and considered the screening force of Third Fleet, which contained the nine aircraft carriers in three carrier divisions.

Until May 1944, the Third Fleet was commanded by Vice Admiral Jisaburō Ozawa, who had replaced Pearl Harbor and Midway commander Admiral Chuichi Nagumo when he was removed from command following the Battle of Santa Cruz. In April 1944, the Navy had reorganized the Combined Fleet as the First Mobile Fleet, composed of Second and Third Fleets. With the death of Koga, Ozawa was moved up to command the Mobile Fleet, retaining command of Third Fleet with his flag aboard the brand-new carrier *Taihō*, an improved Shōkaku-class ship with the first armored flight deck on any Japanese carrier, which had only joined the fleet a little over two months earlier. This reorganization finally placed the carriers as the nucleus of the battle fleet. For the first time in the history of the Imperial Japanese Navy, a carrier admiral now controlled the battleships.

The Mobile Fleet faced two problems. First was the fact that the aviators assigned to the aircraft carriers were largely incapable of performing as carrier aviators, due to their low level of training. Second was the fact that the fleet was forced to base itself near its fuel supplies in Borneo and Sumatra. Throughout the spring of 1944, the Mobile Fleet moved between anchorages in Singapore, Borneo, and the southern Philippines base at Tawi-Tawi in the Sulu Sea. There was a need to keep the carriers near land-based airfields where the under-trained fliers might have the opportunity of further training before going aboard ship. There was an additional problem of the increasing capability of the American submarines, which were now finally equipped with a reliable torpedo, and were using this new capability to attack Japanese warships when found.

Of the nine Japanese aircraft carriers, only three – *Shōkaku*, *Zuikaku*, and *Taihō* – could be considered competitive with their American components. *Junyō* and *Hiyō*, the next two largest carriers, had been converted from passenger ship hulls in 1942 and were only capable of a top speed of 26 knots. Only the first three were fully capable of operating the new D4Y3 *Suisei* dive bomber ("Judy") and B6N2 *Tenzan* ("Jill"), both of which required a wind over the deck to launch that was more than *Junyō* and *Hiyō* could manage unless they were heading into a strong wind. The remaining four light carriers – *Ryūhō*, *Chitose*, *Chiyoda*, and *Zuihō* – were smaller and thus forced to continue to use the obsolete D3Y Val dive bomber and B5N2 Kate torpedo bomber. The failure of Japanese aircraft production meant that the older types were also found in the air groups aboard *Shōkaku*, *Zuikaku*, and *Taihō*.

More importantly, the new bombers were more difficult to fly, which created additional problems with the low level of training for their pilots. They had trouble flying these aircraft from land bases, let alone carriers, and had such a low level of training that they had no gunnery or navigation training and were forced to follow experienced leaders if they were to attack a target.

This lack of ability was demonstrated in late March 1944 when *Zuikaku* and *Shōkaku* had moved from Singapore to the Lingga Roads off Sumatra. The anchorage was near the Palembang oil fields and was spacious enough to allow the carriers to conduct flight operations while the narrow entrance protected them from American submarines. Moving from land bases to carrier decks resulted in a fearsome rise in operational losses. Flying the new bombers at low speed in a carrier approach was dangerous and many simply stalled out and fell into the ocean when turning to final approach due to failure of the pilot to maintain his speed. Many planes that managed to hit the deck failed to hook an arresting wire and careened on into the parked aircraft ahead. The training was ended within a week due to heavy losses and the carriers returned to Singapore where the fliers underwent further land-based training. Significantly, they would receive no further training aboard the carriers before the battle.

With the suspicion that the Americans were possibly in possession of Koga's plan for a fleet action, a detailed new plan, *A-Go*, was devised. It was hoped the battle would take place in the waters off Palau or the western Carolines. The possibility of a battle in the vicinity of the Marianas was not addressed until mid-May. In both cases, the strategy was for the Mobile Fleet to remain in local waters and lure the Americans to them, depending on land-based air units to damage the enemy before the battle.

The fleet was forced to stay in these waters because it could not venture far from its fuel supply since there were insufficient tankers to support operations farther from base. Significantly, due to the loss of refining capability, the fleet now utilized unrefined Tarakan crude oil, which was pure enough to drive the engines but volatile and dirty. The oil was detested by engineering crews for leaving filthy sediment in the boilers as well as greatly increasing the risk of explosions and fires.

Ultimately, the Japanese plan for a battle near the Marianas called for Ozawa's carriers to use the greater range of their aircraft to attack the American carriers while remaining out of range of an American counterstrike, with the poorly trained carrier pilots landing on Guam to be refueled and rearmed for continued attacks against the Americans from the land bases. The First Air Fleet, also called the Base Air Force, on Guam, Tinian (where its HQ was) and Saipan was reinforced in late May to prepare for this eventuality, with an assigned total of 1,750 aircraft. However, due to poor support facilities and a shortage of maintenance personnel, scarcity of ammunition, spare parts, and fuel, First Air Fleet would have only some 407 aircraft available when the invasion came, which was not sufficient to meet the plan that they would take out one-third of the American carriers before the fleet action commenced.

Ozawa expected that once the Mobile Fleet was discovered, the Americans would then move toward the Japanese position, but would not venture far from the invasion fleet they were there to support, which would allow more attacks against the invaders. The Mobile Fleet would utlize the superior range of its aircraft to complete the destruction of Task Force 58 while remaining beyond range of an American strike, after which the survivors of the damaged American fleet would now encounter the battleships of the Second Fleet, which included the two largest battleships in the world, *Yamato* and *Musashi*. The plan was certainly over-optimistic in its expectation that fighting spirit would provide a substitute for trained naval aviators.

Ozawa knew he would be outnumbered. The Imperial Japanese Navy intelligence staff estimated on May 9 that the Americans would sail with 16 battleships, eight of which would be new, with eight large fleet carriers, ten light carriers and 20 CVEs; this was a remarkably accurate assessment.

During April and May, every movement of Ozawa's fleet was under close observation by submarines which covered all the Japanese anchorages. The submarines USS *Lapon* (SS-260) and USS *Bonefish* (SS-223) reported the arrival of the Mobile Fleet at Tawi-Tawi in late May.

Admiral Toyoda at first saw the May 27 American invasion of Biak Island, north of New Guinea, as the attack that must be opposed. As Ozawa prepared to leave Tawi-Tawi, Task Force 58 was spotted at its Majuro anchorage by a Japanese reconnaissance flight. It was unclear to the Japanese whether this fleet would support the invasion that had just happened, or if it was likely to participate in the expected Marianas invasion. Misunderstanding their enemy's overwhelming size and power, most Japanese staff officers thought it very unlikely that the Americans would simultaneously launch two major invasions; however, the recon flight had not spotted the American carriers at Majuro. Thinking the American fleet must be smaller than it was, Admiral Toyoda incorrectly decided the main attack must now be intended for Biak. His change of plans and orders back and forth in response to a quickly changing situation created confusion in the Japanese commanders that reflected his own uncertainty.

The Japanese would be thrown into further disarray in the wake of the fifth patrol of *Harder* (SS-257), the results of which have been described as the most brilliant American submarine action of the war. Three days after Ozawa's fleet had arrived at Tawi-Tawi, the submarine left Fremantle, Australia, on its fifth war patrol, under the command of Lieutenant Commander Sam Dealey. He arrived at his patrol site off Tawi-Tawi on June 6, with orders to report the situation at the Japanese anchorage.

In bright moonlight, *Harder* was spotted on the surface and chased by the destroyer *Minatsuki*. Dealey submerged to periscope depth and held position as the enemy charged forward. At minimum range, he used the "down the throat" shot he had developed and fired three torpedoes at 1,100 yards. Two missed to either side but the third blew up *Minatsuki* and she sank with all hands.

Just after midnight on June 10, Dealey spotted two more destroyers six miles outside the anchorage and fired four torpedoes at the overlapping targets. Both of them exploded and sank quickly, apprehensively watched from the Japanese vessels in the anchorage. Admiral Toyoda decided the submarine risk was too great and ordered the fleet to depart Tawi-Tawi to oppose the American invasion at Biak. As Admiral Matomi Ugaki's force emerged from Tawi-Tawi on the afternoon of June 10, Dealey spotted it and moved in for the attack, sinking one destroyer and narrowly missing another. The next day Ozawa's force also left the anchorage, putting the whole fleet to sea, where Toyoda thought it would be safer, though in fact this left it vulnerable to other American submarines. Dealey reconnoitered the empty anchorage and sent word to Task Force 58 that the Japanese fleet was on its way. The thought that the fleet would be safer at sea was the pivotal error committed by the Japanese since it exposed them to discovery by submarines. It would have a near-fatal result for the Mobile Fleet.

As *Harder* arrived off Tawi-Tawi on June 6, 1944, 54 carriers, battleships, heavy and light cruisers, and destroyers of the Fifth Fleet stood out of Majuro Atoll. It was the largest American battle fleet to set to sea and was bound for the Marianas, a thousand miles distant.

Vice Admiral Marc Mitscher's seven heavy and eight light carriers of Task Force 58 supported an amphibious force of 535 ships of Task Force 51, the Joint Expeditionary Force, and 127,000 assault troops of the 2nd, 3rd, and 4th Marine Divisions and the Army 27th Division aboard the transports under the command of Vice Admiral Richmond Kelly Turner. More than 300,000 men manned the fleet. As the sun set that evening, news spread across the fleet that American and Allied forces had landed on the storm-tossed shores of Normandy, half a world away. The liberation of Europe was finally underway. That the United States could simultaneously launch two such colossal assaults against separate enemies half a world apart was the clearest demonstration of American global military power after only two and a half years of war.

Five days later, the fleet was 200 miles south-southeast of the Marianas when two Japanese snoopers were shot down by the CAPs. Having received the situation report from *Harder* that revealed the enemy had departed Tawi-Tawi, and now that the Japanese knew of the presence of Task Force 58,

Mitscher changed his plans from the traditional dawn strike, which had been scheduled for the morning of June 12. New orders were passed that the first strike would depart for Saipan at 1300 hours.

Air Group 15 took off from the *Essex*, accompanied by air groups from *Cowpens* and *Langley*, and strafed the island from east to west, concentrating on the airfields and seaplane bases, attacking Zekes and floatplanes sent out in the island's defense. Several stationary and airborne Emily seaplanes were destroyed and Dave McCampbell noted the vulnerabilities of the Zeke fighters:

> This was our first encounter as an air group with enemy aircraft. We had heard a great deal about the Zeke. I was pleased to note that the F6F could stay with the Zeke in turns, climbs, and dives, particularly at altitudes above 12,000 feet, where most of the air action took place. I noted two deficiencies of the Zeke: its lack of armor and its unprotected gas tanks. All but one of the three Zekes I saw shot down that day went down in flames.

Returning to the *Essex* from their first combat, the pilots found flak damage on just two Hellcats and nobody had been lost in the air battle. Marpi Point was then hit by a 15-plane strike from Bombing 15, which also sent a 13-plane strike against Pagan after the fighter sweep. Three hangars were leveled, the runway was cratered, and there was an impressive explosion when a building housing ammunition was hit.

Hornet's Air Group 2 was sent to hit airfields on Guam. Commander Dean led the fighter sweep, which was followed 30 minutes later by the Helldivers and Avengers. While the strike force was on the way to Guam, the CAP division over the carrier led by "Tex" Harris dispatched three Japanese Betty snoopers.

Air Group 2's target was the airfield on the Orote peninsula in northwestern Guam. The flak was worse than they had encountered at Truk and two Bombing 2 SB2Cs were shot down while in their dives. Fighting 2's Lieutenant (jg) Howard B. "Duffer" Duff, Jr., was forced to ditch north of the island after taking a flak hit. Danny Carmichael circled to check Duff, but was intercepted by several Zekes at low level. In the melee that followed, Carmichael managed to shoot down two Zekes, but when he returned to the crash scene, Duff was nowhere to be found.

VF-2's CO, Commander Dean, claimed three Ki-61 Tony fighters and a Tojo, to become Fighting 2's first ace to score all victories in the squadron. It should be noted here that there were no Army fighters in the Marianas at this time. US fighter pilot claims throughout the Pacific War were often mistaken as to the exact type of enemy aircraft claimed due to ignorance of Japanese aircraft. A good example is the claiming of JAAF Ki-51 Sonia bombers as Vals. This was due to a similarity of airframe layout, with fixed gear, etc. In David McCampbell's epic 9-victory fight, he claimed both IJNAF and JAAF types, though the formation must have been all IJNAF since the two air forces never flew together and this formation came from the Japanese carriers. Perhaps the most egregious of these claims came from the AVG, where every Ki-43 Oscar they shot down was a Zeke, despite the fact there were no Zekes within 1,000 miles. Those claims continued with vehemence 60 years later when pilots were questioned, similar to the majority of Luftwaffe claims in the Battle of Britain being for Spitfires despite the fact two-thirds of the RAF fighters were Hurricanes. Fighter pilots like to claim the "superior victory."

As well as Dean, Mike Wolf claimed three Tojos. Lieutenant (jg) "Irish" Harrigan, Ensign Davey Park, Lieutenant (jg) Landis E. "Blood" Doner, and Lieutenant (jg) Arthur Van Haren each got two Tojos and Lieutenant (jg) "Butch" Voris, Lieutenant (jg) Leroy Robinson, Lieutenant (jg) "Andy" Skon, Lieutenant (jg) Lester Sipes, and Lieutenant (jg) Charles Carroll scored one each. These might actually have been N1K1-J George-11 fighters from the newly-arrived 343rd Air Group; at the time they were the only IJNAF unit operating this new type, which in the heat of combat could have been mistaken for a Tojo.

With 23 in this first fight and ten more during a second mission, Fighting 2's total score for the day of 52 in the air was a new fleet record and the "Rippers" leaped to the front rank of fighter squadrons in Task Force 58. The victories were tempered by the loss of "Duffer," one of the most popular men in the squadron, a pilot always ready to volunteer for tough missions, with a quick and wicked wit.

On June 12, Air Group 15 performed its first night takeoff for a pre-dawn strike against Marpi Point. On the way, McCampbell spotted a vessel's running lights and a section split off to strafe it. They hit the airstrip and then attacked a convoy offshore amid much flak, dispersing it and sinking four ships.

Air Group 2 went back to northern Guam on June 12 and again ran into Japanese fighters ready to fight, though they were far fewer in number than the day before. The squadron scored 11 enemy fighters. On the second strike, Lieutenant John Searcy was hit by flak but ditched successfully and was quickly picked up by the lifeguard submarine *Stingray* (SS-186). The success was diminished by the loss of Lieutenant (jg) "Demi" Lloyd.

After a second strike, against the runway on Pagan Island, Air Group 15 was preparing for a third launch when a recon flight reported a Japanese convoy, against which McCampbell led a flight from *Cowpens*. After a sustained attack, he saw that four of the cargo ships were on fire and sinking. A further attack from the *Essex* sank two transports and a destroyer and scored damage on all the other ships, dispersing the convoy. Early the next day, McCampbell led another attack, sinking a single cargo ship, then the group spent the rest of the day flying shuttle strikes against Saipan and Pagan.

The strikes decimated Japanese air power in the Marianas. Admiral Spruance ordered Admiral Mitscher to isolate the islands from further aerial reinforcement. The Japanese Mobile Fleet, which had been spotted on June 14 in the western Philippine Sea, was expected to be in range by June 19.

Naval intelligence learned through intercepted Japanese Army communications that aircraft were being flown from Japan to the Bonin Islands north of the Marianas, where they could fly on to Guam and on to other Central Pacific bases from Iwo Jima and Chichi Jima. The island of Iwo Jima, only 600 miles southeast of Tokyo and 700 miles northwest of the Marianas, was a crucial way station for the Japanese defense of the Central Pacific.

Admiral Jocko Clark's Task Group 58.1 *Hornet, Yorktown, Belleau Wood*, and *Bataan* (CVL-29), sailed north on June 14, accompanied by Task Group 58.4, commanded by Rear Admiral William K. Harrill with *Essex* and the light carriers *Langley* and *Cowpens*. The objective was to hit Iwo Jima on June 16–17 and knock out the airfields, then return to the Marianas in time to meet the Mobile Fleet.

A typhoon was moving north of the Bonins and the heavy weather affected the Japanese reinforcement plans. Saburo Sakai, a Flight Petty Officer 1/c and one of the Navy's leading aces despaired for the chances in combat of the young pilots assigned to the Yokosuka Naval Air Group. Badly wounded in combat at Guadalcanal two years earlier, Sakai had lost his right eye. Now that his job as instructor was completed, he expected to be transferred elsewhere, and was surprised when he was told to accompany the inexperienced young men to Iwo Jima.

At the time of the Marianas invasion, Iwo Jima was so lightly defended the Americans could have taken it in a few days. The Yokosuka NAG would reinforce the fighters already on the island and provide air defense there while other units staged through. Weather forced delay after delay in their transfer from Japan.

The carriers reached the target a day early, after Admiral Clark decided to close at high speed, which would allow the carriers to return early for the expected fleet action. Task Group 58.1 launched the first strikes against Iwo Jima and Chichi Jima at 1345 hours.

Fighting 2's skipper Dean only assigned pilots who had yet to score many victories, so they could catch up. Over Iwo Jima, Lieutenant Lloyd G. "Barney" Barnard got lucky and scored five Zekes, then two more in a second mission to become Fighting 2's first "ace in a day" and the squadron's leading ace. Lieutenants (jg) Myrv Noble and Charlie Carroll both got three, while Lieutenants (jg) Byron Johnson and Earling "Zesk" Zaeske shot down two each and Ensigns Connard and Elliott each scored singles. On return, the flight deck rolled and tossed in the increasingly heavy seas and the returning aircraft had trouble getting back aboard. Having taken flak hits, Noble had difficulty maintaining control of his Hellcat at landing speed. Just as he got the cut from the LSO, *Hornet*'s stern dropped several feet and he sheared off a gear leg when he crash landed. One Helldiver was shot down over the island.

Task Group 58.4 also launched strikes. McCampbell led 22 Hellcats from *Essex*, and eight each from *Langley* and *Cowpens*; seeing that several Japanese fighters had been launched, he led the formation north and approached the island from a direction the Japanese were not expecting. The Hellcats nevertheless braved intense antiaircraft fire as they broke into divisions to strafe Iwo, but the surprise of the attack meant that many Japanese planes parked near the runways were sitting ducks, and after six strafing runs the pilots felt they must have disabled half of them.

The runways were targeted by a second strike led by Jim Mini of Bombing 15 – 18 Helldivers and Avengers with eight Hellcats from the *Langley* as escorts. The element of surprise now lost, individual attacks from four of the Helldivers made them easy targets and casualties were high for the Bombing 15 crews. It was a much harder fight than the first strike.

Langley's VT-32 also had a tough mission. Just before takeoff, Lieutenant Dave Marks' good friend, Air Combat Intelligence Officer Lieutenant Hal Payne, asked to come along on the mission "to gather intelligence first-hand." A 1933 graduate of Dartmouth College, Payne was older than most and had been a very successful cosmetics and perfume salesman based in Washington DC, serving a large territory in the Mid-Atlantic states before the war. Like the rest of America, he volunteered after Pearl Harbor and after training in intelligence, became a "plank owner" aboard *Langley*, responsible for debriefing Torpedo 32's aircrews immediately after they returned from a mission.

Payne frequently bummed a ride with the pilots, bringing along a bulky camera to shoot photos of the strike. Despite the admonition of Marks' crewmen, radioman Emil Sellars and gunner Vernon Cravero not to go because it was going to be a bad mission, Payne accepted Marks' invitation and hauled his heavy camera into the space under the greenhouse between pilot and turret gunner.

The strike was launched 150 miles from Iwo Jima. Seventy-five miles out, they hit a nearly impenetrable front and the force broke in two as the pilots attempted to fly around the worst of it. Marks' group went to the south and added 125 miles to their flight so that they arrived over the island after the rest had made their attack.

The target was Motoyama No. 2 Airfield, the northernmost field on the island. The Avengers found holes in the cloud cover and dropped through to initiate their attack. The defending gunners were prepared and flak was heavy as they approached; nearly every airplane took a hit. Marks was number three as he entered his glide bombing run.

Just as he dropped his bombs, the right wing and port elevator were hit by antiaircraft fire. The starboard side of the fuselage and the bomb bay doors were shredded by shell fragments. One shell passed through the trailing edge of the right wing and exploded beside the cockpit, sending chunks of shrapnel into the greenhouse. One piece hit Payne's right chest and exited out the left side of his back. He dropped his camera and crumpled to the deck. Radioman Sellars crawled out of the radio compartment and administered morphine, but it was too late.

Others were also hit. Gunner Aviation Ordnanceman 2/c Arnold "Blackie" Marsh was shredded in the turret of Lieutenant (jg) George Winn's plane, which had its canopy completely shot away, leaving Winn in open air. Lieutenant (jg) Pat Patterson was nearly blinded by flying glass when a shell exploded in front of his windshield. He remained conscious to fly by ammonia-soaked handkerchiefs passed forward by his radioman.

When the Avengers arrived back at the fleet, sea conditions were worse than when they took off. Lieutenant Loren L. Hickerson, described the return in his journal:

> The sea grew rougher by the hour, or so it seemed to me. We heard nothing from any of our planes, although ordinarily the strike frequency was full of plane calls. The sea was at its height when the flight returned. We had had rolls up to 24 degrees and when we turned into the wind to recover our planes, the deck was heaving with tremendous swells, like a lifeboat overturned.

I watched the planes come in from a pilot house porthole, and I have never watched a grimmer or more startling sight. One after another, our TBF's came aboard without mishap; how, I will never know. At least half of them had giant holes in the wings or tail or both, from AA fire. I could see from the pilot house that one pilot's face was covered in blood, and at least two other planes were known to have injured personnel aboard.

The fighter planes looked OK, except for occasional shrapnel holes in the wings or fuselages, but the torpedo planes showed every sign of having had rough going. One plane's port wingtip had been staved in, and the fabric was fluttering as he came in. Another plane came in with the flaps blown to pieces. When I went below I learned that Lt. Hal Payne was taken dead from the greenhouse of Dave Marks' plane. A shell had exploded in his compartment, killing him instantly.

The next afternoon we buried our dead at sea for the first time in our lengthening cruise against Japan. A Marine guard stood stiffly at attention, with officers and men in whites and dungarees, on the hangar deck among the TBFs and fighter planes. The band played a dirge as the pallbearers bore the flag-draped bodies to the starboard gangway opening amidships. The Captain and the Chaplain walked down behind them. The service was brief, and simple, and the bodies were dropped silently into the grey waters 600 miles from Tokyo.

It made me a little sick, the thought of Marks and Winn flying home with those bodies who had been their friends and who had joked with us a few hours before. But there was no deep emotional stir. If there were, none of us, let alone these pilots who fly against the enemy again tomorrow and the next day, would be able to stand it. Today, Hal Payne and Blackie Marsh are forgotten. It can't be any other way. To remember them would be to shake the very foundations upon which we live out here. To live constantly with, but as constantly to ignore, the grim realities which face men and ships, pilots and planes, in enemy waters, this seems to me one of the greatest oddities of all. None of us is asleep to what could happen. There is no fear. Only the inexperienced know fear.

On midday of June 16, once the storm had passed, McCampbell led a strike against Iwo Jima from *Essex* and *Cowpens*. It was clear that the first strike had hit hard, with many of the fires still burning and not much aerial opposition, even though new airplanes appeared to have been delivered overnight. On this occasion, dive bombing from Helldivers and multiple strafing runs resulted in a claim of 63 destroyed Japanese aircraft.

In Japan, the weather forecast on June 16 had seemed to provide the necessary good weather for the neophytes to make the journey. That day, as the US fleet battered Iwo, Sakai and 29 other Zekes left Atsugi bound for Iwo Jima. The formation ran into high winds, thick overcast and torrential rains from the typhoon, which was far too severe for even the experienced pilots in the group and they turned back.

CHAPTER ELEVEN

THE MARIANAS TURKEY SHOOT

The Americans couldn't "read the Japanese mail," but they knew the enemy was coming. *Harder* had reported that the Tawi-Tawi anchorage was empty on June 11, and the Mobile Fleet was spotted for certain by *Redfin* (SS-272) on June 13. The four task groups of Task Force 58 were reunited on June 17. On June 18 all 15 carriers launched searches to find the enemy fleet.

The typical mission involved one Hellcat with either a Helldiver or an Avenger on hours-long searches that tested the endurance of pilots and gunners in cockpits that lacked air conditioning, inside the greenhouse of their plastic canopies under the hot tropic sun. Jim Duffy of Fighting 15 remembered that "The hardest part of a search over the Pacific was staying awake in a hot cockpit with the tropic sun beating through the Plexiglas." Canopies were closed to "clean up" the airplanes and give as much range as possible.

The Japanese were also searching. Several sharp fights happened when searchers spotted their opposite numbers. No American planes were lost but several Japanese snoopers were shot down. Fighting 2's Lieutenant (jg) Bob Shackford scored a Jake floatplane during the afternoon.

Connie Hargreaves remembered:

> Many of us took assignments to search 380 miles out from the carriers with a 50-mile cross leg. This was an unusually long search for fighters. We had to trust that the *Hornet* would be able to continue on its anticipated course and

that we would be able to notice any change in the force or direction of wave caps to enable us to plot more accurately our navigation back to the fleet. Most of the search flights wound up being five hours or more in length, with a maximum fuel supply for just six hours. This meant we required the most accurate navigation, for we might still have to wait for the carrier to respot aircraft on the flight deck before bringing us aboard. It was our best effort, but none of us was able to report a sighting of the Japanese fleet.

Ensign Jim Duffy had reason to remember his mission escorting two Bombing 15 Helldivers, one of which was flown by the recently returned Crellin and Graham:

> We were doing everything we could to extend our range – leaning our engines and flying slow, since we knew how important it was to find the enemy; it was a case of safety and standards be damned. My search group reached the end of one leg of our search pattern, and I was really fighting to stay awake in that warm cockpit. All of a sudden, I noticed one of the Helldivers was rocking his wings and the pilot was pointing down. I saw another airplane below at about our eight o'clock. At first, I thought it was just another of our scouts, but then it hit me that they always flew in pairs, so I decided to take a closer look.

Duffy passed under the plane, seeing the "big red meatballs under the wings", and then positioned at the Jill torpedo bomber's six o'clock, setting it on fire as it ditched into the ocean.

Lieutenant John Strane escorted a Helldiver and attacked a Jake floatplane, which was flamed and fell to the water; a Kate torpedo bomber was his next victim ten minutes later, falling from 3,000 feet straight into the sea after being hit in the wing root.

In the next sector, Lieutenant (jg) Cliff Jordan and gunner Aviation Radioman 2/c Stan Whitby flew in a Helldiver, with Ensign J.D. Bare in his Hellcat. They spotted and destroyed a Kate, Jordan scoring an aerial victory unusual for a Helldiver. Five minutes later they saw another, which Bare quickly dispatched, and on their return to the fleet they chased a more elusive Kate which they eventually brought down under combined fire.

The next day would be remembered in history books as the biggest aerial battle of the Pacific War – the "Marianas Turkey Shoot." The morning of June 19, 1944 was unlike any other Task Force 58's pilots had yet experienced. At 0300 hours, General Quarters sounded. Flight decks and hangar decks

The Battle of the Philippine Sea, June 1944

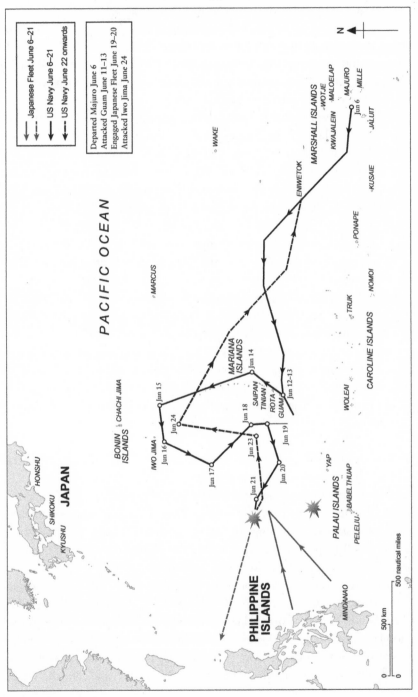

were scenes of bustling activity as the crews sweated the final details to prepare the Hellcats, Helldivers, and Avengers for what lay ahead.

VF-2 intelligence officer Lieutenant (jg) Tom Morrisey, an aspiring writer as were many others who became the keepers of the combat record, wrote of the morning: "We awoke to an ominously placid sea, the night had passed peacefully enough, but the morning dispatches carried with them forebodings of busy and hectic hours ahead."

Pilots were awakened and shuffled into their ready rooms to the electrifying news: they would meet the Japanese Mobile Fleet that day in the first carrier battle since the Battle of the Santa Cruz Islands 20 months earlier.

On Peleliu, several hundred miles southwest of the Marianas, Japanese pilots were called to readiness. Warrant Officer Katsuyoshi Yoshida, a pilot in the Imperial Japanese Navy's 202nd Air Group, recalled:

On 18 June, we were transferred from Kau to Peleliu. It was the night before what was called afterwards The Battle of the Marianas. The 202nd Air Group was to fill the bomber gap, with all our Zeros fitted out with 60-kilogram bombs. We would become a fighter-bomber unit and attack enemy forces landing on Saipan.

The next day, reveille was at 3:30 a.m. We set off, breathing in great lungfuls of the bracing air of Peleliu. After flying for an hour and a half, we landed on Yap, where the ground crews filled us with ammunition, bombs, and fuel. The Z-flag flew, as it had traditionally since the Battle of the Japan Sea in 1905, as if to stress the crucial importance of this battle for our country.

As Yoshida climbed into his cockpit, fellow pilot, Petty Officer Furumura, joked, "I'll show you a good place to die."

Shortly after sunrise, the Mobile Fleet arrived in position. At 0745 hours, *Taihō*, the newest Japanese carrier and Ozawa's flagship, turned into the wind and started launching 16 Zeke fighters, 17 Judy dive bombers, and nine Jill torpedo bombers. Nearby, the flight deck crews of *Zuikaku* and *Shōkaku* readied their aircraft for takeoff.

Below the waves, the submarine *Albacore*, captained by Lieutenant Commander James W. Blanchard, was about to strike a most damaging blow. At 0800 hours Blanchard found himself in the middle of the Japanese Mobile Fleet and at 1,300 yards singled out *Taihō* as the target for a volley of six torpedoes from the bow tubes. Zeke pilot Sakio Kommatsu, who was flying overhead, saw the trails and directed his plane into the water, sacrificing himself in an explosion that took out one of the torpedoes. Four of the others were misses, but one hit *Taihō* starboard, just in front of the island, fracturing the aviation fuel tanks, jamming the forward elevator and bringing her bow down by five feet. Flight operations were halted but as there was no fire and the flight deck was unharmed, Admiral Ozawa remained confident on the flag bridge, taking measures that allowed two more strikes to be launched from the carrier. The vessel seemed safe for the moment, but the unrefined Tarakan crude oil aboard contained volatile fumes that meant disaster loomed.

At 0900 hours, a division of VF-31's CAP was ordered to back up pilots from another carrier who had encountered enemy aircraft over Guam. When Lieutenant Turner, his wingman Ensign Andrews, Lieutenant (jg) Conant, and Lieutenant (jg) Bowie arrived, they saw no friendlies but were jumped by a group of eight Zekes over the enemy air field. In the ensuing fight, they downed six, with Turner shooting down three while Andrews, Conant, and Bowie each scored one. Two of the Hellcats were so badly damaged that all four were taken aboard *Cabot* as soon as they arrived overhead. Once safely on board and below decks, the remaining eight F6Fs of the CAP were ordered to return so they could be replaced by fresh aircraft.

American radar detected the first Japanese strike at 1000 hours at a distance of 150 miles. The 64 aircraft had been launched from the three smallest carriers, *Chitose*, *Chiyoda*, and *Zuihō*. Across Task Force 58, loudspeakers blared, "Pilots! Man your planes!" Alex Vraciu recalled that *Lexington*'s pilots climbed into the first empty cockpit they came across, regardless of assignment. Blue fighters were soon speeding down the flight deck as the pilots pushed throttles through the gate and climbed as steeply as possible with Fighting 16's skipper Paul Buie in the lead. The fighter direction officers manned their microphones and passed the battle cry for all hands to defend the American circus: "Hey Rube!"

Vraciu later recalled the mission:

Our skipper was leading the formation with three divisions of Hellcats and I was leading the second. With him having a new engine in his F6F, he pulled completely out of sight. His wingman's prop froze up trying to keep up with him and he had to ditch it in the ocean.

Suddenly my wingman started pointing at my wing and I found out later that my wings weren't fully locked. Nevertheless, we were directed to return to the carrier and orbit.

Tom Curtis, now a Signalman First Class aboard *Lexington*, remembered, "We men on the ships below could see aerial explosions and fiery trails of smoke trace the sky on the horizon, with contrails above that reminded me of photos of the Battle of Britain over London."

Aboard Admiral Mitscher's flagship *Lexington*, his staff were beside themselves at the situation they were in as a result of the orders given by Fifth Fleet commander Admiral Spruance. Since American carrier aircraft were shorter-ranged than their Japanese opponents, Mitscher had requested permission the previous evening to move Task Force 58 to the west so that they could strike the Japanese carriers as soon as they were spotted. All the experience of four previous carrier battles confirmed that the fleet that struck first would win.

Spruance, however, considered that the ultimate job of the Fifth Fleet and Task Force 58 was to protect the invasion force. He refused Mitscher's request. Now, as the radar screens showed the Japanese first strike approaching, the men who ran the carrier navy were filled with concern: could the carrier force take this first attack and survive to strike the enemy?

Above the fleet, Alex Vraciu received word that radar had bogeys at 75 miles. His division pushed their throttles forward and headed toward the enemy:

About 25 miles away, I saw three bogeys and closed on them immediately. As I got closer, I saw a force of 50 planes flying 2,000 feet below us on the port side and heading toward our ships. The bombers did not have any fighter protection and our position was perfect for a high-side run. I headed for the nearest inboard straggler, which was a Judy. As I closed on him, I caught another Hellcat zeroing in on the same Judy, so I backed off.

I picked another Judy out and came in from the stern, giving him a burst, and he caught fire, heading down in a trail of smoke. Pulling up I spotted two more and sent the first down and maneuvered in from the rear on the second one, with its rear gunner peppering away. It was on fire and as it spiraled into a death dive, the gunner was still firing at me.

The sky was an incredible sight full of smoke, tracer, debris and large bits of fallen enemy planes. We tried to keep the enemy aircraft bunched up and when one broke out of the formation, I broke in behind it and with my oil-soaked windscreen, I gave it a burst. The rounds must have hit the sweet spot on his wing root and probably hit the control cables, because the plane twisted out of control crazily.

The Marianas Turkey Shoot

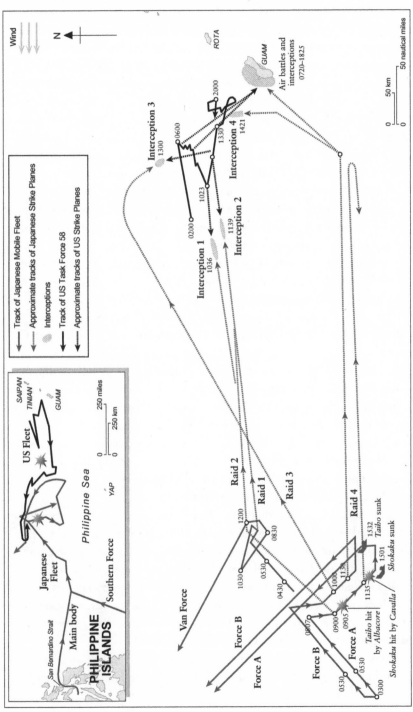

Despite our efforts, the bombers were lining up on their targets. I headed for a group of Judys in a long column. I approached the tail-ender just as the lead was hit by a 5-inch antiaircraft round from a destroyer below. I was in range of number three and a second after opening fire his engine started flying to pieces and he fell off toward the water.

The next one I latched onto was in his dive against one of our destroyers. He was intent on this as I caught up with him and a short burst produced astonishing results. He blew up with a sky-shaking explosion right in front of my face. The heat from the blast belched into my cockpit and I figured to have hit his bomb. I've had planes blow up before but not like this! Yanking up sharply to avoid the flying hot stuff I radioed, "Splash number six; there's another one diving on a battleship, but I don't think he'll make it." Hardly had the words left my mouth when the Judy caught a direct hit that removed it as a factor from the battle. He had flown into a curtain of steel roaring up from the battleship below.

With the Judy gone, I looked around; I could only see a sky full of Hellcats. Glancing back along our route there was a 35-mile long pattern of flaming oil slicks on the water.

Aboard *Cabot*, General Quarters sounded before any replacement CAP could be launched. Radar had picked up the approaching Japanese strike approximately 100 miles distant. Pilots sprinted for the planes and squadron commander Winston beat one of his pilots to the last Hellcat by a matter of feet as he sprang up onto the wing and threw himself into the cockpit. Eleven Hellcats were launched to intercept the Japanese, each catapulted as it was ready. They were soon engaged with the approaching enemy as they dived into more than 50 Zekes at 1047 hours, shooting down 22 in the ensuing fight. Combined with the six shot down earlier, the VF-31's total was 28 enemy aircraft without a single loss.

Essex was a hive of activity; her Helldivers and Avengers were sent on unescorted airfield bombing missions over Guam to keep the decks clear for the ship's fighter aircraft and to make landing harder for Japanese fighters returning to base. Commander Brewer led a CAP above *Essex* that launched with 11 Hellcats at 0910 hours and spotted 24 Japanese fighters, 16 dive bombers, and then a further 15 Judys and 16 Zekes. Brewer turned his attention to this formation and Lieutenant Commander George Duncan took off from the *Essex* to take over the CAP.

Alex Vraciu managed to get through the American flak and land back aboard *Lexington*, where the ordnancemen discovered he had used only 360 rounds of ammunition. Each of the six kills followed a burst lasting less than five seconds. Climbing out of his Hellcat, Vraciu held up two hands with six fingers extended to indicate his score. A photographer's mate on deck caught the moment, which became one of the iconic photos of the war. With 19 victories, Alex Vraciu was now the Navy's leading ace.

Shortly after Duncan's division launched from *Essex*, CAG McCampbell led 11 Hellcats to reinforce Brewer's force. As he later recalled, "By the time my fighters were organized, the fighter controller announced another raid was coming in: 50 bogeys at 150 knots, 45 miles to the east. I was to intercept and stop them." Ensign Spike Borley was number four in his lead division.

Brewer split off from his formation to attack a Zeke and quickly shot it down, only to find a second Zeke on his tail. He quickly reversed the situation and after several bursts from his guns while it wildly maneuvered to escape, the Zeke was downed, making Brewer the first Satan's Playmate to become an ace. His wingman, Ensign Ralph E. Fowler, also fought valiantly and managed to return to *Essex* from his first combat with four Zekes to his name.

Meanwhile, McCampbell's force levelled off at 25,000 feet and reached the enemy formation, where his first target, a Judy, blew up very close, causing him to dodge and change his plan of attack. Back in control, he soon downed two more Judys and concentrated on a Japanese wingman, whose plane exploded on his second pass. He became Fighting 15's first "ace in a day" with his count of seven Judys and became the group's leading ace. Alex Vraciu held his record for the most enemy planes shot down in one mission for only 19 minutes.

Aboard *Essex*, Ted Graham recorded in his diary that, as of 1300 hours, the group's fighters had shot down 36 Japanese aircraft. One Judy got through the screen and dropped a 250-pound bomb 20 feet off the starboard bow, "which scared the hell out of me." That would be the closest any attacker came to hitting an American carrier that day.

Fighting 2 scored early that morning. The "two Tex's" – "Tex" Harris and former Royal Canadian Air Force pilot Merriwell "Tex" Vineyard, who had seen combat on Malta – each knocked down a Zeke when their CAP division was vectored to the snoopers at 0745 hours.

Fighting 2's Commander Dean led eight Hellcats off *Hornet* when the first raid was spotted at 1000 hours. They were ordered to "buster" and climb "Angels 25" to intercept "100-plus" at 25,000 feet. The formation they found was the one launched from *Taihō*. Dean scored a Zeke while

Danny Carmichael claimed two Judys and a Zeke. Butch Voris, Davey Park, Irish Harrigan, Mike Wolf, and Bob Grimes scored a Zeke each.

While Dean was returning to the ship he was jumped by a group of Zekes and took violent evasive action to escape them. They followed and Dean battled for his life. He managed to shoot down two and dive away from the others. "I was fighting for my life for almost an hour out there!" Dean reported.

Leroy Robinson scored two Zekes but was hit and had to put down on the first carrier he spotted, finally getting back to *Hornet* at the end of the day. VF-2's score for the first mission of the day was 12 destroyed.

Shortly after they returned, a second 90-plane bogey was reported. *Hornet* launched all available fighters. Ten Hellcats clawed into the sky and intercepted the Japanese 25 miles out from the fleet between 17,000 and 23,000 feet. Doherty, Redmond, and Van Haren scored two each, while Zesk Zaeske and Carlson each knocked down one.

Hornet launched a strike to hit the airfields on Guam that the enemy would be aiming to land at following their attacks on the fleet, led by Lieutenant William "Hardluck" Blair, a VF-10 veteran. The strike also ran into the inbound strike. Blair – whose nickname came from being scoreless despite numerous fights to date – knocked down two Judys while Ensign Vaughn scored three Zekes, Griff Griffin got two Zekes, and Andy Skon and Charlie Carroll each shot down two Judys. Ensigns Myrv Noble, "Porky" Connard, and "Kid" Lake each scored a Zeke. A 20mm shell exploded in Charlie Carroll's cockpit, while Lake's Hellcat was so completely shot up that the airedales shoved it overboard as soon as he climbed out after landing. Flak over Guam shredded Connard's right wing and it collapsed when he touched down.

The submarine *Cavalla* (SS-244) had left Pearl Harbor on her first patrol on May 31, and at 1048 hours on June 17, Lieutenant Commander Herman J. Kossler raised her periscope right in the midst of the Mobile Fleet in the western Philippine Sea. He chose *Shōkaku* as his target, which was just landing Zekes from a CAP. Three of his six torpedoes hit in the worst possible places: the avgas; the magazines; and the machinery spaces. The damage was substantial, though at first Admiral Hiroshi Matsubara thought the hits non-fatal and ordered aircraft to be launched by the deck crew. All of a sudden, one of the fires ignited some avgas that created a fireball just forward of the bridge, then burning aircraft in the hangar set the rest of the ammunition off. A series of explosions ripped through the ship, littering the deck with body parts as the ship rapidly listed to starboard and fell out of formation. Damage control measures were thrown into disarray, but the crew valiantly fought the fire using extinguishers and even bucket brigades. Finally, at 1408 hours, a three-minute convulsion was to shake her in a series of explosions that took her to the bottom with an appalling loss of 1,263 crew.

Half an hour after *Shōkaku's* demise, the oil fumes that had been spreading through *Taihō* would ignite in a huge explosion, with the ship falling out of formation and settling as Admiral Ozawa reluctantly transferred to another vessel. Fifteen minutes later, *Taihō* blew apart at the seams and went to the bottom with 1,640 officers and crew.

About 150 miles to the east of this, at around midday, the morning CAP landed on *Essex*. Almost immediately two divisions of Hellcats had to be launched in response to the incoming second wave of 109 attack planes from *Zuikaku*, *Taihō* and *Shōkaku* that had been picked up on radar, and a dogged defensive skirmish took place.

At noon a formation of 200 Zekes and Judys of 202nd Air Group took off from Yap, flying east of Guam to attack the American invasion fleet southeast of Saipan. It was met by the American aircraft in a big dogfight, punctuated by intense ack-ack fire from below. Its attack was meant to be augmented by aircraft from Ozawa's Carrier Divisions 1 and 2 but only 64 aircraft were to combine, clear the American defenses and make it into the battle area. Of those who did make it, 30 were downed by the 40 Hellcats and Wildcats defensively flying over the invasion fleet.

Aboard *Essex*, Ted Graham wrote that, as of 1430 hours, the group's Hellcats had shot down 46 attackers. Even as he wrote that, McCampbell led his and George Duncan's divisions on a fighter sweep to Orote Field in west-central Guam, the destination of the surviving attackers. There McCampbell attacked two Zekes, downing one into the fields of Orote Point, before joining Duncan's division and flying back to *Essex*.

Fighting 15 wasn't the only unit over Orote Point. A call had gone out at 1300 hours aboard *Hornet* for volunteers to fly a mission against antiaircraft positions on Guam. Among those who volunteered was Ensign Wilbur B. "Spider" Webb, a former enlisted man who had joined the Navy in October 1938, several months after his 18th birthday, then served in the gunnery and radio divisions aboard the battleship *Colorado* (BB-45) before being assigned to the aviation division as a radioman-gunner flying in Kingfisher scout planes. Following persistent requests for flight training, Webb had finally gotten into flight training at NAS Pensacola, Florida in June 1942, where he earned his Wings of Gold as an enlisted naval aviation pilot in July 1943. Commissioned an ensign a few months later, he joined Fighting 2 in Hawaii in December 1943, following their return from the Gilberts invasion.

Webb later recalled what would go down in the books as one of the outstanding missions flown by any pilot on this day of days:

> I normally flew with Lieutenant (jg) Tex Vineyard, who was the division leader for Ginger-12, our radio call sign. I asked Tex if he wanted to go, but he replied in the negative. I advised the squadron operations officer that I would go. We were assigned as fighter escort for the strike group. I was to fly wing for Lieutenant (jg) Conrad Elliott and was the escort flight's tail-end Charlie.

Surprisingly, Webb ended up flying his "assigned" F6F-3, No. 31. This was almost-unheard of, since pilots were assigned aircraft for missions according to availability on the flight deck:

> Takeoff and rendezvous were normal, and we proceeded to our assigned targets, climbing on course to 28,000 feet. Approaching the target, our division remained as high cover for the torpedo planes and dive-bombers while they made their strikes, then we headed down to drop our 500-pound bombs and strafe our assigned targets around Agana. After the strike on our assigned targets, we proceeded to make a running rendezvous across Guam to just off Orote Peninsula, which was on the west side of the island. We completed our join-up at 3,000 to 4,000 feet, and the entire strike group turned back toward the *Hornet*.

Just at that moment, Webb looked down and saw an American pilot in a rubber life raft in the act of spreading his dye marker, just west of Orote Point. He quickly informed his section leader, and strike leader Commander Jackson Arnold gave permission for Webb to give the pilot cover while section leader Elliott found one of the OS2U Kingfishers and guided it to the pilot:

> I arrived over the life raft and lowered my speed by throttling back and lowering my wheels and flaps, so I could fly a tight circle around the man. My first thought was to throw him some more dye markers in the event he was not picked up before dark, and also to give him another life raft. I opened my canopy, took my knife out, cut two of the dye markers loose

from my Mae West, and threw the markers to the pilot in the water. I was circling him at about 100 feet. After throwing out the dye markers, I proceeded to remove my life raft from under my parachute.

Webb happened to glance at the mountains, where he spotted a long line of airplanes flying through the saddle, headed for the airfields on the island's northern end. "My first thought was, why are our airplanes flying along there with their landing gear down?" In an instant, Webb was aware he had made a mistake in identification:

The first planes were heading for me, and they got to within less than a hundred yards of me before I realized that they were Japanese Val dive bombers, with fixed landing gear, flying in divisions of three. The aircraft above the Vals were Zekes. When they reached the landing pattern for the field, they banked away, and I could see the large red meatballs on their sides. I estimated that there were 30–40 planes in all. I was not very concerned about my position at the time. I just thought, "Boy, this is it. Make it good and get as many as you can before they know you're here!"

Webb called Elliott to let him know of his discovery and turned toward the enemy.

"I had not been detected so far, so I decided not to gain altitude, but to just slide into their traffic pattern and get as many as I could before I was detected." Just before he turned to make a run, Webb picked up his microphone and made a blanket broadcast that would later become famous: "Any American fighter, I have 40 Jap planes surrounded at Orote Airfield. I need some help! Hey Rube!"

He was now less than 20 yards behind three Vals. "I started overrunning them, so I lowered my landing gear and flaps."

Webb swung in behind the Val on the left and squeezed his trigger. His aim was true and the Val exploded. He maneuvered onto the tail of the middle Val and fired. The enemy's vertical stabilizer disintegrated as the rear-seat gunner slumped when hit; the starboard wing flew off when the bomber exploded:

By the time I eased in behind the third plane, my speed had built up and I started overrunning it. The rear-seat gunner was firing directly at me, but he did not hit my aircraft. I was holding down the trigger, but this plane did not seem to want to burn. I kept saying, "Burn, you bastard!" over and over until it finally did explode. If it had not exploded, I would have collided with it, I guess. When it did explode, I flew through the explosion and sustained several holes in my F6F from pieces of it.

Webb set up behind another trio of Vals and again started with the plane to the left:

> The rear-seat gunner of this aircraft was firing directly at me from no farther than 30 yards. I could see the colors of his flight suit, helmet, and skin. Then he seemed to kind of give up. He put his hands up before his face – maybe he thought I was going to run into him – just before several .50-caliber slugs hit him in the chest and face. The aircraft started burning, and the pilot bailed out over the side. We were at no more than 200 feet, so I doubt if he made it.

While the lead Val got away, Webb managed to hit the one on the right. "When I fired, it started shedding pieces and smoking badly. Then his tail disintegrated, and he just fell."

Considerable antiaircraft fire came up from the Orote Peninsula as the battle raged:

> I could see tracers continually coming up in front of me. I guess they had never seen an F6F Hellcat flying so slow. At the time, I did not realize that my plane had been hit. By this point, the sky was filled with planes and several other Hellcats had arrived. No matter where I looked, I could see either a parachute or a burning plane. It seemed like a mad flying circus, only this was real.

Webb's guns stopped firing after the fifth Val went down. He pulled away from the fight and worked the gun chargers until one gun in each wing was working before heading back into the fight. "Almost immediately, I saw a Val coming toward me from above. It was at about 1,000 feet. I got it in my sights and squeezed the trigger. As my guns fired, a third gun started working. This Val seemed to explode in half just behind the pilot, who bailed out."

Webb's guns stopped working again:

> I headed out of the fight until I managed to get two on one side and one on the other working. Then I headed back in. I saw another Val low on the

water, so I nosed over to intercept it and started firing. I killed the rear-seat man, and the plane started smoking. We were heading toward the cliff edge of Orote Peninsula. I had to pull up to avoid the cliff, so I did not see whether this plane crashed or not.

The Hellcat's guns quit a third time, forcing him out of the fight again until he finally managed to get one operating. "At that moment, I spotted one of our Hellcats, which was only about 200 feet over the water, with a Zeke on its tail. The Hellcat was in a bad way. I had only one gun working, but I managed to shoot a few pieces off the Zeke and run him off of the Hellcat, which, it turned out, was flown by Lieutenant (jg) Bill Levering, a night-fighter pilot from my ship."

Though he had only one working gun, Webb stuck in the fight. "I fired at many more Val dive bombers and Zero fighters. I knocked pieces from some and caused others to burn, but none of them was seen to crash. When all my guns became permanently inoperative, I headed out of the fight and toward the open sea."

Out of the fight and able to calm down, Webb realized his Hellcat was the worse for wear with a shot-up canopy and several holes in the wings from ground fire and the Val whose explosion he had flown through:

My goggles were gone, my radio was out, the cylinder-head temperature was high, and oil was all over my cowling and windshield. I found out later that there were over 100 holes in my aircraft. I was beginning to wonder how – or if – I was going to get back to my carrier when a Fighting Two Hellcat joined up on me. I quickly gave him the lead and, by hand code, told him to lead me home. The pilot was Ensign Jack Vaughn, and I was never happier to see anyone than I was to see him at that time.

Elliott had already returned and made his report by the time Webb landed back aboard *Hornet*, "My gun-camera pictures confirmed four of my victories before the camera jammed. For this action, I was recommended for the Congressional Medal of Honor by Admiral Mitscher, but I was awarded the Navy Cross."

Webb was ultimately credited with six Vals destroyed and two probably destroyed. Lieutenant Russ Reisering from *Hornet*'s VF-76 night fighter detachment ran Webb a close second in the same fight with five Vals shot down to become an "ace in a day."

By the end of the day, Satan's Playmates had set an all-time American record of 67.5 victories, and the "Rippers" of Fighting 2 came second with 51 victories. The 15 Hellcat squadrons of Task Force 58 claimed 371 victories; *Lexington*'s Fighting 16 claimed 46; *Yorktown*'s Fighting 1 claimed 37; and newly formed Fighting 27's "Hell Cats" aboard *Princeton* got 30 kills.

June 19, 1944, known as the "Marianas Turkey Shoot", was a mortal blow to Japanese naval aviation, and although the US Navy had won the Battle of the Philippine Sea, it was unaware it had done so because the losses of *Taihō* and *Shōkaku* were not immediately confirmed. Not knowing of these victories and the magnitude of their impact on Japanese naval aviation led to a skewed view of the battle's outcome and played a negative role in American decision-making in the lead-up to the next great battle in October.

CHAPTER TWELVE

THE MISSION BEYOND DARKNESS

June 20, 1944, began early for Task Force 58. Search flights were launched at 0530 hours. The Mobile Fleet was nowhere to be seen, but Fighting 2 pilots Gene Redmond and Arthur Van Haren provided evidence it was out there when each splashed a Jake floatplane, an observation plane usually carried by Japanese heavy cruisers, while a carrier-based Jill fell victim to Zesk Zaeske. Lieutenant Commander Charlie Harbert's search flight found and splashed two more Jills. But enemy surface forces were nowhere to be seen.

At the time the American search flights were launched, Admiral Ozawa's Mobile Fleet was between 330 and 350 miles west of the American fleet, on course to the northwest. Their destination was Okinawa, more than 800 miles distant. Ozawa decided to concentrate his forces, and at 0800 hours, the two carrier groups turned north to join Admiral Kurita's surface force and the two oiler groups. The link-up was accomplished at midday and Ozawa transferred his flag to *Zuikaku*, last of the Pearl Harbor veterans.

The Task Force 58 air staff was close to open revolt with Admiral Spruance after the previous day's defensive battle against Japanese raids, as to what action should now be taken. They had advocated on June 18 that the fleet should head west and intercept the Mobile Fleet before the Japanese could threaten the invasion fleet. Spruance referred to Nimitz's order that the primary duty of Task Force 58 and the Fifth Fleet was defense of the invasion, not destruction of the Japanese fleet.

Spruance believed that if the fleet got too far away from the Marianas and the Japanese found success with their expected strategy of striking while inbound to land on the islands, that then on the return trip the invasion fleet's aerial defense would be compromised.

The staff grumbled that things would be different were Halsey commanding; indeed that difference would be demonstrated four months later at Leyte Gulf. Spruance had demonstrated at Midway he knew when to go "all in" and when to "hold 'em;" he always kept the larger mission in view. This was why Nimitz had chosen him over Halsey as the first commander of the fast carrier fleet.

The air groups flew searches all day. It was clear that, wherever the Japanese were, they would be discovered at maximum range if they were even found at all. The only question was whether the discovery would be in time to close the range in order to launch strikes with sufficient daylight left for the return; there were only a very few aviators in the fleet who were qualified to land aboard at night. Spruance ordered the fleet to steam west throughout the day. Because the prevailing wind was easterly, the carriers would have to turn away from the enemy to launch the strike, which would add to the distance the pilots would have to fly.

At 1528 hours, two Avengers from *Enterprise*'s Torpedo 10 finally found the Mobile Fleet. As he flew through afternoon squalls that reduced visibility, Lieutenant Robert S. Nelson spotted a ripple on the ocean surface. Lieutenant (jg) Edward Laster, who was in the next search sector a few miles south, also spotted the disturbance on the water and investigated. Approaching from opposite sides of a large squall, the two Avenger pilots finally saw something only a very few aviators now in the fleet had ever seen: the Mobile Fleet. Nelson made the first report, sending it twice to insure reception: "Enemy fleet sighted. Latitude 15-00, longitude 135-24. Course 270, speed 20." Laster's radioman tapped out: "Many ships, one carrier 134-12E 14-55N." Seventy miles, a little more than one degree of longitude, separated the sightings. However, both were south and east of the actual Japanese position. Both search teams sent follow-up messages and then Laster turned for home to report in person. Nelson went in close to get a better look. He also corrected his position report.

"My most vivid recollection of the search flight," Nelson later recalled, "was of the Japanese carrier leaving a circular wake as it turned after we had been in view for four or five minutes, double checking the plot of our position." Later, as Nelson flew home, he got confirmation that his sighting report had been received when several air groups passed him, headed west. It was "the most impressive, and the most clearly remembered, event of the day."

When the reports were first received, Admiral Mitscher compared the two and concluded they were the same ships. At approximately 1545 hours he signaled, "Expect to launch everything we have. We will probably have to recover at night." Just after the decision was made, Nelson's corrected position report was received – the enemy was 60 miles farther west than originally reported!

Fighting 2's Lieutenant (jg) Connie Hargreaves recalled, "Air Group 2 contributed 12 fighters to escort 12 dive bombers and nine torpedo planes. Even the fighters were loaded with a 500-pound bomb each, for maximum striking power, since this was the first time a Japanese carrier fleet had come out since October 1942. We could always jettison the bombs in the event we ran into enemy planes."

As the order "Pilots! Man your planes!" echoed across *Hornet*'s flight deck at 1545 hours, Lieutenant (jg) Jack "Dad" Taylor thought for a moment as he strapped into his SB2C-1C Helldiver that this was his 23rd birthday – what a birthday present he had just received. Taylor was second section leader to the senior division leader, Lieutenant Commander Hal Buell. As the Helldivers were pushed into position for launch, the new position was broadcast. Pilots already worried about the distance and their ability to get back as the Japanese were beyond their plotting board's range circles.

Taylor recalled, "We took off and made a running rendezvous at low altitude, heading 285 degrees with the distance to the Japanese being 230 miles." Mixtures were leaned to the maximum and revs were reduced to stretch every possible mile from the gas tanks as they slid their canopies closed to clean up the airplanes and save fuel while they slowly increased their altitude.

Though Ensign Ralph Yaussi, Taylor's wingman, could see no way to fly the mission and return, he held position on his leader. "We went west, and we went west, and then we went west some more. Several times, someone thought they saw the fleet ahead, but it turned out to be cloud shadows on the ocean." Out on the horizon ahead, the sun got lower and lower. The 95 Hellcats, 54 Avengers, 51 Helldivers, and 26 Dauntlesses of three task groups flew on.

The first ships the Americans spotted were the oiler group, which had been left astern by the rest of the Mobile Fleet and was 250 miles west-northwest of Task Force 58. The seven remaining carriers were still in three separate groups: Carrier Division 3 – *Chitose*, *Chiyoda*, and *Zuihō* – was with Admiral Kurita's surface force in the van, 38 miles west-northwest of the oilers; Carrier Division 2 – *Junyō*, *Hiyō*, and *Ryūhō* – was 8 miles north of the van and 40 miles north-northwest of the oilers; Carrier Division 1's survivor, *Zuikaku*, was 18 miles northeast of Carrier Division 2.

Most of the strike groups pressed on to attack the carriers. However, Air Group 14's strike from *Wasp* (CV-18) had been lured southward by radio calls and radar returns; Lieutenant Commander Jack Blitch felt they lacked fuel to fly on and divided his 35 aircraft to attack the oilers, assigning three VB-14 Helldivers to the first four ships with four VT-14 Avengers to attack the fifth, while he held four Avengers in reserve. The 16 VF-14 Hellcats were split between top cover and flak suppression. The attack was successful, with one oiler seen to explode and disintegrate, another set on fire, and a third dead in the water. The first two would sink while the third was saved only by good damage control efforts. As the Helldivers and Avengers came off their targets, they were attacked by six Zekes from *Zuikaku*. One Hellcat and one Helldiver were shot down, and two other SB2C pilots were wounded. On the way home, nine Helldivers and three Avengers were forced to ditch when they ran out of gas.

Future US President and current gunnery officer Lieutenant Gerald R. Ford was among those aboard USS *Monterey* (CVL-26) who watched Lieutenant Roland P. "Rip" Gift lead Air Group 28's strike off the ship. Now, Gift refused to attack the oilers, radioing "To hell with the merchant fleet – let's go get the fighting Navy!" They continued westward and found Kurita's van and Carrier Division 3. Gift led the attack on *Chiyoda* and scored a hit on her stern. It was not enough to sink the light flattop, though 20 men were killed and two planes were destroyed.

While VT-28 was attacking *Chiyoda*, *Cabot*'s VT-31 went after the battleship *Haruna*. The Avengers, led by Lieutenant Edward E. Wood, scored one hit on the dreadnought. *Bunker Hill*'s Bombing 8 and Torpedo 8 also attacked *Chiyoda* and claimed several hits. Nevertheless, she survived, only to be sunk in the Battles of Leyte Gulf. Several Bombing 8 Helldivers also attacked the cruiser *Maya* and scored a near-miss. As they made their escape from the enemy fleet, five of the Helldivers were attacked by Zekes and two were shot down. At the rendezvous, Commander Ralph L. Shifley, *Bunker Hill*'s CAG, and his wingman Lieutenant Gerald R. Rian encountered four Zekes and each claimed one kill and one probable.

Air Group 2 found Carrier Division 1. Hargreaves remembered:

The pilots of Fighting 2 flew out to the sighting area, but there were no Japanese carriers. The CAG ordered us to press on, beyond the safe turn-around point. Finally, just as the sun was setting, we spotted the Jap fleet. There was no aerial opposition, just heavy flak. Bill Dean took his division in first, then my division commenced our dives. After release, we tried to form up, but the darkness was absolute.

Ensign Yaussi recalled, "The Japanese ships were firing what looked like solid flak. It appeared that the sky was covered with gunfire that could not be penetrated without being hit. The smoke was in beautiful colors and patterns, pink and blue and white, and the smoke plumes were spread over huge plots of sky. It was scary."

Hal Buell asked Bombing 2 commander, Lieutenant Commander Grafton Campbell, for permission to dive first. Yaussi remembered, "I wished at that time he hadn't done that. Later he explained to me that he wanted us to go in before they had a chance to get their guns sighted in." The Helldivers dropped down on the largest carrier they saw, which they thought was the now-sunk *Shōkaku* but turned out to be her sister ship and Admiral Ozawa's flagship, *Zuikaku*.

Buell later wrote:

As I pushed over into my dive at about 12,000 feet, the AA fire became so intense that I saw no way of getting through it. My dive brakes were already open and I was well into a good dive, but because of the potent defensive fire, I felt like I was moving in slow motion in quicksand. I would never make it. At this point I did something I had never done before in a dive – I closed my dive brakes. My plane responded by dropping like a stone toward the target below, leaving the heavy AA fire behind. My speed was building up, and in the clean condition without flaps, I could never expect to pull out of the dive after firing my bomb. Shouting a prayer to my guardian angel, I placed the dive brake selector back into the open position at 6,000 feet. The wing brakes did what no manufacturing specs said they would – they opened! It was as if a giant hand grabbed my plane by the tail; my headlong plunge slowed, and there was the enemy carrier dead in my sight below me, turning into my flight path along its lengthwise axis. At the point-blank range of 2,000 feet, I dropped my bombs.

After release I broke my dive and started the pullout, closed the wing flaps, and bent over in the cockpit to activate my bomb bay door lever, which was mounted on the deck of the cockpit. At that precise instant, while bent forward and down in the cockpit, my Helldiver and I were struck a savage blow – a direct hit from an enemy AA shell. The shell struck underneath the starboard wing about eight feet from the side of the plane, and then traveled up through the wing before exploding two or three feet above the upper surface. A large fragment of shell passed through the open cockpit enclosure, striking me in the back where I was hunched up from bending over. This shrapnel piece passed diagonally right to left across my back from my lower right rib cage area to my upper left shoulder, just enough to slice open my flight suit like the cut of a razor. The force of the blow from this fragment, as it tore through my protruding parachute backpack, was like being clubbed from behind with a baseball bat. At the same instant as the blow, I felt a searing stab of pain like a hot iron being pressed against my back. I straightened up in the cockpit and the thought flashed through my mind: "Oh God, I've been hit bad." The burning pain was from a minute bit of the bigger piece of shell, about the size of a .45-caliber bullet, which had buried itself in the middle of my back.

Had Buell been seated normally, he would have been killed.

The Helldivers pulled out of their dives low over the water and jinked wildly as they escaped through the massed antiaircraft fire of battleships, cruisers and destroyers:

> Continuing my pullout, I leveled my stricken Beast at fifty to one hundred feet above the water, and moved between destroyers in the screen that kept blasting away as I passed. The damaged wing was on fire, with a hole about one foot in diameter that was gradually enlarging in size as the edges burned away with a white glow. I still had aileron control with the stick but immediately began having trouble holding the wing up as the size of the burning hole quickly increased. I had to get that fire out fast, before the wing burned away enough to cause a loss of control, or structural failure, but how?

The white heat reminded Buell of watching a blacksmith work during his boyhood. Suddenly, it occurred to him that cutting his speed might put out the fire. He turned left on a heading toward Task Force 58 and began to slow the bomber down and climb slightly:

> But the wing continued to burn and, as the hole grew larger, it became increasingly harder for me to hold the wing up in level flight. I was

becoming really concerned when, at 120 knots airspeed, the fire suddenly snuffed out. By that time the hole was nearly a yard across and, even with full trim tab, I was forced to hold the stick far to the left in order to maintain level flight. In the fading twilight, the outer wing beyond the hole was flexing slightly as we flew along. As there was nothing that could be done about it, I offered up a small prayer that the wing would remain intact.

As for the shrapnel:

I was feeling little actual pain, and was not dizzy or faint, but that could be because my body was still running on natural adrenaline from the excitement of the attack. Reaching behind with my left hand, I felt my lower back – it was wet and sticky. My hand came away covered with blood! While there was a considerable amount of it, I realized that the wound must not be a serious one as I was not feeling weak or having the kind of pain that a major wound would cause. Apparently it was something that I could live with.

Buell led the bombers home. The pilots all believed they had scored two or three hits on their target, having seen what appeared to be explosions and fires aboard the carrier. Bombing 2 commander, Lieutenant Commander G.B. Campbell, who led eight Helldivers down on the carrier after Buell, claimed he saw "one big hole with a fire down inside near the island."

Connie Hargreaves dive-bombed a cruiser. "I think that dive was about the longest I ever made, if not in altitude, then certainly in the time I spent watching my own tracers and trying to distinguish them from all the AA that was coming up at me. It seemed like the point of release for that bomb I had been loaded with would never arrive, even though I had the guns going in short bursts all the way down."

The Hellcats rejoined away from the enemy fleet and turned east in the gathering darkness. "There was no moon, no light reflecting off the clouds, just our instruments and the running lights of other planes. We faced sheer darkness for flying on instruments in and around the clouds. It was a precarious and very scary flight back to our carriers."

Zuikaku, now the last remaining Pearl Harbor veteran after the sinking of *Shokaku* the day before, was attacked by Bombing 2's Helldivers. Bombing 1 arrived overhead as Buell and the others pulled out of their dives and attempted to escape the heavy flak. Squadron leader Lieutenant Commander Joseph Runyon saw "a large hole, rimmed with fire apparently emanating from the hangar deck," the result of Bombing 2's attack. Runyon's Helldivers claimed three hits on Ozawa's flagship and several misses, though the Japanese admitted to only one bomb hitting the ship. However, this one nearly sank *Zuikaku*, when the explosion damaged the aviation fuel system then flooded the hangar deck with avgas. Ignition of the fuel created a fire that spread so quickly that the order to abandon ship was passed. The crew either did not hear or ignored the order, while sailors doggedly fought the fire and it was soon put out.

Belleau Wood's VT-24 scored the greatest aerial success when Lieutenant George Brown, who had sworn before takeoff that he would get a hit at any cost, attacked *Hiyō* with his division of four torpedo-armed Avengers. As he closed in on the enemy carrier, Brown's Avenger was hit several times and caught fire while the outer section of the port wing was shot off. Unable to reach Brown on the intercom, Gunner Aviation Machinist's Mate 2/c George H. Platz and radioman Aviation Radioman 2/c Ellis C. Babcock successfully bailed out and witnessed the attack from the water. Brown continued and the fire in the wing burned itself out. Approaching from the north, he turned to starboard before turning in to drop his torpedo onto *Hiyō's* bow. As he did so, wingmen Lieutenants (jg) Benjamin C. Tate and Warren R. Omark, turned left to attack from the starboard beam and quarter.

Omark later recalled:

Brownie, Ben Tate, and I fanned out to approach from different angles. The attack course took us over the outlying screen of destroyers, then cruisers, and finally the battleships. This screen had to be penetrated in order to reach the proper range for launching torpedoes against the carrier. The antiaircraft fire was very intense, and I took as much evasive action as I could. We came in at about 400 feet over the water to get a satisfactory launch of our torpedoes and dropped them on converging courses which did not allow the enemy carrier to take effective evasive action.

Unable to evade all three torpedoes, *Hiyō* took at least one hit that mortally damaged her. The three Avengers were caught by enemy fighters as they came off the target, but they managed to evade them and make their rendezvous. Brown was just above the surface, flying slowly. Tate remembered, "He held up his right arm, which was all bloodstained. I tried to keep him on my wing to guide him back. I called him on the radio but he didn't answer with anything understandable. I lost him in the dark." Omark reported, "Brown acted stunned, like a football player who had been hit in the head. I turned on my lights to help him, but evidently his light system was shot, because he didn't turn on his. I lost him in the dark about an hour later." Brown was never seen again.

Yorktown's Torpedo 10 Avengers found Carrier Division 2. *Ryūhō* was attacked by five Avengers led by Lieutenant Charles W. Nelson, who was hit by anti-aircraft fire as he overflew the carrier following release of his torpedo. The Avenger was hit badly and crashed, while *Ryūhō* avoided all five torpedoes. Three Avengers armed with bombs claimed three hits and five near-misses when they attacked either *Hiyō* or *Junyō*. Historian Samuel Eliot Morison later speculated that if all the VT-10 Avengers had been armed with torpedoes, they might have sunk *Ryūhō*.

The Torpedo 10 Avenger division led by Lieutenant Van Eason followed a group of Fighting 10 Hellcats led by the CAG, Commander William "Killer" Kane that suppressed antiaircraft fire, but even with help from the "Grim Reapers," the TBMs flew through heavy fire from the battleship *Nagato*. Lieutenant (jg) Joe Doyle reported, "when Eason wobbled his wings and turned left, I looked down and saw we were right on top of two carriers. We were out after carriers, so without looking for details I pulled up in a wing-over to the left and went down on the nearest one." When the carriers were spotted, the Avengers were at 12,000 feet. Their preferred glide-bombing attack had them commence their glide from 8,000 feet, drop their bombs at 5,000 feet and recover at 4,000 feet. With an additional 4,000 feet in the dive, all would find their aim thrown off.

Eason's Avenger hit 330 knots even though he pulled back on his throttle before he released at 3,500 feet. Doyle saw Lieutenant (jg) Aubrey Fife's 1,000-pound bomb near-miss *Ryūhō* to starboard, then saw two splashes from Eason's bombs to port. After releasing his bombs at 4,500 feet, he glanced back and saw two more splashes ahead of *Ryūhō* while his gunner reported two hits on the bow. Lieutenant (jg) Ernie Lawton's dive was so fast that the glass was blown out of his canopy by changing air pressure in a 5,500 foot dive at 350 knots. Two of his bombs near-missed the carrier's bow while the third hit close on the port side and the fourth hung up in his bomb bay. Lieutenant (jg) "Crossbow" Collins walked four bombs from starboard to port with numbers two and three hitting the flight deck. Ensign Ralph Cummings, the last to attack, experienced difficulty opening his bomb bay doors and had to momentarily level off to get them to open before he resumed his dive. Two bombs missed to port, with a possible hit by the third while the fourth failed to release.

The fifth carrier battle of the Pacific War was also the last for the SBD Dauntless, the airplane that had been most responsible for hurting the enemy in the battles of 1942. Bombing 10 and Bombing 16 lived up to their predecessors' reputations.

During his pre-mission briefing, newly promoted Bombing 10 commander Lieutenant Commander James D. "Jig-Dog" Ramage told the pilots "We're going to be gas misers." He was very worried about the distance the Dauntlesses would have to fly and doubted any would return; that was before the word was passed that the Japanese were actually 60 miles farther west than originally reported. With that news, Ramage was convinced it was impossible for his Dauntlesses to make the 297-mile round trip. Even so, he later recalled that "There was no tenseness or nervousness. We were ready, we were good, and we knew it."

At approximately 1815 hours, Lieutenant Commander Ralph Weymouth, leading *Lexington*'s Bombing 16 in company with *Enterprise*'s Bombing 10, spotted an oil slick that led off to the northwest. At 1830, Ramage spotted the oilers. While the oilers were a tempting target, "we were after bigger meat." Forty miles and fifteen minutes later the Dauntlesses found the meat: Carrier Division 2.

Ramage signaled the squadron to break into attack formation and set up for a coordinated attack with Torpedo 10's Avengers. Ramage followed traditional dive-bomber doctrine, leading the first division to strike the farthest carrier, while Lieutenant Louis L. Bangs' second division hit the near carrier in a simultaneous attack. The SBDs pushed into their dives on what Ramage identified as a Zuihō-class carrier. While they were in their dive, a few defending Zekes made a half-hearted attack but were shooed off by the rear gunners. Their target was in fact *Ryūhō*. "The whole flight deck was outlined by tiny candle lights flickering, which was the light AA, punctuated with numerous large-caliber gun bursts. The dive seemed forever, and at 8,000 feet I opened up with my twin .50 caliber nose guns. The tracers disappeared into the deck; however, the Japs didn't for a second leave their guns."

Undaunted, Ramage dove through increasing antiaircraft fire. "I was determined to ride this bomb down to make certain of a hit." Just as he hit the bomb release at 1,500 feet, he saw the stern swing to starboard as she began a turn to port. When he reached to close his dive brakes, he discovered he had never opened them. He was surprised when his gunner opened fire as he pulled out. When he looked back, he was surprised to see a Zeke 15 feet away. An instant later the enemy fighter "stood on its tail and climbed at an impossible angle." As the Zeke climbed away, Ramage's bomb exploded. He looked back and saw black smoke on the flight deck's aft right edge.

Lieutenant (jg) DeTemple was number two behind Ramage and reported his bomb hit almost right on top of Ramage's. Number three Lieutenant (jg) Hubbard near-missed to port while Lieutenant (jg) Schaffer's bomb failed to release and Lieutenant (jg) Schaal claimed a hit on the flight deck's aft port corner.

As Ramage's bombers hit *Ryūhō*, Lieutenant Bangs' three SBDs dived on *Junyō* and the three SBDs led by Lieutenant (jg) Grubiss went after *Hiyō*. Bangs's division claimed three hits – two on *Junyō*'s fantail and one just aft of the island. Grubiss claimed a hit on *Hiyō*'s stern while Lieutenant (jg) Wright scored a near-miss. Lieutenant (jg) Bolton, flying the last "Big E" Dauntless to attack an enemy ship, didn't see the result of his attack. The pilots reported *Junyō* was dead in the water and down by the stern as they turned away.

Following Ramage, Weymouth's Bombing 16 attacked *Hiyō*. Weymouth released his bomb at 1,500 feet and commenced his recovery at 800 feet. His gunner reported he saw black smoke puff up from a hit on the flight deck beside the island.

Using his ailerons during his dive, Ensign Gene Conklin was able to keep the carrier in his sights. He had been warned by Weymouth before takeoff about diving too low, but forgot as he bored in. When he pulled out low, neither he nor his gunner saw the result. The gunners of the last two Dauntlesses, flown by Lieutenant "Pinky" Adams and Ensign Hank Moyers, reported hits. Lieutenant (jg) George Glacken had his view blocked by the four dive bombers ahead of him and ended up diving on *Junyō*.

Leading the second division, Lieutenant Cook Cleland saw Glacken's attack on *Junyō* and came in behind followed by Ensign John F. Caffey. During his dive, Cleland's Dauntless "Old 39" was hit several times, with one putting a 2-foot hole in his starboard wing. He glanced back after dropping and claimed a hit 10 feet forward of *Junyō*'s stern. He turned away and was attacked by a Val, but the enemy dive bomber turned away when Caffey swung his nose towards it. The bomb Cleland dropped was the last hit by a Dauntless on an enemy warship.

While Bombing 16's SBDs attacked the carriers, Alex Vraciu led the eight Fighting 16 Hellcats that escorted the Dauntlesses. He dived on four Zekes intent on going after the dive bombers and caught up with one and downed it. It was his 19th victory. While Vraciu received a nomination for the Medal of Honor for his actions on June 19 and 20, the nomination was downgraded to a Navy Cross when it reached the desk of Admiral George D. Murray at Pacific Fleet Headquarters.

Bombing 2's return to the carriers was described by Ensign Ralph Yaussi: "I found myself alone headed for home. Then I saw another plane and tried to join up on him, but he ran from me apparently thinking I was an enemy. I did not want to expend the fuel to catch him and flew on alone." He then came on two Helldivers flown by his leader Hal Buell and Dave Stear. "We flew along together for some time and I felt that we were not going in the right direction. I communicated my fears through Dave and said that if we didn't change course I was going to leave." Buell turned 2.5 degrees right and convinced him to stick with them, though it was half of what Yaussi suggested. "We arrived just to the left of the fleet but still in sight."

Flying through the pitch dark skies, pilots heard radio calls from planes that couldn't make it. Divisions and sections ditched together to better their chance of surviving the open sea as a group. Individuals called to friends to remember them to loved ones.

Connie Hargreaves remembered:

As we flew on and on in that pitch darkness, I began to question my navigation, for it seemed like we should have found our own carriers a long time ago. But checking my watch indicated that we still had more than half an hour to go before we should be sighting the wakes of our task group, if we had been lucky and plotted our navigation correctly to the Point Option of the moving carriers. All the plotting had to be done in the dull glow of a red-lens flashlight, which was used to help preserve night vision. As I thought about possible navigation errors, I leaned my fuel mixture a little more, as long as the cylinder-head temperatures didn't go beyond acceptable limits.

Forty-three of 51 Helldivers launched survived the attack on the Mobile Fleet. Only ten made it back to the fleet as 32 of those that survived the attack crashed or ran out of fuel and ditched on the return.

At approximately 2015 hours, radar operators aboard the carriers began to see contacts. The fleet had moved 90 miles west in the four hours since launch. At 2030 hours, the ships reversed course to the east and increased speed to 20 knots as they prepared to land aircraft.

Task Group 58.1 commander Rear Admiral Jocko Clark heard the panic in his airmen's voices and ordered the task group's darkened ships to turn on their brightest beams at 2040 hours. Cruisers fired star shells while destroyers turned their searchlights on the carriers.

Seeing Clark's group "lit up like a carnival," Admiral Mitscher gave the famous order, "Turn on the lights." The low clouds reflected light onto the sea below as the ships steamed through the darkness.

Butch Voris was the first to land on *Hornet*, quickly followed by Stinky Davis. From that point on, there was one crash or barrier strike after another as pilots who had never landed aboard a carrier at night tried to get home.

Bombing-2's Jack Taylor remembered:

I got back at 2100 hours with less than 50 gallons of fuel. *Hornet*'s deck was fouled with a crash. We made four passes but were waved off each time. I told my gunner to get the raft ready and prepare for a water landing. After the fourth pass, I pulled the wheels up and flew straight ahead till the engine quit, then ditched. Luckily it was a calm sea so the landing was abrupt but upright. We both got in the raft and, as the night was a dark one, we fired our pistols loaded with tracers to indicate our position.

They were picked up by USS *Bradford* (DD-545) after 20 minutes in their raft.

VF(N)-101's Lieutenant Commander Richard E. Harmer was launched from *Enterprise* in his radar-equipped F4U-2 Corsair. He found three groups and led each home to the task force. As he later remembered, "Prior to this, the deck crews grumbled about not being able to get the deckload ready for the morning launch with our night operations, but afterwards, no one complained about us."

Bunker Hill's Lieutenant Commander Pete Aurand used his radar-equipped F6F-3E Hellcat for the same job. He remembered the return as "a combined Hollywood premiere, Chinese New Year, and Fourth of July." One of those Aurand saved was *Belleau Wood*'s Warren Omark, who had reached Point Option to find "nothing but pitch-black sky." Following Aurand, Omark spotted a carrier and made a straight-in approach. Once he was in the landing pattern, he realized another airplane was right beside him and told himself, "We may have a mid-air collision but I'm not giving up." At the last minute, the other pilot veered off and the LSO gave Omark the cut to land aboard what turned out to be *Lexington*.

Ralph Yaussi remembered that lightning from a thunderstorm 60 miles south of the fleet added to the drama.

We were directed to land on any carrier available. The radio transmissions were chaotic, everyone was talking and therefore no one could be understood. We got in the landing pattern and I went around three times. I was low on fuel so each time I was waved off I retracted my landing gear. On the third approach I was coming in fine when they shined a light and saw my wheels were still retracted so I got a waveoff.

Yaussi told radioman Jim Curry that if they didn't land on the next attempt they would have to ditch. An instant later, the engine cut out and the Helldiver quickly settled onto the ocean from an altitude of 100 feet. The two men struggled free and managed to get into their raft. Yaussi found his Verey pistol after several minutes in the water and fired two flares. USS *Anthony* (DD-515) spotted that and picked them up.

Hal Buell's damaged SB2C's fuel gauges were so low they didn't register. "I had seen some lights come on a short time before off to my right, and right now the ships below me were also lighting up. The first lights were Jocko Clark illuminating *Hornet*; the lights below were from *Lexington*. Soon the ocean was covered with lighted ships speeding through the night. From above it looked like Coney Island on the Fourth of July."

Buell found the nearest carrier and entered the landing pattern. Given a waveoff at the last moment, Buell ignored the LSO and landed aboard. "The plane came down squarely amid the arresting cables, but instead of engaging one of them, the hook bounced and so did my Helldiver. We soared just high enough to clear the first two barriers, came down on top of the final one, then tore loose and slid up the deck toward the parked planes."

The plane just ahead was moving into a tie-down spot. The collision killed the gunner and a sailor in the ship's port catwalk.

Fortunately there was no fire. I cut all engine switches as the crash occurred and, with empty tanks, there was not enough fuel to ignite. The flight deck personnel covered the planes with foam, and began getting us out of the wreckage. Since I was pinned in the cockpit, it took some moments for the deck crew to release me from the tangled metal, but except for minor cuts and bruises I was freed uninjured.

Buell's saviour was *Lexington*.

Connie Hargreaves' ordeal wasn't over after he managed to get back to *Hornet*. "Finally the deck cleared, and I got a chance to land without another waveoff. I picked up the LSO as I turned in for final. I got a

Roger Pass all the way in to the cut and landed without incident on the number-four wire."

After he taxied out of the arrestor gear, Hargreaves was directed to park 50 feet forward of the No. 5 barrier, the last one still usable after all the crashes. After folding his wings and climbing out, he remembered his plotting board was still in the cockpit:

> Suddenly, my plane captain dropped everything and ran to starboard, away from me. For good reason, too! He had glanced back in time to see another Hellcat come barreling up the deck, missing all the landing wires and heading straight for us. For the next few seconds my heart was in my mouth, for I didn't really have any place to go in a hurry. Fortunately, the number five barrier slowed the Hellcat and jerked it to a course crossing to port. It missed my plane by inches but struck another plane, which forced it farther to the left until it slid over the side of the deck and landed on top of the forward port quad-40mm antiaircraft gun mount.

Hornet's newly-promoted CAG, Jackson Arnold, was in the Hellcat's cockpit. Arnold had never flown the Hellcat before taking command of the air group at the end of May and thus had only a few Hellcat daylight carrier landings and had never flown the F6F at night.

Not every pilot was as fortunate as Hargreaves. VF-19's Lieutenant (jg) M.M. Tomme, Jr., had just touched down aboard *Yorktown* when a VF-2 F6F ignored the waveoff as he taxied out of the wires. The *Hornet* Hellcat had been given a waveoff since its tailhook wasn't down; Tomme was killed when it bounced on touchdown and ended up on top of his F6F. *Yorktown* was forced to turn off her lights and close her deck until the wreckage could be cleared. "Jig-Dog" Ramage landed just after the deck was re-opened. His gunner recalled:

> We picked a big one about two miles away and went over to land. There was no one in the pattern and we entered. As we slowed to approach altitude in our SBD, the big radial engine blocked most all of the skipper's forward view. He pulled down his goggles, opened the canopy, and stuck his head way out to the port side. As he did, everything went dark. He had polarized lenses in his goggles! In his effort to get everyone briefed and started this day, he forgot to change to clear lenses. He asked me to help so I read the LSO's signals; he made a perfect approach and we got the cut. As the power came off, we started a beautiful three-point drop and I thought

we were falling into a black hole. The deck was so big it seemed we had to fall three times normal to get down to it.

Air Group 10 was split up with planes landing on five different carriers. The Big-E recovered 17 aircraft from *Bunker Hill*, *Wasp*, *Lexington*, *Hornet*, and *Yorktown*, Torpedo 10 pilot Lieutenant C.B. Collins' made his first approach on what he soon identified as a destroyer! Spotting *Enterprise*, he got into the pattern and was settling into his final approach with incredibly little fuel left when the waveoff came; he ditched alongside a destroyer.

Aboard *San Jacinto* (CVL-30), 19-year-old pilot, Lieutenant (jg) George H.W. Bush, was on the flight deck when an aircraft touched down and the tail hook didn't catch a wire. The plane crashed into a gun mount a few feet away. The pilot's leg, which was severed in the crash, suddenly fell on the deck in front of him. He recalled it was "quivering and separated from the body. The poor guy got cut in half. We young fellows were standing there stunned when this big chief petty officer came along yelling to the crew, 'All right, clean this mess up,' and everybody snapped back."

Two of the four VT-31 TBM Avengers launched from *Cabot* and flown by Lieutenant Wood and Lieutenant Russell, attacked the light carrier *Chiyoda* in the northern group of ships and set it on fire. The other two *Cabot* TBMs, flown by Lieutenant Smith and Ensign Jones, attacked the battleship *Haruna* in the van group. Lieutenants Russell and Wood landed safely back on *Cabot*. Wood had less than 5 gallons in his tank when he touched down, which gave him less than three minutes' flying time. Seven more aircraft from other carriers were also taken aboard *Cabot* that night. Ensign Jones landed on *Bunker Hill* but missed the arresting wires and his TBM crashed into the barrier and caught fire. He and his crew suffered burns getting out of the wreck. Smith ran so low on fuel he was forced to ditch, but he and his two crewmen, Aviation Radioman 1/c McGrath, and Aviation Machinist's Mate 3/c Van Blaircum, were picked up safely two hours later by USS *Hunt* (DD-674) and returned to *Cabot* on June 22.

Bombing 16's Cook Cleland landed aboard *Yorktown*. As he taxied out of the wire, an airedale screamed "Fold them wings!" Cleland replied "This is an SBD!" and the man replied "I don't care what the hell it is! Fold them wings!" The flight deck crews were desperate to find space for the overload of planes coming aboard and decided to push "Ol' 39" overboard since it wasn't one of theirs. Cleland pulled his .45 pistol and aimed it at the flight deck officer. "This airplane stays aboard." "Ol' 39" flew back home to *Lexington* the next morning.

The "Mission Beyond Darkness" was over. Two hundred thirty aircraft were launched and only 115 returned to their carriers. Twenty were lost to flak over the Japanese fleet, while the rest were lost on the return to the fleet from fuel starvation. One hundred pilots and 109 aircrew failed to land aboard a carrier that night. Fifty-one pilots and 50 aircrewmen were pulled out of the water after ditching in the fleet. Fortunately, over the next few days, the planes and destroyers of Task Force 58 were able to search the expanse of the Philippine Sea and an additional 33 pilots and 26 aircrewmen were rescued. Losses for the "Mission Beyond Darkness" were 16 pilots and 33 aircrewmen.

The next morning, *Cabot* had three divisions of VF-31 Hellcats ranged on her flight deck, each carrying a 500-pound armor-piercing bomb and ready for a final mission against the Japanese. By midday, the strike was canceled when it was determined the distance between the fleets was 100 miles farther than the range of the strike aircraft.

With their bombs removed, VF-31 launched the Hellcats to join with other TF 58 aircraft searching for pilots and aircrew who had ditched the night before. When radar picked up a bogey approaching the task force, the Hellcats were diverted from their search and ordered to intercept what turned out to be another of the ubiquitous Betty bombers. Lieutenant (jg) Wilson was first to open fire from above; skipper Lieutenant Commander Winston set the left wing on fire as his wingman, recently-promoted Lieutenant (jg) Conny Nooy, blew off the right wing and Lieutenant (jg) Hancock managed to put a burst into the bomber as it etched a fiery path to the sea below. Winston and his pilots then resumed their search.

On June 29, Robert Winston was promoted to Commander and received orders to take up a position in public information for the Navy Department in Washington. During the squadron's six-month deployment, VF-31 was credited with shooting down 64 enemy aircraft without loss, an admirable achievement for any squadron. Winston would later recount the experience in *Fighter Squadron*, one of the best first-hand accounts of the Central Pacific campaign.

The Navy did not consider what was called the Battle of the Philippine Sea the decisive carrier action that had been sought. As far as was known, only the light carrier *Hiyō* had been sunk, with the carriers *Zuikaku*, *Junyō*, and *Chiyoda*, and the battleship *Haruna* damaged. The results of the submarine attacks on *Shōkaku* and *Taihō* were unknown and it was believed until late September that they had survived to fight another day.

The naval leadership was also not aware that what was left of Japanese naval aviation in the aftermath of the meatgrinder of Rabaul and the depredations by Task Force 58 in the spring of 1944, in addition to the enormous losses sustained on June 19, was now a mere shadow of its former self. The battle had effectively sounded the death knell for the Imperial Japanese Naval Air Force. There would be no time left to replace the losses and provide training to even the very modest level of the pilots who fought at the Marianas.

The lack of understanding of how complete Spruance's victory was would have a momentous effect on the final, and biggest, sea battle of the war, the Battles of Leyte Gulf.

The primary result of the Battle of the Philippine Sea was the establishment of American air supremacy over the western Pacific as the fast carriers ranged where they wished. With the Marianas under American control, the beginning of the end for Japan itself was in view when the B-29 Superfortresses of XXI Bomber Command commenced flying missions against the Home Islands from their Marianas bases in November 1944. From the morning after the Mission Beyond Darkness, the Japanese could do little more than delay the inevitable outcome.

CHAPTER THIRTEEN

THE IWO JIMA DEVELOPMENT CORPORATION

While Air Group 15 was a major participant in the Turkey Shoot, Task Group 58.4 did not participate in the "Mission Beyond Darkness." Nevertheless, the day after the "Mission Beyond Darkness", Lieutenants (jg) John Van Altena and Aviation Radioman 2/c Ray Kataja from Bombing 15 did set off with other planes from the task group to search for survivors from that action, finding some in two rafts at maximum range from the fleet. Van Altena braved high winds and rain to stay airborne above the rafts for some time until a destroyer arrived to rescue the fliers. He ran very low on fuel on his return trip and landed at sunset; as he taxied out of the arresting wires, the engine ran out of fuel and stopped.

Though the Japanese were in retreat, aerial combat continued over the Marianas. David McCampbell led 14 Hellcats, 14 Helldivers and seven Avengers to Guam on June 21, to attack Agana airfield. They hit it hard and during the strike the flak defenses faded into insignificance.

Twelve F6Fs, 15 SB2Cs and seven TBMs went on a second strike, to hit Marpi Point on Saipan – the defense that afternoon was much stronger as the enemy brought replacement guns into action. Ensign William Nolte and his gunner, Aviation Radioman 2/c Lowe dived through heavy flak and the aircraft lost a wing and crashed. Spike Borley remembered "The flak hit the cockpit and I was pretty sure the pilot was killed instantly, but that poor gunner – I watched him try to get out, but the plane was spinning so badly with the wing gone that he couldn't. I've always thought about what must have been going through his mind in those last seconds, knowing there was no alternative but death." They were very popular men and Bombing 15 was hit hard by their loss.

Lieutenant "Beanbag" Barnitz and his gunner, Carl Shelter, also ran into trouble when they were hit over the airfield, but Barnitz was just able to maintain control of his dive bomber and ditch it near the escorting destroyer *Lansdowne* (DD-486), making an escape from their sinking aircraft just in time.

Torpedo 15's lieutenant Bob Cosgrove found his Avenger holed by his own shrapnel when he led his division on a low pass – neither he nor his crew were harmed but back aboard *Essex* the Avenger was no good for anything but spares. Cosgrove received the first of three Distinguished Flying Crosses in September, but the official citation troubled him, as he wrote his wife:

> The whole medal situation is such a farce. I didn't say anything about it. The whole thing is ridiculous. We figure out first who should get a medal and then compose a story that will go through and get the medals for them. Of course, some incident that actually happened is picked to be written up, but it is stretched and dressed up til it is unrecognizable. I'll never again have any respect for a medal ribbon on anyone.

A famous piece of footage was captured on this day when Lieutenant (jg) Baynard Milton crashed his Hellcat aboard the *Essex*. The robustness of his aircraft was demonstrated when flak blew a massive hole in the wing, knocking the right main gear away and severely limiting his aileron control. He had a hard flight back 100 miles to the fleet, with more than 100 holes in the Hellcat, which crushed its single remaining landing gear leg on touchdown and slid across the deck, stopping just short of the island, where an amazingly unharmed Milton stepped out. Milton saw the footage in the newsreel when he went to his hometown movie theater during his post-deployment leave and remembered, "It scared me more to see it than do it."

On June 22, Fighting 15 claimed 12 Zekes while the torpedo and dive bombers damaged the runway at Orote Point on Guam. The snoopers were busy too – a shadowing Emily was shot down by the morning CAP; a Mavis in the afternoon and, at sunset, a second Emily.

The Japanese were being worn down, as Warrant Officer Yoshida noted in his diary, recording his first three days after arriving at Guam:

Day by day, the situation on Saipan grew steadily worse and, here on Guam, we fighter units lost nearly all our usable machines from combat actions and the ceaseless night and day bombing by the enemy. We have had no spare time for repairs on Guam, and by this time there were only two Zeros left. They were guarded the way a tiger guards its cubs.

It was not only the Japanese who were growing tired, as Graham recorded

The boys are tired, some near exhaustion. They're weary, nerves stretched taut. Those who smoke, smoke a lot. Those who fidget, fidget a lot. Most of them are busy though, reading, playing chess, writing, bullshitting. The death of Lowe was sobering. It brought it close to home again. Lowe, newly married, ravenously read his Bible, was well-liked, a hard worker, a humorous, satirical fellow. His getting killed we didn't like at all. It struck me hardest since Smitty's death. Even George Cobbe's going (which was a terrible blow) didn't seem as terrible.

With the threat of a major Japanese attack over, the carriers of Task force 58 set their sights on other Japanese island bases. There was unfinished business at Iwo Jima.

Admiral Clark decided when Task Group 58.1 was ordered to return to Eniwetok the evening of June 22 to refit and rearm, that it would detour north for a second series of strikes at Iwo Jima, with a dawn strike on June 24 laid on.

After four unsuccessful attempts to fly to Iwo Jima with fierce storms traversing the northern Pacific, the Yokosuka Naval Air Group's 80 Zekes finally arrived at Iwo Jima the afternoon of June 23. A hundred aircraft that had also managed the trip that day already packed the runway and parking area, so the Yokosuka NAG pilots landed on a mountainside path without damage. Soldiers stared disbelieving as the fighters taxied past in column as they navigated the mountain path in fog and finally made it to the airfield.

Orote airfield was the target for Dave McCampbell's dawn fighter sweep on June 23. As he led the Hellcats over Agana Field he lost the Zekes he had just seen take off, but then suddenly came across four of them in a Lufbery circle, and six others swept into view as they prepared for the attack. Fortunately, McCampbell had left Bert Morris as high cover with four Hellcats, which swept down to join a half-hour melee over Orote Field, during which Satan's Playmates shot down 11 of the 18 Japanese fighters that had ambushed them.

At 1100 hours a second strike hit positions on Tinian, and a strike was organized on the woods at Orote, where McCampbell had earlier thought he had seen spinning propellers – the jungle was plastered but there were no visible results.

Jim Rigg led a third strike on Orote at 1430 hours, accompanied by members of Bombing 15 who experienced heavy flak and a saw the fighters engage in a dogfight off the beach as they pulled away from their target. Rigg found one to be wily, a useful reminder of the Zeke's performance at low altitude: "he went through every stunt in the books (and some not in) and escaped, unharmed". Yoshida lamented that there were then no aircraft left in 202nd Air Group, though later that night some reinforcements did come in from Yap.

At 0520 hours on June 24, Saburo Sakai and the other pilots were roused by the alarm. American aircraft had been detected inbound on radar. Naval Aviation Pilot 1/c Kinsuke Muto, the leading ace after Sakai, led 42 defenders as they climbed through a break in the clouds into the dawn light while Sakai led the other 38.

At the same time, 15 Fighting 2 Hellcats led by Lieutenant Robert R. Butler broke out of the clouds and spotted Mount Suribachi. Squadrons from *Yorktown*, *Belleau Wood*, and *Bataan* flew through the cloudy sky. Butler's wingman spotted Muto's 42 Zekes as they suddenly burst through the clouds. A swirling dogfight quickly developed. Muto flamed two Hellcats, then chased and quickly set afire a third before turning into a fourth and setting its engine afire.

While an experienced veteran like Muto was still capable of showing what a Japanese fighter pilot could achieve, his fight was notable for achieving the only Japanese victories, as the neophytes were little more than flying targets as the Fighting 2 veterans shot down 28 Zekes in the fast-moving fight.

Connie Hargreaves had been in combat since January and had not seen an enemy airplane until today. "The enemy pilots didn't show a lot of skill. I found a flight of four and just worked from tail-end Charlie to the leader without any of them taking any evasive action." He opened fire on a fifth Zeke, but as the fighter fell away smoking, he was forced to take evasive action and couldn't confirm his fifth victory.

Sakai was surprised by Hellcats that burst out of the clouds as he led his formation toward the battle. As the Americans fastened onto his neophyte pilots, Sakai maneuvered out of the way but momentarily lost sight of the fight; with only one good eye, he was at a disadvantage. Spotting a formation, he flew toward them. He suddenly realized they were enemy, but was too close to turn away.

In the next 20 minutes, Sakai proved his still-superior flying skill as he eluded every attack in a fight that became one of the war's legendary individual air battles. Writing after the war in his autobiography *Samurai*, he recalled:

> The first Grumman tried to match the turn with me. For just that moment I needed, his underside filled the range finder and I squeezed out a burst. The cannon shells exploded along the fuselage. The next second, thick clouds of black smoke poured back from the plane and it went into a wild, uncontrolled dive for the sea. At least a half dozen Grummans were on my tail, their wings sparkling flame as they opened fire. Another left roll – fast! The six fighters ripped past my wing and zoomed in climbing turns to the right.
>
> I slammed the throttle on overboost and rolled right. My Zero closed the distance rapidly. Fifty yards away I opened up with the cannon, watching shells move up the fuselage and disappear into the cockpit. Bright flashes and smoke appeared beneath the glass and the Hellcat swerved crazily and fell off on one wing trailing a growing smoke plume.

The two Hellcats were his 63rd and 64th victories since scoring his first over Clark Air Base on the Pacific War's first day. Now, however, he was boxed in. Twisting and turning, never stopping, the Americans who came at him were disappointed as he flicked away.

Sakai soon realized his opponents weren't as good as their airplanes as he became angered by their clumsy attempts. Turning on one division, he took them head on and hit the leader, who smoked and fell away. The others surrounded him and he only escaped when he threw the Zeke into a spin and fell into a huge cumulus cloud. Suddenly he was in fear of the thunderstorm that shook him, but the maneuver gave him precious seconds to get away because the enemy pilots thought they had gotten him.

Sakai found himself alone in the sky as he fell out of the cloud and recovered. Exhausted, he returned to Iwo Jima, where the mechanics were astonished to find his Zeke untouched by any of the hundreds of rounds the enemy had fired at him. The same could not be said for the rest of the group, since only 30 returned of the 80 who had taken off that morning.

That afternoon, a squadron of Jill torpedo bombers was sent to find and attack the Americans, escorted by Sakai and the surviving pilots he judged able to deal with the weather. They were spotted on radar and were caught by the American CAP before they could get close enough to make an attack.

Hargreaves was one of the defenders. The Zeke he scored made him another of Fighting 2's "aces in a day." June 24, 1944, saw the "Rippers" set a squadron record of 67 victories, just short of Fighting 15's June 19 score of 67.5. In the 90 days since they had entered combat, they were now the top-scoring fighter squadron in the Navy at the moment with 187 victories that had been scored at a faster rate than any other Navy squadron. The day's success was darkened by the loss of Lieutenant (jg) Conrad Elliott, who was one of the most popular pilots, remembered equally for his personal kindness as for his daring. He had fallen to either Muto or Sakai, the only Japanese pilots who scored any victories.

While Admiral Clark's pilots fought over Iwo Jima, an *Essex* strike against Orote Field found no aerial opposition. A ship was discovered offshore that was sunk by Bob Cosgrove with rockets. During a second strike against Agana Airfield led by Jim Mini, Beanbag Barney Barnitz's Helldiver was hit and he had to ditch for the second time in as many days.

Though officially the Americans had declared Japanese air power in the Marianas to be destroyed, enemy aircraft still cropped up. When Ensign Singer went on a third strike to photograph Rota in an F6F-3P photo plane, four Zekes attacked. Luckily he managed to take two down, and evaded the other two.

Warrant Officer Yoshida was one of only eight surviving pilots from 202nd Air Group, and when a Sally landed at Orote Field that night, he convinced the young captain to fly them back to Yap. Yoshida was admitted to hospital on arrival as his malaria had flared up.

As *Essex* headed for Eniwetok at the end of June, Ted Graham committed to paper a song that had been heard around the fleet:

I WANTED WINGS
I wanted wings 'till I got the God-damned things,
Now I don't want 'em anymore!
They taught me how to fly,
Then they brought me here to die
I've had my belly full of war!
You can save all those Zeros
For the God-damned heroes,
'Cause Distinguished Flying Crosses
Don't compensate for losses.

I wanted wings 'till I got the God-damned things,
Now I don't want them anymore!

I'll take the dames while the rest go down in flames,
I've no desire to be burned!
Air combat's no romance
It made me wet my pants,
I'm just an asphalt Arab I have learned.
You can save the Mitsubishis
For the crazy sons of bitches.
I'd rather have a woman,
Than get shot up in a Grumman.
I wanted wings 'till I got the God-damned things,
Now I don't want 'em anymore!

I'm too young to die
Even in a PBY
That's for the eager, not for me!
I wouldn't trust my luck
To be picked up in a Duck
After I'd crashed into the sea.
I'd rather be a bar sop,
Than a flier on a flat-top,
With my hands around a bottle,
Rather than around a throttle.
I wanted wings 'till I got the God-damned things,
Now I don't want 'em anymore!
There is no promotion
On this side of the ocean,
And the guys at home don't really care!
At my bit I'm not a chafin'
For the joy of doin' strafin'
I hate the violent use of tail and rudder!
As for livin' like Flash Gordon,
I'll take boating on the Jordan,
I'm a simple soul and all for home and mudder.
You can have your shoulder holster,
I'll take resting on a bolster,
And I'll trade my long "pig sticker"

For a tall cool drink of likker.
I wanted wings 'till I got the God-damned things,
Now I don't want 'em anymore!
Hey waiter – bring another round!

The bad weather around the Bonins forced Admiral Clark to turn the task group southeast on June 25 and they arrived in Eniwetok on June 28. They departed on July 1 after a quick turnaround and returned to Iwo Jima in company with Task Group 58.4, which was diverted from their return to Eniwetok to join the strikes.

Admiral Harrill's ships slowed to celebrate the Fourth of July that evening, but the aggressive Clark pushed on and his carriers struck Iwo Jima in the late afternoon of July 3. Commander Dean led a 60-plane sweep. They found that more reinforcements had been flown in from the Home Islands, and they were met by Zekes north of the island. They claimed 33 destroyed on return to the *Hornet*. The ill-trained reinforcements had no more success than those who preceded them. Bob Butler and Roy O'Neal failed to return. Since no one had seen what happened to them, they were listed as Missing in Action.

On July 4, both task groups made a coordinated attack on the Bonins in which *Hornet*'s air group attacked Chichi Jima. Torpedo 2 pilot Ken Glass found an enemy destroyer and attacked it with rockets. The ship exploded as he pulled out.

Both task groups withdrew on July 5 to refuel since the weather was too bad for further air strikes. Saburo Sakai received orders to lead his surviving pilots to escort the ten surviving Jills and attack the American fleet. He considered this a death sentence since the force was too small to have any chance of success and the weather was so bad he doubted his pilots could survive. When they were intercepted by the American CAP, all the Jills and seven of the ten Zekes were shot down. Sakai led his two wingmen back to Iwo Jima, where the remaining aircraft were set afire and the pilots were issued rifles in preparation for the expected landings. Had the Americans invaded at this time, it would have been a walkover, given the island's poor defenses. When the invasion didn't happen, Sakai and the other survivors were evacuated to Japan.

Essex and the rest of Task Group 58.4 arrived at Eniwetok on July 6 but only remained until July 14, which was sufficient time to bring supplies aboard and give the crew time on the beach. The enlisted men's ration of two warm beers each, not to mention the sand fleas, failed to impress Ted Graham.

The Battle of the Philippine Sea, July to August 1944

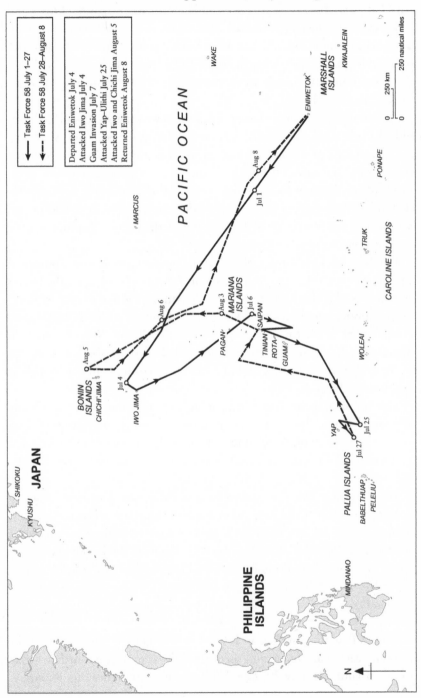

During this stopover, Fighting 15 received the first of the new Grumman F6F-5 Hellcat. They packed considerably more power than the F6F-3 and at first were only given to squadron leaders; however, as they were so much faster than the old planes, it was soon decided it was better to fly divisions arranged by plane type so that they could all move at the same speed. Their glossy sea blue paint made them easy to distinguish from the "tri-color scheme" used on the F6F-3.

Bombing 15 also replaced its planes at this time – the SB2C-1C Helldiver with 3-blade propellers was displaced by the more powerful SB2C-3C with four-blade props and a more powerful engine, making takeoff that much easier and safer. Although the squadron was reduced from 36 to 24 Helldivers, many of the aircrew were able to transfer to the improved Hellcats of Fighting 15, as the F6F-5 could now carry two 1,000-pound bombs and six 5-inch aerial rockets under the wings, improving their capability as a fighter-bomber.

On July 14 Task Group 58.4 left its anchorage – it now comprised *Essex*, *Langley*, and *Cowpens'* replacement, *Princeton* (CVL-23). The latter's captain turned a blind eye to the non-regulation painting of cats' eyes and fangs dripping blood on the cowlings of Fighting 27's F6F-3 "Hell Cats", though Admiral Sherman fully disapproved. Fighting 27 had scored 30 victories at the Marianas Turkey Shoot, their first combat on June 19. By the end of the war, they would be the top-scoring light carrier fighter squadron in the fleet.

Operations against Guam began on July 17 in preparation for the coming invasion of Tinian, and on July 20, Bombing 15 struck southeastern Guam – a wing was blown off the Helldiver flown by Lieutenant Niles Siebert and it fell fast, exploding on impact. A distraught John Bridgers remembered:

> For more than two years, I had been rooming with Lieutenant Niles Raymond Siebert, "Old Sieb," in tents on New Caledonia and Guadalcanal, in a Quonset hut at Creed's Field, and in sea cabins on the *Saratoga*, the *Hornet*, and finally the *Essex*. Our time together, though only a bit less than two years, had seemed much longer in a life paced by carrier flying and combat. Losing Sieb was as close, I suppose, as I'll ever come to losing a brother.

The group flew three strikes on July 24 against gun emplacements on the invasion beaches at Tinian, and spent three days conducting further strikes over the island. On July 29, *Essex* left Tanapag Harbor, heading for strikes against Yap and Palau. The next day they were joined by the fast battleships *Alabama* (BB-60), *New Jersey* (BB-62), *Iowa* (BB-61), *Indiana* (BB-58) and *Wisconsin* (BB-64). Graham wrote that this "battle line" under the command of Rear Admiral Willis Lee "made a stirring sight for all of us."

Guam was invaded on August 1. An average of three air support strikes per day were flown until August 6, when the fast battleships departed.

Hornet and Task Group 58.1 struck a final blow against the Bonins on August 4 and 5. Many aboard the flagship had concluded that their Admiral had a fixation on the islands. As a joke, a "stock certificate" for the "Iwo Jima Development Corp – J.J. Clark, President" was made up and mimeographed. After it had been distributed through the air group, Clark liked it so much he signed copies when asked.

Kid Lake shot down a snooping Emily the morning of August 5 to score his fifth victory. Dick Combs shot down another that afternoon. No other enemy aircraft were encountered. A sweep later that day which found no worthwhile targets and the task group returned to Eniwetok.

Task Group 58.4 continued supporting the Guam invasion until August 9, when Captain Ralph Oftsie departed *Essex*, having been promoted to Rear Admiral. His relief was Captain C.W. Weiber, who would command the ship for the rest of the war. The strike concluded on August 11, when the task group departed for Eniwetok.

The two weeks of relative peace that Air Group 15 had aboard Essex at Eniwetok were welcome – the Pacific War was about to begin its crescendo. The most successful carrier campaign in the war to date had concluded with the invasion and liberation of Saipan, Tinian, and Guam, setting the stage for the final aerial assault on Japan itself.

CHAPTER FOURTEEN

HALSEY'S RAMPAGE

With the Marianas now under American control, the ultimate US strategy for the defeat of Japan reached a turning point in the summer of 1944 that would be resolved as much for the benefit of domestic politics as for the goal of winning the war.

The Japanese conquest of the Philippines was a festering wound to the massive ego of General Douglas MacArthur, the general who had lost half his air force on the ground eight hours after receiving word of the Pearl Harbor attack, who had ordered his men to retreat to the Bataan Peninsula without insuring the necessary food and weapons for a prolonged siege, and who had been ordered to escape by PT Boat, leaving his second in command to surrender to the victorious Japanese. MacArthur left the islands with the promise, "I shall return," and was determined to make good on it. Over the previous two years he had waged a successful campaign first to deny Japan a full conquest of New Guinea and possibly Australia, and then to expel the Imperial Japanese Army from New Guinea. To MacArthur, it was obvious the next advance must be to the Philippines.

What was obvious to Douglas MacArthur was not obvious to everyone else. For the US Navy, the idea of taking the Philippines seemed a diversion from their plan to defeat Japan. Retaking the islands would do nothing to cause irreparable damage to Japan by their loss, while retaking the archipelago from the Japanese forces present would tie down a large ground force for a long campaign which would not affect the ultimate outcome of the war.

The Navy preferred to take Formosa, the island off the Chinese coast that had been colonized by Japan since having seized it at the turn of the century. Such a move made geostrategic sense. Formosa was large, with many airfields. Utilizing it as a base for the Army Air Forces would allow even more air attacks against the Home Islands since it was closer to Japan than the Marianas were. Additionally, its location would allow those air forces to attack Japanese forces in eastern China, which could have a major effect on the war in China that had raged since 1937.

MacArthur was not to be thwarted. When Admiral Nimitz visited the general's Australian headquarters in the spring of 1944, he reported his exchange to Admiral King:

> Then he blew up and made an oration at some length on the impossibility of bypassing the Philippines, his sacred obligations there – redemption of the 17 million people – blood on his soul – deserted by the American people – etc., etc. – and then a criticism of "those gentlemen in Washington who, far from the scene, and having never heard the whistle of bullets, etc., endeavor to set the strategy of the Pacific war."

MacArthur's involvement with the Philippines went back to the original American conquest of the islands in the Spanish-American War. His father, General Arthur MacArthur, had been the military viceroy who defeated the Philippine Insurrection that followed the war, after Filipino nationalists realized they had traded one imperial master for another. Arthur MacArthur's career would eventually founder over his unwillingness to take direction from William Howard Taft after he was appointed Governor General of the Philippines, regarding his policies there. Once Taft became President, Arthur MacArthur was forced into a bitter retirement. The son had been raised to believe himself a "man of destiny" and saw his and his father's involvement with the islands as a personal sacred duty. That he had been chased out by the Japanese was a personal affront that could not go unanswered.

The argument was renewed when the Joint Chiefs adopted the Navy's plan for the invasion of the Marianas to station B-29s there, rather than giving MacArthur the strategic bombers for his Philippines campaign. The decision was seen as a further personal affront by MacArthur, who believed he saw the hand of President Roosevelt in the decision, to deny him the glory of supreme command in the Pacific which he believed was his natural due.

The dispute became intertwined with domestic US politics since the Republican Party was in search of a candidate who might defeat Roosevelt in the fall presidential elections where he was expected to run for an unprecedented fourth term.

MacArthur had long been connected to the right wing of the Republican Party, which was locked in combat with the "internationalists" who were represented by the candidacy of Governor Thomas Dewey. MacArthur was closely allied with Henry Luce, founder of *Time* and *Life* magazines and a power in the conservative wing. Luce and his allies knew of MacArthur's personal dislike of Roosevelt, and his belief that his campaign in the Pacific was being stymied by presidential opposition.

Civilian visitors to MacArthur's headquarters carefully sounded him out on the possibility of resigning his command in opposition to the President, to return to the United States and campaign for the Republican nomination. The general was open to such suggestions.

President Roosevelt was aware of these political moves on the part of his opponents and was well aware of MacArthur's heroic status with the American public due to the careful buildup he had received in Republican newspapers over the previous two years (the largest unit on MacArthur's staff, in terms of number of people assigned, was his publicity department).

The President was also well aware that the Democratic Party had lost the mid-term elections of 1942 due to bad war news over the months preceding the election, which might have changed in his favor had Operation *Torch*, the invasion of North Africa, occurred the weekend before the election, with a consequent national feeling of victory under his leadership, rather than the weekend following. The congressional losses had meant the end of further New Deal legislation when the conservative Midwestern Republicans allied with the conservative Southern Democrats to oppose his final New Deal reform, the nationalization of medical care and the creation of what would have been a "GI Bill of Rights for America," a thoroughgoing democratization of the economic system. For Franklin Roosevelt, the issue of the effect of the timing of military operations on domestic politics was crucially important since he was well aware of the difficulty presented by a campaign for a fourth term.

The disagreement between MacArthur and the Navy over the future course of the Pacific War was so deep it would take personal intervention by President Roosevelt to resolve it. After making a tour of the western states in early July 1944 in preparation for the coming campaign, the President decided to meet his two Pacific military commanders in Hawaii.

MacArthur believed the request was a ploy to get him separated from his command and isolated. At first he claimed operational requirements in the southwest Pacific would prevent his traveling to Hawaii. While Roosevelt hesitated to give his headstrong Commander a direct order, it was made known to MacArthur that this was a request he could not refuse. He made the trip to Pearl Harbor in time to stand on the dock with Admiral Nimitz to welcome the President when he arrived aboard the heavy cruiser *Baltimore* (CA-68).

Once in Hawaii at Nimitz's headquarters, MacArthur listened as Nimitz presented the Navy's proposal that the Philippines be bypassed for an invasion of Formosa which would directly cut off the Home Islands of Japan from the supply of raw materials from Southeast Asia. When Nimitz concluded, MacArthur rose and gave one of his finest performances as he pressed the case for the invasion of the Philippines in purely political terms.

He pointed out that the liberation of America's Asian colony, which was already promised independence at the conclusion of the war, would be popular with the American public, and that the political leader associated with such liberation would reap the benefit. He warned that if Roosevelt did not choose this option, "I dare to say that the American people would be so aroused that they would register most complete resentment against you in the polls."

Seeing that the President still did not appear to agree, he went so far as to privately threaten that if the Philippines strategy was not adopted, he would be morally forced to resign his commission and return to the United States to campaign for the Republican nomination on a claim that the United States government had "abandoned" the people of the Philippines.

It was a political threat Roosevelt could not ignore. He asked what the timetable for such an invasion would be. MacArthur stated that the Army could be on Mindanao by the end of October. When pressed by the President, Nimitz admitted that the Navy would not be able to invade Formosa before January 1945.

Thus, the major decision regarding the future strategy for the defeat of Japan was made on the basis of which action would happen in time to affect the domestic presidential election campaign. The prospect of news that General MacArthur had made good his pledge, "I shall return," by the weekend before the election at the latest was the deciding point in Roosevelt's decision to agree with MacArthur's demand.

President Roosevelt ended the conference with a visit to the wounded at the naval hospital in Pearl Harbor, where he asked the Secret Service to take him through the wards in his wheelchair. Nimitz remembered that "He asked to be wheeled through all the wards that were occupied by men who had lost one or more arms and legs. He insisted on going past each individual bed. He wanted to display himself and his useless legs to those boys who would have to face the same bitterness." It was the only time in his presidency that Franklin Roosevelt made any public acknowledgment of his physical disability.

The Navy was directed to plan its actions in support of the Philippines invasion. Thus, the decision was made to invade the Palaus with a date of mid-September, to provide a footing for land-based air support for the Philippines invasion and a forward operating base for the fleet at Ulithi Atoll. Admiral Halsey, who was set to assume command of the fast carrier fleet at the end of August, was ordered to plan a campaign to isolate the Philippines after supporting the Palau invasion, in preparation for the coming October invasion.

On August 24, 1944, Third Fleet commander Vice Admiral William "Bull" Halsey replaced Fifth Fleet commander Vice Admiral Raymond A. Spruance at the Pacific Fleet anchorage in Eniwetok Atoll. The two were still as friendly as they had been when Spruance had been Halsey's subordinate in 1942, but Halsey saw this change of command differently from Spruance. He hoped the invasion of the Philippines would force the Imperial Japanese Navy to come out for one final battle, and he intended that his victory over them would be the decisive victory Spruance's critics said he had missed in the Marianas.

Throughout the fleet, the sailors took the arrival of "America's fightingest Admiral" as a sign of action to come. While senior officers might prefer Spruance, the common sailors responded to Halsey's charisma and thought of him the way GIs in Europe thought of General George Patton.

There had been several changes aboard the fast carriers as they replenished in the anchorage in the weeks before Halsey's arrival. *Hornet's* Captain Sample was informed of his promotion to Rear Admiral. His replacement was Captain Austin K. Doyle, who assumed command on August 8 and would command the carrier for the rest of the war. Captain Sample was remembered by Air Group 2 as "a fearless leader whose thoughts were always for those in his charge … he proved himself a real friend to the air group."

At an awards ceremony following the change of command, Lieutenant (jg) "Andy" Skon received the Navy Cross for his role the night of Butch O'Hare's loss back in November 1943. Commander Dean received the Distinguished Flying Cross for his leadership of Fighting 2 in the battles on June 11 and 20, 1944.

Connie Hargreaves later recalled Dean's leadership of Fighting 2:

> Commander Bill Dean could have been a very high-scoring pilot, had he
> taken all the flights when opposition was anticipated. But he always tried
> to keep the scores for all his pilots as even as possible, not catering to a

favored few, as some of the other fighter squadron skippers did. Often, he took assignments himself for the CAP or bomber escort instead of leading all the fighter sweeps. That gave us all an opportunity to get into action. Thus, Fighting 2 had 28 aces in our one tour of duty, a Navy record that still stands.

Aboard the task force flagship, *Lexington*, Signalman First Class Tom Curtis was notified he would be promoted to Chief Petty Officer as soon as a vacancy opened up on the ship. When he asked if there was a chance he might be transferred to a different ship, perhaps one that was returning to the United States, his division officer replied that however much he might wish he could do that for his leading petty officer, he couldn't do without Curtis's leadership. Tom Curtis wouldn't return home for another year.

Air Group 16 departed *Lexington* in mid-August. As the leading ace, Alex Vraciu was told he would get the "full treatment" on return home, with a national bond tour as his mentor Butch O'Hare had done two years earlier. "This was just what I didn't want," Vraciu later remembered. Air Group 19, under the command of Commander Thomas H. Winters, Annapolis class of 1935 and a naval aviator since 1936, came aboard *Lexington* as replacements for the veterans of Air Group 16.

On August 24, Air Group 2 learned that their replacement, Air Group 11, had arrived in Hawaii. However, the group would not be able to arrive at Eniwetok to replace them prior to the fleet's departure for the Palau campaign. After five months of nearly continuous combat, the pilots and aircrewmen were ready to go home.

At 0630 hours on August 28, 1944, the fast carriers, now known as Task Force 38 of the Third Fleet, departed Eniwetok headed for the Palaus. *Hornet*, along with *Wasp* and *Hancock*, was accompanied by *Cowpens* and *Monterey* as Task Group 38.1 under the command of Vice Admiral John S. McCain. While the fleet commander was fresh, many of the men he commanded had been at war in the Pacific without break for nearly seven months and some for a year. The majority of the aircrews had been in near-continuous combat since early June, with some having arrived in the combat zone as early as April. Many early groups would be relieved over the next month, leaving the fleet with a combination of tired but experienced and fresh but inexperienced fliers. The combination would lead to operational problems in the final great naval battle of the war, only eight weeks away.

With the change in command from Spruance to Halsey, Fifth Fleet and Task Force 58 became Third Fleet and Task Force 38. The *Essex* task group became Task Group 38.3, composed of *Essex*, Admiral Mitscher's flagship *Lexington*, and the light carrier *Princeton*, joined by the battleships *Washington*, *Massachusetts*, *Indiana*, and *Alabama*.

The task group's escorting destroyers included *Foote*, *Ausburne*, *Spence*, *Aulick*, *Claxton*, *Dyson*, *Converse*, and *Thatcher* of Destroyer Squadron 23. The unit shot to fame as the "Little Beavers" when Captain Arleigh A. Burke assumed command in November 1943. Over the next four months, they were the victors of the Battle of Empress Augusta Bay and the Battle of Cape St. George, as well as 22 lesser engagements. Captain Burke usually operated his destroyers at near-maximum speed; while on their way to rendezvous with other units just before the Battle of Cape St. George, *Spence* suffered damage to a boiler tube, which limited the ships to a top speed of 31 knots, rather than the 34 they were capable of. As a result, their commander gained the nickname "31-knot Burke." Originally meant as a taunt, by the time he left the squadron the following February its record of having sunk one Japanese cruiser, nine destroyers, one submarine, several smaller ships, and shooting down 30 aircraft was such that the nickname became a popular symbol of his hard-charging nature. Following the Battle of Blackett Strait, in which he felt that he had not performed in the way he expected of his officers, Burke asked an ensign what the difference was between a good officer and a poor one. After listening to the young officer's answer, he offered his own view: "The difference between a good officer and a poor one is about ten seconds." Burke had been promoted to Chief of Staff to Admiral Mitscher in March 1944, under Admiral King's policy that an aviation admiral would have a surface officer as chief of staff. His hard-charging attitude permeated through the fleet's officer corps and contributed to its superior performance.

On September 6, Task Force 38 arrived off the Palaus. Pre-invasion strikes concentrated on the strangely shaped island of Peleliu, site of the 1st Marine Division's scheduled landing. Ulithi Atoll was found undefended. The Navy occupied it that week and the first ships of Service Squadron 10 arrived to provide fleet support the next week.

Air Group 2 was in the midst of planning strikes on the Palaus to start the next morning when news arrived that Air Group 11 had departed Pearl Harbor, bound for Eniwetok. The fliers now faced the fact that, while the end of their tour was in sight, they must pass through the gantlet of combat once more, attacking what were certain to be difficult targets in the Philippines, before their relief would happen.

Hornet's first strike took off at 0430 hours on September 7, headed for Angaur. Over the course of the day, three strikes were flown against the islands of Angaur and Ngesibus. A division led by Lieutenant Charlie Carroll, Jack Vaughn, "Razor" Blaydes, and "Randy" Carlson, was assigned to take photographs of the morning strike. Carlson was lost to flak. All losses were felt keenly as everyone looked forward to returning home, but Carlson had been a plank owner in the squadron and the first to score for the squadron.

Admiral Halsey felt by September 8 that his work on the Palaus was done and took three of Task Force 38's task groups off in the direction of the southern Philippines, leaving Admiral Ralph Davison's Task Group 38.4 to support the Palaus invasion. By this time the Japanese had reinforced the Philippines in the months since the Marianas invasion and were ready to put up a stiff resistance.

The Philippines strikes brought Task Force 38's aviators up against the Imperial Japanese Army Air Force in substantial numbers for the first time since the fighting at Rabaul. Because the American pilots were unfamiliar with these Imperial Japanese Army Air Force aircraft, claims were frequently made for shooting down Japanese naval aircraft of similar configuration, though in fact the only Imperial Japanese Naval Air Force unit in the Philippines at this time was the 204th Naval Air Group at Mabalacat, the name the Japanese had given Clark Field on the northern island of Luzon.

Thus, the Nakajima Ki-43 *Hayabusa*, known to the Allies as "Oscar," was often mistaken by pilots for a Zeke, while the Mitsubishi Ki-21 Type 97 heavy bomber "Sally" was claimed as a Betty. The Mitsubishi Ki-51 Type 99 assault plane known as "Sonia" was mis-identified as a Val due to it being a two-seater bomber with fixed landing gear. The obsolete Nakajima Ki-27 "Nate" was also found in surprising numbers, assigned to advanced training units, and was sometimes mis-identified as the A5M "Claude."

Nine airfields on southern Mindanao were the first targets for Air Group 15, supported by *Lexington*'s Air Group 19, when they arrived in the Philippines on September 9 – they first struck the airfields of Lumbia and Cagayan in a strike at 0535 hours. More than 200 Helldivers and Avengers from three task groups were sent against shipping in Macajalar and Bislig bays, sweeping across the island's northern beaches. They also found a convoy and claimed 18 ships sunk.

Fighting 2's Lieutenant Commander Charlie Harbert spotted an Oscar he mis-identified as a Zeke over Cebu which he shot down to become the squadron's 23rd ace. In a four-minute fight, eight more victories were scored and Lieutenant (jg) C.P. "Spit" Spitler got four to become the squadron's 24th ace. Lieutenant (jg) Tom Tillar was hit and his oil line was severed. He ditched east of Leyte Island and swam ashore to be rescued by an SOC Seagull led to his location by Andy Skon.

Fighting 2's second strike went to Negros Island, where eight Hellcats scored six victories and CAG Arnold scored his first. Razor Blaydes became the 25th squadron ace, while Lieutenant (jg) Zaeske scored his fifth moments later to become the unit's 26th ace. Lieutenant (jg) Byron Johnson scored his seventh victory and newly promoted Lieutenant Arthur Van Haren downed his ninth while Barney Barnard chalked up his seventh.

Aviation Radioman 2/c John Miller recorded in his diary Torpedo 15's second strike on the convoy at 1000 hours:

> Sept. 9 – our target this morning was Japanese installations on the island of Mindanao in the Philippines. Our Division Six took off on the second hop with Division Two (Lt. Bridgers' division) at 0900 with a total of 12 Helldivers. Between us and the other carriers, we had six hundred aircraft up that day: SB2Cs, TBMs and F6Fs. We flew 120 miles inland over high mountains, then winding rivers, swamps, and pineapple plantations. We were told that large areas up in the mountains were controlled by Philippine guerrilla bands. These guerrillas would be burning fires in their areas, so if any of us were hit, we should head for the nearest column of smoke rising from the trees and bail out over it. We saw these fires as we headed for the Japanese airfield on the other side of the island. We hit Del Monte Field, Lumbia, and wharves and shipping at Surigao with complete surprise, destroying aircraft on the ground, hangars, and oil storage tanks as well as sinking a large tanker in the harbor.

Destroyer Division 110 and the cruisers *Santa Fe* (CL-60) and *Birmingham* (CL-62) located a convoy off Sanco Point at 1130 hours that had been spotted by one of the earlier air strikes. *Santa Fe* sank four cargo vessels, badly damaged several others and left three aflame before rejoining Task Group 38.3 at 1345 hours.

That day, Cagayan and Lumbia fields had 70 aircraft destroyed, along with a radar installation at San Augustin. 143 sorties had gone up from *Essex* alone, and the Japanese reported that more than 300 enemy planes had attacked Mindanao during the course of the day. It would be hit by further strikes the next day, one of them including ten Hellcats from the *Essex* led by Jim Rigg. By the end of September 10, Japanese air power on Mindanao had been destroyed.

The next target was the Visayan Islands on September 12. The weather was inclement but Jim Rigg led a fighter sweep from *Essex* and *Lexington* towards Cebu airfield and strafed into oblivion 80 fighters that had been lined up for takeoff, before becoming Fighting 15's fourth "ace in a day" by shooting down five Oscars that had taken off from Mactan Field.

Commander Dean led VF-2's first sweep over southern Luzon on September 13. No opposition was found until Dean spotted an Oscar 4,000 feet below him and dispatched it with a single overhead pass. Lieutenant Bill Blair shot down an Oscar while leading a second sweep that afternoon to become the squadron's 27th ace. Banks got another Oscar, while Kid Lake scored two Nates. Ensign Evald Holmgaard, flying his first mission, shot down a third Nate that was the squadron's 245th victory. The Nate claims are surprising, and may have been training aircraft flown by instructor pilots.

Hornet's Task Group 38.2 left Task Force 38 and headed south. On September 15 the carriers were off Halmahera, where they gave air support to MacArthur's forces invading the island of Morotai.

By McCampbell's dawn sweep on October 13, there were few worthwhile targets left on Cebu, though at Negros they found 20 aircraft in revetments at Bacolod Field, which they strafed, shooting down two Sallys and then bringing down a Nate before McCampbell became separated from his wingman and was attacked:

> While waiting for my division to rendezvous, I was attacked from above by a lone Nate that I did not see til it was too late to counter. After his pass, he pulled up in front of me and I got in behind him, but he was out of range by then. I dropped my belly tank and shifted to war emergency power and tried to climb up to him. He started a roll to make an overhead run on me. I split-essed and dived away into a cloud and lost him. The following points stand out: 1) Nate is even more maneuverable than Zeke. 2) Nate can outclimb F6F at 110 to 120 knots airspeed. 3) This "operational student," if he was such, will have no trouble completing the course.

Even someone like McCampbell was able to underestimate the nature of his enemy – he had been caught going low and slow near an unexpectedly maneuverable Japanese plane and it is possible that he only survived the encounter due to its light armament of 7.7mm machine guns.

The CAG found five more Nates at 12,000 feet when he turned to rejoin his flight:

Although I was alone and below, I felt confident (knowing I could dive away into the clouds if necessary) as I tailed behind and below and had almost climbed to their level before the leader spotted me and turned my way. He did not attack immediately, and I held my course and rocked my wings, hoping his recognition was as poor as mine and he would take me for a friendly. He continued on in a lazy climbing circle, then turned toward me again. He wasn't fooled when I rocked my wings this time, and the whole outfit tailed in behind me as I pushed over. In my dive, I saw friendly F6Fs below and turned to drag the enemy in front of them. The fight was on and there were burning airplanes everywhere. We finally rendezvoused at 12,000 feet and chased another Nate into a towering cumulus cloud. As time and gas were running short, we headed for base.

About 40 Oscars and Nates gave VF-15 continuous action for as much as 45 minutes; Wendell Twelves brought down four of these using his climb and dive superiority.

A second strike of 30 bombers led by John Bridgers hit Saravia Field on Leyte, cratering the runway but encountering heavy antiaircraft fire on the return pass, which brought down Gene Golden's Helldiver in a ball of flame. Bridger blamed himself for wanting to "put those heavy 20mm cannon we'd been hauling around to some use. I couldn't help but believe I had signed Gene Golden's death warrant. He'd been a member of the Silent Second since we had first formed."

A third strike left *Essex*, *Lexington* and *Princeton* just before noon and a fourth strike was sent towards Cebu at 1400 hours but turned back due to bad weather conditions.

After four days of strikes, American pilots claimed 170 planes shot down and 300 destroyed on the ground – an absolute disaster for the Japanese in the southern Philippines. Mindanao was now considered low risk and the American invasion forces were to bypass it and head for Leyte two months ahead of schedule.

The Japanese expected the Americans to arrive to invade Luzon around September 20 and busily assembled all their remaining aircraft at Clark Field and Nicholls Field between September 17 and 19, hoping to launch 300 planes against their foe.

After spending September 17 at Peleliu supporting the Marines' invasion, Task Force 38 headed back to Luzon, where they arrived on September 20. Graham recalled their brief that evening:

We'll hit Clark Field and Nichols Field in the morning. In the p.m., the same thing will be repeated. If things go well, we'll do it again the next day. Then hit the Visayans. Jap plane estimate is 500. Bombers will carry torpedoes since they expect two Jap battleships, four light cruisers, nine destroyers, which will be a healthy haul. We all want to go to Manila, and yet we don't. Some of us may get hurt, yet none of us want to miss it. The chief driving force is the hope this will be our last operation!!! Air Group 2, which replaced us on *Hornet*, has orders for home when this is done.

Hargreaves and Banks shot down a snooper over Task Group 38.2 at 0740 hours on September 21, while on CAP. *Hornet*'s strike was launched at 0800 hours in heavy seas.

The weather over Manila Harbor was clear when Ken Glass' Torpedo 2 division made their first-ever combat torpedo strike. As the torpedo bombers and dive bombers attacked the ships, a formation of 20–30 enemy fighters suddenly swept in. Tex Harris recalled:

> The Tonys came in after one flight and completed a run. We scissored, then turned and started climbing, and were soon in position for a tail run from below. The leading Tony turned to the left and dropped its nose – a burst from my guns hit it in the cockpit and it exploded. The second and third were fired on by my wingmen and both went down to watery graves. We then splashed another that tried to outrun us and made a low altitude turn. I saw Gabe in difficulty with three Tonys. We dove on them and they turned away which was a good thing, since we were nearly out of ammo.

The surviving enemy fighters flew off and the torpedo and dive bombers reported destruction of 15 cargo ships.

Several strikes against Clark and Nicholls fields were made by flights led by David McCampbell and Jim Rigg on September 21, often against intense antiaircraft fire. *Lexington* also launched two successful strikes against a convoy 60 miles north of Subic Bay, sinking a destroyer and seriously damaging several other ships. The Japanese reported more than 400 American aircraft over Clark Field that day with the city of Manila, the harbor and the airfields suffering terribly.

Air Group 2's first strike was launched at 0630 hours on September 22 after a night of heavy seas. A Japanese strike force was spotted by radar at 0730 hours and General Quarters was sounded throughout the task group. A bomb-carrying Zeke penetrated the escort screen to strafe *Hornet*'s flight deck. Luckily, its bomb failed to drop until the airplane was shot down. Three of the airedales were wounded in the incident, one seriously. Thirty minutes later, the surviving enemy aircraft escaped after several were shot down by the escorts. Spider Webb shot down a Tony while Tex Vineyard shot the wingman off Webb's tail during the air group's final strike against Manila.

Task Group 38.3 refueled on September 22 as they headed south toward the Visayan Islands. The next day, a big strike was laid on that included 20 fighters and dive bombers from *Essex*, 12 dive bombers from *Lexington*, 24 fighters from *Langley* and *Princeton*, and 32 F6Fs from Admiral McCain's Task Group 38.1. The SB2Cs and TBMs went after shipping and severely damaged six ships in Coron Bay.

McCampbell led a strike against Cebu and Mactan with 24 *Essex* fighters and torpedo bombers and 12 *Lexington* fighters with eight dive bombers. He found two Pete float biplanes over Cebu Harbor, but lost sight of them in the clouds as he went after them. He and his wingman Roy Rushing got both.

A final day of strikes was flown at long range on September 24 against the Visayans. In the first strike, Helldivers and Avengers of Air Group 2 scored two destroyers sunk and a light cruiser badly damaged. During a second strike on Panay, Ensign Frank O'Brien, who had joined the squadron just before they departed Eniwetok at the end of August, was shot down and killed. He was Fighting 2's final casualty. Task Groups 38.1 and 38.3 flew two more strikes against Cebu, but there were no significant targets left.

That night, Task Force 38 withdrew east through the Kossol Passage. In the evening, a Sonia searching for the Americans found the American fleet off Cape Engaño at the northern end of Luzon. Every plane that could still fly was sent off to attack the Americans, but they were unsuccessful since the carriers were heading away from the Philippines.

On September 25, Air Group 2 learned they would be relieved upon arrival in Manus anchorage in the Admiralty Islands. *Hornet* arrived at Manus on September 28. Six months and 14 days after coming aboard, Air Group 2 departed as the band played "Auld Lang Syne" and "California, Here I Come!" The men spent several days at Manus, then went aboard a CVE the afternoon of October 6 and departed at 0745 hours on October 7. They arrived in Majuro fleet anchorage on October 11 and departed for Pearl Harbor the next day, the anniversary of their departure from San Francisco bound for the Pacific. Arriving at Pearl Harbor on October 18, they boarded a troop transport on October 23 and docked in San Francisco on a foggy October 29, tying up at Pier Seven on the Embarcadero at 1600 hours. Ken Glass recalled, "The welcome home party at the Mark Hopkins lasted three days."

Over the course of their year in combat from November 1943 to the end of September 1944, Fighting 2 scored 261 enemy aircraft shot down and 245 destroyed on the ground for a total 506. With 261 aerial victories, Fighting 2 was now the top-ranked fighter squadron, having beaten Fighting 9's 245. Three Hellcats and their pilots were lost in aerial combat for a nearly 9:1 victory-loss ratio, with four planes and pilots lost to enemy antiaircraft fire. Their record of 28 pilots achieving "ace" status during the tour remains the American record. Air Group 2 as a whole was credited with sinking 50,000 tons of enemy shipping in 184 missions.

Air Group 2 was lucky enough to return home on leave, but as much as they might long for home, the rest of Task Force 38 had to content themselves with a no-frills shore leave at Ulithi Atoll.

It didn't help that the supplies situation had become dire by this point – Spike Borley remembered how it was on the *Essex* that fall:

In the wardroom, we were reduced to a breakfast of dehydrated reconstituted eggs, canned beets, and canned asparagus. We could also have toast, but there were weevils in the bread and it was hard. You could tap it on your plate and watch the bugs fall out, which had a negative effect on your appetite. Dinner was more beets and asparagus with Spam. There are only so many ways to cook Spam, and most of us were at the point where the only reason we were eating was to avoid hunger pangs.

CHAPTER FIFTEEN

THE BATTLE OF THE FORMOSA SEA

O n October 6, 1944, the Third Fleet sortied from Ulithi, headed northwest. The new target was the Ryukyus, a chain of islands stretching across the East China Sea from 100 miles south of Kyushu, the southernmost Home Island of Japan proper, to 100 miles north of Taiwan, then known by its Japanese name, Formosa. The series of strikes was aimed at Japanese airpower throughout the region, to separate the Philippines as much as possible prior to the coming invasion.

Not much was known about the Ryukyus except that Okinawa was one of the main Japanese bases and that it was a major waypoint for Japanese Army and Navy planes being funneled into the Philippines, which is why the American fleet intended to attack in this area. Japanese airfield locations and the strengths of the Army and Navy units were nevertheless something of an unknown quantity.

Task Force 38 executed its run-in toward Okinawa on the night of October 9. At 0530 hours on October 10, *Essex* launched a sweep led by McCampbell with 14 VF-15 Hellcats and 16 from *Lexington*'s VF-19. This was followed by Helldivers and Avengers from the task force. The fighter sweep arrived over Yontan North Field in central Okinawa at dawn. It was obvious surprise had been achieved when the defending fighters were spotted still on the ground about to take off, and all were burned. McCampbell led his fights to Yontan South Field, where they again found enemy aircraft still in their revetments. While antiaircraft fire over both targets was fierce, there were no losses.

McCampbell and his wingman Roy Rushing also attacked four cargo ships near Naha with rockets and machine guns, leaving all four dead in the water as the Hellcat sweep departed.

The main strike, composed of 27 Helldivers from *Essex* and *Lexington* and 27 Avengers from *Essex*, *Lexington*, and *Princeton*, were escorted by 32 Hellcats from the three carriers. Yontan North and South were hit solidly, with the runways torn up and hangars and other structures set afire. A second Hellcat sweep launched an hour later led by Bert Morris resulted in four freighters sunk off the port of Naha on the island's east coast.

A thick haze from the fires started by the previous strikes reduced visibility when the third strike arrived over the island. With no major targets still standing on the two fields, the bombers cratered the runways again and the Hellcats shot up everything they could find. McCampbell spotted barges in the channel between Okinawa and the small offshore island of Yahagi Shima. When he called in bombers, several barges filled with fuel caught fire quickly.

It cost them 21 aircraft, five pilots and four aircrew, but by the end of the day Task Force 38 had claimed more than 100 enemy aircraft shot down; they had sunk four ships and badly damaged 13 torpedo boats, two midget submarines and 22 smaller vessels; and they took Yontan airfield right out of action.

As Task Force 38 departed, it split into two groups – Task Groups 38.2 and 38.3 went to the East China Sea South of Ryukyu to refuel, while Task Groups 38.1 and 38.4 went south to northern Luzon to hit Aparri Field. On October 12, 1944, the pilots aboard *Essex* awoke early and took off for a dawn strike with Jim Rigg in the lead. Spike Borley recalled, "The only intelligence material they had on Formosa was photographs taken by submarines, so there really wasn't anything useful. We were told there were as many as 24 enemy airfields and there could be more than three hundred enemy aircraft on the island."

The ports of Kaohsiung on Formosa and the Pescadore Islands were Air Group 15's target. The brightening sky revealed bad weather conditions, with low clouds and a choppy ocean, warning of a typhoon headed across the East China Sea toward the island, of which the Ameriacans were as yet unaware. The rising sun soon revealed the dark shape of the Formosa coast on the western horizon.

Unlike Okinawa, the Americans had not achieved surprise. More than 200 defending fighters were preparing for takeoff or already airborne. However, the defenders were not very experienced pilots and would often split off into individual action rather than fighting as a group, which made them much easier to single out. Jim Rigg remembered the stark difference: "At no time was there noticed a single friendly fighter alone, unless he was joining up on other F6Fs. The enemy aircraft did not follow this procedure; consequently it was easy to pick them off." The fight was fierce and furious nonetheless, leaving the American pilots no time to count their scores.

CAG Tom Winters led a second strike, which took off from *Lexington* at 0815 hours and bombed Bodo Harbor in the Pescadores, scoring a large freighter, a tanker, two destroyers and several smaller vessels. As they returned south they were caught by heavy antiaircraft fire – the TBM of Torpedo 15's Ensign Copeland was brought down in the sea and strafing fire only just managed to sink an enemy freighter before it intercepted his liferaft. He was then safely picked up by a lifeguard submarine.

Toyohara Airfield was the target of the next strike, at 1125 hours, but the weather conditions were not suitable and an unfinished airfield just south of Taichu was chosen as an alternative, most of its installations being destroyed. The same bad weather also hampered the Japanese, who spotted the fleet and sent 55 Jills in a counterattack; the bad weather and the inexperience of their pilots meant that 26 of these failed to return.

For the pilots of Fighting 15, the dawn sweep the next morning was a disappointment. Only three airborne enemy planes were seen, which all ducked into the clouds and avoided the Americans.

McCampbell and Bert Morris led a strike against Ansan naval base at 0800 hours the next morning. Through patchy cloud and antiaircraft fire they scored two hits on a destroyer, strafed other vessels and dropped their bombloads. Working at a lower altitude due to the cloud cover, Lieutenant (jg) Earl Malette and gunner Stan Whitby's Helldiver was hit by flak and they were lost as the plane cartwheeled across the ocean and quickly sank.

A Japanese strike that left Formosa at 1330 hours struck Admiral John S. McCain's Task Group 38.1 and *Canberra* (CA-70) was hit in the stern and disabled before being taken under tow by *Wichita* (CA-45). *Franklin* (CV-13) was also damaged when a Jill crashed into its island, though luckily the flames were extinguished. The Japanese pilots who made it home made wild reports of two carriers sunk, which Toyoda took at face value. The fleet was meant to retire on October 13, but stayed back for another day to provide cover for *Wichita* and *Canberra* as the latter was pulled to safety, and Halsey took the opportunity to launch further strikes against Formosa.

Sixth Base Air Force on Kyushu received orders that morning from Admiral Yoshida to destroy the Americans and when Halsey saw the number of snoopers, the Army Air Force's Bomber Command sent out 100 B-29s at his request to bomb Kaohsiung and Takao.

At 1500 hours a Japanese attack force was launched from Okinawa that arrived in dribs and drabs rather than as one force, which substantially undermined the attack's effectiveness. Seven Jill torpedo bombers made an attack on *Essex*, but though some were able to launch torpedoes, they all missed and the planes were brought down by the carrier's booming guns.

The few returning Japanese pilots conveyed reassuring messages to their superiors, telling them of great successes and nine carriers sunk. A triumphant Admiral Toyoda sent word to Tokyo of the brilliant results of the "Battle of the Formosa Sea," little knowing that the only success of the many aircraft sent into battle was disabling the light cruiser *Houston* (CL-81) and the heavy cruiser *Canberra* (CA-70).

Task Group 38.4 hit airfields on northern Luzon on October 15, to prevent the fleet suffering further attacks. Waiting off Formosa, Task Groups 38.3 and 38.2 hoped to catch the Japanese fleet coming out, but Toyoda had in fact already launched the *Sho-1* plan to defend the Philippines.

At 0800 hours the Japanese found four carriers reported as "damaged" (though they were not) north of Luzon and launched 100 Jills, Judys and Bettys from Kyushu, Okinawa and Formosa to "finish off the cripples". They were surprised to find the American fleet much stronger than had been supposed, and they found no targets because of a typhoon and the general incompetence of the aircrews.

By the morning of October 16, the battle of the Formosa Sea was over and the damaged *Houston* and *Canberra* were safely out of range of Japanese planes. Task Group 38.3 commenced refueling in preparation for the main event to come.

CHAPTER SIXTEEN

THE BATTLES
OF LEYTE GULF

Admiral Toyoda's *Shō Ichigō Sakusen* plan to engage the American Navy in a decisive surface battle was complicated and inflexible, taking no account of the enemy not doing as the Japanese planned, and it worked on the supposition that one killer blow could be struck, rather than slowly wearing their opponent down. It was also based on the erroneous premise that Japanese aviators at the Battle of the Formosa Sea had sunk 11 carriers, two battleships, three cruisers and a destroyer, as well as damaging eight carriers. Such misinformation seriously misled Toyoda in formulating his strategy.

Conversely, American plans tended to adopt a more flexible, ad hoc approach to naval strategy, and their tendency to overestimate rather than underestimate their enemy's power – along with their ignorance of how decisive the June battles had actually been – made them keenly aware of how hard they had to fight. The Americans arrived expecting a "second round" to June's Battle of the Philippine Sea.

Toyoda's plan was essentially to enact a pincer movement that would close on the fleet supporting MacArthur's invasion force in the Leyte Gulf: Vice Admiral Shoji Nishimura and Vice Admiral Kiyohide Shima would lead the fleets of the Southern Force that would advance through the Surigao Strait, attacking the defenseless invasion fleet; Admiral Takeo Kurita's Center Force would advance through San Bernadino Strait and come from the north to close on the American fleet; and meanwhile, Admiral Jisaburō Ozawa's Northern Force would lure Task Force 38 away from northern Luzon to allow the Central and Southern forces to conduct their *coup de grâce*.

Kurita's Center Force was the greatest single fleet of Japanese battleships ever to set to sea; it included the "super battleships" *Musashi* and *Yamato* which were accompanied by older battleships and heavy cruisers. The older "dreadnought" battleships *Fuso* and *Yamashiro* led Nishimura's Southern Force, accompanied by a heavy cruiser and four destroyers; Admiral Shima's 2nd Striking Force comprised two heavy cruisers, a light cruiser and four destroyers.

Division of command would be a problem for both sides. Each Japanese fleet was under the independent command of an admiral who ranked equally with the other commanders. Only Admiral Toyoda outranked the other operational commanders, and he was far removed from the scene and deep in his fantasies. The lack of an admiral equivalent to the US Navy's "Senior Officer Present Afloat" to take overall command on the scene would result in none of the Japanese plans coming close to fruition other than Ozawa's sacrifice.

The American division of command was also complicated: the invasion forces were controlled by General MacArthur, the Southwestern Pacific Area commander, while the defense of these forces was the responsibility of the Third Fleet, controlled by Admiral Nimitz, the Pacific Ocean Area commander. Both were equal in rank and neither liked the other.

The Marianas invasion had been a different matter, since Nimitz had responsibility as overall theater commander and he made it clear to Admiral Spruance that his main responsibility was to protect the invasion forces. At Leyte Gulf, in contrast, Nimitz's order to Admiral Halsey was that destruction of the Japanese fleet – *not* the protection of the invasion forces – was his highest priority. These orders created a situation that favored Halsey's lack of restraint and inability to separate himself and his reputation from the outcome, as Spruance could.

The Battles of Leyte Gulf (officially known to the US Navy as the Second Battle of the Philippine Sea, though now considered a series of separate events) consisted of five actions: the October 23–24 submarine attack on Admiral Kurita's Center Force, known as the Battle of Palawan Passage; the October 24 Battle of the Sibuyan Sea, when Task Force 38 battered the Center Force; the October 24–25 Battle of Surigao Strait; the October 25 Battle off Cape Engaño, and the Battle off Samar on the same day.

The evening of October 22, Admiral Kurita's Center Force left Brunei headed toward the Philippines. The force would enter the Palawan Passage the night of October 23–24, then transit the Sibuyan Sea during the day of

The Battles of Leyte Gulf

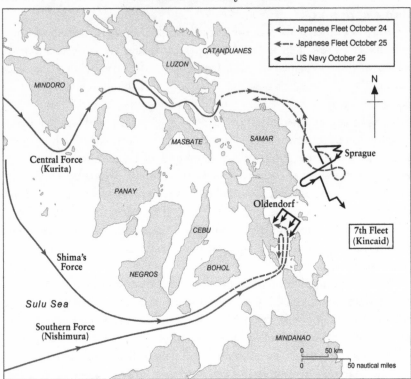

October 24, entering San Bernardino Strait that night, to emerge into the Philippine Sea at dawn and attack the Americans in Leyte Gulf. Admiral Kurita was perhaps the most experienced surface force commander in the Imperial Navy, and had concluded a year earlier following the Solomons campaign that there was little likelihood Japan would be able to end the war on favorable terms. He felt the mission he had been assigned was a waste of men and ships since the invading force had gone ashore five days earlier, which meant any shipping still in Leyte Gulf was likely empty.

Admiral Nishimura departed shortly after Kurita, headed for the Sulu Sea west of Mindanao, where he would then penetrate Surigao Strait for his rendezvous with the Center Force in Leyte Gulf. Shima's cruisers had departed Formosa on October 21 and were approaching the Philippines.

Admiral Ozawa flew his flag on *Zuikaku*, the last of the six carriers which had attacked Pearl Harbor. The same day Kurita departed Singapore, Ozawa's carriers raised anchor at Kure. *Zuikaku* was accompanied by the light carriers *Zuihō*, *Chitose*, and *Chiyoda*; the old dreadnoughts *Hyūga* and *Ise* had been converted to hybrid battleship-carriers though neither carried any aircraft; the light cruisers *Ôyodo*, *Tama*, and *Isuzu*; and eight destroyers forming the Northern Force. The four carriers had only 108 aircraft between then, less than a quarter of what they had entered battle with at the Marianas.

October 23 effectively saw Task Force 38 running at half strength at a critical moment. Task Groups 38.4 and 38.1 had gone to Ulithi to replenish stocks after the Formosa strikes, leaving only Admiral Gerald Bogan's Task Group 38.2 east of Leyte, and Admiral Ted Sherman's Task Group 38.3 200 miles east of Luzon, and northeast of San Bernadino Strait. A last-minute high-speed return by Task Group 38.4 that arrived in the battle area at dawn on October 24 would increase the available force to three-quarter strength.

A wolfpack guarding the Palawan Passage, consisting of Commander David H. McClintock's USS *Darter* (SS-227) and Commander Balden D. Claggett's USS *Dace* (SS-247), was among several submarine formations positioned at strategic locations west of the Philippines, under orders to notify Seventh Fleet if any naval forces were encountered. At 2355 hours on October 23, McClintock reported the approach of Center Force as it passed Palawan Island, informing *Dace* that there were "fast ships on a northeasterly course."

Darter submerged but McClintock kept the radar antenna above the surface as he searched with his periscope. The enemy was zig-zagging, but the ships were still in steaming formation without a properly-deployed defensive antisubmarine screen. Once they passed, McClintock surfaced and warned *Dace*, then sent off a contact report to Commander of Submarines South West Pacific and Seventh and Third Fleets.

Dace's captain Claggett ordered a change of course and brought the engines to full power, planning to pass the enemy and position *Dace* at the far end of Palawan Passage. Both submarines surged through Palawan Passage at 21 knots, close enough that the commanders could communicate by megaphone as they quickly planned a "hammer and anvil" attack at dawn when the enemy entered the Sibuyan Sea. The only way to get into position in time was taking a "short cut" across the "Dangerous Ground," an area with uncharted reefs to either side. They accomplished this difficult feat and separated, with *Darter* moving south of the oncoming enemy and *Dace* north.

McClintock sounded "Battle Stations" at 0500 hours. Ten minutes later, the submarine disappeared into the dark waters and headed toward the enemy fleet. *Dace* submerged five minutes later. The gray pre-dawn light allowed both commanders to spot the targets through their periscopes.

At 0530 hours, *Darter* fired six torpedoes at the nearest cruiser when the fleet zigged toward her. It took barely a minute before numbers two, three, four, and five struck the heavy cruiser *Atago* on her port side from bow to stern. McClintock reported, "Whipped periscope to the first target to see the sight of a lifetime. Cruiser was in so close that all of her could not be seen at once with periscope in high power. She was a mass of billowing black smoke from No. 1 turret to the stern. Cruiser was already going down by the bow."

McClintock then turned and fired the four stern tubes at a second heavy cruiser. They arrowed past the burning *Atago* and hit *Takao* in her stern at 0540 hours, which damaged her engines.

Atago went down with 360 of her crew at 0558 hours. Admiral Kurita chose to go down with her, but was rescued in the water by his staff, who convinced him to carry on. He was pulled from the water by a destroyer, then transferred to *Yamato*. Never a believer in success, Kurita was a shaken man when he ordered two destroyers to escort *Takao* back to Brunei.

Aboard *Dace*, Commander Claggett saw *Atago* sink and *Takao* listing. "It looks like the Fourth of July out there! One is sinking and the other is burning. The Japs are firing all over the place. What a show!" He then took aim at what he identified as a Kongō-class battleship and fired all six bow tubes at 0556 hours. The heavy cruiser *Maya* blew up and sank quickly with heavy loss of life.

Too late, the destroyers went after *Dace* while *Darter* slipped away. Claggett ordered, "Take her deep." Soon *Dace* was shaken by explosions "as if the ocean bottom was blowing up." The explosions were followed by a sound that XO Lieutenant Commander Rafael Benitez described as "Gruesome. It was akin to the noise made by cellophane when it is crumpled." The crackling noise was so loud, it sounded as though *Dace* was breaking up and all compartments were checked. To everyone's relief, there was no damage.

Darter's sound man gave a running narrative of the action. "Four of them are making a run now, Captain." The destroyers "sounded like an electric razor at work on a two-day beard." Everyone heard them approach but only the sound man could tell how many there were. "They were going off all around us and they were close," Benitez recalled. After 90 minutes, the destroyers moved off to rejoin the fleet.

Darter and *Dace* surfaced and spotted the damaged *Takao*. They spent the day maneuvering submerged trying to get a shot. *Takao* finally came to a halt at sunset. Both submarines surfaced after nightfall to attack. Just as they did, *Takao* got underway under her own power. The two captains decided to split their attack: *Darter* would wait to attack from the east while *Dace* made an end run around to attack from the west. Both were moving into position just before midnight. *Takao* picked up more speed and McClintock ordered speed increased to 17 knots, as he attempted to attack before *Takao* could get away.

Both submarines navigated Palawan Passage by dead reckoning. Since they were submerged during daylight, neither navigator was able to get a fix on the mountains of Palawan Island. Thus, both were uncertain of their exact position and the cloudy night prevented either getting a celestial fix.

McClintock planned to remain 7 miles from Bombay Shoal, a coral reef on the passage's western side. Unfortunately, due to a quarter-knot error in the estimate for the current, the submarine was on a collision course with the reef. At 0005 hours on October 25, *Darter's* crew learned why this stretch of water was called the "Dangerous Ground" when she ran hard aground on Bombay Shoal with a tremendous crash.

One of the enemy destroyers immediately headed toward the shoal on hearing the crash and closed to within 12,000 yards before turning away. McClintock later reported "When the Jap destroyer faded on our radar screen we breathed a little easier and went to work in hopes of floating her off at high tide. Desperate to lighten the boat, the crew threw overboard everything movable: anchors, food, furniture." They fired the stern torpedoes. Men gathered on the stern, attempting to raise the bow. Some tried to rock the boat free, running from port to starboard and back again. Nothing worked. *Darter* was high and dry.

When *Dace* received *Darter's* distress call, XO Benitez recalled, "It was hard to give up pursuing a ship that we knew would probably sink with one torpedo hit, but it would have been doubly hard to abandon our comrades to certain death on the shoals of Palawan Passage."

Darter's situation was hopeless. Benitez later wrote, "She was so high that even her screws were out of the water – she seemed like a ship in drydock." As it became evident *Darter* would never get off the reef, her crew burned secret documents and destroyed vital equipment. Rubber rafts brought *Darter's* crew to *Dace*, six at a time over two and a half hours. Benitez wrote, "In the darkness, gnome-like figures on the deck of *Darter* were seen to go down her side into rubber boats awaiting them below. Minutes later, they reappeared at the side of *Dace*, where willing hands hoisted them aboard." Commander McClintock climbed aboard *Dace* at 0439 hours and reported that the demolition charges were set. *Dace* moved away at full speed, but unfortunately only one charge went off with a comical pop. Still intact, *Darter* would be useful if captured.

Dace fired two torpedoes at *Darter* but they hit the reef. She moved directly astern and fired her last two, which also exploded against the reef. By 0530 hours, the sun was rising and the decision was made to destroy *Darter* with *Dace*'s deck gun. The gunners hit *Darter* 21 times, holing the superstructure and hull before the radar operator reported an air contact at 6 miles and closing. Claggett immediately ordered, "Clear the deck!"

Dace started to submerge as the 26 men on deck dashed for the conning tower. Some climbed down the hatch but others fell sideways, dove head first, or were pushed down. The Officer of the Deck closed the hatch seconds before the submarine went under.

Having spotted both submarines, one dead in the water, the other submerging, the enemy pilot attacked the easier target. To the relief of all aboard *Dace*, he bombed *Darter* and flew off. Minutes later the submarine surfaced and set course for Fremantle, Australia. The 11-day voyage was difficult but uneventful, with 81 *Darter* survivors and *Dace*'s 74-man crew aboard. Two days before arrival, the only food left was peanut butter and cream of mushroom soup. *Dace* arrived at Fremantle on November 6. *Darter* remains high atop Bombay Shoal to this day.

As soon as Halsey received the contact report at 0200 hours on October 24, he recalled Admiral Davison and Task Group 38.4, which turned around and rushed back to arrive in position southeast of Luzon, where the three task groups commenced their search for Center Group.

The Battle of the Sibuyan Sea began on October 24 at 1018 hours when Avengers from *Cabot* carrying bombs and torpedoes arrived over the Japanese Center Force. The main attack was on *Musashi*, but *Myōkō*, *Nagato* and *Yamato* were also damaged.

In the first strike, *Musashi*'s Turret No. 1 was hit by a bomb, and the ship was struck to starboard by a torpedo. A second strike from *Intrepid* at 1154 hours scored two hits, the damage creating a list and causing *Musashi* to slow to 22 knots. Task Group 38.3 then sent out a combined force of Helldivers and Avengers from *Essex* and *Lexington*, led by Commander Tom Winters. Flying through heavy cloud, the two formations were separated, but Air Group 15 managed to stick together. The Japanese fleet was spotted and Bombing 15's new XO, Lieutenant Commander John Bridgers, remembered:

We headed there at 15,000 feet, flying above the scattered clouds. The skipper's division was slightly ahead of us and off to starboard when suddenly the enemy announced its presence with a large spread of variously colored bursts of radar-directed antiaircraft fire coming up through the clouds and mostly clustered around the lead planes.

Commander Mini radioed he was preparing to attack a battleship directly ahead, and he directed me to turn east and concentrate on another battleship, which he promised I would see as soon as I reached the edge of the cloud bank I was over ... Suddenly, from beneath the clouds, steamed a dreadnought of vast proportions [*Musashi*], the largest I had ever seen ...

Multiple streams of tracer fire came up at us and the battleship's deck blossomed with muzzle blasts from larger AA guns, presumably the source of the clusters of colored bursts of smoke in the sky, all of which were augmented by similar fire from her screening vessels. I radioed that we were starting our high-speed approach so that the torpedo leader would know to start his let-down to sea level.

We entered a power glide down to 12,000 feet, keeping our target in sight on our port bow. Then I signaled to attack and pulled up slightly across the plane flown by my wingman, Warren Parrish, who was flying stepped down on my port wing. I gradually steepened into my dive and opened my dive flaps.

It was every man for himself, and suddenly I had my hands full. I started my dive stern-to-bow on the target, but my Helldiver was twisted around in a violent skid, which I couldn't control with full rudder pressure and trim-tab adjustment. In this condition, my aircraft was away from its flight path and the trajectory my bomb would follow after its release. I figured if this was how it was to be, then my greatest dropping error would be a deflection laterally and, to wit, not in range, either ahead or behind the target. I did my best to skid down across the length of the ship in order that my major dropping fault would be fore and aft along the ship's greatest dimension. In hundreds of dive-bombing runs I'd made, I'd never experienced this type of wild gyrations from the aircraft. The antiaircraft fire, evidenced by tracers and puffs, was coming from all quarters, from ships large and small.

During my dive, I saw the main battery of heavy guns trained toward our torpedo planes, which were coming in straight, level, and low to the water from either bow. When those guns fired, the ship literally disappeared in a cloud of smoke illuminated by an internal blossom of flame. It was more frightening than dangerous to the torpedo bombers as large-caliber shells meant for heavily armored ships were rather ineffective against small, speeding aircraft unless they ran into a water spout straight on. All that being said, it must have seemed fearsome to the torpedo crews head-on.

My dive, rather than being a smooth and even descent, had been a wild, spiraling ride, thanks to the as-yet-unexplained skid. I released my bomb at 2,500 feet, as usual, but with a sense of fruitlessness in knowing my aim was guesswork at best.

I broke my dive, closed my dive brakes, and, in a full power glide, headed for low altitude just above the wave tops, which we always thought was the safest place in a totally hostile environment. To my surprise, the plane once more flew with good trim and easy control as it should. Fleeing the enemy ships, I couldn't see what happened to our target, but the antiaircraft puffs in the air and the splashes in the sea off our port and starboard let me know the Japanese were still in business. Once I could turn and look back, the big ship looked undamaged and still running at flank speed with guns still blazing at planes coming in behind us. After flying out of range, I started doing gentle "S" turns, which gave the planes of my division a better chance to join up while we climbed for altitude.

Warren Parrish dropped his bomb right amidships on *Musashi*. Pulling out of his dive, he went so low the prop blasted salt spray over the airplane and created a small wake on the ocean's surface. Parrish was so low he had to climb over a Japanese destroyer, all the while evading fire from the ships. Bridgers recalled how happy the five members of the "Silent Second" were to regroup safely:

> None of our other planes were to be seen, not the skipper's division of dive-bombers, not the fighters or torpedo bombers. As we headed home, the pieces began to fall into place. My gunner, Bob Cribb, called me on the intercom and revealed what had happened in our dive. From the rear seat he had been able to see that my dive brakes had opened on only one side, which accounted for the wild ride in the dive, and that the flight returned to normal after my pullout.

While the Helldivers made their attack, Torpedo 15 made attacks on both sides of *Musashi*, as Commander VeeGee Lambert later reported:

> Coming in through the most intense and accurate AA yet experienced, the squadron made three hits on one battleship [*Musashi* recorded four], two hits on another battleship, and two hits each on two different heavy cruisers.

In this action, two planes were lost, but the pilot and turret gunner of one plane, Lieutenant (jg) W.F. Axtman and J.T. O'Donnell, were rescued by friendly forces after watching the entire action from their rubber boat.

One of the more unusual events of the day was precipitated by Morris Markey, a *Liberty* magazine correspondent who had been allowed a seat in the gunner's turret to film the action, displacing gunner David Miller to the radioman's position. As they approached the attack and Miller returned from setting the torpedo, flak burst around them and Markey was jolted around, dropping his camera on Miller and spilling 500 feet of motion picture film:

> All of a sudden, I was surrounded by 16mm film, which was like trying to get out of a spider's web. The more I tried, the more tied up I got! We're bouncing around, flak is going off to either side, shrapnel is flying through the airplane, and there I am, struggling to get free of this movie film! I finally got free just as we dropped the torpedo and pulled up really sharp. I looked out the window and we were maybe 50 feet above the bow of the biggest battleship I ever saw, and I was staring right at these Japanese officers in white uniforms on the bridge!

Bombing 15's four hits and Torpedo 15's four hits spelled *Musashi*'s death, with the fatal blows being the two torpedoes that hit forward and amidships on the port side.

The last *Essex* plane made its escape from the fleet by 1345 hours. *Musashi* was by then *in extremis*. Counter-flooding had cut the starboard list to 1 degree, but the great battleship was down 13 feet at the bow even with nearly all trim tanks and voids flooded. She lagged behind the rest of the fleet while the Sibuyan Sea lapped at her main deck and her speed dropped to 20 knots.

Nagato's defensive fire had hit Jim Mini during his attack. His wingman, Lieutenant (jg) Lauren E. Nelson stuck with him. Despite the severe damage to the Helldiver, he was able to keep the airplane in the air and get back to *Essex*, where he discovered he could not lower his landing gear and was forced to ditch next to *Morrison* (DD-560), which picked up him and his gunner, Aviation Radioman 1/c Arne Frobom. Mini was out of the fight, and would be forced to spend the rest of the battle aboard the destroyer.

While the Americans attacked Kurita's ships in the Sibuyan Sea, Admiral Ozawa's carriers steamed north of Luzon. At 0930 hours, the four carriers launched their one-way strike. The Zekes, Judys, Vals, Kates, and Jills headed south in search of the American carriers.

Ozawa's strike reached *Essex* as its crew prepared for a second strike against Central Force. CAG McCampbell's Hellcat "Minsi III" was being fueled preparatory to his leading the strike. "All fighter pilots! Man your planes! The second strike is canceled!" sounded across the flight deck. McCampbell was specifically commanded not to go. As crewmen ceased fueling his plane and loaded it onto the deck-edge elevator to send it below, a countermanding order for the CAG to fly was heard. Still not fully fueled, *Minsi III* was readied for flight and McCampbell and his wingman Roy Rushing led seven other Hellcats off the *Essex* and set off to intercept the Japanese strike.

McCampbell's Hellcats climbed for altitude under direction from *Essex* fighter direction officer (FDO) Lieutenant John Connally and soon found the incoming enemy warplanes to be dive-bombers protected by 40 fighters. McCampbell announced he and Rushing would go for the escorts. Unaware the others had fallen behind, the two were now the sole defenders of the task force.

The leading enemy fighters, surprised by the appearance of the two Americans, turned away as McCampbell and Rushing climbed on to 30,000 feet. Checking the enemy formation through his binoculars, McCampbell identified them as a mixed Army-Navy formation of Zekes, Oscars and Tonys. He was undoubtedly mistaken, since this was the strike from Ozawa's carriers and they were certainly all Zekes. He banked into a dive and took aim at a trailing Zeke and the fighter exploded. Rushing scored soon after. After two more successful gunnery passes, McCampbell was amazed to see the 37 remaining fighters bend around into a defensive Lufbery Circle.

His next two passes were unsuccessful, but were rewarded when the formation turned and headed for Luzon, a hundred miles away. The Zekes doggedly maintained their course as McCampbell shot down seven of them while Rushing dropped five more. Suddenly, he realized he was nearly out of gas and was forced to break off the fight as Luzon hove into view ahead.

When they arrived back over the fleet, *Essex* was unable to bring the two aboard. When McCampbell put down on the *Langley*, his engine died of fuel starvation as he attempted to taxi out of the arresting wires. He had just set the all-time American record of nine victories in one fight. Admiral Sherman had ordered McCampbell not to "notch victories," and was livid on his return that he had flown contrary to orders, but nobody could work out where the countermand had come from. Considering McCampbell's success, the Admiral let him off with a reprimand and the admonition not to let this happen again.

At 1459 hours, *Essex*'s second strike arrived over the Center Force shortly after *Enterprise*'s Air Group 20 completed their attack. Lieutenant Roger Noyes attacked *Musashi*, *Nagato*, and the heavy cruiser *Chōkai* with 12 Helldivers. Beanbag Barney Barnitz, Crellin, Hall, Talbot, Platt, and Gardner got hits on *Musashi*.

Antiaircraft fire hit the Helldiver flown by Lieutenant (jg) Conrad Crellin and gunner Aviation Radioman 3/c Carl Shelter. Both were killed when the Helldiver flipped over less than 500 feet above the water and hit inverted at 200 miles per hour. Crellin's loss shocked Ted Graham, who had flown many missions with him and only three weeks earlier had convinced the 24-year-old officer to vote to re-elect President Roosevelt. It was the first election in which he was old enough to vote.

On the morning of October 24, Lieutenant James "Red" Shirley and Lieutenant Carl Brown led a two-division CAP from *Princeton* to intercept snoopers, which were quickly brought down, but then an attack of 80 Japanese planes appeared. Brown and Shirley's divisions then engaged in a dogfight above Polilo Island which brought down 20 and 14 planes respectively, before returning to *Princeton*.

Out of nowhere, at 0938 hours the *Princeton* was hit by a 500-kilogram bomb dropped from a Judy, starting a fire in the hangar where fuel and torpedoes were being prepared for the flight deck. While explosion followed explosion, Brown's division of Hellcats was sent out to intercept another raid and other vessels came alongside to try to help *Princeton*. After three hours it looked like the fires were finally under control. Machinist's Mate Harry Popham later described what he saw happen next:

> Damaged by the constant collisions between the two vessels, a hatch door was ripped from *Princeton*'s hull, exposing the interior of what appeared to be a companionway... What I saw was a row of bombs standing upright... Firefighters on *Birmingham* were directing streams of water onto those bombs, causing them to sizzle like a hot frying pan when water is sprinkled onto its surface. This effort by *Birmingham*'s crew to cool down the bombs with fire hoses was desperately hampered because of the narrow quarters and the constant rolling of the ships. The bombs were hissing and generating clouds of steam. My buddies and I watched this activity from our vantage point less than 20 feet away from the nearest bomb. *Birmingham*'s skipper,

Captain Thomas Inglis, was just below us on the flying bridge, directing the entire operation. The grim expression on his face indicated his deep concern at the stress of the situation.

About 90 minutes later, general quarters ended with the all clear. Again *Birmingham* moved alongside *Princeton*. My little group reconvened. Now we perched on the after mushroom ventilator, between the No. 3 and No. 4 turrets, intently watching the activities on *Princeton*. *Birmingham* prepared to rig for towing. From an estimated distance of 50 to 75 yards, absolutely no smoke or fires were observed, only patches of fog-like vapors coming from the numerous openings in *Princeton*'s flight deck. *Princeton* appeared to be serenely drifting with the current. It appeared as if the fires had gone out on their own. Our little group on *Birmingham* figured the excitement was all over. The fires aboard *Princeton* had been extinguished.

The ships were still separated by about 50 feet when sailors shot their messenger lines across in order to secure a spring line between the two ships. George, on my right, suddenly exclaimed, "Look at that flame!" We saw a single tongue of flame shoot out from the area of the after elevator, followed by an enormous puff of white smoke like a billowy cumulus cloud. To our horror, a slender column of pale orange-colored smoke shot several hundred feet straight up. All hell broke loose with an enormous eruption. One hundred and thirty feet of *Princeton*'s stern blew off, as well as 180 feet of her flight deck.

As a high-speed shock wave headed my way, my reflexes took over. I threw myself backward before the concussion could hit me head on. This reflex action undoubtedly saved my life. Still, the force of the shockwave tumbled me backward 30 or 40 feet and about 10 feet into the air before dropping me on the deck. The shockwave hit me a split second before the thunder of the explosion reached my ears.

The fire had finally ignited the bombs in the aft hangar that Popham had seen earlier. At 1523 hours *Princeton*'s stern was blown off in the massive explosion that swept shrapnel across the nearby *Birmingham*, where survivors were being cared for on the open decks – 229 men were killed and 420 wounded. *Princeton* remained afloat until dusk, when the last of her crew were evacuated and she was forcibly sunk by five American torpedoes.

Meanwhile, Brown's group engaged in a protracted dogfight:

I don't know how long the fight lasted. It was a long one; my guess is three to five minutes. I finished with four Zekes on my tail and used my last-ditch maneuver: shove the stick forward as hard as I can with the throttle two-blocked and pitch full low. Nobody can follow and shoot, so you gain at least a few seconds. As soon as I was headed straight down, I put the stick hard to the right and lost them.

He then managed to land his heavily damaged plane aboard *Lexington*, where Bridger had just been reporting to Admiral Sherman the results of his strike from *Essex* on *Musashi*.

Around this time a fifth strike from *Enterprise* and *Franklin* and a sixth from *Intrepid*, *Franklin* and *Cabot*, finally finished off *Musashi* – after hits from 19 torpedoes and 17 bombs, the rest of Center Force abandoned her and continued towards San Bernadino Strait. In the face of these strikes and earlier damage to the cruiser *Myoko* that forced her to turn back, Kurita decided that Center Force must retire, and the last American attackers were able to inform Admiral Halsey that they had seen the ships reverse course.

The seven surviving "Hell Cats" of Fighting 27 landed aboard *Essex* at the end of their defense of *Princeton*. That night, after more than 200 victories since their entry into combat on June 19, Admiral Sherman ordered them amalgamated into Fighting 15. The airplanes' non-regulation cat faces were eradicated under a coat of blue paint to match the rest of the aircraft on the ship per his direction.

Almost straight after hearing of Center Force's withdrawal, Halsey was informed that spotters 150 miles north of Cape Engaño had located Ozawa's carriers – he now laid his plans to destroy Japanese naval air power for good and secure his place in the history books. Before Kurita's withdrawal, Halsey had intended to split his fleet, creating Task Force 34 from four of his fast battleships, five heavy cruisers and two destroyer divisions that he would leave to defend the invasion forces, while the remainder of Task Force 38 headed north to defeat Ozawa's fleet. Now he decided that Task Force 34 was not a necessary expedient and kept these vessels with him as he moved northwards.

The essential problem of the division of American command now came into play. Before he received the sighting report of Ozawa's carriers, Halsey sent an ambiguously worded message to his task group commanders at 1512 hours, detailing his contingency plan:

BATDIV 7 MIAMI, VINCENNES, BILOXI, DESRON 52 LESS STEVEN POTTER, FROM TG 38.2 AND WASHINGTON, ALABAMA, WICHITA, NEW ORLEANS, DESDIV 100, PATTERSON,

BAGLEY FROM TG 38.4 WILL BE FORMED AS TASK FORCE 34 UNDER VICE ADMIRAL LEE, COMMANDER BATTLE LINE. TF 34 TO ENGAGE DECISIVELY AT LONG RANGES. CTG 38.4 CONDUCT CARRIERS OF TG 38.2 AND TG 38.4 CLEAR OF SURFACE FIGHTING. INSTRUCTIONS FOR TG 38.3 AND TG 38.1 LATER. HALSEY, OTC IN NEW JERSEY.

Admiral Nimitz at Pacific Fleet headquarters in Guam and to Admiral King in Washington received information copies of the message, leaving each with the belief that Task Force 34 would definitely be formed and deployed. While Seventh Fleet commander Admiral Kinkaid was not included as an information addressee, the message was nevertheless picked up by Seventh Fleet and passed on to Kinkaid, leaving him also with the impression the force would be formed and deployed.

The problem came from the fact that Halsey's intention in passing this information to his commanders was to inform them that Task Force 34 was a contingency that would be formed and detached on his order. When he wrote "will be formed," he neglected to say "when" Task Force 34 would be formed, or what circumstances would lead to that decision. Unfortunately, when Kinkaid and Nimitz saw the message, both read "will be formed" as being the imperative, rather than the future, tense. Thus both concluded Task Force 34 was already formed and would take station off San Bernardino Strait.

The mistake was compounded at 1710 hours, after Ozawa's carriers were sighted, when Halsey sent a second message by TBS voice radio within Third Fleet which clarified his intentions regarding Task Force 34:

IF THE ENEMY SORTIES (THROUGH SAN BERNARDINO STRAIT) TF 34 WILL BE FORMED WHEN DIRECTED BY ME.

This UHF message could not be intercepted by Seventh Fleet. Unfortunately, Halsey also neglected to update Nimitz or King on the situation, a radio message which would have been intercepted and copied by Seventh Fleet. The result was that the other senior commander present did not have accurate information, due to the first message's ambiguous wording.

This failure on the part of Halsey would have a profound influence on subsequent events.

During October 24, the Japanese had lost over 200 aircraft, *Musashi* had been sunk and six other warships were damaged, yet for all that, Center

Force's overall combat power was not much reduced. When Admiral Toyoda received word that Kurita had turned back in the face of the American attacks, he sent a firm order that Center Force should resume the advance to Leyte Gulf. Unseen by the Americans, the force resumed its original mission and entered the darkness of San Bernardino Strait at approximately 2200 hours.

One hundred fifty miles to the east, Admiral Halsey ordered the Third Fleet to turn north and head for Ozawa's carriers. He radioed Nimitz and Kinkaid:

CENTRAL FORCE HEAVILY DAMAGED ACCORDING TO STRIKE REPORTS.
AM PROCEEDING NORTH WITH THREE GROUPS TO ATTACK CARRIER FORCES AT DAWN

The language of the message was dangerously misleading to anyone unaware of the UHF message. When Nimitz and Kinkaid saw the words "with three groups," both believed Task Force 34 was a separate force now guarding San Bernardino Strait to cover Seventh Fleet's northern flank, while Halsey sent the three carrier task groups to deal with Ozawa's carriers.

There truth was that there was no Task Force 34. Admiral Lee's battleships were at that moment steaming north as part of Task Force 38. There was no way Halsey, aboard his flagship *New Jersey* (BB-62) would not be present to see the final destruction of his sworn enemy.

At 2230 hours, three VT(N)-41 radar-equipped TBM-1Ds led by Lieutenant W.R. Taylor from the specialist night operations Air Group 41 were launched into the dark and stormy skies from *Independence* (CVL-22). At 2330 hours, the flight reported that the navigation lights in San Bernardino Strait had been turned on and that the ships of the Center Force were in the Strait. Ensign Jack D. Dewis went low and close enough that he was able to identify the battleships of Kurita's Center Force steaming toward Leyte Gulf. It is unclear whether this message, which could have changed everything, was either not received due to bad weather that blocked radio communication, or was ignored when received. In any event, Halsey never saw it.

While the Third Fleet headed north, the last fleet action involving American battleships took place a hundred miles south in Surigao Strait. The old battleships *Yamashiro* and *Fuso*, heavy cruiser *Mogami*, and four destroyers assigned to Admiral Nishimura's Southern Force left Brunei at

1500 hours on October 22, following the departure of Admiral Kurita's Center Force. The ships steamed east into the Sulu Sea then northeast past the southern tip of Negros Island into the Mindanao Sea, then headed into the southern entrance of Surigao Strait on the southern side of Leyte Island. The plan called for Nishimura to operate in conjunction with Vice Admiral Kiyohide Shima's Second Striking Force composed of heavy cruisers *Nachi* and *Ashigara*, light cruiser *Abukuma*, and destroyers *Akebono*, *Ushio*, *Kasumi*, and *Shiranui*. This cooperation was prevented by professional jealousy and a pernicious Japanese seniority system that was even more rigid than that of the US Navy.

While Nishimura was a seasoned combat leader who had seen action in the Solomons, former staff officer Shima had never experienced combat. Unfortunately, Shima's promotion to Rear Admiral was just before Nishimura's, which made him the senior officer. Admiral Nishimura refused to submit to command by a man he considered incompetent. Because of this, the Southern Force entered Surigao Strait at 0200 hours, 25 miles and two hours ahead of the Second Striking Force.

American search planes spotted the Southern Force the afternoon of October 24 and it was attacked by American aircraft from TF58, though not with major effect. On receipt of the sighting report, Admiral Jesse Oldendorf ordered the Seventh Fleet's Support Force to prepare for action. The six battleships included *Pennsylvania* (BB-38), *Mississippi* (BB-41), *Tennessee* (BB-43), *California* (BB-44), *Maryland* (BB-46), and *West Virginia* (BB-48). With the exception of *Mississippi*, all had been sunk or damaged at Pearl Harbor; *Tennessee*, *California*, and *West Virginia* had been sunk in the attack, and had then been raised and substantially rebuilt. The four heavy cruisers *Louisville* (CA-28), *Portland* (CA-33), *Minneapolis* (CA-36), and HMAS *Shropshire* and four light cruisers *Phoenix* (CL-46), *Boise* (CL-47) *Columbia* (CL-56) and *Denver* (CL-58), completed the Support Force. Positioned across the northern exit from Surigao Strait, from the outset of contact, the battleships would "cross the T" of Nishimura's battle line.

PT (torpedo) boats stationed in the strait made initial contact with Nishimura's ships at 2236 hours. During the next three and a half hours, they executed attacks, though the Japanese moved north unscathed. Nishimura's luck ran out at 0300 hours on October 25, when American destroyers which had been deployed on both sides of the strait executed torpedo attacks that hit both battleships.

Fuso exploded when she was hit by torpedoes fired by *Melvin* (DD-680) while two of Nishimura's four destroyers with *Asagumo* were hit and forced

The Battle of Surigao Strait

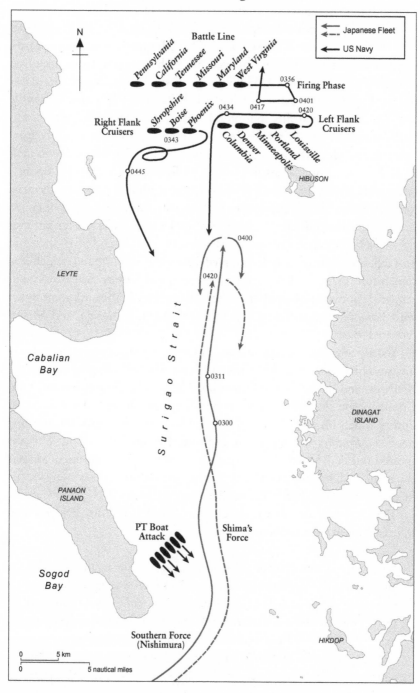

to retire before sinking later. While *Yamashiro* was hit, it was not enough to stop the old dreadnought heading on up the strait.

Nishimura's surviving ships were picked up by *West Virginia*'s radar at 0316 hours, range 42,000 yards. When the range was 30,000 yards, she had a firing solution and opened fire with her eight 16-inch guns at a range of 22,800 yards at 0353 hours. The first salvo hit *Yamashiro* and was followed by 11 more salvos totaling 93 shells. At 0355 hours, *California* and *Tennessee* opened fire, loosing 63 and 69 14-inch shells, respectively. Radar-directed fire control allowed the Americans to fire effectively from a distance at which the Japanese battleships could not respond due to their optical fire control systems not having sufficient range at night. Because *Maryland, Mississippi*, and *Pennsylvania* were equipped with less-advanced gunnery radar, they were unable to take part until *Mississippi* obtained a solution at the end. Her single salvo of 12 14-inch shells was the last ever fired by a battleship against another battleship. The blizzard of 16-inch and 14-inch armor-piercing shells crippled *Yamashiro* and *Mogami*, which also took hits from the flanking cruisers. The destroyer *Shigure* turned away and retreated, but stopped dead after she lost steering. Nishimura went down with *Yamashiro* when she sank at about 0420 hours. *Mogami* and *Shigure* retreated south.

Shortly after Nishimura's defeat, Admiral Shima, who was completely unaware of events, blundered up the strait. PT-137 crippled the cruiser *Abukuma* and she fell out of formation. *Nachi* and *Ashigara* continued on. Coming upon the remnants of the burning *Fuso*, Shima ordered a retreat, during which his flagship *Nachi* collided with the damaged *Mogami* that flooded *Mogami*'s steering room and forced her to fall behind. She was spotted and sunk by American aircraft the next morning. The rest of Shima's ships survived, but all would be lost in air attacks during the coming weeks. History's last classic battle line combat was over.

Two hours before dawn on October 25, 1944, John Bridgers and Warren Parrish were awakened:

A new plan of attack had been devised. During the night, our battleships and some of the cruisers and destroyers had been withdrawn from the fast carrier task force and reassembled as a surface force. These ships were then stationed about a hundred miles north of the carriers, the idea being that we would try to disable their ships by aerial bombardment and leave them for the surface force to sink with their more accurate gunfire. On this day, we were armed with semi-armor-piercing bombs, sharp nosed like a shell for penetration and armed by a delayed-action fuse. They would penetrate and detonate deep in the ship's bowels. We manned our planes under a still-black sky and started our engines with no lights showing.

At 0550 hours, launching commenced:

Our group tactics called for the whole unit to form on the dive-bombers. After the launch, in the blackness of the early morning, we climbed toward 18,000 feet with the torpedo bombers forming up behind and below us at 8,000 feet. The fighters were divided into four-plane divisions and weaved several thousand feet above the formation.

Our CAG, Commander McCampbell, was the target coordinator for the entire strike, with Commander Rigg leading the fighters and Commander Lambert leading the torpedo bombers. Just as the sky started to brighten, we were the first group at the form-up position and started to circle, but in short order the other groups fell in behind. It was the largest formation of planes that I had ever seen, much less in which I had flown, and the amazing thing was that they were all following me! I asked my gunner, Bob Cribb, if he had any idea how many aircraft were with us and he answered "I lost count when I got to 225." There were probably in excess of four hundred planes from all the carriers in the task groups.

When they found the enemy fleet, McCampbell assigned Bridgers the light carrier *Chitose* and he went in for the attack:

Starting my line-up on the bow as my aiming point, I carried my attack down to 1,500 feet before I released my bombs and was low over the water before I leveled out. I found myself completely surrounded by enemy ships and had not noticed the intense AA fire until then. I weaved between the ships, maintaining whatever distance possible from each ship. I took a moment to kick my plane up on one wing and saw two splashes close aboard the carrier's port side and smoke coming up through its flight deck.

As the torpedo bombers went in for a second attack, it was clear the vessel was sinking, so only two of them that were already committed sent in further torpedoes, and the remaining Helldivers and Avengers turned their attention to the *Zuihō*.

As Lieutenant (jg) Warren Kelly came into attack *Zuihō*, problems with the landing gear of his SB2C made for a memorable experience, as his gunner, Aviation Radioman 2/c George "Al" Fowler recorded in his diary:

As Mr. Kelly started our dive on the carrier, my job was to use a K-20 aerial camera to photograph hits to verify damage on the Japanese ships. The Japanese were shooting phosphorous shells at us of various colors, some deep purple, lavender, yellow, and silver. Mr. Kelly put our bombs squarely through the flight deck with direct hits, but the landing gear came down and locked from the force of the pull-out. This in turn caused the Helldiver to seem like it stopped in mid-air, like slamming on the brakes of a car.

By this time, in slow, level flight, we were directly over the battleship *Ise*, which was shooting at us with everything she had. Mr. Kelly was frantically trying to use the hand pump to retract the gear, as well as increase his speed and make violent evasive maneuvers to avoid being hit by all the flak. One of the Japanese shells hit the right wing just forward of the aileron, blowing a hole big enough to crawl through. With the aileron damaged, it was difficult to keep level.

When Kelly arrived back at his carrier, the plane was pushed overboard.

After lunch in the ready room pantry, Bridgers led the "Silent Second" in the day's third and final strike, as he later recalled:

As we made our way back toward the Japanese fleet, we passed a large carrier dead in the water and listing badly. I figured our cruisers and destroyers were on their way to dispatch her in short order. When we arrived back at the Japanese fleet, I saw the target I was assigned, the *Ise*, a very distinctive half-battleship, half-carrier with the Japanese pagoda-style superstructure. My dive was satisfactory, almost directly aft-to-fore, and the target was large.

This time we were greeted with an intense outpouring of tracer fire; it was like upside down rain. As I pulled out of my dive, the plane was nose heavy and I found myself reticent to reach out and spin back the elevator trim-tab to take the pressure off the stick, I didn't want to expose my hand and arm beyond the armor plating behind and beneath my seat. The only hitch was that such armor, present in planes we'd flown early in the war, had long since been removed in the interest of weight reduction. I saw some splashes but didn't take time to count them. Hits were confirmed by the others and *Ise* was seen to be stopped dead in the water by the last retiring aircraft. As I flew home, I thought to myself that the navy's investment in me had been repaid.

The Battle off Samar

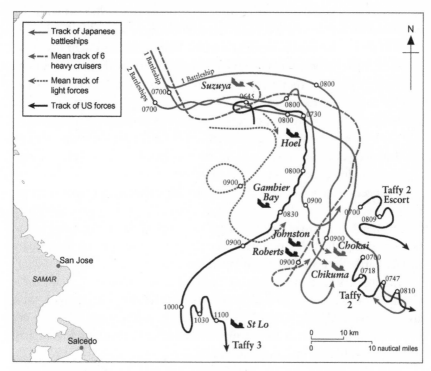

There was also good news for Lieutenant Harold Goodwin and Ensign Alan Hodges when their combined 2,000-pound blockbusters set afire and sunk *Zuikaku*, the last remaining Japanese vessel that had taken part in the Pearl Harbor attack.

While the Third Fleet attacked an enemy that was no longer a threat, the United States Navy fought its last surface action against an enemy fleet. The Battle off Samar has come to be known as the "Navy's finest hour." In the words of Samuel Eliot Morison, the Pacific War's official historian: "In no engagement of its entire history has the United States Navy shown more gallantry, guts and gumption than in those two morning hours between 0730 and 0930 off Samar."

The Battle off Samar is a story of courage of the highest quality in the face of overwhelming odds and is a fitting monument to "Democracy's Navy" – the thousands of reservists, most of whom had never seen an ocean, let alone a ship, before they boarded the ship they took to war. Such a "citizen's navy" as that which was raised in World War II had not existed since Athenian citizens manned the oars of the triremes in the Battle of Salamis, which saved Western civilization 2,000 years earlier. As with the Greek citizen sailors, the US Navy would never have won the Pacific War without those who served with the initials "USNR" behind their name.

Reservists composed the overwhelming majority of those who fought the Pacific War, but they were a near-total majority of the crews in the smaller ships: the escort carriers, destroyers, destroyer-escorts, and fleet auxiliaries without whose support the fast carriers could never have gone to sea. With a captain and senior petty officers from the regular navy (but not always), everyone else aboard was a reservist. Junior officers were "90-day wonder" graduates of officer training programs while junior and mid-level petty officers were promoted to their rank by training and demonstrated ability.

The Battle off Samar involved ships that should never have been in the same ocean with their opponents, let alone battling against the greatest surface battle fleet the Empire of Japan ever sent to sea.

The 16 CVEs of the Seventh Fleet's Carrier Support Group, Task Group 77.4, were commanded by Rear Admiral Thomas L. Sprague, who also commanded Task Unit 77.4.1. The carriers and their escorts were northeast of the island of Samar, just south of San Bernardino Strait. They were further divided into three task units.

Task Unit 77.4.1, known as "Taffy-1" by its radio call sign, included the four larger Sangamon-class early CVEs built on tanker hulls: *Sangamon* (CVE-26), *Suwannee* (CVE-27), *Chenango* (CVE-28), and *Santee* (CVE-29), accompanied by two new Casablanca-class CVEs: *Petrof Bay* (CVE-80) and *Saginaw Bay* (CVE-82); *Chenango* and *Saginaw Bay* departed for Morotai on October 24 with deckloads of "dud" aircraft from the other ships to be replaced and repaired.

Task Unit 77.4.2, "Taffy-2," was commanded by Rear Admiral Felix Stump and comprised *Manila Bay* (CVE-61), *Natoma Bay* (CVE-62), *Kadashan Bay* (CVE-76), *Marcus Island* (CVE-77), *Savo Island* (CVE-78), and *Ommaney Bay* (CVE-79).

Task Unit 77.4.3, "Taffy-3," was commanded by Rear Admiral Clifton "Ziggy" Sprague (no relation to Thomas Sprague) and included *St. Lo* (CVE-63), *White Plains* (CVE-66), *Kalinin Bay* (CVE-68), *Fanshaw Bay* (CVE-70), *Kitkun Bay* (CVE-71), and *Gambier Bay* (CVE-73). With the exception of the four Sangamon-class CVEs, the others had only joined the Navy during the 15 months before the Philippines invasion. Several were Central Pacific campaign veterans that had provided air support for invading soldiers and Marines in the Gilberts, Carolines, and Marianas. *Gambier Bay*, which had only joined the fleet six months earlier, was seeing her first combat operation. The carriers operated approximately 187 TBM-1C Avengers and 292 FM-2 Wildcats and some F6F-5 Hellcats. The squadrons had no anti-shipping ordnance since their assignment was close air support of ground units. Thus they would only be able to impede the enemy during the battle to come, though this harassment would be sufficient to throw the Japanese commander off his stride and convince him he faced a stronger force.

The six CVEs of "Taffy-3," the task unit directly involved in the battle, were escorted by three Fletcher-class destroyers: *Johnston* (DD-557), *Hoel* (DD-533), and *Heermann* (DD-532), and four Butler-class DEs: *John C. Butler* (DE-339), *Dennis* (DE-405), *Raymond* (DE-341), and *Samuel B. Roberts* (DE-413). She had been commissioned less than six months earlier and was seeing combat for the first time.

At about the same time John Bridgers took off from *Essex* 100 miles to the north, a TBM-1C Avenger flown by Ensign Bill Brooks was launched by *St. Lo* on the morning antisubmarine patrol. He retracted his gear and climbed to 3,000 feet. Spotting smoke on the horizon to the northwest at 0647 hours, he turned to investigate. It was the Center Force: four battleships, six heavy and two light cruisers, and 11 destroyers, 17 miles from "Taffy-3" and bearing down on the CVEs at 30 knots.

At about the same moment Brooks spotted the Japanese, lookouts on *St. Lo* reported the unmistakable shapes of "pagoda masts" on the horizon, a sure identification of Japanese battleships. At 0700 hours, Avenger pilot Ensign Hans Jensen reported sighting the fleet, soon confirmed by shipboard radar.

Kurita's ships had just changed to a circular antiaircraft formation when smoke was spotted on the horizon. At about 0700 hours, *Yamato* was first to open fire at a range of 17 nautical miles with her enormous 18-inch main battery. Aboard the carriers and destroyers, the Americans were astonished at the sight of different-colored geysers from the first volleys as succeeding salvos roared overhead and the enemy found the range. Kurita's ships each used a different-colored dye marker to spot their own fire.

On *Yamato*'s flag bridge, no one could find the silhouettes of the American carriers in the identification manuals. Kurita mistakenly took them as fleet carriers and thus assumed he had a task group of the Third Fleet under his guns. He immediately ordered "General Attack." Rather than a carefully orchestrated effort, each division in the Center Force would attack separately.

With his ships limited to a top speed of 18 knots, "Ziggy" Sprague had no hope of outdistancing his pursuers. There was no possibility of out-shooting them. Each carrier had only one 5-inch/38-caliber gun in an open position on the stern. Admiral Sprague ordered the carriers to turn south toward the other carrier groups and ordered the destroyers to make smoke to provide cover while the carriers launched their aircraft.

Despite the fact that *Gambier Bay* was nearest the enemy, she managed to launch most of her aircraft while battleship shells rumbled overhead. Lieutenant Commander Edward J. Huxtable, who commanded Composite Squadron 10, boarded his TBM-1C Avenger and asked his plane captain if he had a bomb load:

> He said no, so I told him to call Lieutenant Commander Buzz Borries, the air officer, to see if I had time to get a load. We had not turned up engines yet and I could not see us going off without some ordnance. I saw Borries talking to Captain Vierwig, who made a sweeping motion with his arm – "Get 'em off!"
>
> About this time, I was startled by what seemed like a rifle shot next to my left ear. I looked out and saw it was a salvo of heavy-caliber stuff splashing alongside *White Plains*. Until this moment, I had no idea the enemy was so near. Now I was more than ready to get on that catapult! We turned up engines and three TBMs launched ahead of me. As I shot off, the lead plane had started his 180-degree turn for a regular carrier join-up. The ceiling was low at about 1,200 feet. I called up Admiral Sprague and asked what our orders were. "Attack immediately!"

Huxtable could just see the DE plane guards in the cloudiness. He broke out into better visibility moments later. "I spotted four cruisers near and what appeared to be four battleships farther back in the gloom. There was no possibility of making a high-altitude attack. I pulled up into the ceiling and started for the cruisers. I had no idea what loads the other planes had, but at least we would give them a good scare."

Huxtable was joined by his Annapolis classmate, Lieutenant Commander Richard Fowler, who led *Kitkun Bay*'s Composite Squadron 5, in attempting coordinated "hot" and "dry" attacks on the Center Force. They kept an unrelenting string of aircraft over Kurita's fleet, giving the Admiral the impression the Americans had far greater resources than they had in fact.

VC-10's Lieutenant (jg) R.L. Crocker had been launched in his Avenger just before his leader. Turret gunner Aviation Machinist's Mate 2/c Charles Westbrook recalled, "We only had four rockets and our guns, but

Mr. Crocker started a run on a cruiser. It turned away and he diverted to a destroyer. He waited till his tracers were bouncing off the deck and then let fly with the rockets. I fired off a full can of ammo on the run. We then got the hell out of there."

The carriers of Taffy-3 could not recover aircraft so the planes were ordered to divert to newly captured Tacloban Airfield on Leyte. "When we landed at Tacloban, we found seven holes in the cowling and a 20mm hole in the port wing. It didn't matter, since a Wildcat landed on top of our Avenger and destroyed both planes."

Lieutenant (jg) Norman Johnson of *Fanshaw Bay*'s Composite Squadron 68 piloted an Avenger with four 500-pound general purpose bombs. He later remembered:

Climbing at full throttle, I penetrated the lower cloud cover and leveled off at 11,000 feet. I took a final look at the enemy ships, which were firing on our ships. When I was about 5 miles away, I nosed down to pick up speed. The Japanese battle force was at that moment occupied in antiaircraft protection against an air attack. Varied colored bursts mushroomed at several levels. It was quite dense and something I had to penetrate. I kept my bomb doors closed as speed increased. I saw three large battleships with rudders hard over and guns spitting flame. At 7,000 feet, I pushed over into my attack, selecting the lead battleship as my target. My radioman reminded me "Open the bomb bay doors!" I opened the doors and the immediate drag was apparent as the airplane was really barreling along now.

I was intent on adjusting the target in my sight. Suddenly the airplane corkscrewed and the right side sliding part of the canopy peeled off. I pressed the bomb release at what seemed the best altitude and concentrated my effort on pulling out. The target was so large the bombs couldn't miss. It was a close call as I leveled off 50 to 100 feet over the water. I pulled up to avoid more AA and then hid in the clouds in case there were any enemy aircraft around.

Johnson and the other *Fanshaw Bay* survivors were also ordered to land at Tacloban. "My TBM touched down on the rough runway and I braked to a halt a foot from a bomb crater. Inspection of the airplane revealed that practically every inspection plate had been blown off!" Later Johnson's turret gunner, a rated Aviation Machinist's Mate, cannibalized a crashed TBM and the Avenger was repaired overnight so that Johnson was able to fly back to *Fanshaw Bay* the next day. "Fortunately, the rumored *banzai* charge didn't happen that night while we were there sleeping in foxholes."

While the pilots desperately attempted to distract the enemy, the "small boys" of "Taffy-3" moved to defend the carriers after Admiral Sprague ordered the three destroyers to attack despite the hopeless odds.

At 0700 hours incoming shell fire bracketed the carriers and *Johnston*'s captain, Commander Ernest E. Evans, the Navy's only full-blooded Native American officer, ordered his destroyer to make smoke to cover the vulnerable CVEs. Ten minutes later, Gunnery Officer Robert Hagen opened fire, registering several hits on the leading heavy cruisers with radar-directed gunfire

Hagen then turned his fire on *Kumano*, scoring several hits on her superstructure and setting her afire. In turn, *Kumano* bracketed the destroyer with colorful shell splashes.

Johnston made smoke and zigzagged as she accelerated to flank speed and headed alone toward the enemy. Hagen had fired over 200 5-inch rounds by the time Evans fired all ten torpedoes when the range closed to 9,000 yards, hitting *Kumano* with one at 0724 hours and blowing the cruiser's bow off. Four of the other torpedoes continued on. *Kongō* was forced to to turn away north to avoid these, which took her out of the fight. *Suzuya*, which had been damaged by attacks launched by aircraft launched from the CVEs, stopped her pursuit to assist *Kumano*, which removed both as a further threat.

The audacity of *Johnston*'s attack confused Admiral Kurita, leading him to conclude he was under attack by cruisers. The CVEs gained precious moments to launch more aircraft when *Johnston*'s torpedoes forced other ships to turn away and lose the integrity of their battle formation.

Evans reversed course back into his own smoke at 0730 hours, but moments later *Kongō* hit her with three 14-inch shells that penetrated her port engine room, reducing her speed by half and cutting power to her three aft gun mounts. Moments later, the bridge was hit by three 6-inch shells fired by *Yamato*. Shrapnel wounded everyone and traumatically amputated the fingers on Evans' left hand.

Johnston's bloody decks were now strewn with dead and dying crewmen. She managed to escape into a rain squall, which gave the damage control parties opportunity to repair the fire control radar and restore power for two of the three aft mounts. With four guns back in operation and hidden by the rain, she fired at a Japanese destroyer before shifting fire to the approaching cruisers.

Minutes later, as *Johnston* retired toward Taffy-3, she came upon *Heermann* and an already-damaged *Hoel* now on their attack run. Had

Evans continued back to the fleet, no one would have faulted him. But he reversed course and made smoke in order to support the others as they headed toward the onrushing Japanese.

Over the next 40 minutes Evans engaged in several duels. At 0820 hours, the destroyer emerged from the smoke and rain squalls to confront *Kongō* at such close range the battleship was unable to depress her main armament sufficiently to take *Johnston* under fire. Hagen fired 40 rounds and scored 15 hits on *Kongō*'s superstructure. Before *Kongō* could respond, Evans reversed course and *Johnston* disappeared back into the smoke. At 0826 hours Evans was ordered to attack the cruisers east of the carriers and took *Chōkai* under fire at 0830 hours while she fired at the helpless *Gambier Bay*. *Johnston* then fired on *Haguro* and scored several hits during a 10-minute engagement.

At 0840 hours, seven enemy destroyers in two columns were spotted closing on the carriers. Hagen opened fire as Evans attempted to "cross the T." *Johnston* hit the lead enemy destroyer 12 times as the Japanese captain realized his tactical disadvantage and turned away. The second destroyer was hit five times before it too veered off, followed by the rest as they turned to avoid *Johnston*'s fire.

The opposing forces were now intertwined in a confused jumble as both *Gambier Bay* and *Hoel* went down. The crippled *Johnston* was now an easy target but she continued to exchange fire with different enemy ships, before finally taking a hit that knocked out the No. 1 gun.

Evans was forced to abandon the bridge at 0920 hours due to exploding ammunition. Taking position on the stern, he shouted orders to the men who manually operated the rudder in the emergency steerage compartment. At 0940 hours, the remaining engine was knocked out and *Johnston* was left dead in the water while her opponents concentrated on her rather than the fleeing carriers. She took so many hits one survivor recalled "they couldn't patch holes fast enough to keep her afloat."

Evans was finally forced to order "Abandon Ship" at 0945 hours and *Johnston* sank at 1005 hours, taking 186 crewmen down with her. Evans, who was last seen going into the water with others, would posthumously be awarded the Medal of Honor. Aboard a raft with other survivors, Seaman Robert Billie remembered watching as an enemy destroyer cruised slowly past while her captain saluted the sinking *Johnston* as an honorable opponent.

If there was a ship which truly did not belong in this naval "Charge of the Light Brigade" (which actually happened on the 90th anniversary of the event immortalized in Tennyson's poem) it was the destroyer-escort

USS *Samuel B. Roberts* (DE-413), known to her crew as "*Sammy-B.*" When he heard that the ship was going to engage the enemy, chief engineer Lieutenant "Lucky" Trowbridge managed to bypass the engines' safety mechanisms and increase speed to 28 knots. As the ship headed toward the enemy, her captain – Lieutenant Commander Robert W. Copeland, USNR – announced: "This will be a fight against overwhelming odds from which survival cannot be expected. We will do what damage we can."

Kongo was forced to turn away from her pursuit of the carriers when *Hoel*, despite damage to her bridge from 14-inch shells, closed to 9,000 yards and fired five torpedos. For the next hour, *Hoel* was to chase shells to distract the enemy from more important carriers, even with three of her five gun mounts out of action and a broken port engine. An 8-inch hit stopped her last engine at 0840 hours, sinking the destroyer and killing 259 of her crew.

Tone and *Chikuma* continued the battle on the carriers and were joined by *Chōkai* and *Kumano*. *Heermann* fired at *Chikuma* and launched five torpedoes at *Haguro* before firing the last three at *Haruna*. None of these scored a hit, but *Yamato* was forced to take evasive action that removed her from the critical area. *Heermann* took hits that flooded her bow and made it sit perilously low in the water as she continued making smoke. Despite losing one gun, she continued firing at *Chikuma* with the others.

"*Sammy-B*" then embarked on the action that would earn her the nickname of "the destroyer escort that fought like a battleship." Closing to within 4,000 yards she launched all three torpedoes and blew off *Chōkai*'s bow, then spent an hour unleashing a torrent of over 600 5-inch shells from her two guns, coming in so close that she could even use her 40mm and 20mm antiaircraft guns. *Sammy-B*'s aft 5-inch gun crew was killed when the gun overheated and exploded at 0851 hours, but she carried on firing at *Chikuma* with her last gun, in concert with *Heermann*. They raked *Chikuma*'s superstructure with armor-piercing shells, high-explosive shells, antiaircraft shells and star shells that started chemical fires which spread through the superstructure. Just before being hit by three 14-inch shells from *Kongō*, *Sammy-B* managed to fire a final shot that knocked out *Chikuma*'s No. 3 Gun turret and then Copeland was forced to order the ship abandoned at 0935 hours. Thirty minutes later, *Samuel B. Roberts* sank with 89 crewmen as 120 survivors took to three life rafts. After a 50-hour ordeal in the open sea, 80 men were finally rescued after being spotted by a passing PBY Catalina patrol plane.

As *Chikuma* turned away from *Heerman* and *Sammy-B*, four Avengers from Taffy-2's *Manila Bay* attacked her. One torpedo hit the stern port quarter, severing the stern while disabling her port screw and rudder. *Chikuma* slowed to 18 knots, then 9 knots as she became unsteerable. The cruiser drifted out of the battle and was unable to respond to Kurita's decision to withdraw. At 1105 hours, five TBMs from *Kitkun Bay* hit her portside amidships with two torpedoes that flooded the engine rooms. At 1400 hours, three TBMs from *Ommaney Bay* and *Natoma Bay* led by Lieutenant Joseph Cady dropped more torpedoes, two of which hit *Chikuma*. This was the final blow and the cruiser sank a short time later, with her survivors being picked up by the destroyer *Nowaki*, which was later sunk by American aircraft on October 27, with loss of the *Chikuma* survivors.

At 0847 hours, *Gambier Bay* was hit in her starboard engine room, while a second hit in the hangar moments later set fueled aircraft afire. Her thin steel wasn't enough to stop the enormous battleship shells that hit her and passed through without exploding, but she went dead at 0900 hours as *Tone*, *Chikuma*, and the damaged *Chōkai* closed in. The CVE capsized at 0907 hours as 800 survivors managed to get off into the water, to become the only American aircraft carrier ever sunk in a surface engagement.

Amazingly, as *Chōkai* turned away from *Gambier Bay*, she was taken under fire at maximum range by the 5-inch gun crew aboard *White Plains*; the third shot hit her torpedo stowage and *Chōkai* exploded and sank. Some historians have argued that she was actually hit by a bomb fortuitously dropped at the same time by one of the attacking Avengers, but the US Navy lists *Chōkai* as the only ship ever sunk by surface gunfire from an aircraft carrier.

At this point in the battle, Admiral Kurita was a shaken man who did not have an accurate picture of his enemy and overestimated the force that opposed him. Over the previous 28 hours, his flagship had been sunk from under him; the "unsinkable" *Musashi* was no more; his fleet was in disarray; and three of his six remaining heavy cruisers had been sunk. He became convinced he was up against TF 38, and that more planes would soon attack as they had the day before while American battleships would appear on the horizon at any minute. Knowing it would take his ships 30 minutes to reorganize and deploy in fighting formation, Admiral Kurita signaled the surviving ships to reverse course and re-enter San Bernardino Strait. At 0920 hours *Yamato* reversed course and the rest of the Center Force followed her.

Had the Japanese pushed on for another 15 minutes, they could have overtaken and sunk the remaining CVEs, which were now defenseless after their aircraft headed to Tacloban. They could then have entered Leyte Gulf and taken on the remaining invasion fleet without opposition. However, this would not have stopped the invasion, since the ground forces were already ashore with their equipment. It is one of history's great what-ifs. From here on, the Japanese Navy would not be a force to be reckoned with, and acted only in support of army actions.

Around an hour after the Battle off Samar concluded, disaster struck when a member of the *kamikaze* Shikishima Unit of the 201st Air Group located the CVE *St. Lo* and flew into the middle of the flight deck with a 250-kilogram bomb. Gasoline fires, explosions and the ignition of the torpedo and bomb magazines sent her to the bottom of the sea half an hour later.

Halsey had made a big mistake and all the high-ranking commanders knew it. Admiral Nimitz, who as a young officer had experienced the divisions within the navy created by the Sampson-Schley controversy over who won the Battle of Santiago in the Spanish-American War, was determined to avoid the problems that might arise if official criticism became public and so forbade any criticism of Halsey, going so far as to ensure that all reproachful comments were removed from official reports.

CHAPTER SEVENTEEN

NO REST FOR THE WEARY

Task Force 38 and the men of Air Group 15 had come out on the winning side of history's greatest sea battle, but although they were absolutely exhausted, on October 27 they returned to normal operations. Attempts were made to keep fatigued pilots out of combat's way by making them fly as radio relays on long-range searches for the enemy. However, this did not work for Lieutenants (jg) Tommy Thompson and Keith West, who bumped into a major attack of 30 planes, engaging Zekes for several minutes before bringing three down and seeing off the Judys and Jills they had been escorting. Admiral Sherman decided by the end of the day that Task Group 38.3 was too low on provisions, bombs and torpedoes and that the crews simply must have a break – finally, the next morning Air Group 15 heard the good news that they would be relieved by Air Group 4 at Ulithi. They would be very disappointed on October 29, when they arrived at the base only to learn they would be heading back to the Philippines the next day with no more than a few replacement aircraft and additional ammunition.

Unfortunately, the good news of the victory at Leyte Gulf did not last as Admiral Ônishi's "divine wind" began to blow with increasing force. On October 29, *Intrepid* became the first fleet carrier hit by a *kamikaze*. Cruising off the coast of the Philippines around noon, a lone Zeke was spotted as it approached from starboard. Her guns opened up fast but the pilot dove straight at the flight deck. A crew of African-American steward's mates manned six 20mm cannon in Gun Tub No. 10. Their combined fire shredded the attacker's wing, but as he lost control, the pilot veered straight into their position, killing ten and wounding ten others in the crash.

As this happened, the CAP splashed a Judy, while three Zekes were shot down by antiaircraft fire from the task group. One Zeke made it through the screen and hit *Lexington* in the rear of her island.

Chief Quartermaster Tom Curtis, who had survived the sinking of the old *Wasp* two years earlier, would never forget the hit:

> I had just gone out on the flight deck side of the island to talk to some of my boys and see how they were, then I started back into a passageway to the other side, when the *kamikaze* hit the base of the island. The force of the explosion blasted me through the passageway, and threw me against a bulkhead, which knocked me out for a few moments and fractured my leg. I came to, and my leg hurt like hell. I managed to drag myself back to where my boys had been, but that whole deck was on fire, and they were all dead.

The kamikaze hit started a fire that resulted in 187 casualties, including Tom Curtis's signalmen. The fire was put out in 20 minutes through quick work by the damage control parties and *Lexington* was able to recover aircraft. The next day, the carrier withdrew to Ulithi for repair, which prematurely ended Air Group 19's highly successful tour. Fighting 19's "Kittens" had scored 155 victories, making them the eighth-ranked Navy fighter squadron for victories in a single deployment, while the Helldivers and Avengers had suffered no losses under their protection.

The next day, it was the turn of *Franklin* (CV-13) and *Belleau Wood* (CVL-24). Task Group 38.4 was cruising in the Philippine Sea, approximately 100 miles east of Samar, with *Enterprise*, *Franklin*, *Belleau Wood*, and *San Jacinto* conducting flight operations. Visibility was over 12 miles and the ceiling was unlimited with scattered high and low cumulus. The wind was from the southeast at 18 knots with a light sea.

Franklin began fueling *Bagley* (DD-386) at 1400 hours. Five minutes later, the carrier commenced launching 12 Hellcats to go to the aid of a fleet tanker force under air attack about 240 miles north. At 1410 hours, a large bogey was picked up on radar, 37 miles distant. At 1417, *Bagley* cast off and General Quarters was sounded. Crews quickly manned all antiaircraft batteries. The last Hellcat left the ship three minutes later. At 1424 hours, *Franklin* turned due east and increased speed to 18 knots when enemy aircraft appeared overhead and commenced their attack.

Three D4Y3 Judys angled down toward the carrier. The first missed and crashed in the water on the starboard side, throwing up a large column of water. The second struck the flight deck in about a 20-degree glide, starboard of the centerline, and crashed through the flight deck and gallery deck spaces below. Parts of this plane were later found in the crew's head. A hole about 30 by 35 feet was blown in the flight deck, with the periphery blown upward. It was recorded in the war diary that "This explosion was of a 'high order' detonation."

The second attacker nearly sank the carrier as disaster spread quickly. Thirteen aircraft on the hangar deck caught fire. The blast demolished the No. 3 bomb elevator trunk above the hangar deck, then continued down the bomb elevator trunk and blew off the counter-weighted door at the third deck level. Flame and dense smoke spread through the down passageway and repair party teams were forced to evacuate. Meanwhile, smoke and flames flashed through the armored hangar deck hatch No. 1-109, which was not closed since the man whose duty it was had been killed by the hangar deck. Flaming gasoline started fires in a second deck living compartment. Smoke and burning gasoline from the hangar deck fire continued down to the third deck where the damage control crew was forced to evacuate with some escaping to the second deck while others worked their way forward along the third deck.

Immediately after the explosion, Hangar Deck Control turned on all hangar sprinklers and water curtains. Soon after, due to dense smoke and heat, all those in Hangar Deck Control were forced to evacuate. About ten minutes after the bomb exploded, two additional explosions occurred on the third deck. The ship's log recorded that "The cause of these two below deck explosions is believed to have been the ignition of gasoline vapors which came down from the hangar deck through the open hatch at frame 109, through the ruptured bomb elevator trunk at frame 127, and down the auxiliary elevator ram cylinder in compartment B-324-L."

Franklin listed three degrees to starboard. Counter-flooding brought the ship back to an even keel before she then took a 2-degree list to port. "It was then realized that the initial list was caused by the tremendous volume of water from the hangar deck sprinklers, water curtains, and fire hoses that were immediately turned on after the initial blast, and which ran down to the second and third decks through the open hatch and bomb elevator trunk. The water collected on the starboard side of the ship initially and caused the increasing list."

The major fires on the flight deck were extinguished by 1530 hours. The hangar deck fire was extinguished by 1625 hours followed minutes later by the gallery deck. There were only a few smoldering fires by 1800 hours. *Franklin* survived, but she was out of the war for an extended period while repairs were completed. Temporary repairs were made at Ulithi before she steamed to San Francisco and more extensive repairs at Hunter's Point Naval Shipyard. A carrier put out of action was the next-best outcome to an outright sinking for a *kamikaze* attack.

Franklin's third attacker dropped a 250-kilogram bomb which landed in the water 30 feet from the ship and exploded, throwing up a large geyser of water. The Judy then crash-landed into the aft end of *Belleau Wood*'s flight deck. Eleven parked aircraft and ready ammunition at the gun mounts to either side of the flight deck caught fire. Before it was controlled, 92 men were dead or missing and 97 wounded. *Belleau Wood* headed for Ulithi with *Franklin*. She would not return until January 1945. Admiral McCain's task group had been cut in half.

Third Fleet was by now becoming used to the terrifying new tactic of *kamikaze* attacks. On November 2 *Claxton* (DD-571) and *Ammen* (DD-527) were hit and survived, but *Abner Read* (DD-526) was sunk. The best form of defense was to spot them inbound as early as possible and intercept them quickly, and to maintain regular attacks on Japanese airfields.

As the time of the US invasion of Leyte, there were only a relative few Imperial Japanese Army troops on the island. However, within a week the Japanese began to quickly transfer troops from Luzon, landing them in Ormoc Bay on Leyte's western side. "Special attack" units were soon operating from the nearby Bacolod air complex on the island of Negros where the fleet was well within range. Because the carrier air groups were the only effective American air force in the Philippines in the weeks immediately following the invasion due to the difficulty of enlarging Tacloban to allow more USAAF units to be flown up from New Guinea, Third Fleet had to remain close to the islands to provide necessary air support, which kept the carriers under kamikaze threat throughout November.

Essex returned to the war on November 5, sending strikes to Clark and Nichols airfields. Fifty-two Hellcats from *Essex*, *Lexington*, *Langley*, and *Ticonderoga* (CV-14) led by VF-15's Jim Rigg strafed the fields ahead of the main strike Dave McCampbell led with 88 Hellcats, Helldivers and Avengers, which cratered the runways and hit the hangars. With quite a few enemy aircraft in the area, George Duncan led another fighter sweep from *Essex* at McCampbell's request. Several Zekes were downed, but the war-weary American airplanes were showing the strain by now and made the American pilots' lives harder – malfunctioning guns, jamming cockpit canopies and instruments that stopped working. The hangar crews performed stirling work at keeping them going, working through the night.

On November 6, the task group launched 98 aircraft at 1130 hours to attack ships in Manila Bay. *Nachi* was attacked by 12 Helldivers that scored three hits while six torpedo-armed Avengers made a hammer-and-anvil attack. Four missed the cruiser but the fifth hit her stern in an enormous explosion which was followed a hit toward the bow by the sixth. *Nachi* was sinking with her crew abandoning ship by the time the Avengers departed.

That afternoon Bob Cosgrove's Avenger was hit in the turret by a 25mm AA burst that blew out the glass and set off the ammunition when he attacked a light cruiser near Cavite Naval Base across the bay from the city. Unable to raise gunner Loyce Deen on the intercom, radioman Digby Denzek confronted a terrible sight when he climbed up to the turret to check his friend with whom he had flown every mission: Deen had been decapitated by the AA burst.

When Cosgrove landed "No. 93" back aboard *Essex* the bomber's damage was so extensive it was impossible to get what was left of Deen out of his turret quickly. As the airedales tried to remove the dead gunner, General Quarters was sounded with *kamikazes* inbound. With no time left, the chaplain was called and the Avenger was pushed to the stern. Crewmen gathered around as the service for the dead was read while a flag was draped over the turret. The bugler blew "Taps" and the airplane went over the stern as Deen's coffin. This was the only time during the war in which an airman was intentionally buried in his plane. In 1952, film of this moving moment was shown publicly in the documentary *Victory at Sea*.

A Judy penetrated *Essex*'s screen, but was shot down and crashed into the sea 100 yards away. Ted Graham wrote that night of the day's events, "I fear they've saved the worst of all this for last."

On November 8, George Duncan led a strike against Clark Field at Manila, bringing down two Bettys and a Frances. The cloud and haze that stemmed from a nearby typhoon north of the Philippines made it hard to find their targets and ships sent up a heavy barrage of antiaircraft fire.

Ted Graham had high hopes when Task Group 38.3 left the coastal area to refuel:

GREAT DAY!! After announcing that Governor Dewey had conceded FDR's victory in presidential race, Lieutenant Mills, in bellowing tones, gave out the dope: *Nimitz ordered Halsey to release Bunker Hill and AG 15!*

So it looks as though we're going home at last! Probably get off at Guam. Dope is we'll get relieved on the 11th in Guam, going home on *Bunker Hill*. Couple of guys packed seabags and other guys tried their blues on. Spirits sky high, but – goddamnit! – we still aren't off this thing. During the night I woke up several times with the ship shaking like hell under full power.

It turned out that American intelligence had learned of an intended Japanese reinforcement near Leyte, and Task Group 38.3 was heading back to locate the convoy and launch strikes against it, much to Graham's disappointment:

> The BUBBLE BURST! We're under full speed to Leyte. The Japs, with assorted BBs, CAs, CLs and DDs, are stirring between Palawan & Borneo. MacArthur's screaming for our support. Bitter day, indeed. It's days like today that makes General Sherman right as rain about war being hell. Scheduled condition two and searches tomorrow. We're supposed to be off Leyte at dawn.

At dawn of Armistice Day 1944, a convoy of four large troop transports and two smaller ones, supported by five destroyers, was spotted rounding Apale Point, bound for Ormoc Bay. The Japanese had managed to land an entire division of the Manchurian Kwantung Army on Leyte between October 27 and November 1, while subsequent convoys were sunk. This one was bigger than the others, bringing in a second division of Kwantung Army troops. PT boats had attacked unsuccessfully at 0310 hours off Asbate Island. The Japanese planned to send troops ashore at noon.

Task Group 38.3's biggest strike ever was launched at 0830 hours. The aircraft arrived over the ships at 1030 hours. The Japanese were within sight of the anchorage and the ships increased speed and scattered while the DDs began to lay a smoke screen.

As McCampbell orbited at 14,000 feet, an Oscar attacked him. He chased it for three minutes before setting it on fire. The Oscar went straight into the sea as his 33rd victory.

The first division attacked the first ship in the convoy, three hits stopping it dead in the water, so the second division turned its attention to the second and third vessels. Against an intense barrage of anitiaircraft fire, the Helldivers managed to distract the defending gunners from firing at the 18 Avengers, which hit the second and third ships, narrowly missing a fourth. Task Force 38 managed to sink the flotilla flagship *Shimikaze*, and all four transports. Of the five destroyers attacked, only *Asashimo* survived, *Hamanami*, *Naganami* and *Wakatsuki* all foundering – a mere 2,000 troops made it ashore, without food or ammunition.

In the face of these tangible results, Bombing 15 unfortunately sustained the largest number of losses on any mission of its tour. Lieutenant (jg) John Foote's Helldiver was shot down, exploding as it hit the water and killing him and Aviation Radioman 2/c Norm Schmidt; Ensign John Avery and gunner Ted Graham were killed when their Helldiver was hit in the engine and cartwheeled inverted across the water before sinking; finally, antiaircraft fire struck the Helldiver flown by Ensign Mel Livesay, bringing the bomber down in a violent spiral, killing him and Aviation Radioman 2/c Chuck Swihart.

The VB-15 gunners assembled once they arrived back at the *Essex* as they realized the three most popular men – Norm Schmidt, Ted Graham, and Chuck Swihart – had all been killed in the attack. In a tension-filled instant, several declared that they had seen enough action now and refused to fly any more missions; soon all the gunners joined in. Jim Mini went below to McCampbell and told him about the rebellion. The incident was officially mutiny in the face of the enemy and McCampbell could not speak directly with the gunners or it would be an acknowledgement of this. Instead, he sent Jim Mini to the men to say that their demands were fair enough and that the pilots would henceforth take to the skies without their gunners, who would be transferred to ship's company. The gunners reconsidered and rescinded their demand, opting to continue flying with the men they had worked with for the last six months. The event was not mentioned again.

Ted Graham's loss was keenly felt and his best friend Aviation Radioman 1/c Paul Sheehan emotionally added a final entry to Graham's diary:

11 November, Armistice Day 1944

Jap reinforcements attempt to land on Leyte and imperil MacArthur's men. 2 DD's, 2 DE's, 4 AK's. At least 20,000 Japs aboard AK's. Task force launched tremendous strike, 20 bombers from *Essex*. Invasion fleet annihilated!

Ted Graham failed to return from this flight. He was shot down while diving through enemy ack–ack. Two other of our bombers are missing.

Today a great blow was struck by the Navy in defending the Army, but it was truly a sad day for VB-15.

We will miss you, Ted Graham, but never forget you.

Aircrewmen of VB-15.

The Japanese reported that Ormoc Bay Convoy No. 2 had been attacked by 260 aircraft. According to American records, 347 aircraft from three air groups of Task Force 38 took part in the attack.

After refueling in rough seas, Task Group 38.3 launched a strike against shipping in Manila Harbor on the morning of November 13, led by McCampbell. Two 1,000-ton cargo ships, an 8,000-ton cargo ship and an 8,000-ton tanker were sunk by his Helldivers. A second strike left at noon, led by VeeGee Lambert; by the end of the day the Americans had left Clark and Nichols fields in great disarray, and a light cruiser, six destroyers and seven freighters had been sunk in Manila Harbor.

Lambert was unaware until after he returned home that one of the Avengers he saw shot down was flown by his brother-in-law, Lieutenant Commander Radcliffe Denniston, who led Torpedo 11 aboard the *Hornet*. Two years earlier Denniston had introduced his sister to Lambert, who later married her.

At 1800 hours, General Quarters sounded aboard *Essex*. Radar had spotted 20 inbound bogeys. The *Essex* CAP shot down two Myrt reconnaissance planes, two Frances bombers, and a Tojo, while the *Hornet* CAP scored five more intruders.

Air Group 15's last two strikes were mounted on November 14. Though 92 aircraft were sent out from *Essex*, *Ticonderoga*, and *Langley* in the first strike, they found that most of the vessels in Manila Harbor were sitting on the harbor bottom and not afloat as they at first appeared to be. There was still heavy antiaircraft fire though, and Lieutenant (jg) Raymond L. Turner (an original member of the "Silent Second") and his gunner Aviation Radioman 2/c Sam Dorosh were shot into the water in their Helldiver – the group's final loss. McCampbell chased and shot down an Oscar, his 34th victory making him the Navy's Ace of Aces, and the third-ranked American ace of the war.

Following an uneventful final strike that afternoon, during which the bombers could not find a target, Admiral Sherman finally gave the order at 1900 hours to head back to Ulithi Harbor, where the *Essex* arrived on November 17, 1944.

Just over two years before Air Group 15 left Task Force 38 and was ferried back to the United States, the US Navy had been on the brink of defeat, yet by October 1944, history's greatest naval campaign was brought to a conclusion in America's favor, as Japan's Navy was decisively defeated.

BIBLIOGRAPHY

Beach, Edward L., *Submarine!* (Henry Holt, 1952)

Boomhower, Ray, *Fighter Pilot: The World War II Career of Alex Vraciu* (Indiana Historical Society Press, 2010)

Borneman, Walter R., *The Admirals: Nimitz, Halsey, Leahy, and King – The Five-Star Admirals Who Won the War at Sea* (Back Bay Books, 2013)

Bradsher, Greg, "The Z Plan Story," *Prologue Magazine*; Vol.37, No. 3, Fall 2005.

Bridgers, John D., MD, "Naval Years," http://www.tk-jk.net/ Bridgers/ Mainpages/ NavalYears.html (2002)

Bryan III, LCDR J., *Mission Beyond Darkness: The Story of USS Lexington's Air Group 16 June 20, 1944 Attack on the Japanese Carrier Fleet as Told by the Men Who Flew That Day* (Duell, Sloan and Pearce, 1945)

Buell, Thomas B., *The Quiet Warrior: A Biography of Admiral Raymond A. Spruance* (Little, Brown, 1974)

Clark, J.J. with Clark G. Reynolds, *Carrier Admiral* (David McKay Co., 1967)

Cleaver, Thomas M., *Fabled Fifteen: The Pacific War Saga of Carrier Air Group 15* (Casemate Publishing, 2014)

Cleaver, Thomas M., *F4F Wildcat and F6F Hellcat Aces of VF-2* (Osprey Publishing, 2015)

Coleman, LCDR Kent Stephen, *Halsey at Leyte Gulf: Command Decision and Disunity of Effort* (Pickle Partners Publishing, 2014)

Cutler, Thomas, *The Battle of Leyte Gulf: 23–26 October 1944* (US Naval Institute Press, 1994)

Dull, Paul S., *A Battle History of the Imperial Japanese Navy, 1941–1945* (US Naval Institute Press, 1978)

Foss, Joe and Brennan, Matthew, *Top Guns: America's Fighter Aces Tell Their Stories* (Pocket Books, 1991)

Frank, Richard B., *Guadalcanal: The Definitive Account of the Landmark Battle* (Penguin, 1990)

Goodwin, Doris Kearns, *No Ordinary Time: Franklin and Eleanor Roosevelt: The Home Front in World War II* (Simon and Schuster, 1995)

Graham, Theodore, *The Diary of Ted Graham: 1943–44* (Unpublished)

Hammel, Eric, *Carrier Clash: The Invasion of Guadalcanal and the Battle of the Eastern Solomons, August 1942* (Pacifica Press, 1997)

Hone, Trent, "Building a Doctrine: U.S. Naval Tactics and Battle Plans in the Interwar Period," *International Journal of Naval History*, Vol. 1, No. 2 (October 2002)

Hornfischer, James D., *The Last Stand of the Tin Can Sailors: The Extraordinary World War II Story of the U.S. Navy's Finest Hour* (Bantam Books, 2005)

Lundstrom, John B., *The First Team and the Guadalcanal Campaign: Naval Fighter Combat from August to November 1942* (new edn), (US Naval Institute Press, 2005)

Markey, Morris, *Well Done! An Aircraft Carrier in Battle Action* (Appleton Century, 1945)

McCampbell, David, *The Reminiscences of Captain David McCampbell, U.S. Navy (Retired)* (US Naval Institute Press, 1992)

Morison, Samuel Eliot, *The Struggle for Guadalcanal, August 1942–February 1943*, Vol. 5 of *History of United States Naval Operations in World War II* (Little, Brown, 1958)

Morison, Samuel Eliot, *The Two-Ocean War: A Short History of the United States Navy in the Second World War* (Little, Brown, 1963)

Noles, James L., Jr., *Twenty-Three Minutes to Eternity: The Final Voyage of the Escort Carrier USS Liscome Bay* (University of Alabama Press, 2004)

Olds, Robert, *Helldiver Squadron: The Story of Carrier Bombing Squadron 17 with Task Force 58* (Dodd, Mead, 1994)

Potter, E.B., "The Command Personality," *US Naval Institute Proceedings*, Vol. 95, No. 1, 19–25 (January 1969)

Potter, E.B., *Bull Halsey* (US Naval Institute Press, 2003)

Potter, E.B., *Nimitz* (US Naval Institute Press, 2008)

Ramage, James D., Lawson, Robert L., and Tillman, Barrett, *The Reminiscences of Rear Admiral James D. Ramage U.S. Navy (Retired)* (US Naval Institute, 1999)

Rems, Alan, "Out of the Jaws of Victory," *Naval History*, Vol. 30, No. 2, 28–35 (April 2016)

Roscoe, Theodore, *History of United States Destroyer Operations in World War II* (US Naval Institute Press, 1949)

Roscoe, Theodore, *History of United States Submarine Operations in World War II* (US Naval Institute Press, 1949)

Rose, Lisle Abbott, *The Ship that Held the Line: The USS Hornet and the First Year of the Pacific War* (Bluejacket Books, 2002)

Sauer, Howard, *The Last Big-Gun Naval Battle: The Battle of Surigao Strait* (Glencannon Press, 1999)

Sears, David, *Pacific Air: How Fearless Flyboys, Peerless Aircraft, and Fast Flattops Conquered the Skies in the War with Japan* (Da Capo Press, 2011)

Shores, Christopher, *Duel for the Sky: Ten Crucial Battles of World War II* (Grub Street, 1985)

Smith, Douglas V., *Carrier Battles: Command Decision in Harm's Way* (US Naval Institute Press, 2006)

Smith, Robert Ross, "Luzon Versus Formosa," *Command Decisions* (United States Army Center of Military History, CMH Pub 70–7, 2000 [1960])

Stafford, Edward P., *The Big E: The Story of the USS Enterprise* (reissue edn), (US Naval Institute Press, 2002)

Stark, Norman, "My True Worth – Ten Gallons of Ice Cream," http://www.ussessexcv9.org/Bravepages/icecream.html (2002)

Thomas, Evan, *Sea of Thunder: Four Commanders and the Last Great Naval Campaign, 1941–1945* (Simon and Schuster, 2006)

Tillman, Barrett, *The Dauntless Dive Bomber in World War II* (US Naval Institute Press, 1976)

Tillman, Barrett, *Corsair: The F4U in World War II* (US Naval Institute Press, 1978)

Tillman, Barrett, *Hellcat: The F6F In World War II* (US Naval Institute Press, 1979)

Tillman, Barrett, *Wildcat: the F4F in World War II* (US Naval Institute Press, 1983)

Tillman, Barrett, *Helldiver Units in World War II* (Osprey Publishing, 1997)

Tillman, Barrett, *Clash of the Carriers: The True Story of the Marianas Turkey Shoot* (New American Library, 2006)

Tillman, Barrett, *Enterprise: America's Fightingest Ship and the Men Who Helped Win World War II* (Simon and Schuster, 2012)

Toll, Ian W., *The Conquering Tide: War in the Pacific Islands, 1942–1944* (W.W. Norton, 2015)

Tuohy, William, *America's Fighting Admirals: Winning the War at Sea in World War II* (Zenith Press, 2007)

Winston, Robert A., *Dive Bomber* (Holiday House, 1939)

Winston, Robert A., *Fighting Squadron: A World War II Fighter Pilot's First-Hand Account* (reprint), (Zenger, 1983)

Woodward, C. Vann, *The Battle for Leyte Gulf: The Incredible Story of World War*

INDEX

References to maps are indicated
by *bold*.